Work and Labour in the Cities of Roman Italy

Liverpool Studies in Ancient History 1

LIVERPOOL STUDIES IN ANCIENT HISTORY

Work and Labour in the Cities of Roman Italy

MIRIAM J. GROEN-VALLINGA

LIVERPOOL UNIVERSITY PRESS

First published 2022 by
Liverpool University Press
4 Cambridge Street
Liverpool
L69 7ZU

British Library Cataloguing-in-Publication data
A British Library CIP record is available

ISBN 978-1-80207-759-9 cased

Typeset by Carnegie Book Production, Lancaster
Printed and bound by CPI Group (UK) Ltd, Croydon CR0 4YY

Contents

Acknowledgements

This book is the revised and updated version of my PhD thesis (Leiden 2017), which was part of the larger research project 'Moving Romans: Urbanisation, Migration and Labour in the Early Roman Principate', funded by the Dutch National Research Organisation (NWO), and conducted at Leiden University under the guidance of Luuk de Ligt and Rens Tacoma. I remain thankful for their support.

Thanks are also due to the Royal Dutch Institute at Rome (KNIR) and the Dutch Institute at Athens (NIA) for their hospitality at various times during the project.

Over the years I have benefited greatly from discussions with colleagues in the field. Thank you for inviting me, for listening, for your constructive criticism, and for sharing your own ideas. I am grateful for the opportunities to share my thoughts with you. I also wish to thank everyone in the academic community who kindly made available their published and as yet unpublished work. My colleagues at Leiden University, the University of Amsterdam, and the Radboud University Nijmegen have been an invaluable source of support. Thank you Clare Litt and everyone at LUP for your guidance in the publication process, and thanks to the anonymous reviewers for their valuable comments.

If I am being unusually brief in this section, it is because I have been truly fortunate to have had so many people help me along the way. They are too many to list, and I would not want to leave anyone unmentioned. To all of you, therefore, my sincere thanks: you know who you are.

Above all, thank you Wouter and Dorian.

Chapter 1

Introduction

Aims, Methods and Sources

> Inter artifices longa differentia est et ingenii et naturae et doctrinae et institutionis.
>
> *Dig.* 46.3.31 (Ulpianus)

Introduction

This study focuses on work and labour in the cities of Roman Italy in the early empire. Work and labour are thereby understood as two distinct concepts. Work includes all economic engagements, which sets the backdrop for analysis of money-making labour activities. In the citation heading this chapter, Ulpian observes that there was great variation in skill and disposition, learning and custom, among Roman artisans. More than that, it can be said that pre-industrial working populations in general were not coherent bodies.[1] An inherent diversity is therefore a priori likely to have been characteristic of the Roman workforce. There is a need for a conceptual framework capable of accommodating this diversity. This book aims to provide that conceptual framework and to investigate the working population of Roman Italy as a whole, through an analysis of the broader social institutions within which work and labour took place: the intersecting axes of family and non-familial labour collectives.

The broader subject of urban labour and labourers in the Roman world is revelling in scholarly attention, as the collections of papers edited by Verboven and Laes (2017), and by Wilson and Flohr (2016), may show. But the papers in them concern largely bits and pieces relevant to the broader picture: despite converging trends they do not present one coherent account. Similarly, Cam Hawkins's monograph, ***Roman Artisans and the Urban Economy***, presents invaluable insights on unstable labour demand and artisans' business strategies, yet his focus is on the skilled artisan.[2]

1 Ehmer (2014) 105.
2 Hawkins (2021) 14–15.

The sizeable freeborn population of Roman Italy has received increasing scholarly attention within accounts of the Roman economy, again with a particular focus on free artisans and craftsmen.[3] Significant progress has also been made in the debate on the nature of Roman slavery and slave labour.[4] New light was shed on the exceptional position of freedmen in Roman society, and in the Roman economy.[5] Economic contributions of women and children have been investigated to some extent.[6] There are monographs and collections of papers on specific topics such as disreputable professions, skills and professionalism, or on particular occupations.[7] These are important publications that show considerable sophistication in the development of the debate. What they have in common, however, is that they focus on a subset of the working population. In virtually all these accounts, moreover, the unremunerated work of women, children, and others is generally not taken into account, although such work contributed significantly to the economic welfare of the larger groups they belonged to, be it the family or a larger collective. There is a need for a coherent, integrated approach to the urban working population that also links up with current developments on the subject of the urban economy in the early Roman empire.[8]

This book sets out from two assumptions derived from recent developments in the study of the Roman economy. First, the notion that work and labour are subject to market forces in society. Markets were not fully integrated, however, and through segmentation guided work patterns in society. Second, all workers were part of the social institutions that made up Roman society. Combining the two, this book argues that individual work and labour patterns were ultimately determined by familial as well

[3] Cf. their incorporation in reference articles by Tacoma (2018); Hawkins (2013); also Brunt (1980).

[4] Vlassopoulos (2021); Bradley and Cartledge eds (2011), particularly the contributions of Morley, "Slavery under the Principate", and Bodel, "Slave Labour and Roman Society"; Scheidel (2008); Bradley (1994), esp. Chapter 4 on slave labour; Harper (2011) on late antiquity includes many valuable observations for the early empire.

[5] On the numerical importance of freedmen based on the album of Herculaneum, see De Ligt and Garnsey (2019); Garnsey and De Ligt (2016); and De Ligt and Garnsey (2012); on the freedman economy, Verboven (2012b); Mouritsen (2011b) provide a full account concerning freedmen, with Chapter 6 (at 206–47) on freedmen in the economy.

[6] On women, e.g. Larsson Lovén (2016); Holleran (2013); Groen-Vallinga (2013); on children, Porena (2016); Laes (2011a) 148–221; Petermandl (1997).

[7] Bond (2016); Stewart et al. eds (2020).

[8] Syntheses like Taylor (1979); Burford (1972); Mossé (1969); Louis (1965); and Calabi Limentani (1958) are outdated in their engagement with the economic background.

as non-familial collectives in a market that was segmented along the lines of gender, status, and skills. By focusing on institutions, an integrated approach to the working population becomes feasible.

Outline of the book

Whereas the presence of market forces in Roman society has become generally accepted, the precise nature of those market forces remains a matter of debate among ancient historians.[9] The question becomes: in what ways and to what extent were work and labour subject to the market? The second chapter of this book therefore discusses the influence of market economics and the existence of an urban labour market in Roman society. It will be argued that such theoretical models are both plausible and useful to think with, provided that the specifics of the Roman case are kept in mind. Economic theories of labour and the labour market should be expanded to an integrated approach of the social and cultural backgrounds of the society under scrutiny. A socio-economic approach serves to highlight factors producing market imperfection and segmentation, and is therefore suited to include unremunerated work.

The ways in which work and labour should be understood are determined by structural factors in society of a social, cultural, economic, and/or legal nature. It is now commonly recognized among Roman economic historians that institutions are crucial determinants of how economies function, in line with the basic tenets of New Institutional Economics (NIE). Roman labour and labourers did not exist in isolation. It is my contention that the daily working life of an individual Roman was decided largely by his or her position within (predominantly) social institutions. The most important of these institutions was the family or household. Family of birth largely determined future economic opportunity, and expectations of, for example, marriage and childbirth were important in negotiating the position of women. Slaves and freedpeople were commonly part of the household. Household members can be expected to have coordinated productive activities as well as consumption patterns with their collective income in mind.[10] Broader, non-familial collectives such as associations should also be factored in and were probably particularly influential for those (temporarily) not surrounded by their family, such as migrants or widows. Associations played a part in directing labour allocation and education, and they had the position to further the economic interests of their members in significant ways.

The remaining chapters of the book are structured in line with the importance of these institutions for understanding urban labour systems

[9] E.g. Temin (2013a); Bang (2008).

[10] Hofmeester (2018) 319; cf. De Vries (2008) 9–19 and *passim*.

in Roman society. Chapters 3 and 4 focus on the social institution of the Roman family in its various shapes and sizes. The discussion of the Roman family in two chapters, rather than one, is prompted by a fundamental difference between small-scale families on the one hand (Chapter 3) and elite households on the other (Chapter 4), in terms of their demographic make-up as well as their motivations for labour participation. It is hoped that this binary classification can do some justice to the contrast between the two, even when it will become clear that both groups were heterogeneous in themselves.

The next chapter considers non-familial labour relations. Social ties and trust networks beyond the family must have been crucial to the way work, and especially labour, was coordinated in a society where much hinged on personal security and *fides*, something that arguably was more difficult to come by within an urban context than in the countryside.[11] An analysis of what I have termed 'the economics of association' will highlight the role played by voluntary associations in labour allocation and economic interaction. The obvious example is the much-debated professional *collegium*. Although this chapter will focus on *collegia*, for which there is a relative abundance of evidence, many of its findings can be understood to reflect broader socio-economic processes of collectivity that had an impact on work. Placing the professional *collegia* within the context of private voluntary associations more generally has already greatly furthered our understanding of the collective.[12] It is now clear that the social and economic functions of associations were seamlessly connected. Associations may thus serve as an example of a broader sense of community that contributed to building trust networks in the cities of Roman Italy and the way that this fostered the Roman economy, and the distribution of labour in particular.

Roman work and labour, finally, did not exist in a historical vacuum: the contribution of the Roman case in the context of a global history of work should be explicitly addressed. In Chapter 6, therefore, the argument is brought together and some of the implications are drawn out. The global perspective may serve to highlight the particularities of Roman labour relations. The discussion of Roman work and labour relations, conversely, brings forth the merits and deficiencies of existing models aiming at universality.

[11] On trust and trust networks in antiquity, generally derived from Tilly (2005), see e.g. Verboven (2017a); Broekaert (2017); Venticinque (2016) 37–38.

[12] E.g. the papers in Kloppenborg and Wilson eds (1996).

Method

The use of theory, models, and comparison has become increasingly common in ancient history since the pioneering works of, among others, Moses Finley and Keith Hopkins, and needs no justification. Much progress in ancient history has been achieved through ever-increasing engagement with other fields of research to develop new theories and models, particularly during the last one or two decades. Very few students currently working in the field of Roman socio-economic history have refrained from the application of economic concepts of, for example, transaction costs or social-network theories. It seems that the editors of *The Cambridge Economic History of the Greco-Roman World* were not wasting their breath when in 2007 they urged the ancient historian to continue "engagements with the social sciences" and "to pursue comparative analyses".[13]

The current investigation thus conforms to a wider trend in ancient history. It takes its cue mainly from NIE. The subject calls for a more multi-faceted approach, however, and I will frequently resort to insights drawn from other socio-economic theories, from simple price theory of supply and demand to human capital theory and family economics. Many of these theories were developed for the early modern or the modern period, opening up various lines of comparison. There may be those who object to this methodological eclecticism. However, the merits of multiple models and comparanda far outweigh the deficits of in-depth knowledge of each. They are introduced mostly to develop models and hypotheses, or to illustrate the inherent (im)plausibility of explanations offered. A full comparison is often unnecessary and beside the point. The same goes for applying only one theory in a rigid way.

The range of topics dealt with in this book in consequence is much wider than work, labour, or the labour market, and includes the Roman family, associations, demography, price theory, slavery, and more. It is my belief that Roman work and labour cannot be understood without taking into account such structural factors in Roman society. Conversely, an understanding of work and labour in Roman Italy is significant for an understanding of the complex web of relations that was Roman society. What is more, ancient historians' exploration of other fields of study should ideally take place along a two-way street. The particularities of Rome have a contribution to make to the larger picture.

Setting boundaries

The chronological scope of the analysis is the early empire, starting from the reign of Octavian Augustus (31 BC–AD 14), up to and including the reign of the emperor Diocletian (284–305), who issued the important Prices

[13] Scheidel et al. (2007) 7.

Edict. That is a period of a little over three centuries. Emphasis is on the structural continuity of the empire as the background for this analysis of the working population of Roman Italy. That is not to deny the fact that political change, social conflict, demographic shocks such as epidemics, and resulting potential market fluctuations occurred in this period. Think only of the many changes which took place during the crisis of the third century. But the impact of conflict or epidemic disease, as well as long-term trends in demography, are virtually impossible to trace through the scattered and fragmentary data for prices and wages, or inscriptions that are not often securely dated. It seems appropriate to opt for a structural approach that incorporates the evidence for the whole period.

The period coincides with the time frame for which ancient sources are most abundant, including the inscriptions that will form the most important body of evidence for this book. The so-called epigraphic habit peaked in the late first and early second centuries AD and the bulk of the inscriptional evidence can be dated to the first three centuries AD.[14] And although the habit of putting up inscriptions continued under Constantine and his followers, the body of epitaphs became more and more Christianized and demonstrates a significant change in labour ethics, evident in Christian perceptions of the family and the labour participation of women.[15] For this reason, Christian inscriptions and other Christian sources are not taken into account. Other evidence for the Roman period is similarly concentrated in the Principate.

This study concentrates on Roman Italy, the core region of the early Roman empire. A high urbanization rate and an unprecedented degree of sophistication of the urban network had consequences for the development and the nature of the Roman Italian labour market. The population of the imperial heartland was more dense than in the provinces, and the wealthy elite was disproportionately based there.[16] Moreover, Roman Italy was where the exceptional city of Rome was located: the capital functioned as an engine generating economic opportunity throughout Roman Italy.[17] Sociopolitical circumstances in the Roman empire were also conducive to economic prosperity. Under the first emperors a relatively stable government was established. The Pax Augusta was firmly in place, and the population of Roman Italy in particular benefited from Italy's exceptional position through exemptions from taxation. From the perspective of NIE,

[14] The term 'epigraphic habit' was coined by MacMullen (1982); see Beltrán Lloris (2015) for a clear explanation of the concept and its interpretive problems; cf. Cherry (1995); Meyer (1990).

[15] On the Christian doctrine of the dignity of labor, e.g. Pleket (1988) 275.

[16] Scheidel (2007a) 47, Table 3.1 at 48.

[17] Cf. Morley (1996).

then, prospects were particularly good for the Italian part of the Roman economy.

Because the scope of this work is considerable and impinges on many other topics, it is important to signal the boundaries of its reach. My focus is specifically on the non-elite. The elite was a relatively closed segment of the population. The boundaries between the elite and the sub-elite were nevertheless permeable. The elite probably needed a continuous influx of newcomers to sustain itself, both in terms of numbers and in terms of wealth; freedmen may not have been allowed in, but their descendants were.[18] The resulting elite was engaged in a very distinct type of work, in a 'labour market' for magistracies, priesthoods, and the like. The elite therefore features mainly on the sidelines of this work, so to speak, as employers, investors, property owners, and heads of household. Much that will be said about elite *domus* holds true as well for that one very particular household, the *familia Caesaris*. But as the imperial household grew into the bureaucracy of an empire, the specific nature of the *familia Caesaris* deserves the more detailed separate treatment that it has received elsewhere.[19]

Most Romans were engaged in agriculture and, to a lesser extent, the exploitation of other natural resources: Roman society had an organic economy.[20] Scheidel's educated guess is that "there is no good reason to believe that more than one person in eight would have been permanently or predominantly engaged in non-agrarian labour".[21] Hence it could easily be argued that a focus on urban labour largely ignores the majority of the population, but this is not, strictly speaking, true. Roman Italian cities survived on the products from the land that surrounded them. Some craftsmen lived in the countryside and some farmers lived in the city. Farmers sold their surplus in the urban market, and potentially hired extra labourers there for the harvest. Conversely, many city dwellers must have been migrants from the countryside who moved to the city for seasonal labour, or who settled there more permanently. The distinction between the urban and rural population therefore was not clear-cut.[22] But a focus on city dwellers in the context of labour is justified by the fact that labour differentiation as a rule takes place in an urban environment, and occupational inscriptions are largely from an urban context.

18 On the Roman Egyptian elite, much of which is also relevant for Roman Italy, cf. Tacoma (2006); on elite and intermarriage with wealthy merchants, Broekaert (2012) 58–60.

19 Schumacher (2001); Boulvert (1974); Weaver (1972); Chantraine (1967); on Julio-Claudian households, see also Penner (2013).

20 This includes mining, and could include glassworks, potteries, and brickmaking.

21 Scheidel (2007a) 80, talking about the whole of Greco-Roman antiquity.

22 Cf. De Ligt (1991).

Work in the army, too, is a world apart that still awaits treatment in a full-length monograph: there were indeed those employed as artisans and craftsmen in the army, travelling or stationed with the legions.[23] Most of them are not part of this discussion for obvious reasons. Occasionally, the army men do feature in this book, but only insofar as they returned home safely and lived out their days in the cities of Roman Italy. Thus a certain Lucius Artorius was a veteran of the legio XIX commemorated in the early second century in Cesena, where he presumably lived out his days as a butcher, judging from the motifs on his funerary relief.[24]

Labor omnia vicit improbus: conceptualizing labour and work

> There was much work and there were many workers in the ancient world but one clear, unequivocal concept, which abstractly and unequivocally denoted labor, was lacking.[25]
>
> Work, as we know it, is a modern invention.[26]

Pleket and Gorz point to a fundamental difficulty in studying Roman labour. What are we studying when we study Roman work, or Roman labour?[27] To the Romans, there was not necessarily a concept of work, as opposed to leisure: the *cum dignitate otium* glorified by Cicero probably was not something the non-elite could really relate to.[28] The linguistic

23 To my knowledge the exceptions that briefly discuss the manual labourers in the army are Strobel (1991); and Rink (1983); cf. Herz (2017); specifically for medics and medicine, Aparaschivei (2019).

24 *CIL* 11.348: "L(ucius) Artorius C(ai) f(ilius) mil(es) / veteran(us) leg(ionis) XIX / Artoria L(uci) l(iberta) Cleopatra / L(ucius) Artorius L(uci) l(ibertus) Licinus"; with Zimmer (1982) no. 8, who argues that the freedman L. Artorius Licinus was the butcher because of the placing of the butcher motifs on the monument; the survival of a veteran of the fated Legio XIX that was almost completely lost at the Battle of the Teutoburg Forest in 9 AD incites questions about the dating of this inscription in the 120s, since the number XIX was never again used for any Roman legion.

25 Pleket (1988) 268–69.

26 Gorz (1989) 14. Cf. also Von Reden, *Der Neue Pauly* (first appeared online 2006), s.v. "Unemployment": "Unemployment was not an economic problem in Antiquity, because concepts such as full employment and working population did not exist." For a good attempt to tackle the issue of unemployment in antiquity, Pleket (1988) 271–75.

27 Verg. *Georg.* I. 145–46, *labor omnia vicit improbus*: "Toil triumphed over every obstacle, unrelenting Toil", translation H. Rushton Fairclough, rev. G.P. Gould (Loeb Classical Library 1999).

28 Cic. *Sest.* 98. Cf. in this context the useful conceptual difference is made by Van der Linden (2011) 27–28: there must have been times of 'non-work', "recovery from work through, for instance, relaxation or sleeping", but probably less time reserved for

antonym of *otium*, *negotium*, does not actually mean 'work', but 'business undertaking'. The citation from Gorz underlines the fact that the historian's understanding of what 'work' is differs over time.

"Obviously, labour history is about labour", Van der Linden and Lucassen write in their programmatic paper, *Prolegomena for a Global Labour History*.[29] But that does not necessarily make it clear what labour is. Is labour the same thing as work? If not, what is work? In common parlance, both labour and work can refer to any variety of activities; in scholarly analysis, they are often used more specifically. Thus labour history has long focused on labour in a relatively restricted sense, specifically referring to wage labour in the context of early capitalism.[30] By contrast, the concept of work appears to be a relatively recent one, which addresses the limitations of the earlier use of 'labour'. Despite the efforts of Verboven, ancient history cannot yet rely on a clear labour–work terminology, and a clear definition of both concepts is urgently called for.[31]

This monograph studies Roman labour in a very specific sense; that is, according to the definition of labour in the *Oxford English Dictionary*: "Work (esp. physical work) considered as a resource or commodity, typically when necessary to supply the needs of the community or for the execution of a particular task; the contribution of the worker to production."[32] Labour in the sense of "work [...] considered as a resource or commodity" has a Marxist ring to it, which in the formulation of the *OED* is probably a reflection of the current Western capitalist interpretation. Its history suggests a distinct difference between the commodification of work and the commodification of workers, however, which would effectively exclude slave labour from the definition. Since enslaved labour is explicitly meant to be included in this analysis, commodified labour should be taken to encompass labourers as a commodity throughout.

"Work [...] considered as a resource or commodity" presumably means that it is a money-making engagement, where in case of a dependent labourer the money may also be made by someone else. Latin *labor* carries the same connotations as its derivatives 'labour', Italian *lavoro*, Spanish *labor*, *et cetera*, associating it with (physical) pain or hardship.[33]

leisure or 'anti-work', "all playful activities that cost a lot of energy but are not meant to produce useful objects or services" – in other words: *otium*.

29 Van der Linden and Lucassen (1999) 8.

30 See Chapter 6 below.

31 Verboven (2017c).

32 *OED* online (March 2022), "Labour", s.v. 10a (accessed 5 May 2022).

33 *OED* online (March 2022), "Labour", s.v 1 and esp. 2a: "Bodily or mental exertion particularly when difficult, painful, or compulsory; (hard) work; toil; *esp.* physical toil" (accessed 5 May 2022). Hofmeester and Moll-Murata (2011) 15 note the ambiguity in early modern vocabulary.

The efforts of labour, specifically hard work and manual labour, may also be indicated by ***opus***; it is no coincidence that condemnation to hard labour is ***damnatio ad opus***. ***Operae***, conversely, indicates service and implies choice.[34] ***Operae*** is also the legal term for the requirement of a certain amount of labour for their former masters that some manumitted slaves had to provide in return for their freedom.[35]

'Work' as a concept would seem to be broader than 'labour', referring to a wide range of actions inclusive of labour.[36] Greek *ergon/ergazesthai* appears to cover a similar width.[37] Labour historians broadly adhere to the definition of work drawn up by the sociologists Chris and Charles Tilly:[38]

> Work includes any human effort adding use value to goods and services. However much their performers may enjoy or loathe the effort, conversation, song, decoration, pornography, table-setting, gardening, house-cleaning, and repair of broken toys, all involve work to the extent that they increase satisfactions their consumers gain from them. Prior to the twentieth century, a vast majority of the world's workers performed the bulk of their work in other settings than the salaried jobs as we know them today. Even today, over the world as a whole, most work takes place outside of regular jobs.[39]

Their definition is important for two reasons: first, Tilly and Tilly correctly emphasize the importance of non-wage labour in many historical societies. The Roman empire is no exception to that. Wage labour may not have been as marginal as it is sometimes thought to have been, but the existence of a large number of slaves and ex-slaves alone significantly complicated the make-up of the working population in Roman society.[40] A highly inclusive definition of work like this is therefore necessary in order to do justice to the complexity and diversity of Roman labour relations, encompassing unfree and free labour, dependent and independent labour, as well as the regularly unremunerated economic contribution of women

[34] Lewis and Short eds (1958) s.v. ***opera***, write, "opus is used mostly of the mechanical activity of work, as that of animals, slaves, and soldiers; operae supposes a free will and desire to serve".

[35] Mouritsen (2011b) 224–26.

[36] ***OED*** online (March 2022), "work", for work being inclusive of labour, s.v. 4 and 5 (accessed 5 May 2022).

[37] Pleket (1988) 268.

[38] Hofmeester (2018) 317–18; Hofmeester and Moll-Murata (2011); Van der Linden and Lucassen (1999); in ancient history, Verboven (2017c) 4–6.

[39] Tilly and Tilly (1998) 22.

[40] On the presumed marginality of free hired labour, famously Finley (1998) 68, 127, 136; on the development and combination of wage labour and slavery in the late republican countryside, Rosafio (2016) 104.

and children.[41] Second, because the definition of Tilly and Tilly is the one that labour historians embarking on the path of global labour history seem to adhere to, opting for the same definition opens up enormous potential for comparison.

In sum, whereas 'work' indicates the recent broadening of scope in the scholarly field, the term 'labour' acknowledges a debt to neo-classical and Marxist labour history. There is a fertile tradition of labour history to build on, and a wealth of comparative material. That said, it is important to acknowledge a fundamental difference in the meaning of labour and work that is conceptually useful, where labour is a 'money-making engagement' and work is "any human effort adding value". This book is about Roman labour, set in the context of Roman work.

The discourse on work: the Roman elite

Most of the ancient evidence was written by and for men from the elite. This is hardly a new observation, nor is it unique to the Roman empire:

> Elite discourses are dominated by members of the elites and by intellectuals. In all the periods under consideration, members of the subordinate classes, and particularly wage dependents and manual workers, participate rather indirectly, as objects, in discourses on work. Very seldom do they appear in the sources as active speakers. The great exception, however, is made up of people of the 'middling sort' such as merchants and artisans, who based their identities, self-esteem, and political demands upon their work.[42]

The study of work through literary sources and legal texts explicitly became a study of 'attitudes towards work' rather than of 'work'.[43] Roman labour was conceptualized mainly through the eyes of those who derived status from the fact that they did not have to work: the Roman elite.

One famous passage that is repeatedly invoked in this context is Cicero's *De Officiis* 1.150–51.[44] In this passage, Cicero distinguishes between trades and employments that are becoming to a gentleman (*liberalis*) on the one hand, and those that are not so becoming (*illiberales*) and are lowly (*sordidae*) on the other. A list of the latter follows, including such jobs "which incur ill-will" (like tax collectors), and all wage workers,

[41] The economic value of unremunerated labour had been stressed earlier by feminist scholars; see the influential work of Tilly and Scott (1978).

[42] Ehmer (2014) 112; with reference to Lis and Soly (2012).

[43] See, for example, the diachronic studies of Lis and Soly (2012); Ehmer and Lis eds (2009); Van den Hoven (1996); Applebaum (1992).

[44] Apart from the aforementioned works (n. 43), also in e.g. Dixon (2001c) 113 ff; Joshel (1992) 66–67; Kampen (1981) 114–15; Treggiari (1980); Finley (1973) 41–57.

"for in their case their very wages are the warrant of their slavery". There is, says Cicero, some merit in the more skilled jobs, particularly those that benefit society "such as medicine or architecture or teaching – they are respectable for those whose status they befit".[45] Ultimately, however, Cicero advocates that agriculture (in the sense of landholding) is the only fitting source of income.

This is just one source, of course, but the reason for its frequent appearance in discussions of the subject is that "Cicero the moralist has proved not a bad guide to prevailing values".[46] The Roman elite as a rule looked down on those who had to work for a living. A very similar attitude regularly prevailed among the higher classes at least up until the Industrial Revolution and even after, when manual labour was still held in relative contempt compared to landholding.[47] For the majority of the population, however, it would be a luxury to engage in philosophical reflections about work or non-work: work to them was a necessity, a simple fact of life. Elite disdain towards the working population would make no one give up their occupation. There is one thing that a strong elite ideology potentially could have done, however: it may have changed the way that individuals arranged to be remembered.[48]

The dignity of work: the non-elite

> [J]ob titles, in contrast to jobs, exist because [...] men and women actually called themselves foot servants, financial agents, silversmiths, and jewelers.[49]

The literary sources appear to show a relatively coherent picture that does not take kindly to work and labourers. It is now realized that this ideology, however, does not match well with the way the labourers themselves refer to their work. De Robertis first pointed to the significant difference of opinion between what he called *l'ambiente volgare* – that is, views toward labour

45 Cic. *Off.* 1.150: "Qui in odia hominum incurrunt [...]; est enim in illis ipsa merces auctoramentum servitutis"; 1.151: "ut medicina, ut architectura, ut doctrina rerum honestarum, eae sunt iis, quorum ordini convenient, honestae." Translation Finley (1973) 41–42.

46 Finley (1973) 57.

47 For pre-industrial Europe, see most extensively Lis and Soly (2012). A substantial section of this impressive volume is devoted to the attitudes towards work and workers in Greek and Roman antiquity.

48 Cristofori (2016) argues that the elite view of work was not entirely uniform, and explores the extent to which the elite and the non-elite views of work complemented and interacted with each other; cf. Cristofori (2004) 79–80.

49 Joshel (1992) 71.

among popular ranks – and *l'ambiente aulico* – or attitudes from within the elite milieu.[50]

Occupational inscriptions

The voice of the non-elite is not lost entirely. From Roman Italy, occupations are known mainly through inscriptions. Epitaphs record an occupational title for between 2,000 and 3,000 Romans from Italy, depending on what criteria are applied (see below); around a hundred monuments had tools of the trade or scenes from work depicted on them instead of, or in addition to, an occupational inscription. Professional associations professed their shared occupation publicly through their very name, adding roughly 200 inscriptions. The occupational inscriptions and reliefs form the most important body of evidence for the current investigation.

My understanding of occupational inscriptions includes epigraphic texts with an indication of employment or job title, including individual job indicators such as 'spinning woman', or 'two brother carpenters', as well as inscriptions set up by a collective like the 'association of bargemen'.[51] Not systematically included are the *instrumentum domesticum* – that is, any writing on artefacts (a great many signatures and/or stamps) – and *inscriptiones parietariae* – that is, wall inscriptions or graffiti – the second type is de facto limited to Pompeii and Herculaneum.[52] These two types of sources are of a fundamentally different nature than the other inscriptions with job title, and on top of that are often fragmentary and offer very little information on the labourers themselves – thus they are not included among the occupational inscriptions. They do feature occasionally as circumstantial evidence for work and labour.

It must be presumed that on a tombstone, occupation was recorded as a result of a conscious choice of the deceased (for a funerary monument constructed *se vivo*) or their heirs: a slab of marble can only contain so much text, so the decision what to record becomes highly significant. Epitaphs are set up at a very particular time: at death. Their importance transcends death, however. Remembering the life of the deceased, with the active participation of the living in setting up the tombstone and the observance of rituals of remembrance thereafter, these texts are highly informative about life in Roman society. An occupational title predictably is added most

[50] De Robertis (1963) 21–97.

[51] *Quasillaria*, e.g. *CIL* 6.6339; *duo fratres fabri tignuarii*, *CIL* 6.9411; *collegium naviculariorum*, *CIL* 6.1740.

[52] *Instrumentum domesticum*, collected in *CIL* volume 15, and see the papers collected in Nicolet and Panciera eds (1994); and in Harris ed. (1993); cf. Salvaterra and Cristofori (2016) 63–64 with n. 42 for additional bibliography; the *inscriptiones parietariae* are collected in *CIL* volume 4.

often for the dedicatee, but not uncommonly for the dedicator as well, and occasionally only for the dedicator to the exclusion of that of the dedicatee.[53] To many artisans, to *collegiati*, and to others, work ostensibly was a source of pride and an important part of their identity.[54] The well-known monument of the baker Eurysaces in Rome traces back his wealth to his occupation in every detail: in the inscription that is rephrased similarly on all four sides, on the elaborate relief like a frieze that runs along the top, and perhaps even in the shape of the actual monument.[55] And not just the ostentatiously successful, like Eurysaces, felt that work was significant enough to record. There are examples of slave, freed, and freeborn workers – men, women, and children – and each category is attested on humble as well as lavish monuments. It is difficult to tell from a job title alone who would be able to afford an inscription, or what their work meant in terms of social status and identity; even an *alipilus*, a 'plucker of armpit hair', was able to set up quite a sizeable tomb and dedicate it to his wife as well as to an unknown number of freedmen.[56]

What one does for a living has become one of the main features of identification in the present day. Roman job titles are evocative and often have a familiar ring to them. It seems to me that this has invoked a certain feeling of identification with these 'ordinary' Romans among historians and their readers.[57] Partly for that reason, perhaps, there has been no lack of scholarly attention to the occupational inscriptions. This is especially noteworthy considering the fact that occupational indicators are found in merely a small minority of all inscriptions. A percentage is difficult to provide, mainly because it is unclear how many inscriptions from Roman Italy have come down to us altogether. Despite that, it seems

[53] Similar findings for the western provinces in Varga (2020) Graph 5.

[54] Joshel (1992) *passim*; Varga (2020) 17: "The complexity and multitude of the occupational titles is hard proof of the fact that certain people identified with their profession regardless of what it was and that sometimes, even if modest, it became an important part of a person's life and being"; Bond (2016) on pride in disreputable professions.

[55] Petersen (2003); cf. George (2006) 23–24 for the exceptional nature of this "blatant celebration of work", but ibid. 24 for the fact that through its scale the monument also conforms to elite views: "The frieze does not memorialize Eurysaces' own work as much as his authority over the work of others".

[56] *CIL* 6.9141. There is a 'job description' of the *alipilus* by Seneca that does not suggest that it was a very respectable occupation: Sen. *Ep.* 56.2, "alipilum cogita tenuem et stridulam vocem, quo sit notabilior, subinde exprimentem nec umquam tacentem, nisi dum vellit alas et alium pro se clamare cogit" – "Think of the hair plucker with his thin, creaking voice, constantly squealing to be more noticeable and never quiet, except when he plucks armpits and forces another to scream for him".

[57] Cf. the humorous title of León (2007): *Working IX to V: Orgy Planners, Funeral Clowns, and Other Prized Professions of the Ancient World*, written for a general audience.

clear that the occupational inscriptions would probably come to well below 5 per cent.[58]

Job title certainly was considered a significant distinctive feature in inscriptions by the ancients, but considering its relative rarity, it is safe to say that job titles have received a disproportionate amount of attention from contemporary students of the ancient world. This is apparent, for example, in large epigraphic corpora that generally include a sub-header for occupational inscriptions.[59] Occupation was also singled out as one of the criteria for the subject-based collection of Hermann Dessau.[60] This long-standing awareness of occupations mentioned in ancient sources greatly facilitates research. However, the inclusion or exclusion of a text in a corpus or under a sub-header depends entirely on the editors' choice, and on their understanding of work. As we will see, the same is true of the selection criteria used for epigraphic investigations into labour and labourers specifically. The fact that this relatively small subset of epigraphic evidence tends to be highlighted may also have distorted historians' understanding of how much we actually know about labour in the Roman empire.

In the last decades of the previous century, the occupational inscriptions became a point of interest in and of themselves. A series of pioneering articles by Susan Treggiari carefully analyses and contextualizes occupational inscriptions from Rome. Treggiari raises many important questions in her considerations of Roman labourers, and of particular groups among them, such as elite households and especially female workers.[61] Astrid

[58] If around half of the approximately 2,500 occupational inscriptions come from Rome, a very rough calculation for that city would come to 1,250/60,000 = 2.1 per cent. Sixty thousand is based on the estimate in Tacoma and Tybout (2016) 358 n. 46; cf. Eck (1998) 32: "Von den rund 35000 funerären Texten, die in CIL VI publiziert sind, geben nur rund 5000 einen genaueren Hinweis auf die soziale Stellung. Doch höchstens rund 1300 von ihnen beziehen sich auf 'normale' Berufe [...]" – that would be 3.7 per cent; Sigismund-Nielsen (2006) 206 for a reassuring finding of 4 per cent in *CIL* 6 (with Table 7 at 211). Her 'random sample' of *CIL* 6 is very problematic, however. Contrast e.g. her finding of 1 per cent with occupational title in the monument of the Statilii with the thorough study of Borbonus (2014) 128, Table 9, who finds no less than 28.8 per cent for that *columbarium*; Huttunen (1974) 48, finally, talks about 9.5 per cent of dedicatees or 4.4 per cent of dedicators. His estimates should in my view be discarded entirely, however, because he works with a radically different understanding of what 'occupation' means, explicitly including senatorial or equestrian status among the occupational indicators for example (ibid., 47).

[59] E.g. *CIL*: "Apparitores et officiales (magistratum, imperatoris, vectigalium); Artes et officia privata."

[60] *Inscriptiones Latinae Selectae* (ILS) (1892).

[61] Treggiari (1973); Treggiari (1975a); Treggiari (1975b); Treggiari (1976); Treggiari (1979a); Treggiari (1979b); Treggiari (1980); cf. also the insightful chapter on written sources on working women in Kampen (1981) 107–29.

Händel employs the epigraphic evidence for preliminary observations about trade and wholesalers in Rome.[62] The fullest exploration of the occupational inscriptions to date remains a monograph by Sandra Joshel called ***Work, Identity, and Legal Status at Rome.***[63] She analyses occupational inscriptions set up by or for individuals from the city of Rome. Joshel's book characterizes the various groups who recorded or were commemorated with occupational title, and sheds light on the motivations to do so. Rather than an investigation into the Roman workforce, her work is all about the inscriptions, and it has become an essential guide to a full understanding of the material.

Since Joshel's book, there have been others who focused on occupational inscriptions in other geographical areas. A valuable thick description of the occupational epigraphy from Picenum was published by Alessandro Cristofori.[64] Outside the Italian peninsula, F.P. Rizzo devoted a book to the occupational epigraphy of Sicily.[65] These works both offer an interpretive framework, but the scarcity of the material makes it difficult to go beyond general observations on labour and the economy, and even their more general observations must therefore remain mostly conjectural. The value of these undertakings lies in Rizzo's and particularly Cristofori's painstaking collection and thorough commentary of the individual inscriptions. Varga has made available the scarce occupational inscriptions for the Latin western provinces.[66] Equally useful material for comparison is Cristofori's article on Epirus and Illyria, and the earlier work of Frézouls on Gallia and Germania.[67] The importance of the observations of Onno van Nijf in his monograph on professional organizations in the Roman East exceeds both professional organizations and the Roman East: especially his finding of a chronological development in the recording of occupation in epitaphs is valuable, though I have not been able to detect a similar trend for Roman Italy.[68] Epigraphic sources regarding *collegia* have been collected in the extensive work of Waltzing, supplemented by Menella and Apicella.[69] Waltzing remains the starting point for sources on the *collegia*, though his careful interpretive volumes have long been superseded by a rich scholarly tradition on associations (see Chapter 5 below).

[62] Händel (1983). Unfortunately, I have not been able to locate the "entstehenden Dissertation, die über die hier vorgelegte Inschriftenanalyse hinaus weitergehende Untersuchungen zum Gegenstand hat", mentioned at 90, but see also Händel (1985).

[63] Joshel (1992).

[64] Cristofori (2004).

[65] Rizzo (1993), to be consulted with the critical review of Clauss (1994) in mind.

[66] Varga (2020).

[67] Cristofori (2011); Frézouls (1991); on the city of Narbonne specifically see Bonsangue (2002); cf. also Tate (1991) for Syria.

[68] Van Nijf (1997) 40–42. At 42 he does suggest regional differences in trends.

[69] Waltzing (1895–1900) 4 vols; Menella and Apicella (2000).

Some Roman professions have attracted more attention in epigraphic studies than others, which must in part be due to the fact that they are the most common in the epigraphic record. Thus the ambitious *Wirtschaftliche Untersuchungen* of Gummerus have resulted in two meticulous epigraphic analyses of doctors, and the more general group of jewellers/metalworkers.[70] Well-documented and well-studied occupations for women are those in the medical sector, with special attention for midwives and – not strictly medical – wet nurses.[71] Other epigraphers have focused not so much on occupation, but on a particular find-spot of the inscriptions. The *columbarium* tombs from Rome and the individual households included among them are relatively easy to demarcate, which is probably why they have received ample scholarly attention.[72] Similarly, the epitaphs from the Isola Sacra necropolis are now readily accessible in a detailed and well-organized monograph.[73] On occasion, there are also more extensive microhistories into one particular labourer or a particularly noteworthy monument.[74]

An extensive catalogue of job titles in Latin is supplied as an a appendix to this book, and has been the starting point for the present analysis. The corpus of inscriptions is ever-expanding, and access to online databases for most of the ancient sources, including inscriptions, papyri, and the entire corpus of known Latin and Greek literary and documentary texts, makes it relatively easy to locate and access the sources for a particular occupation once a job title is known.[75] Having identified the source with its reference, the interested reader will be able to locate the up-to-date bibliography on the document. Identification of the occupations themselves is not straightforward, however, and it is here that my catalogue of job titles is meant to be helpful.

The catalogue itself was derived chiefly from lists provided by Joshel, Treggiari and Von Petrikovits.[76] Their catalogues proved to be complementary, presumably because they each had a distinct workforce in mind.

[70] Gummerus (1915; 1918); medical occupations: Gummerus (1932), with additional material in Cristofori (2006); Rowland (1977). For doctors, see also the archaeological approach of Jackson (2005).

[71] Laes (2011b); Laes (2010) with catalogue; Flemming (2000); Parker (1997); Joshel (1986).

[72] E.g. Borbonus (2014); Hasegawa (2005); Caldelli and Ricci (1999). See Chapter 4 below.

[73] Helttula et al. (2007).

[74] Such as Petersen (2003) on Eurysaces; this tradition, however, has been most prominent in Italian scholarship. Cf. Salvaterra and Cristofori (2016) 63 with n. 10 for additional references.

[75] Elliott (2015) is a useful guide on how to locate current (and future!) epigraphic databases.

[76] See Appendix 1 below. Joshel (1992) 176–82; Von Petrikovits (1981) 83–119; Treggiari (1980) 61–64.

Joshel lists the occupations that are attested in inscriptions for individual Romans in the city of Rome.[77] Treggiari talks about a more specific, but not clearly delineated, group of *opifices* (craftsmen) and *tabernarii* (shopkeepers), again in inscriptions from Rome.[78] Von Petrikovits, finally, seems to have aimed simply to be as inclusive as possible, working with all types of evidence and listing everything that might conceivably be considered a job – yet his list still omits professions found in Joshel and Treggiari.

In addition to consulting the work of Joshel, Treggiari, and Von Petrikovits, the volumes of the *Corpus Inscriptionum Latinarum* (*CIL*) themselves remained a necessary go-to in search of inscriptions with job titles. The *indices* in the bound volumes, and particularly the separate *index vocabulorum* to *CIL* 6, proved an invaluable tool in adding to the catalogue. The resulting catalogue was then further expanded by adding what occupations were discovered in epigraphic, literary, and legal sources or in scholarly literature. The chapter on occupations in a sourcebook by Hemelrijk from 2020, for example, included a number of specialist occupational titles for female musicians that have been added to the catalogue.[79] In compiling a new catalogue of my own, finally, I have occasionally excluded a title from the list that to my mind is not securely attested in epigraphic or other sources from the period or the place under scrutiny.[80] This process has resulted in an extensive list of 580 job titles. I hasten to add, however, that the exact number is elusive: some job titles refer to the same or very similar jobs, and usage may have changed over time.[81] What the catalogue offers is a spectrum of professions and occupational titles that provides a clear window onto the diverse nature of daily work and labour in Roman society.

77 Joshel (1992) 176: "only the titles borne by named individuals".

78 Treggiari (1980) 48: "The area of employment to be discussed is roughly that condemned by Greco-Roman philosophers".

79 Hemelrijk (2020) 124–82.

80 Such as *carnarius* (butcher), only attested in Greek in papyri; *clusor* with no references and Von Petrikovits (1981) 192, "fraglich, ob ein Handwerker"; *paracharactes*, *CTh.* 9.21.9 – 'forger', which is not in my view a job title; or *tomacularius*, supposedly a bratwurst dealer, with Von Petrikovits (1981) 117, only reference to Not. Tir. 103, 80 "(hier irrig *tomatularius*)"; also excluded but highly evocative is the *curator locustae* (locust overseer?) from Africa Proconsularis found in *CIL* 8.26517. The catalogue of the Latin western provinces in Varga (2020) includes a number of additional job titles that are not included here, because they were not attested in Roman Italy.

81 The catalogue also includes a number of decisions on my part: for example, the *hapax anellarius* was included as a variant of the more common *anularius* (ring maker), for example, but *vestifex* is a separate entry from *vestificus* because of the evident variation in job titles for 'tailors'; Gummerus (1932) identifies some chronological changes in usage for medical job titles; more generally, Neumann (1981) and Händel (1985) 501.

This spectrum of occupations ranges from the humble (such as a litter bearer, *lecticarius*) to the more privileged (gem engraver, *gemmarius sculptor*). Even legal infamy was no reason not to record an occupation: a number of male and female entertainers come up in the sources, and there is also a *lanista* (trainer/owner of gladiators).[82] Some wage-earning engagements apparently inspired more pride than others and are far more commonly attested, as indicated for doctors and wet nurses above. Merchants and tradesmen (*mercatores* and *negotiatores/negiotiantes*) of various kinds are also common.

Some members of the working population of Roman Italy used Greek on their tombstone, not Latin. To my knowledge Greek epitaphs from Roman Italy as a rule have not been taken into account by any of the previous studies into Roman labour. The necessary tools are available: there is a catalogue of occupational titles in Greek, albeit compiled for Roman Egypt, and *the Inscriptiones Graecae Urbis Romae* (*IGUR*) and *Inscriptiones Graecae* (*IG*) include in their indices headers for *artes et officia privata*.[83] Although much less numerous than their Latin counterparts, there are various forms of cultural interaction attested. From the Isola Sacra necropolis, for example, comes a beautifully carved inscription set up by Q. Marcios Dem(etrios), *archiatros* – a high-ranking doctor:[84]

> Ἰουλίᾳ Πρ[όκλᾳ]/ Τ. · Μουνατίω · Πρ[όκλῳ] / Μουνατίᾳ · Ἐ[3] / Κ. · Μάρκιος · Δη[μήτριος] / ἀρχιατρος [
>
> To Julia Procla, to Titus Munatius Proclus, [and] to Munatia E[…]. Quintus Marcius Demetrios, physician, [set up this monument]

The inscription is written in latinized Greek, by and for people with Latin or latinized names.[85] These individuals were an integral part of Roman society and their material legacy can contribute to the discussion on Roman labour. They are read together with the Latin inscriptions here, which may be justified by their consistency with what is found in the Latin inscriptions. In this light, it is perhaps reassuring to note that a study on Epirus and Illyria likewise determined that the representations of work and its social

82 *Lanista*: *CIL* 6.10200. Disreputable professions and *infamia*: Bond (2016); Edwards (1997).

83 Catalogue for Roman Egypt: Drexhage (2004); cf. Ruffing (2008) Volume 2.

84 *SEG* 13, 473 = *IPO* A 158 = *ISIS* 149.

85 Compare *IPO* A 184 = *ISIS* 157 ("D(is) M(anibus) / T(ito) Munatio T(iti) f(ilio) Proclo / Quir(ina) Iuliano / fec(it) Iulia Ti(beri) f(ilia) Procla / m(ater) f(ilio) p(iissimo?) vix(it) ann(os) VI die(s) XIIII") and the sarcophagus with inscription *IPO* A 185 = *ISIS* 158: "T(ito) Munat(io) / T(iti) f(ilio) Proclo" – both in Latin, clearly related because both mention Titus Munatius Proclus (Iulianus), son of Titus, and *IPO* A 184 also refers to Julia Procla.

values on Greek and Latin tombstones were largely similar to one another, and to representation in the Italian heartland.[86]

Inscriptions are not without biases. It is well known that the inscription-erecting population was not a direct reflection of the Roman population: men receive commemoration more often than women, and the young are over-represented, to name but a few characteristics.[87] There is local and cultural variation in epigraphic habit.[88] Occupational inscriptions come with a number of additional biases. It should be stressed once more that only a very small minority of epitaphs record an occupation at all (see above). That could theoretically be the result of a general negative view of labour and labourers in Roman society, as encountered in the elite discourse. Monuments inscribed with a job title or with an ornamental representation of work, however, would seem to emphasize pride in, and identification with, a job.[89] It is hard to believe that the elaborate funerary altar of the blacksmiths Lucius Cornelius Atimetus and his freedman Lucius Cornelius Epaphra, for example, represents anything but self-respect: it is a large monument with tools, a vending scene, and a work scene within the smithy on the sides.[90] The view that the small numbers of occupational inscriptions might be due to the fact that entrepreneurs or supervisors of a business in particular are commemorated with job title to the exclusion of their employees, to my mind, is not supported by the evidence.[91] Whereas it is true that the occupation of the head of household is more likely to be mentioned, there are many inscriptions for dependent labourers including those within the family (wives or children), and the extended household (freedmen, *colliberti*, slaves): the monument of Atimetus and Epaphra belongs in that category, too.

In my view, the most logical explanation must lie in a general inclination among the majority of the inscription-erecting population to record familial ties before anything else: this holds true for everyone, men and women, slave, freed, and free. Even so, two clear patterns may be identified. Particularly women were generally commemorated in a familial context, in accordance with Roman ideals: if women were unlikely to put up or

[86] Cristofori (2011).

[87] Hopkins (1966); Hopkins (1987); this difference is particularly marked in Rome, cf. Garnsey and De Ligt (2016) 93 with references.

[88] Hemelrijk (2015) 30–31 with references for a concise, nuanced update on MacMullen (1982), and on the concept of epigraphic density. More extensively but similarly: Beltrán Lloris (2015).

[89] Joshel (1992) 163 and *passim*.

[90] *CIL* 6.16166 (Rome, first century AD), now in the Galleria Lapidaria of the Vatican Museums: "L(ucius) Cornelius / Atimetus / sibi et L(ucio) Cornelio / Epaphrae lib(erto) / bene merenti / ceterisq(ue) libertis / lib(ertabus) posterisque / eorum."

[91] Tran (2007a) 124–25.

receive inscriptions, this phenomenon becomes even more pronounced for inscriptions with job title.[92] Slaves and ex-slaves, conversely, may not have had family to commemorate or to be commemorated by, which helps to explain that they are the ones most likely to have an occupational title in the epigraphic record.

The number of epigraphic sources is impressive, but that should not obscure the fact that their interpretation is not always straightforward. The epitaphs are often brief and offer little or no context, and it is not always clear whether an occupational indicator is meant to be a job title or a cognomen.[93] Thus the common occupation of *faber* (builder) is merely the cognomen of Gaius Petronius Faber, son of Sextus, in *CIL* 11.2067. Fortunately, more often an occupational title is unquestionably an occupational title. But even then it is not always clear what the job entailed. Was a *margaritarius* a dealer in pearls or a pearl setter? Or was he both, selling his own wares in his home–shop *taberna*? What exactly did an *aquarius* do with water?[94] Context matters, and the obscure meaning of the words regularly precludes easy comparison with better-known jobs from later periods.[95]

With certain occupations missing from the record, with other jobs under- or over-represented, and with such a low percentage of 'workers' attested altogether, it is clearly not possible to equate the individuals in the occupational inscriptions with the working population of Roman Italy. Most pieces of that puzzle are probably missing, though definite patterns can still be discerned. Other ancient sources, models, and theories are necessary to decide whether these are patterns of commemoration, accidents of tradition, or reflections of reality.

Reliefs

There is no lack of interest from students of the Roman world, as well as from the general public, in figurative scenes of Romans at work on stone or

92 Cf. Groen-Vallinga (2013); and Chapter 2 below. This pattern is universal, though it is most marked in the city of Rome; similarly, Varga (2020) Graph 4 for the western provinces.

93 Cf. Gummerus (1926).

94 Von Petrikovits (1981) 69. "Die auffallende Tatsache, dass schon seit Plautus im Lateinischen selten zwischen den Produzenten und Händlern einer Ware unterschieden wird, durfte darauf zurückgehen, dass diese Unterscheidung oft auch in der Wirklichkeit nicht existierte". Cf. Morel (1992) 232. Händel's brave attempt to identify jobs ending in *-tor* as executive employees and those in *-arius* as owners/wholesalers simply does not hold; think e.g. of the *aerarius* (coppersmith), *albarius* (stucco worker), *brattiarius* (gold leaf beater), and so on.

95 See Chapter 6 below for integrating Roman job titles in the historical classification of occupations (HISCO), with Varga (2020) Chapter 3.

frescos; the scenes of fulling from the walls of a fullery in Pompeii have been reproduced countless times, for example.[96] Occupational reliefs, however, are considerably less numerous than occupational inscriptions. They signify a more expensive form of funerary commemoration, which goes a long way to explaining their smaller numbers. Probably for the same reason, slaves are hardly ever commemorated on a monument with a relief, and that includes occupational reliefs. Freedmen predominate. It is interesting that the Gallic provinces are best represented in scholarly literature: occupational reliefs seem to have been part of the commemorative habit there more than anywhere else.[97] The Italian heartland nevertheless brought forth many pictorial sources for work.

Zimmer's collection of *Römische Berufsdarstellungen* (1982) contains about 100 funerary reliefs, shop signs, stones, and frescos from Roman Italy portraying scenes from work, and monuments depicting tools. It is the only illustrated catalogue of this type of evidence to date, and as such remains invaluable.[98] Kampen also includes a catalogue of work reliefs in her book on working women in Ostia, though her criteria for inclusion are significantly different.[99] Her catalogue includes women from Italy and the provinces, and men only from Ostia. Kampen chose to include only scenes of work, not tools, but she does include the category of mythological illustrations of work, such as an image of Amores and Psychae with garlands. In my view, this category of mythological work is mainly that: mythological. The Amores and Psychae may hint at the occupation of garland making, but they does not necessarily refer to the occupation of the deceased. Nevertheless, her catalogue adds a number of reliefs not covered in the work of Zimmer. Neither collection can – or does – claim completeness.[100]

Collecting all occupational illustrations for Roman Italy would be a different endeavour altogether, and it is my contention that doing so would not have added much to the argument of this book. Originally, however,

96 The fullery is VI. 8.20.

97 Larsson Lovén (2007); Langner (2001); Béal (2000); Chevallier (1997); also Rose (2007), particularly on Metz. George (2006) 28 suggests that the prevalence of the imagery of work in the north-western provinces was due to the fact that the elite ideology, which was after all developed in and extended out from Rome, carried less weight there.

98 Zimmer (1982) is more inclusive than Gummerus' pioneering study of 1913; Schulze (1998) offers a diachronic catalogue for all types of ancient images of child-minders (***nutrix*** and ***paedagogus***). The findings from the Roman period are small in number in both absolute and relative terms.

99 Kampen (1981) 137–61.

100 The occasional relief is still being published; see e.g. Wilson and Schörle (2009) for a funerary relief with scenes from a bakery.

inscription and relief were part of the same funerary monument, and they should be studied as such wherever possible. As often as not, only one of the two remains. Whenever we are fortunate enough to find both preserved, profession as a rule is not mentioned in the text, but is conveyed solely through the image – or vice versa. The earliest freedmen monument with explicit reference to work is the lavish tomb of the Gavii, depicting four life-size portrait busts of the family. Only in the inscription, added in uneven writing in the right-hand corner, as if it were an afterthought, is the text "duo fratres fabrei tignuares", "two brothers, who were carpenters".[101] George tentatively suggested that the freedmen monuments show a swift development throughout the first century AD, from the modest monument of the Gavii, to increasing visibility of work in emblematic motives added to the stones, to vending scenes – that is, an honourable perspective on industry – to the ostentatious pride shown on the monument of Atimetus and Epaphra.[102] In my view, the perceived 'evolution' must remain conjectural, because it relies on very precise dating based on stylistic rather than factual aspects, and these examples all fall within the broad first century AD. In epigraphy, however, dating is even more problematic. For these and other reasons it is a pity that inscription and monument are not consistently studied together; in spite of converging trends, iconography still is mostly the prerogative of art historians and archaeologists, whereas textual evidence tends to be reserved for historians and classicists. Bridging the gap is not easy, especially when dealing with large numbers of data.

Although digital humanities greatly facilitate the search for occupational inscriptions, the problem with an online database is that much information is lost in the process: a careful note from the editors of *CIL* that a sickle or a comb is depicted on the monument, for example, is as yet untraceable online. Pictures of the inscriptions and their monuments are thankfully becoming available in greater numbers, and this is a great help. But there is a long way to go before every single monument with an inscription can also be viewed. The images that are currently available are not searchable; the photos accompanying inscriptions often lack quality, and regularly do not present a full view of all sides of a monument.

[101] *CIL* 6.9411, Rome, 40 BC, now in the S. Giovanni in Laterano, Chiostro; George (2006) 20–21 for dating and discussion of how this monument highlights socially conservative values (the family) rather than occupation, under the influence of elite views on labour. For occupation only on the relief, not in the text, e.g. the altar of Lucius Cornelius Atimetus and Epaphra, discussed above, with *CIL* 6.16166; also *IPO* A 273–75, all three part of the same monument for a smith in the Isola Sacra necropolis, in this instance rather well documented: see D'Ambra (1988); Helttula et al. (2007) nos 37–39.

[102] George (2006).

Literature, law, and material remains

There is other, more indirect, evidence available as well. Glimpses of working life may be found in fragments from the satirists, like Martial 2.17 remarking on the practice of a *tonstrix* (barber) in the Subura:

> Mart. *Ep.* 2.17
>
> Tonstrix Suburae faucibus sedet primis,
> cruenta pendent qua flagella tortorum
> Argique Letum multus obsidet sutor:
> sed ista tonstrix, Ammiane, non tondet,
> non tondet, inquam. Quid igitur facit? Radit.
>
> A female barber sits just at the entrance of the Subura, where the blood-stained scourges of the executioners hang, and many a cobbler faces the Potter's Field. But that female barber, Ammianus, does not crop you: she does not crop you, I say. What, then, does she do? She skins you.[103]

The text paints a rather vivid picture of a woman who has her business well in order, and incidentally tells us that in Martial's social universe at least one *tonstrix* worked in the Subura.[104] Similarly, a novelist like Apuleius brings to the stage more than one labourer as part of the lively décor to his story of Lucius the Ass.[105]

Roman labour law or, to put it less anachronistically, the evidence from passages that refer to labour and labour relations in the Roman legal texts, is also an invaluable source. Law is at the heart of the influential monographs of Francesco Maria De Robertis.[106] Mima Maxey based her work on occupations of the lower classes in Roman society on attestations of job titles in Justinian's *Digest*.[107] The Corpus Iuris provides a wealth of information about the possibilities for hiring labour or labourers, and about liability and enforcement. Roman wage labour and labourers (*mercennarii*) can only be fully understood against the legal backdrop of the existence of labour contracts: *locatio conductio operis* and *locatio conductio operarum*. The position of slaves and freedmen in the economy is also illuminated greatly by the knowledge that their legal position of dependence makes

[103] Translation Delphi Classics 2013. The meaning of *radit* is crucial to the interpretation of the epigram; it is likely to be a pun on finances: one gets ripped off, cf. the commentary of Williams (2004) 83.

[104] There are four *tonstrices* in the occupational inscriptions, three from Rome: *CIL* 6.941, 5865, and 9493 = 33809; one from Venafrum, *AE* (1999) 473.

[105] Bradley (2012) is a wonderful collection of papers on the historical value of Apuleius' work.

[106] De Robertis (1946); De Robertis (1963); Salvaterra and Cristofori (2016) 57–59.

[107] Maxey (1938).

them particularly well suited as agents for their masters.[108] The question always remains to what extent written law can be equated with actual practice. Many labour contracts may have been mere verbal agreements, and one can wonder to what extent an unskilled labourer could resort to (expensive) measures of contract enforcement. Even so, the legal framework remains vital for an understanding of the economy more generally, for it, as Broekaert put it so aptly, determined "the norm under which trade should be conducted".[109]

Apart from textual evidence, there is also a wealth of archaeological data available, ranging from the remains of settlements, industry, and *tabernae* in the town plan to artefacts, tools, stamps, availability of raw materials, and finished product. Archaeological finds initially led to a wealth of studies on the more technological aspects of the production processes that actually created the artefact,[110] on the organization of particular workshops like the potteries at La Graufesenque, and on the patterns of trade that can be discerned in the distribution of finds. The building trade in particular, as well as other individual trades, has become the subject of intensive scholarship.[111] Monographs and articles with an archaeological outlook on particular trades or products increasingly have become engaged with the debate on the economy more generally and contain important additions to that debate.[112]

The archaeological record is being linked up with the broader questions of economic growth in the imperial period, and with important questions of supply and demand – including the demand for labour.[113] Material remains also offer additional indicators for living standards, for example moving past the question of how much food the Romans could buy, as calculated from documentary records of wages and prices, to what they actually ate, as evidenced by their skeletal remains.[114] Finds from houses are being considered as economic evidence for the household, which adds a new and

108 Rosafio (2016) 101, 107–9; Garnauf (2009); De Ligt (1999); Aubert (1994); Kirschenbaum (1987).

109 Broekaert (2017) 410 and *passim*, illustrating that the legal norm was leading in extra-legal solutions as well. Cf. also Terpstra (2008), Hawkins (2021) 101–24 on *collegia* as private order enforcement networks.

110 E.g. various contributions to *The Oxford Handbook of Engineering and Technology* ed. J.P. Oleson (2009); pioneering work in Strong and Brown (1976).

111 Building trade: Bernard (2017); DeLaine (1997); other trades, see e.g. Ulrich (2008) on woodworking; or the papers in MacMahon and Price (2005).

112 E.g. Ellis (2018) on retail; Flohr (2013) on fulling.

113 E.g. the variety of the papers in Flohr and Wilson eds (2017); labour demand, e.g. Flohr (2019).

114 Most explicitly in Rowan (2017); Lazer (2017); health also in Laurence (2005); and see below.

exciting avenue of research that sheds light on households as an economic unit from a very different perspective than household structure can.[115] The recent focus on urban (commercial) space, particularly on workshops and shops (*tabernae*), is equally relevant to the discussion in this book: if we wish to repopulate the urban landscape, the existence of *tabernae* points to urban networks of elite owners of shops, as well as a broader social context in which work and labour, workers and labourers, were markedly present in their own neighbourhood collective: people could be heard and seen; they could be approached to be contracted or reproached; their products were on display; their businesses advertised through sight and sound, as well as scent.[116]

The renewed dialogue between historians of the Roman economy and archaeologists has opened the way to new and fruitful approaches of labour and work in Roman Italy starting from the material remains.[117] Throughout this book, it has been my aim to align my findings from occupational inscriptions and reliefs with these new insights from the urban archaeological record, but also with legal, literary, and material sources in order to draft a more complete picture.

Urbanization

A focus on the urban context of labour and work requires some discussion of urbanization. What is urban and what is not? Up to a point, the choice of what counts as urban is based on the evidence: most inscriptions are commonly thought to originate in or near towns. This principle works both ways, however. If many inscriptions are found in one place, it will likely be termed 'urban'. To opt for the epigraphic approach, as is also the point of departure for this book, is to settle for an urban outlook. Occupational inscriptions thus cover mainly individuals who worked and/or died in the city. The implications of choosing an urban outlook are profound and deserve to be dealt with in some detail.

The urbanization of Roman Italy is a much-debated topic. From a historical perspective, the urban landscape of Roman Italy was well developed.[118] From a contemporary perspective, too, Roman Italy was

115 Ray (2017); Berg (2016); Allison (2004); still seminal is the work of Laurence and Wallace-Hadrill eds. (1997).

116 See Miko Flohr's *Building Tabernae* project; Ellis (2018); Schoevaert (2018); Holleran (2012); Bond (2016) for an interesting take on scent and sound of professions.

117 See Wilson and Flohr eds (2016); also the contributions of Bond, Flohr, and Murphy in Verboven and Laes eds (2017); Flohr (2012); Flohr (2007).

118 Erdkamp (2012) is a useful introduction to the 'urbanism' of the urban economy; cf. Patterson (2006); Jongman (1990) 43; cf. De Vries (1984) for early modern Europe.

flourishing: Italy could boast a population that was more dense than in the provinces, plus higher urbanization rates and a greater concentration of urban settlements than anywhere else in the empire.[119]

Overall urbanization rates for Roman Italy have been estimated at 15 to 20 per cent, without taking into account the supercity of Rome, and its harbour city, Ostia.[120] Rome of the first century AD, with its 800,000 to 1 million inhabitants, was one of a kind: the city would not be surpassed by any other city in the West until the rise of London around the year 1800.[121] The next city in line was Capua, which was significantly smaller with a population of between 40,000 and 50,000 people.[122] These are exceptions to the general pattern, however: there were only a few large towns in the Italian peninsula.[123] The urban landscape can therefore be characterized by a great variation of settlements of medium and small sizes. Regional differentiation was probably significant as well: Campania was more urbanized than Picenum, for example.[124] Apart from variation in settlement sizes, it is likely that there was also variation in their nature. While the economies of most cities seem to have been sustained by governmental or elite expenditure, entrepôt trade or production of manufactured goods for export played an important part in at least some cities. The existence of an intricate road network unlocked at least the potential for urban integration and migration towards the cities.[125]

The diversity of the urban network is reflected in the sources: about half of the occupational inscriptions come from Rome or Ostia, whereas the sizeable city of Hatria in Picenum only brought forth one.[126] The number

119 Scheidel (2007a) 47 with Table 3.1 at 48. His Map 3.2 at 76 shows the cities of the empire with greater clustering of cities in Roman Italy.

120 De Ligt (2012) Chapter 5, esp. 213, 239–40. De Ligt's findings are therefore not quite so irreconcilable with the 25 to 30 per cent urbanization rate found by Hanson and Ortman (2017) as these authors seem to suggest at 323.

121 E.g. Jongman (1990) 43. In the Eastern world a counterpart existed far earlier in Baghdad at the turn of the tenth century AD.

122 De Ligt (2012) 236; Scheidel (2007a) 78.

123 De Ligt (2012) 235–38 with Map 5.2 at 237. Cf. Erdkamp (2012) 244 without reference to De Ligt. See also Patterson (2006) 38–39; and Morley (1996) 182, both emphasizing wide variation in urban population sizes. This was apparently still true for Italy in the late twentieth century, see Garnsey (1998) 112–13.

124 De Ligt (2012) 231; this was predicted by Garnsey (1998) 113.

125 Laurence (1999).

126 *CIL* 9.5018 from Hatria records a freeborn scribe (*scriba*). Cf. Cristofori (2004). According to De Ligt (2012) 312 Hatria is one of two large towns in Picenum, but see De Ligt (2016) 55 for a correction of its estimated size from 45 to 37 hectares, which makes it a 'medium-sized' settlement. The remaining large town is Asculum, which has six occupational inscriptions (to the list in Cristofori 2004 should be added *CIL* 9.5189).

of occupational inscriptions is not always related to settlement size. Cities of roughly equal size sometimes also spawned rather different evidence for employment. It remains to be seen whether this is because of a distinctive nature of the towns, because of variation in epigraphical patterns, or simply due to the accidents of survival.

The urban population

> The city's inhabitants were always changing; at any one time they could include tourists, merchants on a regular visit, farmers in for market, immigrants who were likely to die there and natives who still hoped to get out.[127]

This passage was written about Rome. Even so, the words probably hold true for other urban settlements to some extent, many of which were performing the role of market centre where goods and services were manufactured and/or exchanged. Reading such comments, it would appear that the urban population was a rather heterogeneous body.

An urbanization rate of about 25 per cent (Rome included) and the existence of a number of sizeable cities in Roman Italy both imply a significant level of migration to towns. Urban migration theory dictates that cities need a continuous influx of migrants to keep up their population. One tier of the theory is known as urban graveyard theory, based on the fact that preindustrial cities were notoriously unhealthy places. For that reason preindustrial cities have often been portrayed as 'population sinks' in need of massive numbers of immigrants to keep up their dwindling population numbers. The second argument is thought to reinforce the first. It is based on migrant fertility, assuming that a lower marriage rate and therefore a lower fertility rate among migrants – who were mostly young males – must be postulated, leading to excess mortality rates and the need for yet more immigrants. It has convincingly been argued that urban migration theory was applicable to ancient Rome, and it can be presumed that this argument extends to the largest cities of Roman Italy.[128] It may not necessarily hold for all, or even for most, of the cities in Roman Italy, however. Whereas there is no apparent population threshold for the migrant fertility problem to apply, some settlements may have been too small to actually become population sinks.[129] If part of urban migration theory does not apply to all settlements in Roman Italy, however, that

[127] Morley (1996) 33.

[128] Tacoma (2016) esp. Chapter 5; cf. De Ligt (2013) 155; Holleran (2011) for migration into the city of Rome; Jongman (2003) 106.

[129] Tacoma (2016) 247–53 for the applicability of urban migration theory to cities

does not mean that there was no migration into towns. The promise of employment opportunities and better wages was a sure draw.

The subject of migration in the Roman world has experienced an upsurge of interest in the last decade or two.[130] The relationship between migration and labour, however, is not straightforward, all the more so because the Roman world was familiar with both forced and voluntary migration.[131] Were migrants able to find work in the city? Their options depended largely on the openness of the labour market. Was all work open to migrants? Information about labour opportunities and actual vacancies in the city must have affected migration patterns; conversely, the size and nature of migration flows will have influenced the structure of the urban population and workforce. The dominance of slavery in some sectors of the urban economy, especially in the domestic sector, may have reduced labour opportunities for free women; the presence (and influx) of slaves and ex-slaves in towns more generally could have severely impeded the opportunities for voluntary labour migration.[132] An analysis of the openness or segmentation of the labour market is one of the underlying goals of this work.

Rome and the rest

There was no place like Rome. Rome potentially accounted for up to 18 per cent of the entire population of Roman Italy.[133] The existence of a primate city is not in itself anomalous in history; it is the absence of secondary centres in Roman Italy that makes Rome so extraordinary.[134] Therefore the structure of the population and the nature of institutions in the capital may also have been very different from any other urban settlement in Roman Italy. Rome is where the emperor and the imperial government resided. Rome was also the main attraction for both the elite and the poor. The elite spent lavishly, and their taste for luxury goods and services created money-making opportunities for a whole segment of urban labourers. The clustering of urban poor in the capital, the (imperial) building trade and other jobs in which they scraped a living, and the grain

other than Rome; Hin (2016) for a nuanced view of migrant fertility; De Ligt (2012) 245–46; the threshold for population sinks is traditionally thought to be 10,000 people.

130 See e.g. the edited volumes by Lo Cascio and Tacoma (2017); De Ligt and Tacoma (2016); and the monograph by Tacoma (2016); cf. Noy (2000); Scheidel (2004); Scheidel (2005a).

131 See Chapter 2 below; cf. Tacoma (2016) Chapter 6; Holleran (2011) for voluntary migration to Rome.

132 Garnsey and De Ligt (2016) for Herculaneum (and other cities in the Bay of Naples by proxy, at 71): imported slaves may have been the majority of migrants, ibid., 94.

133 De Ligt (2012) 195.

134 Outside Roman Italy, one might mention Alexandria and Carthage, although it remains to be seen exactly how sizeable these cities were.

distributions to help support them are well known and have been the subject of many scholarly works to date.[135]

The nature of the ancient evidence from the capital should also be considered. Contemporary Rome still is a cosmopolis and home to some 2.9 million inhabitants in the city proper in the year 2021.[136] The current built-up area obscures much of the ancient city, and much has yet to be uncovered. The other side of the coin is that much of the ancient city remains visible in the shape of the present-day town plan. Moreover, there is no other city that has been studied and excavated so extensively.[137] Ancient Rome was exceptional, and because it has also been treated as such by many generations of scholars it is much better documented than any other settlement. The fact that about half of the occupational inscriptions from Roman Italy actually originate from Rome is therefore more than a reflection of an ancient reality. The gap between Rome and the rest deepens.

That Rome was a very distinct place should be kept in mind throughout this analysis. There are good reasons to believe that the functioning of *collegia*, for example, was different in Rome than in other cities.[138] Subterranean *columbaria* are attested virtually exclusively in the capital.[139] Rome had a large free proletariat, which is why the proportion of slaves among the population is likely to have been lower in the capital than in other urban settlements.[140] The only settlement that approximates Rome at all is Ostia, which to some extent might be viewed as an extension of the capital itself.[141] Even though the occupational inscriptions and reliefs for individuals are comparable in many ways to those from the city of Rome, however, it should be noted that the role of associations in Ostian society appears to have been specific to Ostia, not only different from Rome, which might be explained by the imperial presence in the capital, but also to be distinguished from associations attested for other cities.[142]

Ostia itself has inspired many avenues of research and may be considered on a par with Pompeii and Herculaneum: this archaeological triad is well represented in the evidentiary body and in scholarly literature on any subject considered 'urban', for the obvious reason that they comprise the best-preserved, best-documented specimens of Roman urban settlements in

135 E.g. Bernard (2017); Holleran (2011); Aldrete and Mattingly (1999); Brunt (1980).

136 See https://worldpopulationreview.com/world-cities/rome-population (accessed 2 July 2021).

137 With the possible exception of Ostia, Pompeii, and Herculaneum, but see below.

138 See Chapter 5 below.

139 See Chapter 4 below.

140 Cf. Garnsey and De Ligt (2016).

141 Not everyone agrees, e.g. Bruun (2011) 110–11 with n. 5.

142 See Chapter 5 below.

Roman Italy that we know of.[143] Besides the remains of the ancient cities themselves, it is also where the archive of the Sulpicii was recovered, as were the wax tablets of Iucundus, to name but two examples. New avenues of investigation are likely to amplify their prominent position in the debate despite an increasing awareness of their specific nature.[144]

It is generally conceded that no single town can be understood without consideration of its regional context. Unsurprisingly, a number of studies and conferences have focused on (parts of) Campania.[145] Campania must have been a fertile region with a welcome healthy climate; the region had close connections with the capital and for that reason many elite citizens had country estates there. Its harbour town of Puteoli provided easy access for trade and commerce in basic and luxury goods to satisfy its privileged population.[146] Campania appears to have been relatively wealthy and therefore cannot stand as representative for Roman Italy as a whole. Conversely, some of the other regions – such as region II Apulia and Calabria, or III Lucania and Brutii – show a dearth of (occupational) evidence, leading to results that also cannot be typical of the general Italian population. Our knowledge of the economic integration of Roman Italy and regional urban systems, however, is rapidly expanding.[147]

Acknowledging regional and local differences, then, a number of reasons to look at Roman Italy as a whole remains, as I have pointed out above: urbanization rates and an urban infrastructure, population density, and to a lesser extent also peace and prosperity. Roman Italy shows an internal coherence that sets it apart from the rest of the empire. In what follows, the homogeneity of the epigraphic data have led me to assume that most of my observations on work and labour are valid for the whole of Roman Italy. It will become clear that many sources demonstrably have a wider relevance to warrant such an assumption. The evidence from Rome and Ostia has much to contribute, though the differences between the eternal city and smaller settlements should always be kept in mind, particularly with a focus on the social fabric of the city. To be sure, some documents are so exceptional as to be specifically attuned to one highly specific context, such as the Album of Herculaneum – they will be treated as such, but they may still be connected with the larger picture. This book can be said to offer an insight into a universal spectrum of social ties, the relative influence of which will have been different in distinctive localities.

143 See the introduction of Ellis (2018) esp. 14, 18.

144 On Pompeii, see the introduction to Flohr and Wilson eds (2017).

145 Maiuro and Balbo eds (2019); Camodeca and Giglio eds (2016).

146 On Puteoli, Jaschke (2010).

147 Deliberate references to the titles of Tol and De Haas eds (2017); De Ligt and Bintliff eds (2019).

Urbanization and labour differentiation

Urbanization is often causally linked with economic growth and complexity, and vice versa.[148] Economic prosperity may lead to a division of labour between town and country: Adam Smith in the *Wealth of Nations* noted that job differentiation develops when sufficient agricultural surplus is produced to allow part of the labour population to take up other occupations than agriculture.[149] Urbanization therefore leads to increased job differentiation and specialization.[150] Hanson, Ortman, and Lobo confirmed this observation for the Roman empire, within the recent developments of settlement-scaling theory from contemporary urban-systems scholarship: settlement-scaling theory predicts an increase in levels of functional diversity for larger settlements, whereby functional diversity is an indicator of the division of labour.[151]

It is tempting to conceptually locate the labourers with an 'urban' occupation in towns, and to place farmers and farmhands on the land. That idea is in fact corroborated by Garnsey's answer to the question 'where Italian peasants lived' – that is, mostly on the land – and it is also the distinction that Hopkins used for his calculation of urbanization rates in Roman Italy.[152] To be sure, the division between the urban and rural workforce of Roman Italy was not as convenient as that. Not all artisans and craftsmen lived in the city, and not all farmers lived on the land. There was industrial activity in the rural areas, too.[153] There certainly was plenty of movement between town and country. But the nature of the evidence in this book legitimates a model of non-agricultural cities and an agricultural countryside.[154]

Occupational differentiation is a defining feature of the urban labour market in Roman Italy. My catalogue of job titles records no less than

148 Erdkamp (2012) 243–44; Scheidel (2007a) 81: "institutional arrangements and even moderate levels of intensive economic growth appear to have been the main driving force behind the success of urbanism". Cf. Hanson et al. (2017) 3.

149 On the rural–urban distinction, but starting from Procopius rather than Adam Smith, see also Erdkamp (2012) 241–43.

150 With 'specialization' in the sense of breaking up the production process, cf. Van Minnen (1987) 45.

151 Hanson et al. (2017). I concur with their general findings, though in my view their statistics should be read as very rough estimates.

152 Garnsey (1998) 107–33, contra the concept of agro-towns, cf. Lo Cascio (2009) 89–91; Hopkins (1978) 68–69.

153 Cf. De Ligt (1991); Rowan (2017) 127 notes the possibility of a shift in the food economy of Pompeii of the mid-second century BC from intramural to extramural crop processing based on the finds of carbonized chaff (or lack thereof).

154 Hanson and Ortman (2017) 309–10 include it as a criterion for what constitutes an urban settlement: "sites that are more likely to have engaged in secondary and tertiary activities than primary activities" – admittedly adapted to match the more conventional arguments of settlement and population size or civic status of the settlement.

580 different occupations.[155] Treggiari remarks for the city of Rome, "The opportunities available contrast favourably with the 101 jobs [...] for which regulations were made in 13th-century Paris (where specialisation went far enough to allow three types of rosary-makers)".[156] This phenomenon has been noted by many scholars, but it has led to radically different explanations.

The high degree of specialization attested has been connected to the existence of large workshops exhibiting extreme specialization: such specialization in the sense of breaking up the production process demanded only low levels of skill, because all workers made only a tiny contribution to create a complex final product that nobody knew how to manufacture any more.[157] The most eloquent ancient source for this type of decentralization, perhaps, is Augustine's *De Civitate Dei* 7.4 from the early fifth century, which has relevance for the early empire too. Augustine notes how polytheistic deities are all active within a specific territory, "like craftsmen in the quarter of the silversmiths, where one vessel passes through the hands of many artisans in order to come out perfect, even though it could have been completed by one perfect artisan".[158] Further on in the text, Augustine's description of the silversmiths hints at the existence of industrial districts, where those in the same line of work clustered together to facilitate subcontracting.[159] It is more a metaphor than it is an actual attestation concerning the work of silversmiths, but in order for the metaphor to work it must reflect reality to some extent.[160] The fact that Augustine seems to prefer the work of the one skilled artisan is not always noted but, having said that, it likely reflects religious rather than worldly matters for him.

155 See Appendix 1, catalogue of job titles.

156 Treggiari (1980) 56; cf. Tran (2007a); cf. Harris (2002) for the extensive differentiation of occupational designations in classical Athens.

157 Morel (1992) 232–34 on the existence of this type of decentralization; Hawkins (2017) 44–45 for the option of decentralization on the level of the 'firm' (i.e. workshop).

158 Translation Hawkins (2021) 66, with 66–68 on this text and its relevance for the early empire; Aug. *Civ. Dei* 7.4: "tamquam opifices in uico argentario, ubi unum uasculum, ut perfectum exeat, per multos artifices transit, cum ab uno perfecto perfici posset". It is not difficult to identify the tenor of the 'one perfect artisan' of the metaphor.

159 Topographical names hinting at clustering like this are well attested for the early empire: Holleran (2012) 51–60, MacMullen (1974) 70–79. The extent to which economic zoning existed despite these names may be debated, however. See Chapter 5 below.

160 Hawkins (2021) 67 notes that the text might alternatively be read as evidence for intensive investment by each artisan in "mastering a relatively narrow but technically demanding skill that could only be acquired with long practice". The comparison with one perfect artisan suggests to me that intensive investment is not what is meant in the text.

It is likely that this – what has been referred to as the vertical division of labour, i.e. specialization or breaking up the production process – accounts for some of the job differentiation attested in the cities, but there is more to it. There was also a horizontal division of labour, in the sense that urbanization also created a market for more, and more varied, occupations.[161] It should be noted, however, that both types of labour differentiation are related: "As settlements grow in population, individuals tend to concentrate on a narrower range of tasks, even as the overall set of possible economic tasks expands".[162]

Highly specialized jobs attested regularly are also highly skilled, such as a *gemmarius* (gem setter) or *caelator* (engraver); their high skill levels are also to be argued on the basis of the quality of products that have come down to us. In a similar vein, evidence for the intake of a more diverse diet suggests a prosperity that required an increasingly varied and large non-agricultural working population.[163] Large-scale and factory-like settings where decentralization may have taken place are solely attested in Rome and Ostia, and even then only to a limited degree.[164] There are fulleries where it does seem that some employees were either trampling clothes or rinsing them all day. More generally, however, it appears that fullers were engaged with the whole process from A to Z.[165] The modest mean size of shops and workshops in the urban landscape suggests that very often one artisan or craftsman did possess the complete set of skills. Occupational variation as a reflection of economic complexity therefore should not be overlooked, all the more since it is generally thought that the Roman economy was thriving.[166]

Some of the attested job differentiation must also be a result of conspicuous consumption; that is, the fact that elite owners liked to show off by employing a slave for every single task one can think of, however petty or insignificant.[167] The elite *domus* thus accounts for a large share of the occupational differentiation, particularly in the city of Rome.[168] There is a *margaritarius* who

[161] Ruffing (2016) on horizontal and vertical division of labour.

[162] Hanson et al. (2017) n.p.

[163] Rowan (2017) 127: "The overall increase in dietary variety must have corresponded to an increase in the number of people working in the food industry: a larger variety of fish meant more fishermen and more equipment (and, in turn, more people making the equipment) while the increased imports [...] presuppose more merchants and ships".

[164] Flohr (2007).

[165] Flohr (2013).

[166] Jongman (2014); Scheidel et al. eds (2007) 5–6; Temin (2006); or Saller (2002); without sustained economic growth: Hawkins (2021).

[167] It can also be understood as part of the slaving strategy that Vlassopoulos (2021) 64–65 calls 'prestige creation'.

[168] For elite domus and occupational differentiation, see also Chapter 4. Cf. Joshel (1992)

appears to be a caretaker of pearls, a *cubicularius* (bedchamber servant), and a *capsarius* (carrier of scroll holders), for example, none of whom we might perhaps expect to have spent all day at their appointed tasks.[169] Not all of these occupations fell to slaves, but the fact that freedmen and the occasional freeman are also attested in the elite household does not diminish the conspicuousness of a large and differentiated household.[170]

Each of these explanations accounts for part of the attested occupational differentiation, and none of them is exclusive of the others. In other words: these factors taken together account for the wide range of occupations attested.

The Roman economy and New Institutional Economics

The enormous influence of Moses Finley can perhaps largely be held responsible for the fact that it has taken so long for ancient historians to catch up with economic theory. It is no secret that Finley propagated the ancient economy as something fundamentally different from modern economies. In the eyes of Finley and his followers, Roman society had an economy that was embedded socially and culturally. The publication of Finley's *The Ancient Economy* initiated a debate between those who agreed that the ancient economy should be studied by itself, and those who chose to make the link with economics.[171] Recent decades have seen important converging trends in this primitivist–modernist debate, which has lost much of its intensity.[172]

The ultimate reconciliation between the two came, perhaps, with the introduction of NIE to ancient history.[173] Douglass North introduced the concept of institutions to economics, at a time when economics was concerned chiefly with performance, particularly the performance of contemporary entities: North held that contemporary economies as well as historical economies are embedded.[174] This approach opens up all of history as comparative material for economic theory. A focus on institutions stems from an interest in the structural determinants of economic performance, and therefore takes into account both structure and performance:

73–76, Bradley (1994) 57–80, who mentions at 58 that in the *familia rustica* as well as the *familia urbana* "the number of occupations discharged was virtually limitless".

169 Bradley (1994) 60 takes as examples an *ostiarius* and a *scoparius*.

170 Harper and Scheidel (2018) 99–100.

171 Cf. Jongman (1988) for a Finleyan analysis that does make use of modern economic theory.

172 E.g. Saller (2002).

173 For a useful introductory piece, Bang (2009).

174 Esp. North (1990). See also North (2005).

> If neo-institutional economics can be seen as an attempt to bring history to the attention of economists, it may equally well be a way to make economic theory serve the interests of historians; it is situated at the crossroads of the two disciplines.[175]

NIE is therefore well suited to the needs of ancient historians and has been taken up with enthusiasm. NIE was implemented, for example, in both Bang's influential *The Roman Bazaar* and its theoretical opposite, Temin's *Roman Market Economy* – two main contributions to the discussion on the nature of the Roman economy.[176] Others have engaged with the institutional framework provided by Roman law, transaction cost theory, or the *collegia* as social institutions.[177] New Institutional Ancient Economics has become an established, vibrant field of research.

NIE itself has gone through important developments, and is now better suited for the Roman case.[178] A full understanding of institutions includes the ways in which they furthered market forces, as well as the ways in which they may have restricted them. A distinction was made between formal and informal institutions, the latter based on social and cultural beliefs. It is simple enough to underline that relevant institutions existed, but the mere existence of institutions does not imply that they were economically efficient.[179] Cultural beliefs and social circumstances largely determine the shaping of institutions and an individual's choices, recognition of which led NIE to branch out into behavioural economics.

The advantages of applying NIE to studies of labour in antiquity specifically were advocated by Zuiderhoek:

> Focussing on institutions/organisations allows us to bring some analytical order to the great variety of different categories of labour and types of labourers which we come across in ancient sources. This is so because institutions/organisations functioned as structuring actors, that might simultaneously 'consume', i.e. buy/hire and employ, and supply labour to third parties. Thus, they in effect operated as allocation mechanisms (or channels) via which labour and labour power were distributed in ancient society. An institutional/organisational focus, moreover, can also provide us with some rationale for the great diversity of labour statuses which we encounter in antiquity, since within a given institutional/organizational context, different status positions and the specific labour relations associated

175 Bang (2009) 197.

176 Bang (2008); Temin (2013a).

177 Roman law: Terpstra (2008) and Hawkins (2017); transaction costs: Hawkins (2021); Liu (2017).

178 Verboven (2015), which is a programmatic article.

179 E.g. Ogilvie (2007); Liu (2017) 204–6, Bang (2009) 203.

> with them might well serve to reduce costs of oversight, transaction and information so as to maximize 'efficiency', in terms of output, profit or, indeed, exploitation (rent-seeking, predation).[180]

The number of institutions that are relevant to Roman labour are probably too numerous to list. For a very brief exploration, Zuiderhoek selects the institutions of the household, associations, and cities. In my analysis of work and labour, too, I have opted to deal with the family and associations, both in an urban context. That is not to deny the importance of other institutions or organizing principles, like Roman law. But in Roman labour history that ground has been covered relatively well. Verboven acknowledged the widespread use of many aspects of NIE amongst ancient historians, but emphasized the need to incorporate more fully the impact of cultural beliefs.[181] They had an influence on familial norms and values, on family form, and on the social and more formal characteristics of associations.

Discovering the Roman family[182]

"People usually do not work alone. Seldom do they only work for themselves".[183] Easily the most important structural factor that determines work and labour is the family.[184] This pattern can be perceived in many historical societies. In the modern labour taxonomy of the Global Collaboratory on the History of Labour Relations, for example, the family, "defined as a group of kin or a *household*, who pool their income and mostly live and eat together", is considered the first goal of production.[185] In other words, the suggestion seems to be that the first priority and the primary recipient of any economic gain was the family, generally before any considerations of profit in the market. The family decided on the balance between work, aimed at the maintenance and self-sufficiency of the household, and labour, directed towards the market. The interaction between the household and the market allowed for substantial household autonomy of decisions in economic strategies.[186] Considering the hypothesis that the family was

180 Zuiderhoek (2013) 43.

181 Verboven (2012a) 599: "Historians of antiquity are now familiar with several key concepts of the New Institutional Economics – such as transaction costs or path dependence – but until now they have paid very little attention to the role of cultural values and norms". See now more fully Verboven (2015).

182 With reference to the title of Bradley's influential 1991 monograph on the Roman family.

183 Hofmeester (2018) 319.

184 Cf. the preliminary observations of Saller (2007).

185 Hofmeester (2018) 319, her emphasis. The taxonomy of labour relations is dealt with in more detail especially in Chapter 6 below, and included here as Appendix 3.

186 De Vries (2008) 10–11.

so crucial in labour economics, the first question that should really be addressed is what we mean by 'family' in the Roman context.

In modern-day English, 'family' can denote basically any group of individuals, or even any group of things, all according to context.[187] It is used, for example, in the expression 'having a family' – that is, having children – or in a 'family weekend', indicating a meeting attended by what could be any random selection of close as well as more distant relatives, and sometimes even of unrelated friends from outside the family.[188] Generally, however, family is defined by kinship. Whereas the English word 'family' is certainly derived from Latin *familia*, *familia* is not equivalent to family.[189] The Romans, however, were no less versatile in their use of both *familia* and *domus*.[190]

Familia can cover a wide variety of meanings. With reference to persons, not things, *familia* may refer to the agnatic kin group, which appears relatively familiar to us. More exclusively, it may also indicate the slaves of the household. Throughout this book, however, I will limit the use of *familia* to one of its more specific legal definitions: the *familia* encompasses all persons under the power (*potestas*) of the *paterfamilias*, including wife, children, slaves, and freedmen:

> *Dig.* 50.16.195.2
>
> Familiae appellatio refertur et ad corporis cuiusdam significationem, quod aut iure proprio ipsorum aut communi universae cognationis continentur. Iure proprio familiam dicimus plures personas, quae sunt sub unius potestate aut natura aut iure subiectae, ut puta patrem familias, matrem familias, filium familias, filiam familias quique deinceps vicem eorum sequuntur, ut puta nepotes et neptes et deinceps.
>
> The term *familia* also refers to a collection of persons, connected either by their own legal rights vis-à-vis each other, or by a more general kinship relationship. We say that a family is connected by its own legal bond when several persons are either by nature or by law subjected to the *potestas* of

[187] *OED* online (March 2022) s.v. *family*: A. I "Senses relating to a group of people or animals", A. II "Senses relating to things" (accessed 5 May 2022).

[188] Bradley (1991) 3–4: "even at the level of ordinary discourse, *family* is an ambiguous, elusive term, whose meaning for any individual is shaped primarily by the variables of age and marital status, and if divorce and remarriage have anywhere entered the picture, the complications of understanding and defining are greater still".

[189] It is interesting that the lemma of the *OED* online (March 2022) s.v. *family* still includes a historical definition that does sometimes approximate the Latin *OLD* s.v. *familia* (accessed 5 May 2022).

[190] Saller (1994) Chapter 4 offers a good analysis of Roman 'family, *familia*, and *domus*'; See also Dixon (1992) 1–12; and Saller (1984).

> one person – for example, the *paterfamilias*, *materfamilias*, and son and daughter under paternal control, as well as their descendants, such as grandsons, granddaughters, and their successors.[191]

Technically a wife was only part of the *familia* if married *cum manu*, whereas *sine manu* marriage was common during the Principate. It is nevertheless likely that she was often implicitly considered a part of the *familia*.

Latin *domus* can include both cognate and agnate kin, and is perhaps a better approximation to our broader understanding of 'family'. But it, too, has a variety of other meanings, and was also used to refer to the household and everyone in it (including servants), or merely to the physical house.[192] For this reason I have limited the use of *domus* to the elite *domus* of Chapter 4.

Households may be defined concisely as "those sets of relationships, historically variable yet relatively constant, that have as one of their principal features the sharing of sustenance gained from the widest possible variety of sources".[193] In terms of economic functionality, then, the household provides a better focus than the family. It includes non-kin living in the household.[194] The addition of non-kin is significant for the current analysis of the Roman situation as well, where many households contained a number of slaves and freedmen.[195] It should be noted that the criterion of co-residence is applied more loosely here than in various other publications.[196] Household members who are temporarily away for seasonal labour or apprenticeships, and who may contribute substantially to the family income by doing so, are to be included.[197] It may be referred to as the 'family-based household'.[198]

The economic unity of the family has been well established in scholarly literature, and requires little further elucidation.[199] The study of the family

[191] *Dig.* 50.16.195.2 (Ulpian). Translation Dillon and Garland (2005) 342.

[192] See, for example, Harlow and Laurence (2002) Chapter 2.

[193] McGuire et al. (1986) 76; quoted by Van der Linden (2002) 4.

[194] An important notion found first in Laslett (1972) 24–25.

[195] Conversely, "Most slaves have been part of households." Vlassopoulos (2021) 74.

[196] Laslett (1972) 27 speaks not of household, but of 'coresident domestic group' – still opting for a co-residence criterion. His wish to uphold this measure results primarily from the fact that non-co-resident individuals would not have been registered in the census records that are the main source of evidence for many sociologists, rather than from any functional criterion.

[197] E.g. Netting et al. (1984) Introduction; also Van der Linden (2002) 4: "households do not necessarily entail co-residence".

[198] De Vries (2008) 10 n. 28 for a definition, although he does not explicitly coin this somewhat awkward but useful term before applying it.

[199] Hofmeester (2018); De Vries (2008); Van der Linden and Lucassen (1999) 9: "workers simply cannot be understood as individuals"; Cigno (1991) 2: "It is not, therefore, the economic relevance of household organization and behaviour – even when looked at

as an economic unit of individuals working and acting together took off with the development of New Home Economics in the second half of the twentieth century.[200] It was recognized that within the family, decisions on family expenses are made, the demand for which is in turn determined by the structure of the family. Production, consumption, how to manage the family income, labour allocation, and investment in human capital are typically decided within the family group.[201] With reference to occupation, family was important to everyone: to an emperor who inherited his position, to a slave or a slave's slave bound to their master's family, and to everyone in between.

There was a significant variety of family forms within Roman society, not all of which may be equally recognizable in view of modern family structures: the suggestion that the dominant family form in Roman society was the nuclear family has been long since refuted.[202] Each family form had a distinctive relation to labour and labourers:

> there were considerable differences in household composition between the elite and the lower classes, and between urban and village populations. Composition and size of households depended on the economic basis from which the family made its living, since different forms of property and economic activities required different kinds of labor. Families that were smaller and simpler in organization have been observed for day laborers, small traders, craftsmen, and fishermen, whereas peasant farmers usually lived in larger, more complex families because they needed a sufficient pool of labor to meet peak periods of labor demand.[203]

It seems reasonable to distinguish between broad categories of urban families: the non-elite family features in Chapter 3, and elite *domus* in Chapter 4. The simple dichotomy glosses over great variation within each of these two chapters, but it at least allows for a more general economic differentiation between non-elite and elite wants and needs. In both instances, it will be argued that adaptive family strategies can account for the choices that were made in their engagements with the labour market. Family, in whatever shape or size, was an important indicator of economic success and development. This monograph focuses on urban labourers. The larger rural families also referred to in the passage from Hübner therefore largely fall outside the scope of my research, except at

from the narrow point of view of the traditional interests of economists – that can be in any doubt." For Rome, e.g. Broekaert (2012) 45; Saller (2007).

200 The development is summarized in Engelen, Knotter et al. (2004) 124.

201 De Vries (2008); Mincer and Polachek (1974) 397.

202 Hübner (2011); Saller and Shaw (1984); see Chapter 3 below.

203 Hübner (2011) 82.

those times when their individual family members migrated to the city for (seasonal) labour.

Non-familial labour collectives: private associations

The Roman empire expanded to encompass increasingly more people, people who thronged together in cities and settlements to find an income through work. The town population was woven together in a complex web of social relations that made up the community, and just as most people today obtain a job through personal connections, similar networks in Roman society surely contributed to the coordination of work and labour supply and demand. Besides familial bonds, then, the social context of neighbours and neighbourhood, of patrons and patronage, and of the Roman *collegia* should be considered here.

Associations provided a solution to the anonymity of being part of a large population, a situation that we may envisage as particularly vivid for the city of Rome.[204] The *collegia* gained momentum over the course of the second and third centuries, when the formation of the empire transformed the civic make-up to give pride of place to the associations and their members.[205] *Collegium* membership was a privilege and was always reserved for a minority of the population.

The associations are generally referred to as 'voluntary' or 'private' associations in scholarly research, a useful terminology that was "designed to distinguish them from institutions such as the state, city, or family, where membership was automatic – a question of birth rather than choice".[206] I deliberately adhere to this broad definition. The advantage of an open approach like this is that it includes all relevant social collectives: for current purposes, the gains of understanding the workings of group formation and group processes trump the loss of the specific. Needless to say, this does not obviate a general need for investigations into particular associations in any way.[207]

The Latin terminology of association is varied. Most common both in Roman antiquity and in secondary literature on the subject today is

[204] This view is eloquently summarized by MacMullen (1966) 174: "Their objects were simple, summed up in the phrase 'social security': to have a refuge from loneliness in a very big world." Cf. Hopkins (1983) 214.

[205] Patterson (2006) esp. Chapter 3; see also Patterson (1992) 23.

[206] Wilson (1996) 1, defining 'voluntary' in the 'voluntary associations' of the title of Kloppenborg and Wilson (1996). On the same page, Wilson writes, "the term 'private association', which some prefer, is a possible alternative, though it too would have required careful definition".

[207] Liu (2009) 4–11 on the merits of a synthetic analysis, and on the need for complementary investigations into particular *collegia*, to which her study of the *collegia centonariorum* is an important contribution.

collegium, but in antiquity *corpus*, *sodalitas*, *sodalicium*, *koinon*, and other synonyms in both Latin and Greek were also widespread, which in itself indicates the reality of a large variety in social collectives.[208] Not all associations were recognized by the law as formal *collegia*. It has proven virtually impossible to distinguish formal from informal associations and most scholars include most or all recognizable collectives in their analysis; because all types of collective are meaningful contributions to an individual's economic and social network I will do the same here. For the sake of clarity, throughout this work the current terms *collegium* and 'association' will be used to indicate any private collective.

Roman private associations were named according to religious affiliation, location (either current location or place of origin), or occupation. A strict distinction into separate categories, however, will not hold: religious, funerary, convivial/congregational/social, and economic functions often overlapped.[209] Even the primary identity reflected in the names of associations may not be an indication of their main activities, as members of the cult for Asclepius and Hygieia were very likely doctors, for example.[210] Perry's conceptual deconstruction of *collegia funeraticia* (burial colleges), as identified by Mommsen, "calls into question the need to 'categorize' colleges at all, a notion owed, in great measure, to this exposition of the subject in the *De collegiis* [Mommsen (1843)]".[211] In sum, in order to investigate the structural influence of associations on the labour market, it is not sufficient to take into account only *collegia* identified by a common occupation.

The category of 'professional' or 'occupational' *collegia* when singled out in secondary literature generally collects *collegia* that were occupational in name. Similarly, in this monograph, the terms 'professional' and 'occupational' *collegia* will be used to refer to such associations. It bears repeating, however, that there was no clear dividing line between professional and other associations: scholars have become increasingly aware of the social function of occupational *collegia* and, conversely, of the economic activities also of *collegia* that – at least in name – were not trade-based.[212]

208 For a brief overview of terminology, see Ausbüttel (1982) 16–22, with n. 10 for earlier references; Bruun (2015) 613–14 includes membership lists of the *familia publica*.

209 Van Nijf (2002) 311–15; Van Nijf (1997) 10–11; Van Minnen (1987) 51–52 on Roman Egypt; Ausbüttel (1982) 29, 30.

210 Verboven (2017b) 176 n. 12 with reference to *CIL* 6.10234, Rome second century AD. Compare *AE* 1937, 161, for a *collegium Aesculapi et Hygiae structorum Caes(aris) n(ostri)*, who were apparently not doctors, but masons.

211 Perry (2006) 32, with reference to his dissertation from 1999 on *collegia funeraticia*.

212 Verboven (2017b).

Conclusion

The daily labour of the people in the Roman empire has left many traces for a historian to follow. From an ancient historian's viewpoint in particular, the sources for workers are very promising. Documentary texts including occupational inscriptions, law, contracts, letters; anecdotes from a literary context that refer to labour in passing; a wealth of material remains such as tools, the countless artefacts that are the result of unflagging industry, reliefs or frescos of people at work; and the archaeological remains of shops and workshops have come down to us. The wealth of evidence has, of course, not gone unnoticed, and many ancient historians have been motivated by this remarkable opportunity to explore what life was like below the elite.

Although many valuable studies exist on work in the ancient world, and although many of the sources that I will be using are well known in themselves, a systematic analysis placing occupational inscriptions and reliefs firmly in their historical context is lacking. The aim of this monograph is to offer such an analysis for the cities of Roman Italy in roughly the first three centuries AD.

This study has the advantage that much of the evidence has been made available before and that many of the biases in the evidence are now known. This makes it possible to include an exceedingly wide range of sources. Constructing an image of Roman labourers from the ancient sources alone, however, can only go so far. In my opinion, the advance of the use of New Institutional Economics makes it possible to use comparative material from other historical periods in order to delineate interpretive frameworks. In other words, comparative history should be a tool, not to accept without thinking that the situation in Rome must have been similar, but rather to build hypotheses and models, always to be tested against the evidence.

One inscriptions tells us very little about the economy as a whole, but a few thousand texts that document workers may well further our understanding of the labour market by uncovering underlying patterns. There are indeed guesstimates, percentages, and statistics in this book, but perhaps not as many as might be expected in a book on work and labour. The choice is deliberate. Others have been engaged with number crunching, and their data have gratefully been used to confirm the more general patterns and orders of magnitude that will be presented for various aspects under discussion. It is my contention, however, that the evidence does not allow for decisive statistics. It will be argued that work and labour are as much a part of the dynamic life cycle of individuals as they are influenced by changeable cycles of supply and demand. Because of this, and because this is a synchronic approach to the ancient evidence, the inclusion of too-specific numbers would provide the reader with a false sense of security. The overall patterns are nevertheless clear. As such, I believe that the context of social structures will provide a rich and insightful picture of the place of work and labour, and of workers and labourers, in Roman society.

Chapter 2

Labour and Labour Market Theories

Introduction

The heterogeneous nature of the people at work in Roman Italy should be clear from the introductory chapter. This finding fits in quite well with investigations into labour history and labour market theory. This chapter will elaborate on the ways in which economic theories may aid us in our understanding of Roman labour and labourers, and it will apply them to identify the most important distinctions among workers that governed the lived reality of the ancient Romans. Understanding these factors governing the labour market in turn sheds light on the workers outside the market.

Labour market theory revolves around the commodification of free labour, and the understanding that labour and labourers can move to the market. The existence of forced labour – slavery – in a historical society in theory effectively negates the existence of a labour market. However, scholars are increasingly aware that price theory is subject to various non-economic restraints. The most important of these is labour market segmentation: restrictions and limitations will occur in any given labour market on the basis of various socially and culturally determined factors for discrimination, such as gender. It is my contention that in Roman society, legal status was just another such discriminating factor. Slave, freed, and free may not always have been interchangeable, but they were certainly part of the same labour market.[1] Therefore I believe that an integrated analysis of the labour force in its entirety is the only way to comprehend the workings of the Roman labour market and to bring out the options available to any one individual.

That there was such a thing as a Roman labour market is not commonly accepted. *Der Neue Pauly* offers an entry under "Arbeitsmarkt" that may serve to illustrate this:

> Mit Bohannan und Dalton ist zwischen dem Markt a) als Ort und b) als preisregulierendem Mechanismus von Angebot und Nachfrage

[1] Cf. Temin (2004); Temin (2013a) 114–38.

> zu unterscheiden. Während sich ein A. im Sinne von b) in der Ant. nicht herausbildete, war Arbeit wie andere Waren auf dem Marktplatz erhältlich. Entweder konnte sie dauerhaft in Form eines Sklaven gekauft, oder temporär von einem freien Lohnarbeiter "geliehen" werden (lat. *locatio*; …). Umgekehrt konnte jeder seine Arbeit auf dem Markt anbieten.[2]

This reference article may be labelled 'job market', but it negates the existence of a labour market in antiquity, as opposed to a market for labour. In this view, moreover, the market for labour appears to be limited to the actual marketplace. The author is a well-respected scholar working on the ancient economy, whose views may be expected to have wider support. This chapter therefore argues that it is useful to analyse Roman labour and labourers in terms of a Roman labour market, taking into consideration that the concept of a labour market is more complex than merely serving the law of supply and demand. And if we can speak of a labour market, then in what ways can labour market theory contribute to our understanding of Roman society, in terms of both the urban labour market and the work and labour systems outside it?

Chapter outline

Neither the active presence of market economics, nor the reality of an integrated labour market, is entirely self-evident in a slave society that predominantly leant on agriculture.[3] It is therefore necessary to justify the use of such modern economic concepts in a Roman context. I will argue that the question whether or not the Roman economy was a market economy is the wrong question to ask. Few historians would deny that sources for the Roman economy attest to market transactions and market forces at work. The focus of research should be on how the Roman market functioned, and in what way economic theory can contribute to an understanding of it. It will become clear that Roman market economics demonstrate the existence of market regions rather than an integrated market economy.

According to economic price theory, a labour market is characterized by freedom of movement and wages that move in response to supply and demand.[4] This narrow definition does not take into account that societies are governed by social and cultural factors that will always lead to market segmentation, and it will therefore be argued that a broader concept of labour market is necessary to operationalize it for the Roman world. The subsequent investigations into labour mobility, therefore, focus not only on

[2] Von Reden, ***Der Neue Pauly*** (first appeared online 2006) s.v. "Arbeitsmarkt". The English version translates it as 'job market'.

[3] Harper and Scheidel (2018) on the Roman slave society.

[4] E.g. Temin (2013a); Temin (2004) 515.

possibilities and factors that facilitated movement, but also on restrictions to (labour) migration within Roman Italy.

The very idea of a free labour market, with wages that move in accordance with the laws of supply and demand, seems irreconcilable with forced labour in a slave economy. The question of the extent to which slave and free can be considered to have been part of a unified labour force will therefore have to be dealt with in some detail. The percentage of slaves is thought to have been significantly higher in Roman Italy than in the rest of the empire, which makes the matter all the more interesting in this context.[5] It is not just the dichotomy between slave and free, however, that might preclude full labour market integration. The same holds true of the historically unstable balance between male and female workers, and that between skilled and unskilled work. The Roman labour market is likely to have been made up of multiple local labour markets with limited movement between them. Market segmentation explains this pattern of restrictions to individual movement and opportunities within the Roman labour market.

The last section of this chapter deals with labour supply and labour demand. The combination of a dense population and a high urbanization rate in Roman Italy made for a thick urban labour market: in other words, there were more workers than work. This is likely to have been particularly relevant for unskilled wage labourers. A copious labour supply in this sector is underlined by the scarce evidence for remuneration, which suggests that wages were low; for the majority of people, living standards were therefore probably low. Labour demand in Rome was variable due to fluctuations and seasonality of consumer demand and the building/shipping trades, which were conducive to cyclical unemployment or underemployment. It was difficult to scrape a living in the city. But the city was the place to do it.

The Roman economy

Since the early 1980s, the debate on the nature of the Roman economy has moved on considerably, and this has freed the way for a novel interpretation of labour.[6] There probably are not many ancient historians who would deny that there were market forces at work in Roman society. The regular attestation of prices, contracts, rents, and wages points to the existence of market forces in the Roman economy. The plentiful use of coinage in the Roman empire is well known and does not require further elaboration

[5] De Ligt (2012) 190, Table 4.3 for a tentative percentage of 40 per cent slaves in the cities of Roman Italy, cf. Hopkins (1978) 68.

[6] See, e.g., de Callatay ed. (2014); Scheidel ed. (2012a); Temin (2013a); Bowman ed. (2009); Scheidel et al. eds (2007); Scheidel and Von Reden eds (2002); The papers in Garnsey ed. (1980) in my view formed an important turning point in Roman labour studies.

here.[7] The one document that provides most of the Roman price data we know, Diocletian's Prices Edict of AD 301, is price regulation on a massive scale that was likely a response to market-driven inflation; moreover, market forces were so strong that they may well have caused the Edict's failure.[8] In the words of Von Reden, "That the Roman economy was not simple – that it set market prices, sustained development, and had room for growth – is old news".[9] But what form this took, and to what extent economic theories can be applied, is still the subject of debate.

The Roman market economy

> There is a lot of information, but hardly any of what economists call data.[10]

Roman historians have not shied away from using various economic principles in their analysis of the Roman economy.[11] Many of such economic principles rest upon the null hypothesis of a functioning market economy in the society under scrutiny.[12] The logical corollary that the Roman economy therefore may have functioned like a market economy, however, has only found a true protagonist in Peter Temin over the last two decades, culminating in his 2013 monograph *The Roman Market Economy*.[13] It is worth pointing out that the initiative to promulgate the more general view of a Roman market economy came from an economist rather than an ancient historian.[14] Economists seem to accept the view that Rome had a market economy.[15] Responses from scholars of the ancient world, however, are more reserved than the economist reviewers. One ancient historian reviewed the book for the *Times Literary Supplement*, concluding that "Temin has, I fear,

[7] E.g. Howgego (1992); cf. Verboven (2017a); and Harris (2006) on other means of payment.

[8] Temin (2001) 173; Groen-Vallinga and Tacoma (2017).

[9] Von Reden (2014) 536.

[10] Temin (2006) 134.

[11] Contrary to what Temin (2006) 133 writes: "Ancient economic history is in its infancy, both because few economists have learned much about the ancient world and because ancient historians have typically not incorporated economics into their analysis".

[12] Temin (2001) 170, repeated verbatim in Temin (2013a) 6: "This is a problem for the study of the Roman economy, because it is precisely this typical null hypothesis that needs to be tested".

[13] Temin (2013a); Temin (2001).

[14] Cf. Temin (2013a) 1: "The application of economic reasoning to ancient history is growing, but more ancient historians than economists are interested in ancient economies".

[15] E.g. Berg (2014) 37; also Grantham, unpublished paper for the Work, Labor and Professions conference, Ghent, 31 May 2013.

done a good job of persuading me that there was really nothing resembling an integrated Roman market economy".[16] In the reviewer's opinion, the Roman economy does not lend itself to 'new economic history', because it leaves the social aspect of economic transactions out of the equation.

In my view the problem with Temin's work can, perhaps, be summarized as follows: the market economy is too theoretical, too abstract and all-encompassing a concept and it cannot simply be imposed on the Roman empire. It needs to be tailored to fit the specifics of that empire. The question is not whether or not the Roman economy was a market economy – there is no yes or no answer – but to what extent the market economy model, and the closely related presumption of a functioning labour market, may have explanatory power for the Roman empire. It does not matter whether or not Finley was wrong. We need to progress from the theoretical model of a market economy to the specifics of market forces in the empire, from the existential question whether Rome had a market economy to a utilitarian perspective that can usefully apply the economics of the market to Roman Italy.

The value of Temin's *The Roman Market Economy* to my mind lies in the far-reaching hypothesis of an integrated market in the Roman empire. Precisely this extreme attempt to emphasize a supposed complete interconnectedness within the early Roman empire in my view brings out how the market was broken up into segments and regions.

With market integration comes price correlation. Temin suggested that the wages for work in the mines of the Roman empire support the existence of a functioning, empire-wide labour market, since the wages of the miners at Mons Claudianus in Egypt resemble those for gold miners in Dacia (Alburnus Maior). The mining trade, however, is likely to have been largely under imperial control. The imperial administration would have set standard wages which may even have limited labour migration.[17] To illustrate that the Roman empire constituted an integrated market, moreover, Temin places much emphasis on his analysis of the grain trade. On the basis of just six references to grain prices, he establishes a supposed correlation between price and distance to Rome, which would illustrate an integrated market for wheat.[18] This argument does not hold and has been

[16] Thonemann (2013). The review by Ivanov (2013), trained as an economist, interestingly does not fit into the category of work by economists nor that by ancient historians and is quite insightful.

[17] Nuanced critique in Holleran (2016) 96–97, with references. For the approximation of wages in Egypt and Dacia: Cuvigny (1996) 142–45, as evidence for integrated labour market Temin (2013a) 118, who does note the possibility of intervention of the Roman state.

[18] Temin (2013a) Chapters 2, 5.

the focus of justified criticism. “No amount of regression analysis is going to convince many ancient historians that six pieces of data, taken from a period of more than two centuries, are sufficient to demonstrate the integration of the entire Roman wheat market”.[19] In a thorough analysis of the (qualitative as well as quantitative) evidence for the grain trade, Erdkamp demonstrated that market integration was regional rather than empire-wide.[20] The grain trade may serve as an illustration of a more general pattern. In antiquity, the infrastructure for goods and, more importantly, information was slow and therefore largely unsuitable for full empire-wide integration.[21] Market integration therefore was also slow, and may rather have been compartmentalized into smaller market regions within the empire.

Market forces are also identified by Temin in the instrumental behaviour that shows from Roman literature. Instrumental – that is, economically rational – behaviour would be indicative of free competition in a market economy.[22] In a famous anecdote, Plutarch speaks both of Cato the Elder’s clever way of investing in shipping enterprises, minimizing risk by taking on only 1/50 share, and of the way he bought slaves to sell them for double after a year of solid education.[23] There is no way of knowing whether Cato’s behaviour was truly economically rational, however, and to what extent his decisions were also determined by considerations of reputation or social capital, and of convention. Seeking profit is no evidence for market integration.

The historical circumstances of the early Roman empire facilitated market exchange. The trading opportunities that came with the foundation of the empire were unprecedented. Formal institutions created the necessary infrastructure to maximize profit: the Pax Romana, a relatively stable government, and an empire-wide legal system greatly contributed to the increase and the success of business enterprises and commercial

19 Morley (2013) n.p., with reference to Temin’s “tendency to adopt unrealistically sharp distinctions and polarities”. The economist reviewers, too, invariably mention these six data. See Bransbourg (2012) s.v. “the law of small numbers”; with response by Temin (2013b); for a very different analysis of the grain market see Erdkamp (2014); Erdkamp (2005).

20 Erdkamp (2005); Erdkamp (2008).

21 As Temin himself notes, e.g. (2001) 179. See also Bang (2008); Terpstra (2008) esp. 352–54.

22 Temin (1980) on instrumental behaviour, which is to be expected in market exchanges, as opposed to customary and command behaviour – see also the brief summary in Temin (2001) 171–72.

23 The reference is to Plut. *Cat.Mai.* 21. Temin (2001) 175; Temin (2006) 134; Temin (2013a) 103, 129, 188. Columella’s careful description of the vineyard business and the cost involved is another choice illustration; Colum. *RR* 3.3, 7–11, cited in Temin (2006) 143; cf. Temin (2013a) 136.

partnerships.[24] Not every historian is convinced of the effectiveness of these institutions, however. The role of formal institutions was regularly complemented or replaced by informal networks of family, friendship (*amicitia*), patronage, and (professional and other) associations.[25] The following chapters will provide ample proof of that. The social structure of society was crucial in the development and maintenance of networks, and these are likely to have been of a local, or at most regional, nature. This pattern is demonstrable in trade, but also in human mobility; that is, migration patterns. Temin's chapter on financial intermediation and Roman banks and loans incidentally provides an excellent illustration of this phenomenon.[26]

The evidence for market activity typically originated from an urban context, and the literary and juristic references sprung from the top layers of society. The peasant farmers of the Roman empire are hardly represented at all, and it remains to be seen how market-oriented they were.[27] As Temin points out, "Although market activity was only a minority of all productive activity, it was the dominant mode of activity of 'literate Rome'".[28] In other words, the presumption of market activity goes a long way to explain the evidence that has come down to us, much of which is in written form. With that, accepting the possibility of market exchange in Rome becomes essential to our interpretation.

Integration and market forces in the Roman empire were probably strongest among the cities of the Italian heartland, with the city of Rome in particular taking centre stage. The concept of a market economy has explanatory power for the Roman empire, if only because much of the ancient evidence comes from market transactions. That is all the more valid for Roman Italy, where there may have been more of a market economy than anywhere else in the empire, because of its high degree of urbanization and strongly integrated city networks. Rome itself functioned as the single biggest market for food, goods, and people in the empire.[29] Even within the boundaries of Roman Italy, however, regional differences occurred and we

[24] Temin (2013a) 100; cf. Woolf (1992) for the view that it was the expansion of empire in the last centuries BC rather than the stable empire that created the largest integrated markets.

[25] Cf. Hawkins (2021); Broekaert (2012); Broekaert (2011); Verboven (2012b); Verboven (2002); Terpstra (2008).

[26] Temin (2013a) 157–89.

[27] De Ligt (1993) argues that they were not market-dependent.

[28] Temin (2001) 180.

[29] One economist writes, "To my mind the existence of the city of Rome with a population of close to a million pointed to the existence of a sophisticated division of labour that was inconceivable without a flourishing market economy." Koyama (2013) 270.

have to allow for variation in the degree of market integration within and between cities, and between city and countryside.

The Roman labour market

The labour market deals in a particularly elusive good. Labour is immaterial, unlike physical capital, which can change hands. That distinctive feature is complicated by the existence of slavery in Rome: slaves and slave labour are material and *can* change hands. The Roman labour market therefore is not only an interesting subject that deserves closer scrutiny in itself, but as a pre-industrial labour market with slave labour it is also a particularly instructive case study to test labour market theories.

It is necessary to identify first and foremost what is meant by the designation 'labour market'. Temin characterizes a labour market in economic terms:

> A functioning labor market couples a labor demand with a labor supply. Two conditions must be filled, at least partially: workers must be free to change their economic activity and/or their location, and they must be paid something commensurate with their labor productivity to indicate to them which kind of work to choose.[30]

This definition readily presents two guidelines for testing whether there was a labour market or not: the extent of labour mobility, and market integration for wages and labourers. An analysis of Roman labour mobility and market integration in accordance with price theory cannot present the full picture, so I suggest opting for a socio-economic interpretation of the concept of 'labour market'. The *Dictionary of Sociology* offers some insightful additions to this principal definition and is worth quoting at length:

> In a labour-market, human effort (or labour power) is made into a commodity, which is bought and sold under terms which in law are deemed to constitute a contract. The purchase and sale of formally free labour developed extensively with capitalism, but alternative paths to industrialization [...] have entailed wage employment, though not strictly a free market for labour. Economists argue that, as with other factors of production, the market for labour can be understood as a special case of the general theory of prices, with the price (wages or salaries) being determined by supply and demand. However, research on actual labour-markets has shown that, in practice, many of the basic conditions assumed by price theory are usually absent. Mobility of workers

[30] Temin (2013a) 115.

> between jobs is often sluggish or non-existent; the anarchic structure of earnings differentials bears only the loosest relation to labour supply and demand; discrimination, labelling, racism, and sexism are rife. Economic explanations of labour-market processes have to be supplemented, and sometimes replaced, by sociological analysis, creating a promising field for interdisciplinary research.[31]

Market imperfections will be a recurrent theme in the following investigation into the Roman labour market. Thus distinct patterns of mobility will become apparent that may have facilitated or restricted labour movement. Labour market segmentation will therefore have limited market integration. Seen in this way, the Roman case may not present us with the numbers or statistics for a strictly economic analysis, but there is plenty of qualitative evidence that can increase our understanding of the Roman urban labour market, and that adds to its value in a historical comparison.

Labour mobility

Economic theory, then, holds that a functioning labour market requires freedom of movement for labourers.[32] Freedom of movement includes geographical movement, as well as movement between employers, or between occupations. The socio-economic concept of a labour market furthermore predicts that there will be certain restrictions and governing principles to labour mobility.

Geographical mobility: labour migration

The pull of the city was strong. Overall living standards were probably better in the urban centres than in the countryside of Roman Italy – even if inequality was high and a large part of the urban population lived in poverty. The hope of a better life must have been irresistible to many. Many of the rural–urban migrants in Roman Italy will have been attracted by the (expectation of) labour opportunities in towns.[33] That is particularly true for Rome, but the expectation of better wages is likely to have drawn labour migrants to smaller urban settlements, too.[34]

[31] Scott and Marshall (2009) s.v. "labour-market".

[32] Temin (2013a) 115: "labor needs to be mobile enough to bring wages for work of equal skill near equality", or rather "approximately equal", (ibid. 120).

[33] Tacoma (2016) 172: "Much – though certainly not all – migration is related to work." For an indication that wages were higher in the city of Rome than in the Egyptian countryside, see Temin (2013a) 254; on inequality in towns generally see Gilbert (2013) 685; cf. Holleran (2011) on the city of Rome; Holleran (2016) offers an insightful account of labour migration to mining centres.

[34] The analysis of Herculaneum in Garnsey and De Ligt (2016) indicates that there may have been few options left open to free labour migrants in smaller centres like

There appears to have been no fundamental predisposition favouring local labour over migrant labour in Roman Italy.[35] That does not necessarily mean that migrants' chances in the labour market were equal to those of city-born Romans. Labour-induced migration is governed by different factors than trade or market integration. Human mobility of the free population is guided by social networks, institutions, and services, both in the place of origin and in the place of destination.[36] In Roman cities, this networking is substantiated by the (professional) associations, and by a close-knit system of patronage, both of which may not have been easy to access, which potentially made it difficult for migrants to resettle permanently. The necessary reputation to gain credit to set up a business, or credibility as a business partner or employee, was generally built on these very same networks. Migrant networks and family were therefore the supporting instruments of chain migration.[37] Indeed, the chapters below discuss some of the evidence for migrant networks or family in this role, such as merchant associations or the more regional social connections for apprenticeships.[38]

There were perhaps more opportunities for migrants seeking temporary hired labour, especially for the unskilled labourer.[39] The temporary and seasonal nature of much of the available work in this category made slave labour unprofitable.[40] Instead, many of these temporary labourers will have been freeborn farmhands from the surrounding countryside. The life cycle of rural families and the seasonal cycle of agricultural work left many able workers underemployed for extensive periods of time.[41] As a result, many farmhands would attempt to find some additional form of income in the city. These cyclical migrants were not just the poor; it has been reasonably argued that especially those farmers who were better off could profit most from these opportunities.[42] Patterns of (seasonal) occupational pluralism

Herculaneum (ibid. 84) – though Herculaneum appears to be something of a special case: see De Ligt and Garnsey (2019); Mouritsen (2019). Cf. Holleran (2016) 98 n. 16.

35 Tacoma (2016) Chapter 6. Most of his analysis for Rome holds true for Roman Italy.

36 On labour migration in general see L. Lucassen (2013); in Roman antiquity, Holleran (2017) 96–97.

37 Tacoma (2016) 201–2, 232–40; Zuiderhoek (2013) on these allocative institutions; Holleran (2016) 96–100 on the importance of migrant networks for finding work in Rome.

38 Family networks are discussed in Chapter 3, associations in Chapter 5, below.

39 Cf. Zuiderhoek (2013) 47. Holleran (2011) is pessimistic about migrants' chances in the capital.

40 Erdkamp (2016) 37–38.

41 Erdkamp (2016); Erdkamp (2008); Erdkamp (1999).

42 Erdkamp (2016) 37–38.

are also attested in other historical societies.[43] Many of the available urban labour opportunities, however, were found in sectors that did not always match the seasonal cycle of the work of the farm: the building trade and the shipping trade are likely to have been their main employers and were also subject to a seasonal cycle of their own. The building trade could nevertheless support a number of workers for around nine months a year. It is likely that there were some vacancies left for wage workers who wanted to settle, or who already lived, in the city.[44]

Humans typically move over shorter distances than goods, which implies that free labour markets were probably local, or regional at most.[45] Unfree labour, conversely, may have moved over somewhat greater distances, similar to perceived market patterns for goods. This concerns soldiers, convict labour, and, above all, slaves.[46] Slaves were a much-needed addition to the urban population. In all likelihood they were purchased and then moved to the city in order to fulfil labour demands for domestic service in an elite *domus*, or to work in smaller workshops: slave migrants were thus a direct result of urban job opportunities and this will have meant significant competition for free labourers looking to find work.[47] This supposition holds even if some slaves were primarily acquired to add to the prestige of their owner and were only engaged in work as a secondary aim.[48] It has even been suggested that voluntary slavery could be a means for some to bypass the significant cost of migration.[49] Arguably, that would put such forced labourers directly at the heart of the job market.

The nature of the urban labour market also determined the character of labour-induced migration.[50] Urban labour demand in Roman Italy is likely to have been volatile. This was due to the seasonal trades, but also because of fluctuating demand for (luxury) goods.[51] High mortality in an urban environment theoretically leads to job openings.[52] But there was no lack of

43 McCann (1999) on nineteenth-century Nova Scotia.

44 Garnsey and De Ligt (2016) 84, 90–91.

45 For local labour markets, cf. Holleran (2013) 238.

46 Woolf (2017); convict labour: Groen-Vallinga and Tacoma (2015).

47 Garnsey and De Ligt (2016) 82–84; De Ligt (2013) 155: "the vast majority of the cities of the Roman empire seem to have grown as a result of local or regional processes of migration and as a result of elite expenditure on urban slaves"; for the elite *domus*, see Chapter 4 below. The pattern is most clear for the capital, but there are indications that it is also realistic for other cities; see De Ligt and Garnsey (2012).

48 Bodel (2011) 312: "Everything a slave did, except what was done at the master's sufferance, was done for the master and thus constituted work".

49 Silver (2016).

50 L. Lucassen (2013).

51 Hawkins (2021) esp. Chapter 1.

52 Garnsey and De Ligt (2016) 91.

job applicants either. Not for every fortune seeker could a year-round stable occupation be found. Because of unstable labour demand, there must have been a large group of unskilled labourers who migrated to the city only temporarily. Such unskilled wage workers historically were mostly young males.[53] The Roman city had very little to offer in terms of social security or security of employment, and the *annona* in Rome was an exceptional arrangement for which most labour migrants would not have been eligible.[54] To cushion these insecurities, migrants generally maintained close bonds with their family in the countryside, and many must have returned there. To skilled workers, however, the cities of Roman Italy may have provided a more stable environment to settle permanently. Skills strengthened their position in the labour market, and they may also have benefited more from the institutional framework of voluntary associations, such as the manifold professional *collegia*.[55]

Job hopping

Changing employers or changing jobs in the Roman city was not particularly difficult, at least in theory. Much of the available labour was hired labour performed under limited-term contracts, varying from day labour and bespoke assignments to longer-term agreements.[56] Various passages in the *Digest*, for example, discuss the theoretical situation of a slave apparently rented out for a period of a year.[57] The problem, then, was not the theoretical possibility of changing jobs, but the practical implications of finding work.[58]

Slavery, it seems, did not preclude freedom of movement in the labour market. There is some evidence suggesting that slaves were allowed to

[53] Tacoma (2016) 113–23 argues that migrants to the city of Rome were mostly young males. On (the limits of) female mobility in Roman society, cf. Woolf (2013); and various publications of Foubert, e.g. (2013).

[54] Erdkamp (2016) 47; Brunt (1980) 94–95; Holleran (2017) 87. But compare Jongman (2007) 605 who believes that "public subsistence support was indeed one of the salient features of Roman life"; conversely, Silver (2016) suggests that a lack of resources and networks could be a motive for self-sale for, e.g., migrants from the Near East, by which they would gain an entirely different kind of 'social network'.

[55] Compare Tacoma (2016) 202: "In practice this meant that those who had already had success at home would be the best placed to make the move, but at the same time they were exactly the persons who might have had the least incentive to do so: they would have already have settled and might have started a family." Holleran (2016) 114; see also Chapter 5 below.

[56] Groen-Vallinga and Tacoma (2017) on the predominance of hired labour and the various forms of remuneration in Diocletian's Prices Edict; Holleran (2016) 95–96; Treggiari (1980) 51.

[57] *Dig.* 24.3.7.10 (Ulpian book 31 ad Sabinum); *Dig.* 33.7.19 (Paul).

[58] Holleran (2017) for the mechanisms of finding work in the city of Rome.

exploit their own labour for a wage during the times their owner had no work for them. In such instances, the slave apparently paid his owner a set remittance each day; if he earned more than he owed, the slave could thereby enhance his own assets (the *peculium*).[59] This was a mutually beneficial arrangement: the slave could earn money, and saved his owner the trouble of finding employment for him. Hiring out slaves, by their masters or by slaves themselves, was a common way of cutting costs in other slave societies: in British and antebellum America, as well as in ancient Athens.[60] The *Digest* presents a number of clear references to such practices in the Roman empire.[61] Labeo, for example, discusses liability in the case of an incompetent muleteer:

> *Dig.* 19.2.60.7
>
> Servum meum mulionem conduxisti: neglegentia eius mulus tuus perit. si ipse se locasset, ex peculio dumtaxat et in rem versum damnum tibi praestaturum dico: si autem ipse eum locassem, non ultra me tibi praestaturum, quam dolum malum et culpam meam abesse: quod si sine definitione personae mulionem a me conduxisti et ego eum tibi dedissem, cuius neglegentia iumentum perierit, illam quoque culpam me tibi praestaturum aio, quod eum elegissem, qui eiusmodi damno te adficeret.
>
> You hired my slave as a muleteer; your mule died because of his carelessness. If he leased himself out, I say that I will be responsible to you only up to the value of his *peculium* or the amount of my enrichment. If, however, I leased him out, I will not be responsible to you for more than the absence of my bad faith and fault. If you hired a muleteer from me without specification of the individual, and I gave you the man from whose carelessness the mule died, I think that I will be responsible to you also for that fault, because I chose the one who caused you the loss in question.[62]

[59] Cf. Hawkins (2021) 143–46, citing Colum. *RR* 1 pr. 12. Columella seems to refer to a self-hiring slave when he mentions a wage worker's daily tribute (*quotidianum tributum* = remittance?). Incidentally, a slave could also hire out his/her under-slaves (*vicarii*) and make a profit from that (*Dig.* 14.3.11.8).

[60] Hawkins (2021) 143–46 with references; Vlassopoulos (2021) 62–64 includes it among slaving strategies for revenue extraction.

[61] For other indications of slave self-hire in the *Digest*, see the references in Brunt (1980) 88 n. 42 and in Hawkins (2021) 143–46; for both hire and self-hire of slaves, see especially Jonkers (1933) 112 n. 1; Bürge (1990) has argued at length that the term *mercennarius* refers exclusively to another man's slave, renting himself out. Möller (1993), however, argues convincingly that the converse is true and that *mercennarius* refers to freeborn wage labourers, unless the addendum *servus* (vel sim.) appears. See also the comments of Scheidel (1994) 153–202 *passim*.

[62] Translation Martin (2001) 112–13 n. 17.

The text specifically discusses the possibility that the slave hired out his own labour, contrasting it with the option in which the slave was hired out by his owner.

Changing occupations was perhaps more difficult for a freeborn specialist, an artisan or craftsman. Tied to one skill set and possibly also to work-related property, changing jobs was reserved for the next generation. In the early empire, occupation was not always inherited. On the one hand, there is ample evidence for family businesses and for sons following in their fathers' footsteps; such intergenerational continuity would be the obvious strategy when the family owned a workshop. On the other hand, many children had a different occupation from their father or mother. If a workshop was rented rather than owned, this would have facilitated career changes.[63] The family business could not always be handed down to biological children, which could be remedied by apprenticeship, adoption, or even manumission. Families with more than one child (that is, more than one heir) might seek to differentiate in order to spread the risk of unemployment or underemployment.[64]

There were no guild restrictions in Roman Italy that would have impeded a change of occupation, or of location. The comparison between professional associations and medieval guilds has proven useful in some respects, but the Roman associations did not entertain a monopoly like the medieval guild may have done.[65] Affiliation with an association was not an inherited right, but was based on individual merit. Significant numbers of artisans and craftsmen did not even join the associations and operated independently or through separate networks. That situation only changed in the late third and early fourth centuries.

Despite the fact that there were no structural inhibitions to labour mobility, actual evidence of Romans switching jobs is scarce. The fact that there are few people whose careers we can trace is in line with the nature of the evidence: someone like Lucian, for example, would not be commemorated for his brief endeavour as an apprentice sculptor in his epitaph.[66] The closest thing to a 'career' perhaps is a provocative graffito from Pompeii scolding someone who held various jobs in the past, and supposedly would do anything for money now: *nunc facis si cummu(m) linx<s>e<e>ris, consummaris omnia*. "The joke would surely only work if changing occupations were possible".[67] The most obvious advancement,

63 Tacoma (2016) 196.

64 The hereditary nature of jobs and intergenerational persistence will be discussed in more detail in Chapter 3 below.

65 But see Chapter 5 below for the fact that medieval guilds may not have had such a monopoly either.

66 Luc. *Somn.* 1, discussed in Chapter 3 below.

67 *CIL* 4.10150, Holleran (2017) 88 n. 12. It is the only example of changing occupations that she adduces.

however, is a career within the elite household, from slavery to freedom. There is some evidence for slaves moving between jobs (or tasks?) in the *Digest* and in epigraphy; similarly, Petronius outlines the fictional career of Trimalchio in some detail – pageboy, apprentice accountant, and paymaster, as well as his engagements in business as a freedman.[68]

Market integration and labour market segmentation

Previous studies on Roman labour have tended to pay much attention to status distinctions of labourers. This has prompted many scholars to concentrate either on free independent artisans and craftsmen, or on slavery. As a result, the artisans and craftsmen, for example, have sometimes been understood as a Roman 'middle class', and were sometimes equated with wealthy freedmen – a stance that was reaffirmed by Mayer's influential monograph of 2012.[69] Strong distinctions like these, however, do not hold in face of the evidence from occupational inscriptions and are likely to distort a broader view of workers and labourers in Roman society. It is my contention that the entire working population can and should be studied together.

The distinction between slave and free workers was important in the notoriously hierarchical society that was Rome, and will receive due attention in the analysis. But in addition two other dichotomies seem to govern the discussion about the Roman labour market: between skilled and unskilled, and between male and female, workers.[70] Economic theory of a functioning labour market predicts full market integration. Labour segmentation theory, however, predicts that the labour market was not fully integrated, but divided into corresponding 'segments' or smaller 'labour markets', that were not automatically interlinked. Consequently, these dichotomies are likely to reflect real restrictions to what jobs were open to an individual.

Slave and free labour

Slavery was crucial in the economic development of the Roman empire, and it permeated all aspects of society. In many ways, therefore, Roman society can be seen as a slave society.[71] The division between free and unfree

[68] For multitasking slaves, see Chapter 4 below; Trimalchio's career is outlined in Petr. *Sat.* 29, cf. the summary in Petersen (2006) 3–4.

[69] Mayer (2012); the less burdened terminology of 'non-poor, non-elite' that is applied in Flohr and Wilson (2017) 15 is much preferable.

[70] See also Tacoma (2016) 170–203 for the same three basic distinctions plus a paragraph (195–99) on permanent, temporary, and seasonal work; Tacoma (2018) distinguishes also between dependent and independent labour; Hawkins (2013) singles out only gender and legal status.

[71] Harper and Scheidel (2018); Bradley (1994) 10–30; cf. the objections of Vlassopoulos (2021) 1–6.

labour is not always clear-cut in the ancient discourse, and that (deliberate) fuzziness has implicitly been taken up in scholarly literature.

The Roman elite likened wage employment to slavery. Cicero wrote of wage labourers that "their very wages are the warrant of their slavery".[72] The close connection between working for wages and slavery is reinforced also when Chrysippus tries to soften the position of a slave by calling him a "perpetual wage-labourer".[73] These passages may be among the first uses of the concept of 'wage slavery' that would become prominent in the late nineteenth and twentieth centuries.

The elite openly expressed their loathing of manual labour in general: agriculture was the only decent way to earn a livelihood.[74] Joshel sums up nicely the picture painted in the ancient sources: "Doctors kill their patients, and teachers corrupt their students [...] Businessmen always cheat, and rich auctioneers are usually crass. Men who make their living in commerce are materialistic, and they will try to use their wealth to claim precedence."[75] On closer inspection, however, some occupations apparently were not deemed quite as disreputable as others. Jobs can be perfectly respectable for those "whose status they befit" ("quorum ordini conveniunt"), such as architects.[76] Elite disdain of work focuses "on the relationship of dependency that work signified rather than on the status of who performed it".[77] The equation of workers and slaves perceived in ancient literature is therefore largely superficial.

A more literal reading of the Roman elite view of manual labour, however, has coloured historians' perception of labour in the Roman world in the past:[78]

> Economists sometimes express surprise that free labour should have played so small a part in the Roman world, whilst besides the slaves a *plebs* of

[72] Cic. *De Off.* 1.150: "est enim in illis ipsa merces auctoramentum servitutis". Translation Finley (1973) 57. Cf. Treggiari (1980) 52: "most of the passages cited to prove [that the Romans equated wage earning with slavery] seem insubstantial or ambiguous, except for Cicero's famous and rhetorical phrase". For Cic. *De Off.* 1.150 and elite views on labour, see also the Introduction above.

[73] "Mercennarius perpetuus"; Chrysippus in Sen. *De ben.* 3.22.1.

[74] Cf. Chapter 1 and, e.g., Van den Hoven (1996) 49.

[75] Joshel (1992) 63–64. Similarly, Van den Hoven (1996) 49: "This train of thought in both pagan and Christian authors often resulted in not so much a dislike of trade as a dislike of traders. This is, of course, very similar to the traditional opinion of the Greeks and Romans concerning crafts: the product of the craftsman was not frowned upon, nor his skills, but the craftsman himself was".

[76] Cic. *De Off.* 1.151. Compare Or. 9

[77] Bodel (2011) 317.

[78] See also Holleran (2017) 87 with references; Tacoma (2016) 176 n. 34.

> several hundred thousand men inhabited the capital and other *plebes* not subject to the authority of any owner lived in all the large towns under both the Republic and the Empire. But all surprise is removed when one considers the institutions [i.e. the *annona*] which permitted this proletariat to live in idleness [...] Free labour, which however never completely yielded to servile labour, lost its power of resistance in proportion to the ability of the *civis romanus* to live at the expense of the State.[79]

The opinion voiced here by Louis downplays the contribution of free labour to the economy. In this view, the freeborn in the countryside – the majority of the population – were thought to have been farmers;[80] the idle poor in the city did not work; they were mollycoddled by means of bread and circuses instead – at best, they could be employed in the imperial building projects.[81] Note that in this, once again, the situation of the city of Rome is extrapolated to assumptions about the Roman empire.

The conjecture that all manual labour was performed by slaves was supported by the fact that ancient evidence on slave labour and working freedmen is more abundant than that on free labour: slaves and ex-slaves predominate in the occupational inscriptions by a wide margin. It is now known, however, that this is partly the result of biases in the material. Slaves nevertheless made up a significant percentage of the urban population, perhaps over 40 per cent. The percentage may well have been lower for the city of Rome, but it would still amount to between 25 and 30 per cent.[82] Percentages of this order of magnitude clearly indicate the importance of slave labour within the urban economy. But they also illustrate that the majority of the working population must have consisted of free labour.[83]

In Roman society, overall welfare levels were low (see below). It was only in the city of Rome itself that the dole satisfied (or partly satisfied) a basic need for grain, and that was only for a select group of the urban non-elite; even the dole, moreover, will have left people in need of additional income.[84]

[79] Louis (1965) 2. Cf. Sall. *Cat.* 37.7.

[80] Also, e.g., Treggiari (1969b) 90: "leaving [the free Romans] two occupations only, farming and war", although she hastens to add that "displaced and unemployed citizens were often glad to undertake ['servile' work]".

[81] On the importance of the building trade, e.g. Brunt (1980). But see Holleran (2011) 171–72.

[82] Cf. De Ligt (2012) 190, Table 4.3; De Ligt and Garnsey (2012) for Herculaneum; Joshel (1992) 46–49.

[83] Holleran (2017) 87–90; Tacoma (2016) 176–78; cf. Temin (2004) 526: "slaves were not the dominant labor force either in the city or the countryside of the early Roman empire".

[84] Erdkamp (2016) 46–47; cf. Brunt (1980); LeGall (1971). On the dole, see e.g. Aldrete and Mattingly (1999).

Common sense dictates that the group of free labourers in the cities must have been substantial, if only because a life of leisure in accordance with elite ideals was probably out of reach for most. The urban labour market therefore was not solely populated by slaves, although it is clear that slaves held an important share in it. The existence of a large urban slave population, combined with the hypothesis that the free urban population had to work for a living, leads to the expectation that slave and free often must have worked side by side. Slaves thus constituted not an economic, but primarily a legal, category.[85] If slavery is regarded as just one type of labour relation among a spectrum of possible labour relationships, the question remains: why was this quite extreme type so popular?

In many instances, more than one objective was met through slave-holding, and such 'slaving strategies' must often have overlapped.[86] Since the seminal work of Orlando Patterson, *Slavery and Social Death*, the importance of asymmetric relationships of power between enslaved and enslaver has become universally recognized in studies of Roman slavery.[87] It is difficult to estimate the value of prestige and social capital gained through slave-holding in the eyes of the Romans, or their perception of the economic security of access to dependent labour.[88] The various ways in which slaves and freedpeople contributed to the Roman economy, however, can nevertheless be investigated. Servile labourers' economic position could provide them with some measure of power over their own lives. Occupational inscriptions indicate that (ex-)slaves experienced work as a source of pride, shaping their identity as well as ties of association among their peers. Their labour was the driving force not only of agricultural estates, but also of the domestic households of the elite. Non-elite households too will often have included one or two slaves who actively participated in work and labour. Slaves were not infrequently placed in positions of trust and authority, which made them virtually indistinguishable from free hired labourers.[89] The range of occupations attested for slave, freed, and free persons is broadly similar. If some slaves were acquired with the goal of prestige or gratification in mind, in many instances they were purchased with an eye to the extraction of labour and revenue.[90]

Slave and free were therefore part of the same labour market, and if that labour market functioned according to economic price theory, they would have had to compete in price. There is little evidence for wages from

85 Bradley (1994); Temin (2004).

86 Vlassopoulos (2021) 58–74.

87 Patterson (1982); cf. its reception through the lens of Bodel and Scheidel eds (2017).

88 Scheidel (2005b); Scheidel (2008); cf. Hawkins (2017) 48 ff.

89 Vlassopoulos (2021) 64.

90 Slaving strategies in Vlassopoulos (2021) 58–74.

Roman antiquity to work with.[91] Even if there were more attestations to wages, slaves do not always receive any. The relative price of slave labour is hard, if not impossible, to calculate. An attempt to account for the price of freedom (which is invaluable) from a modern perspective, as undertaken by White, may be morally sound but it is also anachronistic and cannot lead to an understanding of the economic contribution of slavery within Roman society.[92] An interest in the economic value of slave labour is nevertheless reflected in slave prices: male slaves commanded higher prices than female slaves under the Roman empire. If slavery were based merely on traditions of honour and prestige involved in owning slaves, rather than on their economic value, we should expect prices to be similar for all slaves.[93] A definite awareness of the profitability of slave labour is also present in, for example, Columella's careful calculations of how many slaves and supervisors are needed to work a vineyard, or in Varro's advice to hire doctors, fullers, or builders rather than provide expensive job training for slaves to do those jobs.[94] The antique authors never explicitly compare the cost and benefits of slave versus free labour, however.

It should be emphasized at this point that slave and free were not static categories. An individual could move from one to the other category: slaves could be granted their freedom through manumission, and free men could be enslaved through debt bondage, penal slavery, and self-sale. Freed status was not permanent either, because the next generation would be freeborn.

One could say that slavery offered additional labour opportunities. Self-enslavement is in essence simply a particularly striking form of freedom of labour movement and economic strategy. Historically it is a desperate measure for individuals to turn to when there is no other option for sustenance left – "rather as when in seventeenth-century India, as Braudel records, a Persian ambassador acquired 'innumerable slaves [...] for almost nothing because of the famine'".[95] It has indeed been argued, unconvincingly in my view, that in Roman Italy the prospect of enslavement may have been desirable when compared to the life of the free urban poor, though the incidence of self-enslavement remains the subject of debate.[96]

91 Groen-Vallinga and Tacoma (2017); Scheidel (2014); Allen (2009); Drexhage (1991).

92 White (2008).

93 Harper (2010) 234; historically, female slaves were often more expensive than males, more prestigious and more numerous.

94 Colum. *RR* 1.9.1–5; Varro *RR* 1.16.4.

95 Braudel (1981), quoted by Harris (1999) 73.

96 Silver (2011); Silver (2016) on contractual slavery; see also Ramin and Veyne (1981); Temin (2013a) 132–33; Temin (2004) 526.

A remarkably open slave system and frequent manumission are commonly listed as the core characteristics of Roman slavery.[97] In some noticeably optimistic approaches to Roman slavery – undoubtedly inspired by a willingness to see the Roman empire as the sophisticated forerunner of modern civilization – it has been argued that virtually all slaves were freed eventually, and that when they were freed they could expect full social integration in an open slave system.[98] Urban slaves in particular do seem to have stood a good chance of being manumitted once they had reached the legal age of manumission, though manumission was certainly not universal.[99] The frequency of manumission and the openness of the Roman slave system will be discussed more elaborately in the context of the elite *domus* below.

It is undoubtedly true that the Roman ex-slave was accepted into society to a remarkable degree.[100] I would argue that this acceptance is the result of the overall integration of slaves within Roman society, and of an ex-slave's continued bonds with his or her former owner. Both these facts secured freedmen a place within Rome's hierarchy. Acceptance was emphatically not the result of assimilation of the freed among the freeborn. Freedmen were never wholly free from stigma. A freedman became a Roman citizen, but he did not have full citizen rights.[101] He was barred from the senatorial, equestrian, and decurial classes, and thereby excluded from a number of political offices; intermarriage with the senatorial order was restricted.[102] More importantly, freedmen remained dependent on their patron, although the practical implications of that bond could differ.[103]

To a certain extent, then, slave, freed, and freeborn were interchangeable. Kyle Harper noted, "It is an open question, and one which has not been posed often or explicitly enough, to what extent slave and free labor acted as

[97] E.g. Kleijwegt (2006) 22. See Chapter 4 below for a more detailed discussion of manumission practices.

[98] Watson (1980) on open and closed slave systems. Quasi-universal manumission: Alföldy (1986); Weaver (1972); Harper (1972).

[99] Perhaps more than 50 per cent: see Garnsey and De Ligt (2012); Garnsey and De Ligt (2016); see also Chapter 4 below. Lopez Barja de Quiroga (1998) on Iunian Latins.

[100] Kleijwegt (2006) 56: "In no other slave society do we observe so many freedmen reaching important political positions and accumulating capital and property in commerce and entrepreneurship as we see in ancient Rome."

[101] Cf. Lopez Barja de Quiroga (1998) on possibly numerous Iunian Latins, who gained their freedom but not Roman citizenship.

[102] Mouritsen (2011b) 12, 268–69; Kleijwegt (2006) 3: "In ancient Rome, enslavement automatically wiped out free birth [...] In contrast, manumission documents from Brazil contain the standard clause that the act of manumission turned the slave into a free man, 'as if free from birth'." See also ibid. 38 ff, specifically 41 on the "incomplete transition from slave to free" throughout history, and in Rome.

[103] For continued dependence on patrons, see especially Mouritsen (2011b), and see Chapter 4 below.

substitutes in the Roman economy".[104] Although most jobs appear to have been open to all, regardless of legal status, some sectors were predominantly staffed by either slave or free, and they should therefore be seen as "*imperfect* economic substitutes".[105]

Skilled and unskilled labour

Occupational inscriptions testify to high job differentiation in Roman Italy and some of the recorded jobs were clearly highly skilled.[106] There were surgeons and ophthalmologists, architects and gem engravers.[107] The fine quality of many material remains from Roman antiquity also attests to the fact that there were highly skilled artisans and craftsmen in Roman Italy. No one could deny the skills of the architects of the harbour facilities at Portus or the Baths of Caracalla, or the talent of the sculptor who copied the Greek original of the Apollo of Belvedere, or that of the vase maker who decorated the Warren cup. It is therefore unlikely that high job differentiation was merely the result of low levels of skill in Roman society, in a scenario where all workers merely made a tiny contribution to the manufacture of a more complex final product.[108]

The dichotomy between skilled and unskilled crosses the boundaries of legal status.[109] This is a point that deserves emphasis, because – like manual labour – skills are sometimes thought to have been exclusive to slaves.[110] The perseverance of that idea may once again be attributed to the overwhelming predominance of slaves and freedmen in the occupational inscriptions. Occupational inscriptions, but also other evidence like the chapter on wage in Diocletian's Prices Edict, chiefly attest to skilled labour.[111] Reasons why skilled occupations should be over-represented in the occupational inscriptions are not difficult to come up with. It may be assumed that people took pride in a job they had trained for. Moreover, it

[104] Harper (2010) 213.

[105] Tacoma (2016) 183, his emphasis; also Tacoma (2018); Bradley (1994) 65; Temin (2004) 518.

[106] Tacoma (2016) 184 on a spectrum of skills; cf. Tacoma (2018); Stewart et al. eds (2020) on skilled labour and professionalism in Greece and Rome.

[107] *Medicus chirurgus*: *CIL* 6.3986, *CIL* 11.5400; *medicus ocularius*: *CIL* 5.3156, *CIL* 6.33880; *architectus*: *CIL* 5.3464, *CIL* 6.8724 – examples for these three occupations could be multiplied. There is only one *gemmarius sculptor*: *CIL* 6.9436.

[108] As argued by Morel (1992). On labour differentiation, see Introduction above and Chapter 4 below.

[109] Temin (2004) 538: "The fundamental economic division in the early Roman empire [...] was between educated and uneducated – skilled and unskilled – not between slave and free".

[110] E.g. Casson (1978) 45; and see Chapter 4 below.

[111] Cf. Groen-Vallinga and Tacoma (2017).

was a job that earned more money than unskilled wage labour, so that it allowed them to set up an epitaph in stone more often than their unskilled counterparts. Even if they were commemorated in an inscription, many unskilled labourers were probably more like jacks of all trades and not easily collected under the heading of a single job title.

Most people commemorated with a job title on their epitaph were both skilled and of servile background – but that does not mean that all skilled labourers were of a servile background. No doubt it is true that some of the men and women who were enslaved during the expansion of the empire were clever Greeks.[112] Moreover, investment in the education of home-born and bought slaves could certainly be a profitable undertaking and it must be assumed that many slaves were trained in the household. Conversely, the prospect of manumission might also have encouraged some slaves to actively pursue an education.[113] It will be argued here that skills were also accessible to the free population. Job training was available to slave and free alike, and to both men and (if not as regularly) women. Investment in human capital was not exclusive to slaves and slave-owners. Slaves and ex-slaves just had better reasons to record their skills in stone – or less to substitute it with on their epitaphs, in terms of family ties.[114]

Skilled labour paid at least twice as much as unskilled work, which could theoretically indicate that it was in relatively short supply.[115] Investment in education was costly, and despite the skill premium it was not an investment that everyone could afford. A low life expectancy (and thus a shorter time span to cash in on the investment), and competition for employment between slave and free workers, made job training less alluring for the freeborn. The evidence for investment in human capital by the freeborn, however, is better than that for slave education. Moreover, intergenerational persistence predicts that skilled labourers will often have been able to provide similar training for their children.

[112] As suggested by, e.g., Garnsey (1980) 44; cf. Silver (2016); see Tacoma (2016) 201 for (exceptional) trades that were "associated with foreignness": (Eastern) astrologers and (Greek) doctors. See also Cristofori (2006) on suspicion of 'exotic' healers. Of course, origin can be faked to create the same effect. I wonder if the owl statuette at the National Museum of Antiquities (RMO) in Leiden belongs in that category, with a Greek inscription signposting the seer Achates Petrios' business in Rome.

[113] Or to pursue it with more enthusiasm, insofar as they had any choice in the matter. Temin (2013a) 131: "The observation that educated people became slaves reverses the causation noted earlier in this chapter that open systems of slavery with manumission promoted education. The earlier statement was that manumission led to education; the previous paragraph asserts that educated slaves led to manumission. Which is correct?" Temin argues that both were caused by the conquest of the Mediterranean.

[114] Joshel (1992).

[115] Hawkins (2017) 44–48.

It also indicates that unskilled workers very likely could not do the same for their offspring. In sum, job training presumably was not as common or as self-evident as it is in the Western world today – but that does not mean that skilled labour was necessarily scarce.[116] Scarcity depends on labour demand as well.

Roman society must have had a significantly higher demand for the muscle power of unskilled labourers than for the work of specialists: interesting research avenues in archaeology exploring the market for skilled work from the perspective of both supply and demand seem to indicate that the specialist work we find could generally be done by few labourers, making any investment in human capital less attractive.[117] Combined with the limited scope for job training just outlined, a large group of unskilled labourers must therefore be postulated. Indeed, despite the difficulties of quantification, scholars agree that, especially in the capital, employers had at their disposal a virtually limitless pool of unskilled workers.[118] The market for unskilled labour in the city may have been more casual, temporary, and seasonal in nature than that for skilled labour, since labour demands were relatively unstable. The building trade and the transport sector should be highlighted in this context. This demand for unskilled labour power was probably not only met by urban residents, but must have been supplemented by the temporary, cyclical labour migrants discussed above.

Skilled labour and human capital have dominated scholarship as they do the ancient evidence, but the wider economic contributions of the unskilled and semi-skilled population may be underlined by their importance (numerical and otherwise) to the family and in voluntary associations, and through them in Roman society.

Male and female labour

Gender distinctions are present within the other two distinctions of slave and free, skilled and unskilled. In virtually every type of job men are more prominent and more often attested than women. It will become clear that this holds true even for a number of historically 'feminine' engagements, such as childcare, and that this is valid for slave and free alike. For most families, however, the additional income of women must have been an economic necessity, not to mention its importance for single women or widows who may also have been household heads. Many

[116] See Chapter 3 below for investment in human capital of the freeborn, Chapter 4 for investment in human capital of slaves.

[117] Flohr (2019) for a demand approach; Esposito (2017) for a supply approach, in dialogue on the subject of painters/domestic decoration in Pompeii.

[118] Holleran (2017) 102–3.

Roman women will have engaged not only in unremunerated work but also in paid labour.

Scholarly discourse on Roman labour implicitly or explicitly focuses on male labour, for which the sources are much better. The current work is not entirely free of this fault. Whereas 'gender' indicates the balance between male and female, the fact that everything else is mostly based on sources about men's work turns this section about male and female labour into one that is really mostly about women's work.

As recently as 2012, Ray Laurence signalled a correlation between developments in the study of the Roman family, and the fact that it was pioneered by women: "Female academics have been shown to study to a greater degree activities associated with 'the home'; whereas male academics have chosen to turn their attention to 'the street'".[119] Roman women have indeed often been researched with a focus on their familial role, defining the women by the men in their lives – just as the Romans seem to have done.[120] Accordingly, when looking at female labour in the context of the Roman family, it is often assumed that women, when they were economically active, did not have a money-earning occupation, but assisted their husbands in the family business.[121] The conclusion is noteworthy, because working women in Rome are not particularly uncommon in the sources and they have certainly not lacked scholarly attention.[122] There is a tendency to explain away evidence for independent and skilled women in favour of these generalizations. Female academics, incidentally, are still predominant in studies of Roman women (and the family), but they are increasingly turning to 'the street' and women's role in it.[123]

Women's contribution to the family income, like that of children, is difficult to measure. In many historical as well as contemporary societies, women's primary involvement with family economics has been with domestic housekeeping and childcare, which is generally unremunerated. Because of

119 Laurence (2012) 3.

120 E.g. Hübner and Ratzan (2021), *Missing Mothers*; Petersen and Salzman (2012), *Mothering and Motherhood in the Ancient World*; Dixon (1988), *The Roman Mother*; Hallett (1984), *Fathers and Daughters in Roman Society* – the titles are telling.

121 E.g. Hawkins (2021) 242–67; Saller (2007) 105–7; Saller (2003) 194; Kampen (1981) 112–13, 125; Treggiari (1979a) 73, 76; Treggiari (1976).

122 Hemelrijk (2020) 124–82; Groen-Vallinga (2013); Holleran (2013); Malaspina (2003); Dixon (2001a); and the important methodological chapter on working women in Dixon (2001c) 113–34; Eichenauer (1988); Günther (1987) for freedwomen; Kampen (1981); LeGall (1970); worth mentioning here is especially the work of Treggiari (1976); Treggiari (1979a); and Treggiari (1979b), which already poses many fundamental questions.

123 Holleran (2013); Holleran (2012) Chapter 5 populates the streets partly with women retailers.

that, "The woman at home was said to be economically nonfunctional".[124] Though historical analyses of past economies and labour have started to take the economic value of domestic work into consideration, the time-consuming and significant nature of it is not always acknowledged.[125] What is more, Roman women were not always at home. I would argue that it is likely that most women had a money-earning occupation at some point in their lives, though the family life cycle will also have put many of them in the home during the early years of marriage and childbirth.

Women's engagement with the labour market is therefore heavily influenced by the family life cycle; their actual position in the market, however, all the more so when viewed in the pre-industrial context of Rome, is still often underexposed. There were important differences between male and female labour that need to be taken into account, but these differences first have to be addressed to be able to integrate these women who were such an important part of the working population into the account. This section reveals that a focus on men is only partly justified, and that when speaking of Roman labourers, this really does include many women.

Roman society was governed by men, and male dominance pervaded the organization of labour and the economy as well. Referring to such social systems as 'patriarchy' often carries a pejorative connotation, but it also facilitates comparison.[126] Patriarchy is not unique to Rome. In other historical societies, patriarchy did not so much ban women from the labour market, as it kept women confined to inferior, often unskilled, jobs, with lower wages and fewer opportunities in what is called a secondary, or dual, labour market – calling to mind the glass ceiling that is still a serious issue today.[127] Such an engendered dual labour market limited women's opportunities of employment, and it was firmly in place in Roman society.[128] In the words of Richard Saller, "A gendered division of labor makes Rome no different from nearly every other human society, but it is worth reflecting

[124] Tilly and Scott (1978) 5; Berg (2016) 175 similarly notes that a "lack of attention to such non-monetary activities has, in fact, meant that women have had little visibility in the study of ancient economics".

[125] Berg (2016) 185–89, specifically at 185. Although she mostly discusses households that were relatively well off, I think this is a valid argument overall.

[126] Groen-Vallinga (2013) 297–98; Honeyman and Goodman (1991) on patriarchy in general.

[127] See e.g. Ridgeway (2011) 92–126, "Gendering at Work". The glass ceiling is in fact a phenomenon of an engendered, but not of a dual, labour market. The historical development from the industrious household to the breadwinner–homemaker household suggested in De Vries (2008) is debatable.

[128] Groen-Vallinga (2013); see also Gardner (1995); and Dixon (1984) for women's position in Roman law.

on the consequences of the particular configuration of gendered labor in Rome's slave society".[129]

A gendered labour market is a result, as well as a reflection, of gender ideals: the Roman elite endorsed the ideal that a woman should not need to work. This ideal image became widespread among the rest of the population and, as a result, women's work is not usually recorded in the ancient evidence.[130] Because of a widespread gender bias and the resulting lower wages, as well as the expectation of a relatively early marriage which may have shortened their time in the labour market and limited returns on investment in their human capital, it is likely that girls had fewer opportunities for job training than boys.[131] Their economic prospects therefore were limited, discouraging investment in female human capital even more.

Women had a biological comparative advantage in the home when they were tending to young children; men had a comparative advantage in the labour market because they generally commanded higher wages.[132] Regardless of their weak position in the labour market, it should be emphasized that the majority of women will still have had to contribute to the family income to make ends meet. There were various ways of scraping a living, and some will have done so in the informal economy of the home, where others were actively seeking to be part of the labour market. But when a woman was trained in an occupation, her profession was not the first thing she was remembered for in an epitaph.[133] It is noteworthy that these are broader patterns that come to the fore in the epigraphic evidence for slave women as much as for free women.[134]

For all these reasons, working women are likely to be under-represented, which goes a long way to explain the relative scarcity of the epigraphic evidence from ancient Rome. The material we do have, however, shows that women were operating in a remarkably broad range of jobs. There is no reason why they should not be: there was no law against women in commerce, production and business, and their income presumably presented a welcome addition to the family budget.[135]

[129] Saller (2003) 201.

[130] Groen-Vallinga (2013) 295–99.

[131] Women's wages are seldom attested, and when they are, gender differentiations are not clear; on wages for women in Diocletian's Prices Edict, Groen-Vallinga and Tacoma (2017) 113; on investment in human capital of women, see Chapter 3 below.

[132] Cf. Cigno (1991) 28.

[133] Larsson Lovén (2016); Groen-Vallinga (2013) 295–99; Hemelrijk (2004) on the *Laudatio Turiae*; Larsson Lovén (1998).

[134] Cf. Vlassopoulos (2021) 76, with references.

[135] Larsson Lovén (2016); Groen-Vallinga (2013); and on the family as a whole see Chapter 3 below.

Labour supply and demand

According to economic price theory, "A functioning labor market couples a labor demand with a labor supply".[136] This section therefore takes a closer look at labour demand and labour supply in Roman Italy. The expectation here, too, is that there will have been sociocultural constraints to reaching an equilibrium between supply and demand.

Urbanization rates in Roman Italy were high. That fact prompts a number of suppositions about supply and demand within the urban labour market: it suggests that there were plenty of workers available in what would be considered a thick urban labour market. If so, the ample availability of labour would then reduce the value of labour, implying low wages. Low wages led to an increase in labour supply, because people will have sought to increase their income by looking for more work. However, a large urban population also means that there was a larger pool of consumers: people have to eat and so a large population raises product demand. Urbanization was linked to labour differentiation above, for these reasons. But was the increase in product demand enough to increase labour demand, and to increase it sufficiently to satisfy everyone's need to find an income? Was it idle hope to find a new life or a better income in the city?

Living standards and the working population

Aggregate labour supply in economic theory is determined by the numbers of the working population, multiplied by the hours worked and the intensity of effort in those hours, taking into consideration such factors as demography and human capital. Obviously, no such sophisticated cliometric analysis is possible for ancient Rome. But there is much to be said about the numbers and the structure of the total urban population of Roman Italy, which is the maximum potential work force. It will be argued that most of the Italian population lived at or under subsistence level, and that therefore the potential working population at least roughly approximates the actual workforce: everyone who could do so, had to work for a living.

It has been stated that "ordinary Romans lived well".[137] The amount of scholarship trying to make sense of the scarce data on Roman living standards indicates that the argument is not easy to substantiate, however. In recent years, students of the Roman economy have presented various efforts to calculate Roman gross domestic product (GDP) for the early empire, mostly in the context of analysis of Roman economic

[136] Temin (2013a) 115.

[137] Temin (2013a) 2 and Chapter 11; cf. Temin (2006) 133: "Many inhabitants of ancient Rome lived well"; cf. Jongman (2007).

growth, but also in connection with investigations into Roman living standards.[138] There is no way to identify per capita GDP accurately for the Roman empire. Some findings are suggestive for our current investigation, however. Comparative evidence suggests that regional differences in the distribution of GDP occur; in the case of the Roman empire it is likely that wealth was concentrated in Roman Italy, raising GDP there. As a rule, GDP and urbanization rates are linked, and indeed the high urbanization rate of Roman Italy matches the higher GDP suggested for the Italian heartland.[139] Within Roman Italy, too, it is likely that there were regional differences, as Campania is generally considered to have been relatively wealthy.[140]

The proposition that Roman Italy had a higher GDP than the rest of the empire does not necessarily mean that the inhabitants of Roman Italy were well off, nor does it imply that they were any better off than those in the provinces. Temin's assumption that Roman Italy can best be compared to the blossoming economy of the Netherlands in 1600, rather than to the less wealthy 'early modern European economy' proposed as comparandum by others, does not prove the hypothesis that "ordinary Romans lived well". Calculations of per capita or aggregate GDP effectively mask income inequality, and the distribution of income may well have been more unequal in Roman Italy than elsewhere, because wealth tended to concentrate in the hands of a small group of people.[141] It begs the question what is meant by an 'ordinary Roman'. The 'middling' group of non-poor, non-elite households remains elusive and difficult to define or quantify, although scholars seem to agree that they lived comfortably – relatively speaking.[142] But this still leaves a large group of poor people unaccounted for.

Real wages are perhaps a better indication of living standards than per capita GDP. The most comprehensive data set of prices and wages to calculate real wages is the list contained in Diocletian's Prices Edict. The conclusions drawn on the basis of the wage of an unskilled worker

[138] Temin (2013a); Lo Cascio and Malanima (2009); Scheidel and Friesen (2009); Bang (2008); Maddison (2007); Temin (2006); Goldsmith (1984); Hopkins (1980).

[139] Temin (2013a) 253, 256; whereas the correlation is clear, Temin notes that the causality is unclear – is it wealth that leads to urbanization, or does that work the other way around?

[140] Flohr and Wilson eds (2017), throughout, in their Introduction, and particularly the contributions of Ray, Rowan, and Lazer.

[141] Temin (2013a) 256–57. Cf. De Ligt (2012) 19, with reference to Van Bavel (2008) and Maat (2005) for income inequality in the Dutch Republic of the Golden Age; Groen-Vallinga and Tacoma (2017) 118–22 note that Diocletian's Prices Edict points to high income variation.

[142] Flohr (2019) 121; Ray (2017) for a concrete approach to non-poor, non-elite households in Pompeii.

in the Edict are consistent: real wages were low in comparison with other historical societies.[143] The more abundant wage data from Roman Egypt lead to the same inference.[144] It was postulated here that a large part of the urban population consisted of these unskilled labourers who had to get by on a very low wage. Most ancient historians therefore infer that "the majority of the Romans were not very well off".[145] The effects of low real wages may theoretically be cushioned by the regular participation of all family members, not just the male head of household.[146] This phenomenon also suggests that the supply of labour was high. But in fact labour supply may have been so high that it could not always be satisfied, in which case large groups of people were underemployed, or unemployed at any one time.[147] This presumption supports the argument that the large majority of the Italian population may still have been living at or under subsistence levels.[148] Somewhat paradoxically, a city like Rome was the best place to live in structural poverty, because it offered the largest variety of casual and informal ways to survive.[149]

Price theory suggests that low real wages indicate an abundant supply of labour. This is supported by the evidence: the urban population in the Italian peninsula was substantial by any calculation. There were quite simply very many people in Roman Italy, no matter whether we choose to adhere to the so-called 'low count' – 6 million or 7 million people – or the 'high count' – 15 million or 16 million – of the Italian population. It has been plausibly suggested that perhaps 25 per cent of the numerous Italians lived in cities.[150] Warfare and other unnatural population checks did not interfere greatly with the population of Italy in the period under scrutiny. It

143 Allen (2009); and Duncan-Jones (1978); Scheidel (2014) for a less clear-cut negative answer. See also Groen-Vallinga and Tacoma (2017) 118 with further references.

144 Scheidel (2010b) 433; cf. Drexhage (1991) Chapter 9.

145 Groen-Vallinga and Tacoma (2017) 118. But see Jongman (2007) for a rather more optimistic view on the standard of living under the early empire; and Rathbone (2006), who holds that Roman Egypt in the early empire was relatively prosperous overall.

146 Groen-Vallinga and Tacoma (2017) 119–20; Groen-Vallinga (2013) on female labour participation; Scheidel (2010b) 433–35, 451.

147 Holleran (2011) 165: "Cities in developing countries typically demonstrate high levels of unemployment, underemployment and poverty".

148 Gilbert (2013) on rising inequality in cities throughout history; Temin (2013a) 250 on the subjectivity of the term 'subsistence'; Holleran (2011) for the concept of chronic poverty in Rome; Scheidel and Friesen (2009) for income distributions and a percentage of 84–90 per cent just above, at or below subsistence levels; on poverty in the Roman world see also Harris (2011) 27–54, 'Poverty and Destitution in the Roman Empire'; Scheidel (2006); Garnsey (1988).

149 Holleran (2011) 177–78.

150 De Ligt (2012) 231–33, 238–46.

is clear that there was no shortage of labour in the urban labour market, at least in terms of population numbers.[151]

The value of these people's human capital – the intensity of work – was also dependent on health: in line with what was said before about the material well-being of the urban population, Jongman wrote, "Many inhabitants of the Roman empire only eked out a meager living, their skeletons grim testimonies to malnutrition and disease".[152] In times of food shortages, the state had only limited resources to intervene.[153] By contrast, slaves may have been fed relatively well, since caring for slaves was equivalent to preserving property. The suggestion is difficult to prove and unlikely to have been universal, of course. It does bring out nicely how implicit assumptions guide scientific results, however, when the remains of a 14-year-old girl from Herculaneum, conversely, are hypothesized to have been those of a slave, because her teeth show signs of malnutrition and her knees show wear.[154] A different interpretation of such skeletal evidence is open now that scholars have started to explore the possibility that women and children may not always have been fed as well as the men of the family.[155]

Bioarchaeology as well as less direct approaches to analyse the physical well-being of the ancient Romans form an expanding and promising new area of research.[156] This developing research into skeletal evidence and the physique of the ancient Romans does not yet allow for firm conclusions on topics like malnutrition or stature, although a review of Pompeian skeletal evidence suggests perhaps a more optimistic view of the health of at least the local population.[157] Similarly, dietary variety in Herculaneum and Pompeii was apparently highly diverse, and therefore conducive to healthier

151 Cf. Holleran (2017) 103, who notes that there is no mention of labour shortages in Rome in the ancient sources. See also Suet. *Vesp.* 18, where Vespasian refuses a labour-saving device with the argument that he needs to feed his people – suggesting that there were many in need of work.

152 Jongman (2007) 594; that said, note that Jongman argues that the majority of Romans in the early empire were actually relatively well off, and that increasing inequality and poverty was a thing of late antiquity.

153 Holleran (2018); Erdkamp (2018) esp. 298–300.

154 The example is Erc10 with explanation in Bisel and Bisel (2002) 464–65.

155 Laes (2018).

156 For its possibilities and limitations see, e.g., the *Routledge Handbook of Diet and Nutrition in the Roman World* (Erdkamp and Holleran eds (2018)), particularly the contributions of Killgrove, Kron, and Flohr. The contributions of both Jongman ("Consumption") and Sallares ("Ecology") to the *Cambridge Economic History of the Greco-Roman World* (Scheidel et al. eds (2007)) illustrate its incorporation in studies of the ancient economy; see also the edited volume by King (2005); Bisel and Bisel (2002); and Tacoma (2017) for its use in migration studies.

157 Lazer (2017).

living in this region.[158] Even as knowledge about the practicalities of the food supply adds up, however, the question remains whether society allowed everyone – poorer people, enslaved persons, women, or children – equal access to these food reserves.[159]

Some more general patterns may still be sketched out. In the unhealthy environment of a pre-industrial city, endemic diseases were omnipresent and will have decreased the efficiency and ability of people to work: their human capital.[160] The urban population was also more likely to be susceptible to epidemic disease than the rural population, a fact the Romans themselves were aware of and which led the elite to spend parts of the year on their country estates.[161] Escape from the city was not an option for all, however. If an epidemic led to a sudden drop in population numbers, the labour supply dwindled and that would have led to higher labour participation of women and children; it would also have raised wages, at least in a functioning labour market. Too little is known about epidemics in the ancient world to determine their effects with any certainty. It is only the great Antonine Plague of the later second century AD for which scholars have attempted to find some tentative answers about its economic effects: population losses of perhaps as much as 20 to 30 per cent seem to have doubled the price of labour in Roman Egypt.[162]

Economic insecurity and fluctuating demands

Labour demand is a derived demand, based on demand for services and products. It has been noted several times in passing in this chapter that labour demand is likely to have been particularly unstable in the cities of Roman Italy, as argued by Hawkins.[163] This has been attributed in part to the seasonality of the building and transport sectors, where many unskilled city dwellers and temporary migrants should be located. The influx of cyclical labour migrants in turn added to the general consumer

158 Rowan (2017), but marking the exceptionality of the region at 116.

159 E.g. Laes (2018) on women and children; Holleran (2018) on state interventions in food supply.

160 Oerlemans and Tacoma (2014) for imperial Rome; Gowland and Garnsey (2010) on the correlation between urbanization and disease. Eventually the problem 'solved' itself – Parkin (2003) 235: "When a person's failing state of physical and mental health led to total inability to be self-supporting, then, in the absence of effective medication [...] dependence on others may have been short-lived anyway".

161 Duncan-Jones (1996) 109–11; Sallares (2002) on endemic malaria; Scheidel (2003) for Rome; Laurence (2005) for Herculaneum and Pompeii.

162 Temin (2013a) 118, 84–85; Rathbone (2009) 305; Scheidel (2012d); and Scheidel (2002) to be read with the critical comments of Bagnall (2002); cf. Duncan-Jones (1996).

163 Hawkins (2021) esp. Chapter 1, who derives this model from a comparison with medieval and early modern cities. More briefly, Hawkins (2013) 339–46.

demand in the cities. Conversely, there is a possibility that some of the unskilled urban population moved away from the city in summer to assist on farms during the harvesting season.[164] Though seasonality and instability certainly apply, the trough in demand during the off season was perhaps not as severe as we might expect. The building sector is thought to have continued throughout nine months a year; the shipping trade, with due acknowledgement of the dangers involved, may have been not as strictly limited to the sailing season (traditionally April to October) as has generally been thought.[165] The sailing season, of course, also influenced mobility in general, and tourism and migration may have spiked in the safer period. The seasons or, more accurately, the weather obviously affected many trades more generally.

Equally cyclical were religious festivals and other festivities on the calendar, which presented a major incentive in demand, be it for the required ritual clothing or through the habit of exchanging gifts; the crowd of people in itself will have increased consumption and attracted itinerant merchants.[166] Especially in the city of Rome, celebrations such as triumphal processions, and the mere presence of the emperor, will have attracted many people. The elections of the magistrates in January apparently drew many to the city; Augustus implemented a summer low period for the Senate and a recess for the courts which had the opposite effect:[167] outside the political high season, many nobles moved to the countryside to survive the (literally) murderous summer heat.

These seasonal and cyclical peaks and troughs in demand required a certain flexibility of the workers, but at least they were to a certain extent predictable. Throughout the year, workshops produced on commission, however, which was largely unpredictable. Many of the luxury trades catered specifically to the needs of the elite – much of the money that went round in the city simply was spent by the elite.[168] Larger (building) projects

164 So Hawkins (2013) 341; but see Erdkamp (2016): it is probable that the rural population had enough manpower for the harvest without the help of urban residents. A brief stay on a farm in the north of the Netherlands taught me that even today farmers work together, rotating the machinery and manpower for grass silage within the one week that this had to be brought in.

165 The building trade: Erdkamp (2016) 39, with reference to the work of DeLaine (1997), adding up to roughly 220 days of work a year spread out during these nine months. On the sailing season, Hawkins (2013) writes it was from May to September, but see now Gambash (2017); and especially Beresford (2012).

166 De Ligt (1993) 60 for markets during the *ludi* in Rome.

167 Plin. *Ep.* 2.11.10 (the crowd in January); Suet. *Aug.* 32 (recess of the courts in November and December), 35 (only the presence of a minimum of senators, which ones was determined by lot, was required in September and October).

168 On the correlation between urbanization and elite expenditure, see Chapter 4 below.

could present entrepreneurs with a sudden peak in labour demand.[169] For day labourers, insecurity was a daily fact of life: even if they had regular employment with one employer, his sudden leave of absence could mean a day without work – and without pay: Apuleius has a poor carpenter return home unsuccessfully from work, stating proudly that "although our shopkeeper, wrapped up in a public matter, has made this a holiday for us, still I have raked in our daily bread" – in this case, by selling an unused *dolium*.[170] The implications are twofold: first, he expected to leave for work like every other day, but was unexpectedly sent away, and second, because he was sent away for the day he did not get paid and had to resort to other means to purchase food.

The city was the place where supply and demand for labour could meet.[171] The congregation of people looking for workers, or work, in itself was also a powerful generator of consumer demand, increasing the pull of the city even more. Fluctuating demand increased the insecurities of the urban economy, prompting various economic strategies that would increase flexibility for labourers and employers alike. It will be argued in this book that social institutions were key to that flexibility.

Conclusion

Labour in the Roman empire clearly was subject to market forces and it is therefore possible to speak of a Roman urban labour market. This chapter has illustrated that market integration was far from perfect, however. The Roman market economy is likely to have been local or regional in many instances. Moreover, the importance of social structures that determined and restricted the integration of a market for labour should be emphasized. In the chapters that follow it will be argued that family ties and non-familial networks were the chief determinant of an individual's labour opportunities in the market, and governed their role in unremunerated work. Again, these socio-economic networks will generally have been of a local, or at most regional, nature. The section on labour migration showed a similar dependence on institutions: there was movement, but there were certain restrictions as to who moved, and as to what options were open in the receiving labour market.

169 Erdkamp (2016) 48: "the labour demand of the urban economy fluctuated, in part following a pattern of predictable and regular, seasonal cycles, in part as a result of less predictable and less short-term trends that were primarily caused by imperial spending".

170 Apul. *Mot.* 9.5–6: "licet forensi negotio officinator noster attentus ferias nobis fecerit, tamen hodiernae cenulae nostrae propexi."

171 Holleran (2017) on the ways in which employer and employee may have found each other.

Labour mobility is likely to have accounted for a large part of migration streams in Roman Italy. Migrants moved to the city in the hope of finding additional income or better wages. Rural–urban migration flows kept the urban population intact, including forced migration and free workers alike – even if many free labour migrants were only temporary guests. The urban infrastructure was probably more conducive to permanent settlement of skilled labourers than to that of unskilled wage workers, but the city had an appeal for both groups. The possibility of movement between jobs was enough to allow for some flexibility in the light of labour demand, which holds true for slave workers as well as for free labourers. Changing or finding jobs was easier in theory than in practice, however.

Opportunities on the labour market were governed by legal status, skills, and gender. Perhaps contrary to expectations, it was not the split between slave and free that stands out as the most important limiting factor. Most occupations appear to have been open to slaves, freedmen, and the freeborn alike. It is only in domestic service that a strong preference for slave labour comes to the fore, closely connected to the phenomenon of conspicuous consumption. Because women historically often find work in this sector and Roman society was familiar with a similar gender ideal, this is likely to have impacted most on free women's chances to find paid work.

Skills were highly valued in Roman society, and here, too, there is little to indicate that chances were better for slave or free – both seem to have had access to job training. The one group that is less well represented, again, is that of freeborn women. There were certainly women who were trained as artisans, or who gained other skills, and they should not be explained away – still it is safe to say that gender was the most distinctive criterion that determined one's potential in the labour market.

Labour was undoubtedly the most widely available production factor in antiquity.[172] Labour supply often was greater than labour demand in Roman Italy, leaving large parts of the free urban population under- or unemployed for regular periods of time. The urban population was large. The cities of Roman Italy were the home of the freeborn, freed, and slaves, and of men, women, and children. The individuals that made up the urban population were not equal, in the sense of perfectly interchangeable. For example, it is likely that elite *domus* simply employed slaves to fulfil vacancies in their household, effectively closing off part of the service sector for the freeborn. In very many instances, however, labour demand was met by both slave and free labourers. That should not be surprising, considering the fact that the majority of the working population effectively consisted of free labourers. Some of the labourers possessed a particular skill set; others were unskilled wage labourers. It was postulated that skilled labour may

172 *Pace* Rosafio (2016) 112, who stresses the importance of the production factor land.

have been relatively scarce, and very valuable because of it. Investment in occupational skills was not risk-free, however, dealing with fluctuating and unstable demands.

The labour supply for unskilled wage work, in particular, is likely to have been abundant. Since the supply of labour was at times more profuse than labour demand, wages tended to be low. Roman Italy may have demonstrated a relatively high per capita GDP, but income inequality was also high, particularly in the Italian heartland; comparative evidence suggests that inequality was likely to be most pronounced in an urban context. The evidence indicates that the majority of the urban population in Roman society did indeed work for low wages and that their living standards were low. Quite possibly many of them were living in chronic poverty. The emperor and the urban elite needed to provide more than bread and circuses to keep the people happy: work, in the form of large building projects, for example, was vital.

Strong labour segmentation within an urban labour market that was characterized by fluctuating demand and high labour participation, a large proletariat of unskilled labourers that is poorly reflected in the epigraphic evidence, and a small group of highly skilled workers that is well represented, are the backbone for the rest of this book.

Chapter 3

Family Economics

Non-elite Households

Introduction

More often than not we have little or no knowledge of the context of an occupational inscription: we do not know the monument it was part of, and it is often unclear precisely where or when the text was set up. Many of these inscriptions probably belonged to the modest environment of the non-elite household, which is the focus of this chapter. Naturally, some households will have been a little less modest than others. The *aurifex brattiarius* from Rome whose statue base is now in the Galleria delle Statue of the Vatican can hardly be considered modest.[1] Similarly, the conspicuous monument to the famous baker M. Vergilius Eurysaces, still standing at the Porta Maggiore in Rome today, shows that he was not exactly unpretentious, nor of modest means.[2] Their households may have contained a significant number of slaves and freedmen, but they were not comparable to the sizeable elite *domus* of T. Statilius Taurus or Livia Augusta, whose domestic staff members were buried in large *columbarium* tombs.

What, then, is the non-elite household? For want of a better distinguishing criterion, I would define 'non-elite households' broadly as family units in which family members contributed their labour power for the well-being of the collective. This group is thus noticeably broader than any perceived 'Roman middle class', and more inclusive than the non-poor, non-elite households so elegantly identified in the evidence for Pompeii.[3] I refer to these family units as non-elite households, or small families, to draw an explicit contrast with the large elite *domus* of Chapter 4, where the principal family could afford not to get their own hands dirty and have others perform all kinds of work necessary. The non-elite made up the vast

[1] *CIL* 6.9210.

[2] On the monument see Mayer (2012) 112–14; Petersen (2003); the inscription preserved on three sides of the monument is *CIL* 6.1958a.

[3] Mayer (2012); Flohr and Wilson (2017) 15; also Ray (2017).

majority of the total population of Roman Italy, perhaps up to 98.5 per cent.[4] Because my definition concerns such great numbers, it includes a noticeably broad range of non-elite families: they came in many shapes and sizes, ranging from Eurysaces' successful business to a street vendor and his family. A non-elite family of freedmen may also have originated from an elite *domus*. Not only was there a great variety of family forms, but also individual households changed over time in a life cycle of their own.

This chapter starts out from the hypothesis that the dynamics of the family are fundamental to understanding the Romans' engagement with work, labour, and the labour market. The family unit is likely to have engaged both in largely unremunerated work, directed at maintenance and self-sufficiency of the household, and in wage labour and production directed towards the market.[5] The balance between the two is likely to have shifted over time. The dynamics of the family include the demographics of family structure and the family life cycle, as well as fluctuations in family economics. The aim of this chapter is to illuminate how these factors interlinked to eventually determine the economic strategies, or household living strategies, that a Roman family adopted.[6]

Economic analyses of the family in early modern Europe generally consider the pre-industrial family as "the unit of production and consumption and the household the locus of work and residence".[7] This model of convergence of supply and demand within the family has been called the 'family economy'. This premise is also implicit in studies on the Roman family.[8] Agricultural families are thought to have been largely self-sufficient, for example.[9] In the context of urban commerce and production, the family economy model is met by the widespread view that small-scale *tabernae*/workshops were the dominant production units in the ancient Roman economy, under the assumption that people lived where they worked.[10] It

[4] Scheidel and Friesen (2009) 76, Table 6, estimate roughly 1.5 per cent of households belonged to the economic elite (senators, *equites*, and *decuriones*), leaving no less than 98.5 per cent non-elite households.

[5] Cf. the first and the third goals of production in the taxonomy of labour relations of the Global Collaboratory on the History of Labour Relations, Hofmeester (2018) 319, introduced above.

[6] For the term 'household living strategies', or 'coping strategies', cf. Engelen (2002).

[7] Wall (1986) 265.

[8] Or explicit, as in the case of Saller (2011); Saller (2007) 87, where he opens his paper: "In the Greco-Roman world the household was the basic unit of production as well as consumption." See also Saller (2003) 189.

[9] Implicit in e.g. Dyson (2011), a sweeping overview of scholarship on rural families.

[10] People living where they worked, in *tabernae*: Ellis (2018) 9 with references; Holleran (2012) 27, 125; Händel (1985) 499; Loane (1938) 63; on small-scale *tabernae* and larger workshops, see most elaborately Flohr (2017).

will become clear throughout this chapter that this perception of the family can explain much, though not all, of the ancient evidence.

The Industrial Revolution profoundly changed the nature of the family economy. A new model was introduced to accommodate the fact that many workers were now employed as wage workers in large-scale factories: the new nineteenth-century standard was labelled the 'family wage economy'. Although this model has firm origins in historical analysis of the Industrial Revolution, even in pre-industrial families the family was not necessarily the locus of work, and hiring out labour outside the family was also a very real possibility.[11] Thus the model of a family wage economy could perhaps be detached from its industrial origins and be applied to earlier societies. In Rome and Ostia, large production facilities have been recovered archaeologically, even if they are only attested sporadically.[12] But we shall see that wage labour in general was more widespread in Roman society than has been assumed, and that there were many wage-earning families in Rome.

The historical demographer Richard Wall felt that both the family economy and the family wage economy could not account for the historical data he found for his research into nineteenth-century Colyton, and so he came up with a new model: the 'adaptive family economy'.[13] The model of the adaptive family economy allows for diversification of labour and for flexible economic strategies of the family, both inside and outside the confines of the house, with the aim of maximizing "economic well-being".[14] Jan de Vries expanded this theoretical framework to include the fact that consumption goals could extend beyond mere 'needs' of the household to include its 'wants'.[15] Consumer aspirations, in his view, functioned as a powerful stimulant to increase labour supply, motivating the allocation of time between the household and the market, and inspiring economic choices.

Virtually the same solution was reached through scholarly endeavours into the concept of 'family strategy':[16] the study of strategy was the natural

[11] De Vries (2008) traces his 'industrious household' to at least a century before the Industrial Revolution, but many aspects of household negotiation with the market that he identifies may be valid for Roman society as well.

[12] E.g. Flohr (2007) on the differences between Pompei and Ostia; Saller (2013) considers the large *domus* as productive units – but they are also unique to Rome, at least in an urban context.

[13] Wall (1986) 265; and see Groen-Vallinga (2013) for an earlier introduction of the adaptive family economy to the ancient Roman evidence for female labour.

[14] Wall (1986) 265.

[15] De Vries (2008).

[16] For a conceptual approach to family strategy, see especially the research program on family and labour of the NW Posthumus Institute (the Dutch National Research School for Social and Economic History); the results of the research group were published in

result of a scholarly shift from investigating structural functionalism to individualism and agency.[17] In other words, families became historical actors with an active contribution to make to the course of history, rather than objects whose life course was determined solely by external circumstances. Family members "coordinate their activities, so we can speak of a collective strategy, also called 'household living strategy'".[18] As with the adaptive family economy, the addition of 'adaptive' to family strategies emphasizes flexibility in the way that families may 'adapt' to their circumstances.[19] The focus in this chapter therefore lies on what could be called 'family adaptive labour strategies': a family's economic actions on the labour market and the unremunerated work that supported those actions.

Family strategy is the outcome of a process of decision making within the family. That process is guided by internal power structures on the one hand, and by the larger cultural, social, and economic factors in society on the other. The decision-making process itself is fundamental in understanding subjects like marriage, investment in human capital, or labour allocation, and will be brought in whenever appropriate.[20] Out of necessity, on the lower end of the scale, household strategies were directed primarily towards the modest goal of staying alive. As a result, in the poorer households motivations were chiefly economic and choices were relatively limited.

Chapter outline

Families had various economic strategies open to them in theory, the range of which varied according to the situation they were in. Can actual forms of economic strategy be detected in the ancient sources, and how does that help to interpret and explain the ancient evidence?

Economic strategies of the family in my view can be divided into two categories: quantitative and qualitative. The quantity of the family concerns the demographic make-up of the family. Family demography to a large extent was a conscious choice, as in the case of marriage, or buying

special volumes: ***Economic and Social History in the Netherlands*** 6 (1994); ***History of the Family: An International Quarterly***, special issue, ***Structure or Strategy?*** (1997), and ***History of the Family*** 9 (2004), special issue, ***Labor Strategies of Families***. Contrast, e.g., the loose application of family strategy in Judd (2010) on contemporary rural west China, or Ornstein and Stalker (2013) on modern Canadian families.

[17] E.g. Engelen (2002) 453–54.

[18] Hofmeester (2018) 319.

[19] Moen and Wethington (1992).

[20] By incorporating the decision-making process, and structural factors in the decision-making process, this analysis counters the most fundamental points of critique of 'family strategy' that led Theo Engelen to suggest we abandon it altogether – Engelen (2002) esp. 464. Engelen seems to have come back from that, however; see Engelen, Knotter et al. (2004).

a slave. However, conscious decisions about the structure of the family can go much further: it starts with marriage and the choice whether to raise a child or not. The quality of the family, conversely, encompasses decisions concerning the labour allocation of the various family members, and the related matter of investment in education and the family's collective stock of human capital. This chapter discusses the various possibilities within both types of strategies in turn.

Quantitative strategies: family structure and the family life cycle

What did the Roman family look like? It will be argued here that there was such a thing as a preferred family form – the family form that people strove for in the cities of the early Roman empire – despite the various forms the family took in reality. An awareness of the particularities of the urban Roman family could prove to be helpful in determining the parameters for family labour supply and demand.

The very family dynamics that have made the Roman family such an intangible concept are key to our understanding of the family unit. Families come in all shapes and sizes, and because the make-up of a family is always in flux, that family's economic needs and abilities also change over time. This so-called household cycle, or family life cycle, is a great influence on economic choices of the family. Although we usually do not have the data to follow a historical family over the life cycle, many demographic parameters can be modelled. The section on the dynamics of demography therefore focuses on the life-changing events of marriage, the birth of a child, and both kin and non-kin additions to the family. Marriage forged important bonds, and also made for the most efficient economic cooperation. Children were considered to be an economically valuable asset to the family. In a high-mortality environment, however, family ties were unstable and death led to continuous reconfigurations. Widows and widowers, orphans, solitary households, and other live-in kin should be taken into account. In many families, and in skilled work in particular, the family firm often extended itself with one or more slaves.

Qualitative strategies: human capital and the allocation of labour

If labour was the most important production factor in antiquity, as it is widely assumed to have been, it follows that significant profit could be gained principally through investment in population quality; that is, human capital. Human capital is a convenient term for the combined characteristics of an individual worker. Such characteristics may include age, sex, health and physique, and innate ability, as well as levels of education and opportunities for migration. Significantly, then, human capital concerns more than schooling – although, to my mind, education remains its most powerful aspect. Human-capital theory breaks down labour as a factor of production into more specific components, in order to give due credit to personal ability and output of labourers – which can then be taken into consideration when calculating profit and investment. Adam Smith in his *Wealth of Nations* was the first to mention "a capital fixed and realized, as it were, in his person".[21] As an economic concept, however, human capital was developed fully only in the second half of the twentieth century.[22]

The application of human-capital theory to Roman history of necessity must remain very basic.[23] It is my contention that, fortunately, it is precisely these basic principles that may help us understand the predominantly qualitative evidence for investment in human capital in the Roman period. Physical well-being and health are important to economics, and this subject receives increasing attention from ancient historians.[24] Life expectancy, generally unhealthy urban environments, and the Antonine Plague were briefly referred to in the previous chapter. In the context of work and labour, however, it seems justified to focus on education and the acquisition of skills.

In human capital theory, "The individual is assumed to maximize the present value of future expected lifetime net earnings, where net earnings are take-home pay [...] minus any direct human capital investment costs incurred, such as the costs of training".[25] The expectation of private returns differs per person: men, for example, would expect to spend more active time in the labour market than women in many historical periods; women often dropped out of the labour force (temporarily) upon marriage or just before the birth of a first child.[26] Future expected earnings are dependent on market demands as well. Labour demand, as stated before, is a derived demand, in that it depends upon product demand – which will have influenced the choice of an occupation.[27] For example, there is no reason to train a child as a scribe when the current local scribes have years ahead of them, and when there is a strong demand for potters in the city instead.

[21] Smith (1776) 335.

[22] Eide and Showalter (2010) is a useful introductory piece on human capital. Key works are Schultz (1961); Schultz (1980); Becker (1964); Becker (1985).

[23] Pioneering works by Hawkins (2021); Saller (2013); Saller (2007); and Verboven (2012b). For an indication of the full complexity of human capital in economics see, e.g., the handbook by Burton-Jones and Spender eds (2011).

[24] E.g. Rowan (2017); Lazer (2017); Scheidel (2012c); Jongman (2007); Laurence (2005).

[25] Bosworth et al. (1996) 35.

[26] The literature about women and human capital is extensive, but see e.g. Schultz ed. (1995); Becker (1985); Mincer and Polachek (1974).

[27] Eide and Showalter (2010) 283: "Observed outcomes in the marketplace will be the result of an equilibrium process where the demand for specific skills and abilities is balanced with its supply".

The resulting balance predicts that investing in human capital also has social returns: effects that benefit society, like the security of having enough doctors to service everyone.

Demography of the family: family structure

The demography of the family has been steadily gathering ground in ancient history.[28] Family and family structure have become integral to the subject of ancient demography.[29] The parameters of high mortality and high fertility are well known;[30] the effects of high mortality on the population and the reality of high fertility are only measurable in the context of the Roman family. Conversely, demography will have affected Roman family life and the social and cultural preferences surrounding it. This section deals with the preferred family structure in the cities of Roman Italy. In a similar undertaking for Roman Egypt, Hübner has expressed well what is at stake:

> Decisions about the marriage of a daughter, a new family enterprise, the purchase of more land, sending a son away for an apprenticeship, and provision for old age and death did not affect only one individual, but all the family members who lived together. The timing of those decisions was the response to the opportunities or needs that arose from certain household constellations. On the other hand, certain cultural patterns of predominant living form influenced decision-making to achieve the household form that was considered the ideal for traditional and economic reasons. Household composition also affected the way an individual or family coped with situations of crisis, the death of a spouse, divorce, orphanhood, or childless old age.[31]

Family form therefore must have had economic implications as well. The addition of slaves and freedmen in the household will also have had important consequences in view of the family labour supply.

Family form

In search of what the Roman family generally looked like, ancient historians turned to household structure and family typology. A classic progress paradigm was proffered by early modern historians, with the nuclear family at its apex.[32] Within this paradigm, the extended family was thought to

28 Holleran and Pudsey (2011b); Scheidel ed. (2001a); Parkin (1992).

29 Holleran and Pudsey (2011b) 2.

30 E.g. Scheidel (1996); Scheidel ed. (2001a); Scheidel (2001b); Parkin (1992).

31 Hübner (2013) 31.

32 LePlay (1871), who deserves credit for having established research into family typology; cf. Saller (1997) on the parallel discussion on the Roman concept of kinship.

have been the norm before the period of industrialization and modernization. That hypothesis predicted that in ancient Rome most families would have consisted of two or more generations of conjugal couples. However, with the work of Peter Laslett and the widely influential Cambridge Group for the History of Population and Social Structure, it was argued that the nuclear family, also termed the 'stem family' or 'simple family household' in the Cambridge typology of household forms, had in fact been the most important family focus as far back as AD 1300.[33] Ancient historians readily picked up on this. A leading article published by Saller and Shaw in 1984 shifted consensus towards the supposition of a dominant nuclear Roman family system. Saller and Shaw demonstrated a clear predominance of nuclear family ties in commemorative inscriptions.[34] This was taken by many scholars to imply a predominance of the nuclear family form more generally, rather than merely among the family relations on the inscriptions.[35]

The conclusion is understandable, because the ideal of the nuclear family was indeed valued greatly in Rome.[36] Marriage appears to have been mainly neo-local, which means that the newly-weds set up their own household after the wedding – starting out as a simple family unit. It is suggestive that the wedding ceremony consisted of a procession with which the bride would leave her birth home and enter the marital home.[37] It is possible that there sometimes were economic reasons to start out married life in the household of the groom's father instead; however, I know of very little evidence for such arrangements outside Roman Egypt, where patrilocal marriage appears to have been the norm.[38]

Ideal and reality are not quite the same thing, however.[39] Keith Bradley discovered that families were often of a composite nature, and included

[33] Laslett and Wall eds (1972). Saller and Shaw (1984) on the predominance of the nuclear family in Rome.

[34] For a critique of their work see Martin (1996); Scheidel (2012b). See also Gallivan and Wilkins (1997) for regional differences in family structure.

[35] As Edmondson (2015) 568 notes that Saller and Shaw "were careful to emphasize that their data did not allow the reconstruction of family structures, still less the shape and size of households".

[36] For the focus of sentimentality on the nuclear family, Dixon (1991) *passim* and 111: the ideal "ignored the reality that family life frequently included people beyond the nuclear, idealized group".

[37] Hin (2013) 186–90 cautions against the assumption that neo-local marriage was universal (her argument was made for the second and first centuries BC but has relevance for the imperial period). On the wedding ceremony see, e.g., Dixon (1992) 64–65.

[38] Economic reasons, cf. Hin (2011) 113. On Roman Egypt see Hübner (2013) 48–50.

[39] Hübner (2011) 78.

others besides the nuclear triad of father, mother, and children. Composite families were shaped by death, birth, marriage, divorce, and remarriage.[40] The implications are profound in a society familiar with high mortality rates. Individuals could easily end up alone, and singles subsequently joined with others to create new or compound family groups.[41] An increasing awareness of ancient demography has led in turn to thought-provoking studies on the practical (and psychological) impact of singles in the ancient world, or maternal absence in antiquity, for example, which must have had a profound influence on children and on family life more generally.[42] The places of resultant 'missing mothers' and, I might add, those of absent fathers, too, were filled by others, such as enslaved caretakers. The servile component of the family, moreover, only adds to the changeability of the Roman family. The dynamic nature of family structure, incidentally, is also the reason why one should be very cautious with estimates of standard household size – tentatively put at five persons – and even more so with any calculations based on that number.[43]

Roman epigraphy offers a great many illustrations of what the family could look like at a fixed moment in time. In funerary epigraphy that moment is marked by the death of a family member. *CIL* 6.18404 is a good example of a household tomb:[44]

CIL 6.18404

D(is) M(anibus) / Flaviae Primae fecit / T(itus) Flav(iu)s Daphnus vern(a)e / suae q(ui) v(ixit) a(nnos) XII m(enses) VIII d(ies) XXV / et sibi et Flaviae Eu{E}<f>ro/syne coniugi suae et L(ucio) / Laberio Hermeti cogna/to suo et Cassiae Synethe / amic(a)e optim(a)e et liber{t}/tis libertabusque / suis posterisque eorum / h(oc) m(onumentum) h(eredem) n(on) s(equetur)

40 Bradley (1991). In this light LePlay's terminology for the nuclear family – he calls it the "unstable family" – is actually very much to the point, although he elected to name it unstable rather because the family dissolved when children moved out and the parents died. LePlay (1871) 17.

41 Hübner (2019) demonstrates that most households in the Roman Egyptian census records document an adult family member who was not, or was no longer, married.

42 Laes and Hübner eds (2019); Hübner and Ratzan eds (2021).

43 Hanson and Ortman (2017) 308–9 for standard household size, as a parameter for wide-ranging calculations about the Hellenistic and Roman urban population.

44 This particular example of a household tomb was brought to my attention by Sigismund Nielsen (2013) 295–96, who at 296 notes that "all these persons did not necessarily live in the same house". Sigismund-Nielsen (2006) 202 suggests that the term 'household tomb' is used too widely ("despite the scarcity of close kin"), but my interpretation of the Roman family does the opposite and argues that those included in a 'household inscription', like the one cited here, provide clues to help us find who should be included in our understanding of the Roman family.

> To the divine spirits. Titus Flavius Daphnus [set up this monument] for Flavia Prima, his *verna* who lived 12 years 8 months and 25 days; and for himself and Flavia Eufrosyne his wife, and for Lucius Laberius Hermetus his kinsman, and for Cassia Synethe best of friends, and for his freedmen and freedwomen and their descendants. This monument shall not go to the heirs.

The example shows a conjugal couple (as yet) without children, in whose household lived a freed girl, Flavia Prima, a *verna* whose death at age twelve was the incentive to build the tomb, a male relative (*cognatus*) and a female friend (*amica*). The formula *libertis libertabusque suis posterisque eorum* is a commonplace that can occur in a variety of similar forms; it allows a place in the tomb for any up until now nonexistent offspring, as well as all freedmen of the family.[45] I would classify this example as an extension of the simple family, where 'extended' is a relatively elastic notion.

The Cambridge typology may provide a useful way to characterize a family at a fixed point in time, but it does not allow for changes in family structure.[46] Regional differences in preferred family form can be significant and need to be taken into account. Moreover, Hübner cautions against the value of inscriptions for the analysis of household structures: her comparison of Roman Egyptian inscriptions on the one hand, and the census documents on the other, show wholly different patterns, and Hübner implies that the census documents are to be preferred over the epigraphic evidence. By analogy, she argues that family structure in the Roman West is virtually impossible to reconstruct, since there are only inscriptions and no census documents to work with.[47] Hübner, however, is also the one who demonstrates most clearly that Roman Egypt is not Roman Italy – particularly in matters of the family.[48]

Roman Egypt shows a clear preference for a multiple family form, at least in the census documents. However, the urban context of the *metropoleis* shows a marked preference for simple families. Significantly, the pattern of smaller households and simple family forms in the city is not restricted to

45 Crook (1967) 136 suggests that the *liberti* clause is not mere generosity, but should also be understood as a disguised commission to maintain the monument.

46 Pudsey (2011) 82: "The evidence reveals that the Cambridge typology of households is particularly useful to the extent that it categorises a household at a particular point in its life course". Hübner (2011) 78: "It must be stressed here that these different types of household forms – solitary, nuclear, extended or multiple – should not be seen so much as alternatives rather than as stages in a household cycle reflecting the age and reproductive status of its members".

47 Hübner (2011) 90; cf. Hübner (2013) 31–57.

48 This to me is the essence of Hübner (2013).

Roman Egypt, but recurs everywhere throughout history.[49] It appears that urbanization is the dominant determinant of the prevalent family form. The sources therefore suggest to me that the predominant family form, in the cities of Roman Italy at least, was the nuclear family, regularly extended by co-resident kin or slaves and ex-slaves. There is a considerable variety in the attestations, because of the dislocation and recomposition of the family, as well as the element of extension. In my view, it is precisely this variety that characterizes the Roman family, more than any family in a non-slave society after the demographic transition. The likelihood that many urban families were of the simple family type, but with extensions, matches the model of the family economy, the idea of the small workshops where an artisan worked with the help of his nuclear family and one or two slaves. However, it can also account for more divergent family strategies.[50] The composition of the family is likely to have reflected its livelihood. But its livelihood, conversely, is also likely to have been tailored to its composition.

Slaves and freedmen in the family

The Roman family often included slaves.[51] Slaves are part of the household in the legal definition of *familia*, which encompassed everyone under the power of the *paterfamilias*.[52] Slaves generally lived in with their masters. A well-known example from Apuleius' *Metamorphoses* is the servant-girl Photis, the girl who tells the protagonist about her mistress's magic – an event that eventually leads to Lucius' metamorphosis into an ass. Non-fictional instances can be found in epigraphy, as in *CIL* 6.12366:

> *CIL* 6.12366
>
> D(is) M(anibus) / Cn(aeo) Arrio Agapeto / Arria Agapete mater / et Bostrychus pater / et Helpis mamma et / Filete(?) nutrix filio / pientissimo b(ene) m(erenti) f(ecit) / vixit a(nnis) III diebus / XXXXV
>
> To the spirits of the dead. To Cnaius Arrius Agapetus, their well-deserving, dutiful son. He lived 3 years and 45 days. Arria Agapete his mother, and Bostrychus his father, and Helpis his *mamma* and Filete his wet nurse set up [this monument].[53]

[49] Hübner (2013) 32–33 with references, cf. Hin (2013) 100–09.

[50] Cf. De Vries (2008) 17.

[51] Vlassopoulos (2021) 74 for the 'household' as the main 'slaving context' in ancient history.

[52] *Dig.* 50.195.16.1–4 (Ulpian). In a *sine manu* marriage there could be two *familiae* in the family. the slaves of the husband, and the slaves of the (legally independent) wife, which, as Edmondson (2011) 343 notes, adds to the complexity of the family unit.

[53] See Bradley (1991) 76–102 on *tatae* and *mammae* in the Roman family. The reading of *filete* is uncertain.

A nurse and a second child minder (labelled *mamma*) are given a prominent place in a family commemoration of a three-year-old boy. Their inclusion in the inscription makes it probable that both these women lived in with the family, and it can be assumed from their single names that they were slave women.[54]

Bagnall and Frier's analysis of the Roman Egyptian census data shows that metropolitan households were more likely to own slaves than agricultural families.[55] It may well be that this was also true for Roman Italy; the majority of slaves in Roman Italy lived in cities and not all of them were employed by the elite *domus*.[56] It is quite likely that many households owned one or two slaves. The frequency of the formulaic *libertis libertabus posterisque eorum* is further evidence of that.

Hawkins has argued that entrepreneurs were likely to employ slaves rather than hire free labourers in the small permanent workforce of their family undertaking.[57] He offers various reasons for this: whereas the Romans may not have calculated the actual cost-effectiveness of having a slave rather than hiring labour, they would know that educating their slave greatly enhanced his or her value, and that it would ensure them of skilled labour in a labour market where such skilled labour was not in ample supply. If the cost of maintenance became too high, manumission could alleviate, if not fully abolish, this cost item – an attractive option since the freedman's labour might still be available (see below).[58] The slave presence in the household thus supports the idea of a small workshop-based economy in the Roman cities and thus in the family economy, but it also underlines the importance of flexibility – adaptive family strategies – in the face of economic change.

Dynamics of demography: the family life cycle

Family structure changes over time as the family goes through its own 'family life cycle'. The concept works differently with regard to the labour force of elite households and non-elite families, because whereas the elite *domus* were reliant chiefly on dependent labour, non-elite families were actively engaged in the labour market. As a result, in the elite *domus*

[54] The father of the boy, Bostrychus, appears to be a slave as well.

[55] Bagnall and Frier (2006) 48–49, 70–71.

[56] Edmondson (2011) 339–40. He does not extend his paper on 'slavery and the Roman family' much beyond the elite families; Harper (2011) 49–53 is insightful for sub-elite slaveholding in late antiquity.

[57] Hawkins (2017) 51 ff.

[58] Hawkins (forthcoming). This is in line with Scheidel (2005b) 13, who postulates that Roman slaves were relatively expensive compared to free labour. Therefore there had to be other reasons why so many still preferred to employ slave labour.

changes in family structure and the family labour force took place mainly in the larger slave segment of the family. The demographic realities of the enslaved population will therefore be dealt with in more detail in Chapter 4 below. Some of those findings undoubtedly are also relevant to the non-elite family. But for the non-elite household, economic relevance lies primarily in the demography of the freeborn family members.

The economic actions and decisions of the family are influenced greatly by family structure, and vice versa. What the family looks like at any one point is determined by the family life cycle, and this in turn affects the range of options open to a family when they choose whether or not, and how, to employ the various family members. Moen and Wethington argue for a life course approach of family strategies:[59]

> Families move in and out of positions that make it possible to mobilize effectively in the face of external and internal threats. Their spheres of control, and their corresponding repertoire of strategies, shift over the life course, along with shifts in household composition, family needs, and family resources as well as external supports, demands, constraints, and opportunities.[60]

In other words, at various stages in the family life cycle, family demands change, as does the family's collective supply of labour. Demand for sustenance increases when young children are born into the family, for example, and labour power increases as these children start to contribute to the family income. The changeability of the family structure means that labour power of the family could differ greatly over time and that expectations of prospective earnings and future time allocations were governed by "internal threats"; that is, uncertainties of their supply of labour, through illnesses, for example, as well as by "external threats", such as uncertainties in labour demand in the market. The family life cycle was not just governed by threats, however. It is significant that a deliberate alteration in family structure, through marriage, for example, also provided economic opportunity, and could add to capital, status, and networks.[61]

The standard family life cycle automatically induces a number of life cycle squeezes, when there are more mouths to feed than there is income:[62]

59 A life course approach of family strategies is implemented by e.g. Paping (2004); and Knotter (2004) for later periods.

60 Moen and Wethington (1992) 246–47.

61 Cf. Brockaert (2012) 12.

62 E.g. Knotter (2004), who identifies a pattern for families of Amsterdam (casual) dockworkers in the twentieth century. The term 'life cycle squeeze' appears to have been coined by Wilensky (1963).

> At three points in the life cycle of a household, tensions emerge between the income of the male head and household expenditure: when the family is being established, in the years when the children are not yet generating income, and as the parents reach old age.[63]

A life cycle squeeze necessitates additional forms of income, such as additional family members starting to do paid work, and/or resorting to the grain dole, loans, and so on. It is clear that in Rome high mortality, particularly the potentially early demise of the *paterfamilias* and the resulting loss of the main income, would present a major life cycle squeeze for many young families. Under these circumstances, it may be expected that children were put to work as soon as possible. A life cycle peak, as observed in early modern households when children matured, was perhaps also less likely to be significant in light of this high-mortality regime.[64] In many ways, therefore, it can be seen that the family life cycle determined the individual life course of family members and vice versa.[65]

A life course approach has compellingly found its way into ancient history.[66] The problem is that the evidence is generally inadequate to follow a particular Roman family through the family life cycle. There are some examples in the census documents from Roman Egypt, and also in Roman Egypt some family archives have been found;[67] in Roman Italy, conversely, we are fairly well informed about the life of a few well-known (but not very representative) families such as that of Cicero, but there is not much else to go on.[68] The ancient evidence provides snapshots, frozen moments in time that reflect the family situation at a specific moment. Most occupational inscriptions thus are a snapshot of the family at the death of a family member.

[63] Engelen, Knotter et al. (2004) 128, with reference to Oppenheimer (1974); Oppenheimer (1982).

[64] De Vries (2008) 109–10.

[65] Cf. Dixon (1992) 6: "Hareven (1987) insists that *life course* is more appropriate than *life cycle*, which presupposes that each generation eventually repeats the pattern of earlier generations, but there is a sense in which household composition does go through a fairly predictable cycle" (her italics); reference to Hareven (1987) xiii.

[66] Various of the contributions to Harlow and Larsson Lovén eds (2012), e.g. Laurence and Trifilò (2012); Parkin (2011); Pudsey (2011); Laurence (2005); Harlow and Laurence (2002). Note that the basic notion of a family life cycle was already included in Dixon (1992) 133–59 and Rawson's introduction to her influential edited volume of 1991, 5: "the family in their household must have been differently constituted at different times – not because of life-cycle changes due to the changing age of parents and children but also because of death, divorce, remarriage, and adoption or (more likely in the lower classes) fostering of young children".

[67] For Greco-Roman Egypt, see Bagnall and Frier (2006); Pudsey (2011) on eight recurring families in the census returns from Roman Egypt; and Hübner (2013).

[68] E.g. Bradley (1991) Chapter 8: "A Roman Family", on the Tullii Cicerones.

The closest thing we have to following a family over time perhaps is a micro-simulation of the Roman population that was presented by Richard Saller.[69] Saller's micro-simulation gives an overview of chances of survival and the chance for an individual at a certain age of having a living grandfather, sister, uncle, niece, and so on: the result is a tabulated blueprint for the demography of the family life cycle. The kinship universe of the simulation is restricted, and some of the parameters used can be questioned, but the simulation offers a valuable insight into family structure and the implications of a high-mortality regime that has not been possible before.[70] However useful, tables, numbers, and chances without context tell us little about the implications of changes in family demography. Rather than sketching out the myriad possible life courses of the family, it is more sensible for my current purposes to focus on specific transition points in family formation and the economic implications that come with it. Marriage is one of those benchmarks in the development of the family, as is the birth of a child, or the addition of other individuals to the family through adoption. A transition point of the life cycle that significantly does not occur in the Roman life cycle is institutionalized retirement.[71]

Marriage

Marriage is crucial to family formation: Roman marriage *is* the formation of a family. It was already mentioned that Roman marriage was largely neo-local. Thus in Rome the new household unit was established on the wedding day. Conversely, the ending of marriage through death or divorce equalled the dissolution of the family.[72] The event of a girl's first marriage signified her transition into adulthood.[73] What the family looked like at any one point in time can best be extrapolated from what it looked like at the beginning.

In Roman society, marriage is thought to have been practically universal. Augustan marriage legislation required all citizens between the ages of 25

[69] Saller (1994) with the help of James Smith and his CAMSIM simulation programme.

[70] Saller is right to emphasize that changing parameters, like age at marriage, do not significantly alter the general patterns that the simulation brings forth. However, these parameters do change the life course of individuals considerably.

[71] See Ehmer (2014) for this transition point in the economic life cycle. Parkin (2003) 234–35 for its absence in Rome, even if he connects that to a supposed absence of wage work, with which I disagree. His conclusion at 235 holds: "When a person's failing state of physical and mental health led to total inability to be self-supporting, then, in the absence of effective medication [...] dependence on others may have been short-lived anyway". There was one type of retirement: for soldiers.

[72] Noted also by Pudsey (2011) 64.

[73] Harlow and Laurence (2002) Chapter 4.

and 50 (for men) or 20 and 50 (for women) to be married. The effects and success of these laws are unknown, and it is clear that they were part of Augustus' imperial ideology. Nevertheless, they do seem to have built on existing social norms and remained in effect for several centuries.[74] The Gnomon of the Idios Logos from Roman Egypt confirms that marriage and childbearing were socially besought.[75]

The age at which the Romans married is much debated in spite (or because) of the relatively rich evidence for it from epitaphs, legal sources, and literature. The estimates for age at first marriage vary, from roughly 15 to 20 years for women, and 20 to 30 years for men.[76] The dominant marriage pattern can have important demographic consequences. A significant age gap between spouses seems likely, which will have led to a large number of relatively young widows, who can be expected to have participated in the labour market more extensively than married women.[77] It may not seem like such a great difference whether a girl married at age 15 or at age 20, but it is exactly those years that would allow or preclude an education or apprenticeship (see below). In this context it is significant that the attestation of early marriage ages for both men and women has been explained as evidence for the existence of an elite pattern of early marriage, as opposed to a more general later marriage pattern for the non-elite.[78] If girls were commonly married in their late teens rather than in their early teens, the time constraint to women's job training is thereby removed. Moreover, marriage may have been costly, which is especially true for neo-local marriage, so some may have chosen to postpone it until finances were sufficient.[79] This accounts for a later age at marriage for males, who were generally expected to be the family breadwinner.

Marriage was a family matter. In general the union was arranged by the ***paterfamilias*** in quasi-formal consultation with his own family, and the family of an eligible bachelor(-ette).[80] Marriage, divorce, and remarriage have long been recognized as strategies of the elite to forge political alliances.[81]

74 Evans Grubbs (2013) 83–87.

75 Thoma (2016).

76 The debate is ongoing, mostly on the basis of epigraphic data. Scheidel (2007b); Lelis et al. (2003) with review by De Ligt (2005); Saller (1994) 25–41; Treggiari (1991) 39–43 for legal sources; Saller (1987) for men; Shaw (1987a) for women; Syme (1987) for elite males; cf. Bagnall and Frier (2006) 111–18 for Roman Egypt; Hopkins (1965), a follow-up on the efforts of Harkness (1896).

77 Young widows: Tacoma (2016) 111–12; Pudsey (2011) 61.

78 Saller (1994) 37; Shaw (1987a).

79 Hin (2011) 112.

80 Cantarella (2005) 28–29; Bradley (1991) 112–13; Dixon (1992) 62–64 and index s.v. *consilium*.

81 Corbier (1991).

Conversely, for the majority of the population there may well have been economic motives in marriage policies: the lack of a male heir or a suitable candidate to take over the family business, or a need for economic allies, may have guided the choice of marriage partner. "Marriage extended familial ties: on divorce or bereavement, remarriage was expected by other blood relatives to ensure that their collective network of affinity and kinship was maintained".[82] Marriages could consolidate business connections or forge local or supra-local economic networks, and sometimes allowed for socially upward mobility.[83] The desire to prevent fragmentation and keep the property within the family, for example, was a major incentive for the formation of consanguineous unions in Roman Egypt.[84] The potential of marriage alliances underlines the hypothesis that despite a cultural ideal of the 'one-husband woman' (*univira*), remarriage of women after divorce or the death of a spouse will have been quite common in the pre-Christian Principate, if not as customary as has been suggested in the past.[85]

Economic theory offers additional reasons why it is economically rational to form a marriage bond. Simply put, two can produce more than one, three more than two, and so on.[86] However, the bond of marriage is not the same as simply putting together two (or more) individuals. A family unit has "a double advantage over a non-family household with comparable membership and resources".[87] Through intimate and long-term familiarity with each other's capabilities, immediate availability, and bonds of trust, a family firm saves on transaction costs for finding labour. Within this theoretical framework, an internal division of labour allows the conjugal couple to benefit even more from their respective comparative advantages.[88] The argument is quite nuanced on paper, but crudely speaking it can be read to predict that one partner will take up full responsibility for the unremunerated domestic work if their wage in the labour market is lower than that of the other, leading to a classic dichotomy between men in the public domain and women at home. That said, the ideal of preserving separate domains for husband and wife must have been largely an elite prerogative, as in many instances the additional income of women was

82 Harlow and Laurence (2002) 104.

83 Most elaborately Broekaert (2012); briefly noted by Cantarella (2005) 28.

84 Hübner (2013) Chapter 7; Hübner (2007) on the likelihood that the brother–sister marriages concern adoptive children and biological children, contra Remijsen and Clarysse (2008); Rowlandson and Takahashi (2009).

85 On *univira* see Lightman and Zeisel (1977); on singles, Hübner (2019).

86 Cigno (1991) 37–38, and Chapter 5. The economic benefit of growth in household size is not infinite.

87 Cigno (1991) 38.

88 Cigno (1991) Part I, e.g., 24, 41–42.

vital to the family.[89] Another economic privilege of marriage is that the expectancy of a stable, long-term liaison allows the family to engage in "lengthy production processes", such as raising a child.[90] Children are an important structural addition to the family.

Children

Once it has been initiated through marriage, the natural way of expanding a family is through having a child. Children ensured continuity: the importance of children had everything to do with passing on the family name and the family assets.[91] The birth of a biological child to the *paterfamilias* was not the only way in which infants came into the family, however, nor was it the only manner to beget heirs, or the only means of passing on the family name.[92] The family could also be expanded through adoption, fosterage, and care for foundlings.

Raising and killing children[93]

In Western developed countries today, when a couple think about the possibility of having children, economic considerations regularly play a part in the decision to try and go for it or not, but also in the timing, spacing, and number of children they would hope for. Many potential parents want to be able to provide for their children, covering primary needs such as food and clothing, but also secondary needs like a college education. This decision-making process must have been comparable in ancient Rome, even if it was informed by very different sociocultural and demographic circumstances. Moreover, the actual element of 'choice' was limited, considering the lack of reliable methods of contraception.

When a child was born to the freeborn couple at the head of the household, that child had much to offer. Emotions and affection must have had a large part to play.[94] Quite apart from being heir in name and property, necessary for the continuity of the family line, an infant also had economic potential. The son or daughter would become a labourer who could supply the family with additional income or who could increase

[89] Groen-Vallinga (2013) 295; Hemelrijk (2015) 9–12 for a brief overview with references on the fluid notions of the public versus the private domains of men and women (or perhaps rather, as she puts it, *forum/domus*); cf. Scheidel (1995) 205–6.

[90] Cigno (1991) 37.

[91] E.g. Rawson (2003) 108: "The political, social and inheritance value of a child, especially a son, is clearest for the upper classes". Informed overviews on the various types of children in the Roman family are Rawson (1986a); Rawson (2003); Dixon (1992) 98–132; and more recently Sigismund-Nielsen (2013).

[92] Manumission would also continue the family name; see below.

[93] A reference to the title of Shaw (2001).

[94] The *locus classicus* is Golden (1988).

production. An extra pair of hands could make all the difference in some families. A correlation between income and the number of children in a family – the poorer the family, the more children – is not unlikely, though virtually impossible to substantiate for the Roman empire.[95] A child may also have meant insurance against the possible economic hardships of old age, which is one of the life cycle squeezes identified earlier.[96] "Even a rough understanding of ancient Mediterranean demography suggests that [...] women and children were important potential sources of labor", writes Saller.[97] It was therefore economically beneficial in many ways for the family to raise a child.

Various scholars have nuanced the importance of economic motivations for having children, however.[98] They point out that having children is a decision typically governed by cultural norms rather than economic rationality. Certainly a Roman marriage was contracted with the ideal of reproduction in mind.[99] Girls were expected to marry, and bear children. For Roman women, motherhood was clearly valued over occupation: a preference for commemorating familial roles rather than economic contribution surely is one of the reasons why occupational inscriptions of women are relatively rare.

The birth of a child is another life cycle squeeze: a rise in costs, and a drop in income. The 'break-even point' – that is, the moment when the total income generated by a child starts to outweigh the costs incurred in their upbringing – was possibly never reached in a society with a life expectancy at birth that may not have exceeded 25 years.[100] Bringing up an infant required substantial investment in food and shelter, and potentially in education as well. As childcare would limit the parents' (or rather the mother's) time working, a lower-class family that already had a number of children may not have been able to feed another mouth. That pattern would be exacerbated if the mother died in childbirth. A wealthy, higher-class family, conversely, may not have wanted to raise another heir at the risk of having to split up the family property any more than necessary.[101] It is

95 Knotter (2004) 235 with references to early modern examples of this pattern.

96 Old age came with economic as well as social hardship. Cf. Hübner (2013) for Roman Egypt; Parkin (2003) esp. 203–35; Rawson (2003) 108; Harlow and Laurence (2002).

97 Saller (2007) 87.

98 Hin (2011) esp. 100–4; De Ligt (2004) 750–51.

99 E.g. Dixon (1992) 61–62.

100 Hin (2011) 101. Significantly, at 102 she suggests that perhaps an urban environment is the one place where children could find the employment that would earn enough to break even.

101 The Romans endorsed partible inheritance, so all children male and female inherited equally from their parents. Rawson (2003) 114; cf. Champlin (1991) 114–17

not too difficult to think of other reasons, such as divorce, adultery, or a pregnancy out of wedlock, why an unborn child was less than welcome.[102] Dangers to the health of the mother that were inherent in pregnancy could also have played a part. For all these reasons the Romans may have wanted to exercise some form of family planning one way or another, either to stimulate or to prevent further births in the family.

Contraception was not unheard of in ancient Rome, but the methods used were not always safe or reliable.[103] Continued breastfeeding ensured only partial protection (and there is some discussion whether Roman women generally breastfed their own infants or not); a kind of condom made of sheep's bladders was expensive; and the herbs that were used as abortifacients were inefficient at best, and could also be dangerous to the mother.[104] Many of these forms of contraception may have been reserved for the elite.[105] As a result, there were Romans who turned to other, more secure, methods of family planning: infant exposure and infanticide.

The Roman practices of infanticide and exposure have been accentuated in scholarly literature, because they go directly against contemporary norms and values.[106] It is likely that a number of Roman infants were indeed exposed, abandoned, or in a few extreme cases even killed shortly after birth, but the exact numbers cannot be known. However, I would argue that this was not so much a sign that there was a large number of 'unwanted children': exposure did not preclude emotional attachment to their living offspring. Many of the newborns who were abandoned were swaddled for protection. They were sometimes provided with some kind of token, indicating the parents' hope to reclaim their child when they had the opportunity. Moreover, it seems plausible that in Rome, as in later historical periods, infants were regularly left in a public place where they stood a very real chance of being found – that is to say, the parents did not wish for them to die.[107] This points to a predominantly economic

for the fact that Roman wills show a tendency to bequeath the bulk of an inheritance to one son.

102 E.g. Evans Grubbs (2013) 84–92 for motivations that might lead to exposure of an infant. Many of these arguments hold for slave babies, too (ibid., 89), though it is likely that slave births were less common in smaller families than in elite households.

103 Contra Riddle (1992); see, e.g., the critique by Frier (1994); Hin (2011).

104 Contraception: Bracher (1992). On a possible low level of breastfeeding Parkin (2013) 52, and at 53: "In preindustrial societies, to feed an infant unpasteurized animal milk was tantamount to manslaughter" – but wet nurses were also common in Roman society; on the dangers involved for the woman, most vividly Ov. *Am.* 2.13.

105 Hin (2011) 108–9.

106 Evans Grubbs (2013); Garnsey (1991); Harris (1994); Corbier (2001); Shaw (2001).

107 Corbier (2001) 69, taking into consideration what she considers a good chance for the exposed infant to survive, writes, "Roman parents probably did not consider exposure

motivation behind exposure.[108] Infanticide seems to have been rarely applied.[109]

The 'social birth' of the infant – that is, its acceptance into the family – took place after eight days (in the case of a girl) or nine days (for a boy).[110] The decision to raise a child presumably lay with the *paterfamilias.* It has long been thought that the father would literally raise the child (*tollere/suscipere liberum*) up from the ground to indicate his willingness to raise the newborn. The fact that the existence of this particular ritual acceptance of the child is now seriously in doubt probably does not change the father's influence in this matter.[111] If he chose not to bring up the newborn infant, we may presume that the child would be exposed or perhaps even killed. It has been convincingly argued that this is the context in which we should read the *paterfamilias*'s power of life and death (*ius vitae necisque*), where the power of death was probably acted out sporadically, and then predominantly in the case of serious health problems that would complicate life for the newborn.[112]

With all this talk of exposure and infanticide, it should not be forgotten that most children were treasured in Roman society.[113] Where for some a child had become a difficulty that ultimately led to exposure or abandonment, for others it was crucial to beget a child. "In a society where childbearing and the passing on of property were considered the primary purposes of marriage, women were under enormous pressure to produce a healthy heir."[114] And that may not always have been self-evident.[115]

a form of 'infanticide'". Cf. also her references to literary recognition scenes, and legal texts relating to the possible continued influence of the biological father over a child exposed at birth and raised by another.

108 Porena (2016) 676 suggests that the economic insecurity for families "in alcune aree urbanizzate dell'Impero" ("in some urbanized areas of the empire") could have led to increased numbers of child exposure – and increased attestations of child labour as a result, for which see below.

109 Evans Grubbs and Parkin (2013) 1 bring to mind that DeMause as recently as 1974 (at 51) still classified "Antiquity to the Fourth Century AD" as part of the "Infanticidal Mode", a notion that has long since been refuted. When infanticide did occur, it may have been for reasons of serious health problems and deformity, although some disabled infants were brought up. See Laes (2013) 129–31; O'Hara (1998) 211.

110 Hänninen (2005) 56–59.

111 Köves-Zulauf (1990); Shaw (2001) 32–56. It is, however, certain that the decision remained with the *paterfamilias*, says Corbier (2001) 58.

112 Laes (2013); O'Hara (1998). For a different explanation of the *ius*, see Shaw (2001) 56–77.

113 Dixon (1991) 109–11.

114 Evans Grubbs (2013) 87.

115 Corbier (1991) 67; Hänninen (2005) 49 on the very real danger of the death of the child, mother, or both in childbed.

The *Laudatio Turiae* is a famous funerary text for an infertile woman who allegedly offered to divorce her husband so that he might have children with another.[116] Roman society, like many pre-industrial populations, was characterized by high fertility rates on the one hand, and high mortality on the other.[117] Mortality was particularly high during infancy and early childhood, and mortality rates were elevated by the unsanitary circumstances of the larger cities.[118] Raising a child until maturity was not guaranteed.

The wish for a baby or the need for an heir might theoretically lead Romans to turn to 'non-natural' methods of begetting a child, such as adopting, or taking up a foundling. Neither of these options appear to have been very common in ancient Rome, however. Foundlings could theoretically be picked up and raised as one's own. As far as can be known, however, most foundlings were raised as slaves.[119] Having said that, there is a distinct possibility that the evidence would not explicitly identify a foundling brought up as a natural son or daughter. Even more likely to go undetected, when successful, is supposition. Evans Grubbs notes the possible supposition of babies, who might also be foundlings.[120] If only because of its highly specific requirements, however – an infant of the same age available at just the right time through just the right channels to ensure secrecy – supposition is unlikely to have been common.[121] Adoption of infants was legally recognized, but it was rare.[122] Corbier thinks that the childless 'Turia' and her husband may have considered adoption of a baby girl, but that was only after the husband decided that the apparently more customary response to infertility – divorce and remarriage – was not an option for him.[123] It is in fact characteristic of adoption in Roman society that it typically took place at a later age.[124]

[116] Right-hand column, lines 25–50; Hemelrijk (2004); Hemelrijk (2001b); Hemelrijk (2001a) with Dutch translation and commentary.

[117] Parkin (2013) 44: "Children in classical antiquity were a very large proportion of the population, and a lot of them were dying."

[118] Parkin (2013).

[119] Porena (2016) 674–75; Corbier (2001) 66–67. For more on foundlings as a source of slaves, see Chapter 4 below.

[120] Evans Grubbs (2013) 87.

[121] Corbier (1991) 65: "Precautions would be taken at the time of a widow's confinement to prevent the substitution of the child", with reference to *Dig.* 37.9.1.15 (Ulpian).

[122] Lindsay (2009) 69–70 briefly considers adoption of minors.

[123] Corbier (1991) 63; but Lindsay (2009) 153 disagrees.

[124] Lindsay (2009) makes extensive use of cross-cultural comparisons, esp. Chapter one at 4–28. An earlier, more pointed version of this chapter was published as Lindsay (2001), with 201–4 specifically on ancient Rome. See Hübner (2013) for the significant differences with the practice of adoption in the ancient eastern Mediterranean.

Other additions to the family

It has already been emphasized that many Roman families consisted of a free and a slave segment. It is known that at least some urban households in addition also contained lodgers. Both house owners and lodgers can be identified in the Egyptian census data; these lodgers are mainly male adults.[125] If a similar pattern existed in Roman Italy, the rent will have been a welcome addition to the family income. The evidence does not permit me to conclude any more on this strategy, however. Two other categories of family members, however, do deserve to be mentioned in somewhat more detail. It is likely that there were more children in the house than the children we just considered. The elusive category of *alumni*, or foster-children, contains some who were raised in the household from birth, and others who found a temporary home there. More secure family ties were constructed by adoption. Adoption could be an effective family strategy, at least for free citizens.[126] It was a means to transfer an adult into another family in the eyes of the law, as a natural son or grandson.[127]

Alumni

Alumni were children who were raised from infancy by people who were not their biological parents.[128] This much can be said, as well as the fact that the term *alumnus/-a* professes affection and quasi-familial bonds.[129] Other than that, they make for a heterogeneous and complex group that defies direct definition. Some were raised as slaves, others were free; despite obvious similarities with children who were exposed or abandoned, *alumni* may or may not have been foundlings.[130] It is their status that was fundamentally different from foundlings who were adopted as a natural child: free *alumni* were not legally kin. The designation *alumnus* may merely indicate that

[125] Pudsey (2012) 167: "Lodgers were a feature of households in the large towns and metropoleis", and in n. 22 she gives the example of Bagnall and Frier (2006): 103–Ar–1 (nine lodgers).

[126] An excellent, concise account of adoption as familial strategy, is Corbier (1991). I have not been able to access Corbier ed. (1999). The technicalities of adoption by life or testamentary adoption, and adrogation, are deliberately left out of my discussion. These aspects do not change the nature of the resulting kinship bond, which is decisive for adoption as a family strategy. For those interested in these details, I recommend Lindsay (2009) esp. Chapters 4, 5.

[127] For the adoption of a grandson, Lindsay (2009) 66; Corbier (1991) 67–68.

[128] Sigismund-Nielsen (2013) 289. On *alumni*, see especially Sigismund-Nielsen (1987); Bellemore and Rawson (1990).

[129] Dixon (1992) 129: "The term *alumnus* and its cognates are less likely to be employed of an adult than of a child, which suggests that the special relationship might vary over the life cycle."

[130] Sigismund-Nielsen (2013) 289 argues that they were not.

the child was literally 'nurtured' by a wet nurse. There is some evidence to suggest that sometimes its meaning comes closer to 'apprentice' than to 'nursling', however, as in the following inscription from Puteoli:[131]

> *CIL* 10.1922
>
> D(is) M(anibus) / G. Atilius Fortu/natus faber in/testinarius q(ui) v(ixit) / an(n)is XXXI f(ecit) Iulius Felicis/simus alum(no) mere(nti)
>
> To the spirits of the dead. [Here lies] Gaius Atilius Fortunatus, inlayer/cabinet maker, who lived 31 years. Iulius Felicissimus set up [this monument] for his well-deserving student.

Fortunatus died relatively young, at the age of 31. At that time he was fully educated as a *faber intestinarius*. He was commemorated by one Iulius Felicissimus. Therefore it appears that Felicissimus either raised Fortunatus or taught him the trade of fine carpentry, or indeed a combination of the two: the term *alumnus* can point in both directions. The lack of any mention of other family bonds suggests that Fortunatus was unmarried, and that his biological parents were out of the picture. Perhaps Felicissimus was indeed a surrogate father to Fortunatus. Both their *cognomina*, Felicissimus and Fortunatus, are names that suggest a servile background. Although the *duo* and *tria nomina* could technically also indicate freeborn status, it would not be surprising that libertinization is not explicitly mentioned if Fortunatus were a Iunian Latin. Scholars have generally assumed that Iunian Latins were not allowed to boast libertinization.[132] Fortunatus' age suggests that he may well have been manumitted before the legal minimum age of 30 and thereby became a Iunian Latin. This would also explain why Fortunatus was not formally adrogated by Felicissimus, a fact that can be gathered from the dissimilarity of their *gentilicia*. As an ex-slave, Felicissimus was legally able to adrogate (though not technically adopt) another citizen, but Iunian Latins were not considered to be citizens.[133] In this instance it appears that Fortunatus was educated to be Felicissimus' successor in the business, which was expressed in the inscription by the term *alumnus* as a replacement for formal adrogation. At other times apprentices were taken in temporarily to master a trade, only for them to

[131] Sigismund-Nielsen (2013) 289 mentions this option, but with reference to the rather unconvincing examples of *CIL* 6.10158, *CIL* 6.8454, and *CIL* 6.8697 (in this last case no *alumnus* is mentioned).

[132] But see Mouritsen (2019) 221–22. There and in Mouritsen (2011b) 39 he also defends a preference for the term 'pseudo-filiation' to emphasize the social relation between patron and freedman that was created; I will adhere throughout to the terminology of *liberti* and libertinization that the epigraphs and legal texts demonstrate.

[133] Lopez Barja de Quiroga (1998).

return to their family of birth, an investment of the birth family that will be dealt with in detail below.

Adoption

The main motive for adoption in Rome appears to have been the need for an heir. It generally concerned adult males who were adopted in the event that no heir was present. Adopting when a (male) heir existed, or even when the adopter was still under 60 – which was the age before which he might reasonably expect to still beget children of his own according to the law – was frowned upon.[134] Close relatives were the preferred choice for adoption, but it was also possible to adopt the child of a friend, for example.[135] In theory, the adopted son became heir to his new family. In practice, ties with the family of origin were simultaneously recognized. This enabled the procedure to function as a way of strengthening the bond between two families. A patron might choose to adopt a freedman, to solidify a claim to the freedman's wealth, for example.[136] For the freedman himself, his new status as a 'natural' son to his patron did not remove the practical consequences of the freedman stigma, however. Apparently even adoption could not change that. Corbier illustrates that the possibilities for rearranging lineage provided by adoption were virtually endless; the practice "recognized [the] right of a father to reshape his relationships".[137] The evidence is heavily biased towards the imperial elite, however, and even then adoption does not appear to have been very common.[138] There is no way of knowing whether a legal construct like this was ever exploited by the rest of the population, though the benefits of adopting a particularly talented apprentice to continue the family business, to name but one possibility, are obvious.

Human capital

Just like many other life-changing events such as marriage, investment in a child's human capital was decided on by the family.[139] If decisions on raising a child or buying a slave concern the quantity of the family labour supply, investment in human capital involves the quality of the family.

Modern economists have demonstrated that there is a direct correlation

134 Corbier (1991) 66–67.

135 Corbier (1991) 67.

136 Lindsay (2009) 132–36 offers a very brief account that mostly raises questions rather than answers them. He only hints at the possibility that freedmen may have wanted to use adoption to bring together their natural family born in slavery.

137 Corbier (1991) 76.

138 Lindsay (2009) 2–3 mentions a few estimates by previous scholars that range from 2 to 9 per cent.

139 Bradley (1991) 112–13.

between years of schooling and income.[140] This correlation appears to be equally valid for ancient Rome, although we have few numerical data on wages in Rome.[141] The example of Diocletian's Prices Edict of AD 301 illustrates that skilled labour typically brought in twice as much as unskilled daily wages, or more.[142] This points to significant returns on education. Why, then, did not everyone attempt to obtain an education for themselves, their children or their slaves?[143] Economic theory predicts that "[i]n principle, we would expect all individuals to be grouped at the highest educational level, to benefit from the increased income opportunities".[144] This is obviously not the case today, and it was not in ancient Rome – quite the reverse. Several possible answers can be found in modern economic theory. Investment in schooling can be restricted through high child mortality, financial constraints, and what is called 'intergenerational persistence'.

Intergenerational persistence refers to the fact that a poor family regularly could not afford job training for their children, so that the next generation remained poor, in perpetual self-confirmation; conversely, skilled workers earned more and hence they could more likely afford their children's education, and so on.[145] In the calculations of Scheidel and Friesen, close to 90 per cent of the population lived at or under subsistence levels, which surely means that these people did not have the resources to ensure an education for themselves or their children.[146] Family background mattered. The fact that job training was not available to everyone in the freeborn population therefore largely is the result of intergenerational persistence, although the same principle also implies that freeborn skilled labourers were a continuous presence.

The comparatively high mortality rate in the Roman empire meant that on average there were relatively few years left to reap the benefits of an education, or to develop human capital further through experience. In other words, investing in any kind of training did not always pay off. As

140 E.g. Checchi (2006) 5–10.

141 Szilágyi (1963); Mrozek (1975); Corbier (1980); and see Szaivert and Wolters (2005) for the literary wage data. Roman Egypt: Johnson (1936); Drexhage (1991).

142 Groen-Vallinga and Tacoma (2017) 113–14, 118–22 with references. Rathbone (2009) 214 for two- to threefold differentials, and the suggestion that the latter was more common in urban contexts. Bernard (2017) 83 points out that the Roman skill premium is normal in comparative perspective.

143 Similarly, Saller (2013) 76–77: "If an apprenticeship [...] doubled his daily wage [...] why did more parents and slave masters not apprentice their sons and slaves [...] I have no answer." This section is an attempt to answer the question.

144 Checchi (2006) 10.

145 Checchi (2006) Chapter 7 on intergenerational persistence.

146 Scheidel and Friesen (2009) 82–88.

a result, high (child) mortality probably was an additional factor limiting investment in, and accumulation of, human capital.[147]

Specific to Rome is the fact that much skilled work was carried out by slaves, thereby restricting job opportunities for freeborn skilled workers. Since investment in human capital correlates with expectations of prospective earnings, the competition of slave labourers in the market has a direct effect on the time, effort, and money spent on education by the freeborn population. Hawkins concludes that apprencticeship was not easily affordable and, on the assumption that employers were more likely to hire or buy slaves than to hire the freeborn to do their skilled work, "those who could afford to pay for such training probably did so with an eye to establishing their sons as independent producers rather than as wage workers".[148]

Even without slave competition, general labour demands predict that there cannot have been an unlimited demand for skilled labour, and that there was a definite need for menial labour as well. For many it was more profitable to step in where there was work in the unskilled sector, rather than to be trained but unemployed.

It is likely that such factors had a limiting effect on the total amount of time and effort spent by the free population on acquiring occupational skills in ancient Rome, and as a result skilled hired free labour became harder to come by.[149] Despite these limiting factors, aggregate investment in human capital in the Roman world was far from negligible, even if it was not in any way comparable to the modern Western world.[150] There were opportunities for slaves as well as the freeborn, both boys and girls, to receive some kind of basic education. Although there was no formal schooling system, let alone an educational program set up by the government, in theory the class of the *ludimagister* was open to all from about age seven.[151] Rates of literacy for Roman Italy were unprecedented, especially taking into account basic literacy or craft literacy.[152]

147 And vice versa: it has been demonstrated that at least in the late twentieth century, lower-educated people had a lower life expectancy as well. Checchi (2006) 18 with references; cf. Saller (2013) 76: "In order to derive the greatest return on the investment in training, it should be provided at that developmental moment after the ravages of childhood diseases when the children have the physical and mental capacity to learn the skills and pull their weight in the workshop".

148 Hawkins (2017) 46–48, quote at 48.

149 On the scarcity of skilled labour, see also Hawkins (2017).

150 Saller (2013) 71–72; Verboven (2012b) 95 suggests that "freedmanship may have been the decisive factor explaining the significantly higher investment in human capital in the Roman empire than would be seen for a thousand years to come".

151 Laes (2011a) 107–47, which is actually most illustrative of what we do *not* know about Roman (primary) education; Laes and Strubbe (2008) 75ff.

152 Woolf (2000) provides a useful overview of the debate on literacy.

Arts and crafts

Some children went on to learn a trade. The theory of intergenerational continuity predicts that they were predominantly the children of artisans and craftsmen, who could afford to provide their descendants with job training. Many will have eased into the business, taking up more tasks within the household as they grew older and stronger.[153] If parents were master artisans, they were well capable of teaching their children to become master artisans themselves. The benefits of educating a child at home are simple: there would be virtually no loss of labour input, and therefore no forgone earnings, while building human capital. Specialist job training was not necessarily based in the household, however, and it remains to be seen just how many children followed in their parents' footsteps (see below). Just like a basic primary education, job training regularly was obtained elsewhere: children, both slave and free, could be apprenticed out. The boundaries between formal apprenticeship, and arrangements to have a child trained in the household of birth, or that of a relative or friend, are not clear-cut. Formal apprenticeship contracts might a priori be considered a relatively straightforward source for investment in education, but as it turns out these documents provide evidence for much more varied investment strategies.

Apprenticeship

Formal job training is relatively well attested for the Roman empire, particularly in apprenticeship contracts from Roman Egypt. The contracts provide a valuable insight into the considerations of investing in human capital, and it is well worth taking a closer look at these documents here.[154] There are no apprenticeship contracts from outside Roman Egypt, however, and one may wonder whether they present a picture that is representative of Roman Italy as well. Scattered references in Roman law, literature, and epigraphy suggest to me that the practice was not reserved to Roman Egypt.

Ulpian mentions a rather unfortunate apprentice in *Digest* 9.2.5.3: "A shoemaker struck with a last the neck of a freeborn apprentice (*puero discenti ingenuo filio familias*), who did not do what the shoemaker instructed well enough. The boy's eye was knocked out."[155]

[153] Saller (2013) 73–75 assumes that this kind of informal learning was the way most Romans gained their skills, certainly in agriculture but also in the arts and crafts.

[154] For a general overview, most recently Bergamasco (1995); see also Zambon (1935).

[155] Ulpian takes the example from Julian. "Sutor [inquit] puero discenti ingenuo filio familias, parum bene facienti quod demonstraverit, forma calcei cervicem percussit, ut oculus puero perfunderetur."

In epigraphy the rare attestations include a medical apprentice from Pula:[156]

CIL 5.89

D(is) M(anibus) / P(ublio) Coesio Ortensi[a]/no medico / ann(orum) XVIII(?) / Miluso Primo / discipulo

To the divine spirits. To Publius Coesius Ortensianus, doctor, who lived 18(?) years. To Milusus Primus, his student.

Lucian recounts his brief experience as an apprentice sculptor in his 'autobiography', *The Dream*:

Luc. *Somn.* 1

Ἄρτι μὲν ἐπεπαύμην εἰς τὰ διδασκαλεῖα φοιτῶν ἤδη τὴν ἡλικίαν πρόσηβος ὤν, ὁ δὲ πατὴρ ἐσκοπεῖτο μετὰ τῶν φίλων ὅ τι καὶ διδάξαιτό με. τοῖς πλείστοις οὖν ἔδοξεν παιδεία μὲν καὶ πόνου πολλοῦ καὶ χρόνου μακροῦ καὶ δαπάνης οὐ μικρᾶς καὶ τύχης δεῖσθαι λαμπρᾶς, τὰ δ' ἡμέτερα μικρά τε εἶναι καὶ ταχεῖάν τινα τὴν ἐπικουρίαν ἀπαιτεῖν· εἰ δέ τινα τέχνην τῶν βαναύσων τούτων ἐκμάθοιμι, τὸ μὲν πρῶτον εὐθὺς ἂν αὐτὸς ἔχειν τὰ ἀρκοῦντα παρὰ τῆς τέχνης καὶ μηκέτ' οἰκόσιτος εἶναι τηλικοῦτος ὤν, οὐκ εἰς μακρὰν δὲ καὶ τὸν πατέρα εὐφρανεῖν ἀποφέρων ἀεὶ τὸ γιγνόμενον.

No sooner had I left off school, being then well on in my teens, than my father and his friends began to discuss what he should have me taught next. Most of them thought that higher education required great labour, much time, considerable expense, and conspicuous social position, while our circumstances were but moderate and demanded speedy relief; but that if I were to learn one of the handicrafts, in the first place I myself would immediately receive my support from the trade instead of continuing to share the family table at my age; besides, at no distant day I would delight my father by bringing home my earnings regularly.[157]

The passage is highly instructive of the possible considerations involved for the family when deciding on an apprenticeship. Among the 'friends' present is Lucian's uncle, a sculptor – and indeed it is decided that Lucian should be apprenticed out to him to become a sculptor too. The arrangement is economically motivated: there is no money for higher education. Through an apprenticeship Lucian would no longer burden the family income ("continuing to share the family table") – he would even contribute to it ("bringing home my earnings regularly"). It may also be significant that

156 Schulz-Falkenthal (1972) collects references for *discipuli* and *discentes*.
157 Translation Harmon (1913, Loeb Classical Library).

sculpting runs in the family, with two uncles and his grandfather in the trade. The example is from second-century Syria, but it will become clear that it is representative of a wider context in many respects.

The job of hairdresser (*ornatrix*) apparently required a training of at least two months to qualify, judging from *Digest* 32.65.3, which states that only those who have trained with a *magister* for at least two months qualify as legated hairdressers. The women in this text are clearly slaves.[158]

From these examples I conclude that even in the absence of apprenticeship contracts from Roman Italy, it can safely be assumed that a similar apprenticeship system existed in there.[159] As far as can be ascertained, it seems that the contracts come from an urban context: the majority come from Oxyrhynchus. This underlines the relevance of these documents to the present inquiry into the Roman urban labour market.

The number of Egyptian apprenticeship contracts currently known lies around 50 for the early Roman empire, but the list is ever-expanding.[160] They refer mostly to apprentice weavers, which appears to be the result of coincidence rather than a reflection of any particular aspect of the weaving trade. The majority of the contracts that have survived were set up for freeborn children: roughly 40 out of 50 contracts. These numbers strongly suggest that job training was not reserved exclusively for slaves, and that the freeborn did have a chance to receive an education. So what considerations for investing in job training can be gathered from apprenticeship contracts?

Because of the nature of the documents we are well informed about the cost of apprenticeship. None of the master artisans receives an instruction fee for a freeborn apprentice. Even for slave apprentices, only in two instances does the master artisan receive a fee for the instruction.[161] In *BGU* 4.1125 from Alexandria, in 13 BC, a certain C. Iulius Philios pays 100 drachmae to have his slave boy Narkissos instructed in the art of flute

158 *Dig.* 32.65.3: "Ornatricibus legatis Celsus scripsit eas, quae duos tantum menses apud magistrum fuerunt, legato non cedere, alii et has cedere, ne necesse sit nullam cedere, cum omnes adhuc discere possint et omne artificium incrementum recipit: quod magis optinere debet, quia humanae naturae congruum est."

159 Bradley (1991) 112–16; Laes (2015b).

160 See Appendix 2 for a catalogue. The most recent collection is Bergamasco (1995), who lists 42 documents (Ptolemaic and Roman), to which should be added *SB* 24.16186 (Bergamasco (2004)), *P.Col. Inv.* 164 (Bergamasco (2006a)), *P.Oxy.* 67.4596 (Bergamasco (2004)), *P. Mich. Inv.* 4238 (Eckerman (2011)). Bergamasco has announced that work on a new collection of the apprenticeship contracts and apprenticeship registrations is currently under way. Bergamasco (2004) 31 n. 1; Bergamasco (2006a) 207 n. 1.

161 This difference in remuneration caused a desire to separate the apprenticeship contracts analytically into two groups. Cf. Bergamasco (1995) 100–4 for the various typologies that have been applied, e.g. *Lehrvertrag* und *Unterrichtsvertrag* (Adams (1964)), or *Lehrvertrag* and *Lehrlingsvertrag* (Berger (1911)).

playing over the course of a year. And in AD 155 a certain Apollonius from Oxyrhynchus receives 120 drachmae to have his son teach the slave boy Chairammon shorthand writing in two years.[162] In all likelihood this can be related to the type of employment: the pupil of a flute player or stenographer cannot perhaps be immediately put to work as easily as an apprentice weaver during the teaching period.

Economic theory suggests that the main expense of education, however, is not so much the instruction fee as forgone earnings: the income not collected during the time spent in training. In Roman Egypt, forgone earnings were mitigated by the fact that the apprentices were usually paid for their efforts, in accordance with Lucian's remark: "at no distant day I would delight my father by bringing home my earnings regularly".[163] This could be either in the form of a lump sum to be paid at the beginning or the end of the contract, or in the form of a monthly wage. The master craftswoman Aurelia Libouke pays the lump sum of 60 drachmae for a year in return for the efforts of a slave girl apprentice, in a third-century document.[164] When a monthly wage is specified, sometimes the contracts take account of the fact that a student accumulates ever more skills over time. For example, the slave girl Thermoution from late second-century Oxyrhynchus earns eight drachmae a month in the first year of her apprenticeship, but this modest figure is raised to 12 in the second year and 16 in the third year, and to 20 drachmae a month in the final year when she earns quite a respectable monthly wage.[165] In most instances the master artisan also met the cost for food, clothing, taxes, and all other expenses related to the trade, again just like Lucian: "I myself would immediately receive my support from the trade instead of continuing to share the family table at my age".[166] Having a child or a slave in job training would thus seem to be an

[162] *P.Oxy*. 4.724.

[163] See also Hengstl (1972) 92–95. Payment is not always specified, but then not all documents are complete. In *P. Mich*. 5.346a the apprentice is fed and clothed by the master, but she does not receive a wage; cost or payment is unknown for *St. Pal*. 22.40.

[164] *P. Mich. Inv*. 5195a.

[165] *P.Oxy*. 14.1647. Cf. Drexhage (1991) 425–29 for monthly wages attested in contracts on papyrus. Twenty drachmae appears to be about the average monthly wage for unskilled work in the first two centuries AD; a similar regular wage increase can be observed in *P. Oxy*. 41.2977 (AD 239). *PSI* 3.241 (third century) documents a contract where the apprentice does not receive a wage for the first six months, which is a different way to account for her inexperience at the outset. These examples are all for slave apprentices, but the principle is no different for free boys and girls, e.g. *P. Oxy*. 4.725 (five-year contract for a weaver's apprentice; wages of 12 rising to 24 drachmae a month from the seventh month of the second year onwards).

[166] Lucian *Somn*. 1, quoted above; Bergamasco (1995) 149 on remuneration; *P. Oxy*. 67.4596 even specifies that the apprentice receives food and clothing from the master

economically sound investment.[167] It would have been attractive for parents/carers or masters because as a rule the child was fed and clothed, brought home wages, and learnt a trade, which would bring in more money than menial labour at a later age.

Apprenticeship could be a compelling option for another reasons. Freeborn children were sometimes apprenticed out in connection with loans contracted by their parents or relatives. It appears that the labour of the apprentice was a security pledge that the advanced sum would be repaid, that it was traded for the interest on the loan, or perhaps both. A good example is *P. Tebt.* 2.384 (AD 10):

***P. Tebt.* 2.384, 15–25**

[Ἁ]ρμιῦσις καὶ Παπνεβ[τῦ]ν̣ις οἱ δο(*) Ὀρσενούφι[ος Πέρσαι]
τῆς ἐπιγονῆς ὁμολογοῦμεν ἔχειν π̣[αρὰ Πασώ-]
νιος τοῦ Ὀρσενούφιος ἀργυρίου δραχμὰς [δεκά-]
εξ [καὶ] ἀ̣ν̣τὶ τῶν τούτων τόκων καὶ [τρο]φ[είων](*)[καὶ]
ἱ̣ματισμοῦ καὶ λαογραφίας κώμης Ὀξυρύνχω̣[ν καὶ]
τέλους γερδίων καὶ τῶν τούτων μισθῶ[ν παρ-]
εξόμεθα τὸν ἀδελφὸν ὑμῶν(*) Π̣α̣σ̣ίωνα π̣[αραμέ-]
νοντα αὐτῷ ἐνιαυτὸν ἕνα ἀπὸ̣ τ̣ο̣ῦ̣ τ̣ε[σσα-]
ρακοστοῦ ἔτου[ς] Καίσαρ[ος ἐ]ργαζόμενον [κατὰ τὴν]
γερδιακὴν τέχνην καὶ ποιοῦντα τὰ ἐ̣π̣[ιταχθη-]
σόμε[να] πάντα

[…] We, Harmiysis and Papnebtynis, both sons of Orsenouphis, Persians of the Epigone, acknowledge that we have received from Pasonis, son of Orsenouphis, 16 drachmas of silver, and in return for the (remission of) interest upon this sum and the boy's keep and clothing and poll-tax at the village of Oxyrhyncha and weavers' tax and wages will produce our brother Pasion to stay with Pasonis for one year from the 40th year of Caesar and to work at the weaver's trade and perform all that he is bidden […][168]

artisan "instead of wages" (l. 15, ἀντὶ μισθῶν). A slave apprentice often moved in with the master, e.g. *P. Mich.* 346a (13 BC), *P.Oxy.* 41.2977 (AD 239).

[167] *P. Wisc.* 1.4 is the one exception that proves the rule. The apprentice's father provided the master artisan with 14 drachmae for clothing, and five silver drachmae a month for food. No other costs or wages are specified. *Pace* Hawkins (2017), who adduces *P. Oxy.* 4.725 as an example of the assumption that the cost of apprenticeship was considerable (his n. 32). Although the parents pay for food, and the apprentice starts earning wages only after two years and four months, the master still pays for clothing. It is also the single most unfavourable example from the parents' perspective; therefore I believe the actual costs generally may have been less substantial than Hawkins suggests.

[168] Translation by the editors of *P. Tebt.* 2.

In this text, two brothers 'hand over', or 'entrust' (the verb is a form of *parechomai*, commonly used for 'apprenticing out'), their brother Pasion to a master weaver, Pasonis, for the duration of one year, in exchange for a loan of 16 silver drachmae; Pasonis in return will charge no interest on this sum, and see to Pasion's food and clothing as well as the weaver's tax. The advantages to the family are evident: Pasion's brothers save the expense of his keep, and they stand to gain not only from the remission of interest on the silver drachmae, but also from their brother's (unspecified) wages.

There are other such instances. It appears that Hermaiskos, son of Herakleides, was apprenticed out to the nailsmith Nilus in return for a loan of 100 drachmae, made out to his father and a certain Taurion. This we learn from *BGU* 4.1124 (Alexandria, 18 BC), a document specifying the annulment of the teaching contract (which has not been preserved), because Herakleides and Taurion had paid off their debt to Nilos.[169] Similarly, *P. Oxy.* 67.4596 (AD 264) is an apprenticeship contract for four years, where the instruction takes place in return for a loan of 400 drachmae to be returned – explicitly without interest – at the conclusion of the contract.[170] In this contract, a girl is to be educated as a weaver.[171] The text adds the significant clause that the father "is not allowed to take away his daughter within this period nor after the end of this period until he repays the four hundred silver drachmae in full".[172] An apprentice as surety for a loan therefore seems to me the more conclusive reading of these particular texts.[173] These loans have sometimes been explained the other way around; that is, as caution money ensuring that the master craftsman fulfilled his obligations to the parents/carers. The clause of *P. Oxy.* 4596 is clear, however. The explanation of caution money does not clarify the early termination of Hermaiskos' teaching contract either (*BGU* 4.1124).

[169] In my opinion this document is about a loan, not a return of an advance payment of wages, as (very) tentatively suggested by Sijpesteijn (1967) in his commentary of *P. Wisc.* I. 4, lines 9–10. Compare *BGU* 4.1154 (Alexandria, 10 BC) which demonstrates a similar construction, the *synchoresis* explicitly drafted to pay back a loan. *P. Oxy.* 31.2586 also includes the sum of 400 drachmae from master to father, to be returned at the end of the contract; unlike the other examples, however, this contract also specifies wages for the apprentice.

[170] See J. David Thomas's 2001 edition of the papyrus; and Bergamasco (2004) 35–38 for its date.

[171] An interesting detail is that she is taught in the weaving trade by an overseer (*histonarches*) rather than a weaver, on which see Migliardi Zingale (2007) 207–8.

[172] Lines 21–25: "ọụκ [ἐξόντος αὐ-] τῳ ἐντὸς του χρόνου ἀποσπạ[ν τὴν θυ-]γατέρạ ạụ̣του οὐδẹ̀ μετὰ τὸν χρọ́νọν [-ca.?-] πρịὶν ἂṿ ἀποδῷ τὰς τοῦ ἀργυρί[ου] δ̣[ραχμὰς] [τετρ]ạκọσịạς πλήρη[ς]." Translation David Thomas, editor.

[173] Compare Pudsey (2013) 503–4 for pledging of children, with references in n. 20.

In line with this interpretation, it may be pointed out that the master artisan had most to lose in case of an early termination of the contract, not the parents or carers: the students' labour input becomes more valuable after some time of training. The implication may be that artisans were not always keen on accepting apprentices. However, I believe that apprenticeship was actually appealing for craftsmen too, because it added a relatively cheap pair of extra hands in the workshop. There is no other way to explain why Pasonis, for example, would agree to bear all the costs for Pasion in a relatively short-term contract.[174] The fact that many apprentices, Pasion included, receive wages from day one is a clue that their labour was valuable, even if their wage usually only increases with time spent in training.[175] As an extra precaution, there usually is a monetary penalty set to the parents or owners in case they should take the child away before the contract ends.

The cost of apprenticeship may therefore have been relatively low compared to the benefits, at least for families who had a little money to begin with. This underlines the effects of intergenerational continuity. The costs of forgone earnings are mitigated by an apprentice's wages, the option of a loan could be desirable in itself, and future earnings for a skilled labourer were certainly promising. The exception seems to lie in the luxury trades on the one hand, as exemplified by the costly education of an enslaved apprentice flute player, which fits in nicely with our understanding of the concept of conspicuous consumption. The expense of training a stenographer on the other hand may perhaps be seen as an investment in a highly skilled slave that may fetch a nice price on the market or prove his worth in the household itself. The non-economic, social benefits of apprenticeship should not be underestimated either.[176] But there were still restrictions in access to job training. One of them was the availability of positions and the social network to get in; the other was gender.

Pausiris

The relative abundance of documentary papyri results in the added advantage that we can sometimes trace the same person in several documents over time. Four first-century documents pertaining to apprenticeship mention the same man: Pausiris, son of Ammonios, who lived in

[174] Unless of course Pasion was already experienced to a degree, continuing the apprenticeship he started elsewhere with Pasonis. Hermaiskos the nailsmith's apprentice (*BGU* 4.1124), whose contract was terminated, would also have to engage in another apprenticeship to finish his training, so this is a possible scenario.

[175] *P. Oslo Inv.* 1470; *PSI* 10.1110 verso 1; *P. Oxy* 14 .1647; *P. Oxy*. 38.2875; *P. Oxy*. 31.2586; *PSI* 3.241.

[176] Liu (2017) 219; Freu (2016); Munck et al. (2007) 5.

the Cavalry Parade Quarter of Oxyrhynchus.[177] This set of documents offers an interesting insight in family economic strategy over (part of) the life cycle. One is an apprenticeship contract, the others concern apprenticeship registrations – apparently for tax purposes, since two texts are explicitly addressed to the *eklemptoreis gerdiôn*, tax farmers of the weavers' tax. Let us take a closer look at Pausiris and his family.

In *P. Mich.* 3.170 from AD 49, Pausiris asks for registration of his eldest(?) son, Ammonios, as the apprentice of Apollonios, master weaver. Because it concerns a registration, the particulars of the contract itself, other than the year it commenced, are unknown. It is specified, however, that both Pausiris and the master artisan are based in the same part of the city. Four years later, an apprenticeship contract (*P. Wisc.* 1.4) testifies to the fact that Pausiris sends another son, Dioskous, to the same master artisan, Apollonios. The boy is to learn from Apollonios "the whole weaver's trade, as he also knows it himself".[178] Apparently Dioskous stays with Apollonios for the year of his apprenticeship despite their physical proximity, because the master is compensated by Pausiris for the boy's maintenance.

So far there is little that is unusual about these arrangements. As it turns out, however, Pausiris is a master weaver himself.[179] *P. Mich.* 3.171 (AD 58) is a copy of a letter to Panechotes and Ischyrion, farmers of the weaver's tax. It is a request from a certain Helen to register her orphaned nephew, Amoitas, as apprentice to Pausiris. And in AD 62, Pausiris writes to register a third son, Pausiris junior, as apprentice in the weaver's trade. This time, however, Pausiris entrusts his son not to Apollonios, but to Epinikos son of Theon – the aforementioned Helen's husband (*P. Mich.* 3.172).

It is clear that Pausiris had his sons trained in the weavers' trade, presumably to succeed him in the family business when the time came. But if Pausiris was a master weaver, why did he not instruct his sons himself? Similarly, why did Epinikos not take on his wife's nephew as an apprentice, rather than entrust him to Pausiris?

Reputation and quality control have been suggested as reasons not to train one's own child.[180] There is no denying that the proposition makes good sense. The suggestion that some sort of minimum standard was upheld

[177] The family archive of 23 documents, referred to as the archive of Pausiris Jr, son of Pausiris, is the subject of Gagos et al. (1992). The documents are listed in their Appendix II at 201–4. There is a family tree at 181. At 181–82 they announce work on a forthcoming text edition.

[178] Lines 5–7: ὥστ̣[ε μ]ạθεῖṿ τὴν γερδιακὴν τ̣έχνην πᾶσ̣[αν αὐτὸ]ṿ ὡ[ς] καὶ αὐτὸς ἐπίσταται. Translation Sijpesteijn (1967) 13.

[179] This can also be gathered from *P. Mich.* 10.598 from AD 49, which is a receipt for four installments of Pausiris' payment of the weaver's tax.

[180] Laes (2011a) 191; see also Schulz-Falkenthal (1972) 210.

would be corroborated if the apprenticeship contracts offered evidence for something like a final exam to assess the acquired skills – as scholars have tentatively suggested that they do.[181] However, a closer look at the four texts adduced by Bergamasco in this context illustrates that the passages are at the very least ambiguous and in need of careful reconsideration.

In *P. Fouad.* 1.37 (AD 48) the master writes in lines 7–8 that he will present (ἐπιδείξομαι) the apprentice weaver to his father "before [*vel sim*] three colleagues" (ἐπὶ ὁμοτέχνων τριῶν). It may be that a similar wording occurs in *SB* 22.15538 (13 BC), where a slave boy is to be taught how to play the flute. The heavily damaged text is reconstructed as [...] ἐξετασθήσεται ὑφ' ὁμοτέχ]ṿων τριῶν (line 10), in which case the boy would "be examined by three colleagues", but the reference to an exam remains conjectural.[182] The *epideixis* – demonstration – of *P. Fouad.* 1.37 could of course refer to an exam. But both phrases may just as well have been included to prevent favouritism from the master. If what is meant in these two texts, therefore, is not an exam, but the simple clause that the apprentice is to be treated equally to the other apprentices, then there is an unambiguous example which illustrates that this is a good possibility: this principle is also known from *P. Oxy.* 4.725.[183] The other two texts that may indicate the existence of a master exam are difficult to interpret for other reasons. The apprenticeship contract for a slave girl in *P. Mich.* 5.346a (AD 13) states the consequences for the master "if she is judged unfledged" (ἐὰν ... κρίνηται μὴ εἰδυειαι, lines 9–10).[184] Bergamasco concedes that *krinetai* here does not necessarily refer to an official judgement, but may merely mean that the owner is dissatisfied with the slave's progress.[185] The last possible reference to a master exam is *P. Aberd.* 59, which is not only a late example (late fifth or early sixth century AD) but also extremely fragmentary. I am hesitant to use this text to substantiate any argument.[186]

The attestations are few, and at least two of them refer to slave apprentices. While it is therefore difficult to exclude the possibility of a master exam altogether, I do not believe that it was very common, or that

181 Bergamasco (1995) 133–34; Laes (2015b) 476; Laes (2011a) 191. Laes also adds *P. Oxy.* 2.275, but in it I see no references to the apprentice undergoing a test; Freu (2011) 34–35.

182 *BGU* 4.1125, lines 1–15.

183 AD 183; this similarity was pointed out by Scherer, the editor of *P. Fouad.* 1.37. In *P. Oxy.* 4.725 the possibility of an exam is unlikely because of the context. It should be noted, however, that unlike myself and (in his view) contrary to *P. Oxy.* 4.725, Scherer believes that *P. Fouad* 1.37 does refer to an exam of sorts.

184 Interestingly, the penalty is to pay what he has received, but an instruction fee is not specified.

185 Bergamasco (1995) 134.

186 For the date, see *BL* 5, p. 1.

the quality control it exemplifies could be the reason to apprentice out a son to another weaver.[187]

Perhaps part of the answer to why Pausiris did not tutor his own sons should rather be sought in fluctuations in labour supply and demand.[188] In the household of Epinikos and Helen, for example, Helen's nephew probably was an unexpected addition to their family when Amoitas' father suddenly passed away. It is therefore not unlikely that Epinikos already had apprentices and labourers under contract at that time, which is why for them it was more profitable to apprentice out their nephew Amoitas.[189] Although we do not have such contextual evidence in the documents concerning Pausiris, if he, too, had a sufficient number of labourers at work in his workshop, then that might have been a reason to send his sons elsewhere to learn the trade. We can at least infer that when Pausiris took in Helen's nephew, Pausiris junior was still too young to add anything to the weaving business: He must have been under ten years of age in AD 58, because he was still referred to as a minor (in Roman Egypt that means under 14 years of age) in his own registration as an apprentice in AD 62.[190]

Alternatively, having a son apprenticed out to another weaver might refer to different types of weaving, which points to specialization and diversification of the weaver's trade, partly to preclude competition.[191] This suggestion cannot be substantiated, however. To my knowledge only one apprenticeship contract casually refers to a specific type of weaving: *P. Fouad* I.37 speaks of 'horizontal' weaving.[192] Moreover, the history of another family of weavers suggests that it is legitimate to speak of a family business, regardless of whether a son was educated in the craft at home or not.

Whereas these explanations may all be true to some extent, I believe that the most convincing explanation is in socio-economic networks. Recently there has been considerable attention paid to guilds as professional

187 Cf. Freu (2011) 31 for a different refutation with similar conclusions.

188 Hawkins (2021) 233–38; cf. Saller (2013) 75–76: "Apprenticeship was a mechanism that allowed labor to be moved from the natal family to a household where it was needed and could be supported with food".

189 This may be the reason why orphan apprentices are relatively prominent, a pattern that is more often attested historically (Lemercier (2012) for nineteenth-century France); cf. Freu (2011) 30. However, Laes (2015b) 476 points out that the percentage of apprentices without a father is in line with the expected percentage of boys without a father at that age.

190 *P. Mich.* 3.172, l.8.

191 Sijpesteijn (1967) 14 in his commentary on *P. Wisc.* 1.4; Biscottini on Tryphon-archive (1966) 65 ff.

192 Sitting down as opposed to standing up.

networks, and the social and familial ties of guild members, all of which are relevant here.[193] It is obvious that the exchange of apprentices between Pausiris and Apollonios on the one hand, and Pausiris and Epinikos on the other, indicates the existence of social and economic bonds between the weavers of Oxyrhynchus.[194] This does not preclude the interpretation that these documents offer glimpses of the professional network provided by guilds, through which the weavers found each other and which helped to minimize production costs and transaction costs. In the case of Pausiris and Apollonios, we may presume that weavers in the same part of town knew each other well; as we have seen, both were from the Cavalry Parade Quarter.[195] It should, however, be emphasized that there is no explicit reference to *collegia*.

Tryphon

The weaver Tryphon was born in AD 8 or 9; like Pausiris and his family, this family lived in the first century AD. It is a stroke of luck that much of the family archive has survived.[196] It tells us that Tryphon's grandfather, Dionysios, was a weaver, and so were his father, also named Dionysios, his uncle, and one of his two brothers (who were both younger than him). Therefore it comes as no surprise when we learn that Tryphon's eldest son started paying the weaver's tax from age ten.[197] For Tryphon himself, and for his eldest son, however, there is no apprenticeship contract. Therefore it is possible that in this family we have two instances of the eldest son learning the trade at home, from his father.

For the other weavers in the family, an apprenticeship contract was recorded. By the time Tryphon's younger brother Onnophris was of an age to start his apprenticeship, in AD 36, Tryphon's father may have passed away: the contract, *P. Oxy.* 2.322, was drawn up by their mother, with Tryphon acting as a guardian. Tryphon was now of an age to take on apprentices of his own (27–28 years old), yet it was decided that Onnophris should be apprenticed out to another weaver.[198] In AD 66 Tryphon's second son, Thoonis, was apprenticed out (*P. Oxy.* 2.275). This decision may have had to do with Tryphon's advancing age, or the fact that he lost

193 Liu (2017); Freu (2016); Venticinque (2016); Venticinque (2010). See also Chapter 5 below.

194 Liu (2017) 217–21; Venticinque (2010) 291.

195 Hawkins (2021) 109–10; Liu (2017) 217–24, Figure 10.1 at 218.

196 Piccolo (2003); Pestman and Clarysse (1989) 74–80; Vandoni (1974); Biscottini (1966); Brewster (1927).

197 *P. Oxy.* 2.310, AD 56; cf. Brewster (1927) 147, Chart B.

198 It is not specified at what age artisans could take apprentices, which in any case had to do with skill, not age, but the master carpenter in *P. Mich. Inv.* 4238 is 25 years old, and the master weaver of *P. Tebt.* 2.385 is about the same age as Tryphon was here.

part of his eyesight some years before.[199] Other considerations unknown to us may have played a part as well: the network theories outlined above with the more elaborate example of Pausiris are evocative. It appears that some learnt their trade within the family, and others were apprenticed out – but all save one remained in the family business.[200] Perhaps the simplest solution is also the most elegant: whenever a son was his father's apprentice, there was no apprenticeship contract. But absence of evidence is not evidence of absence.

The archives of Pausiris and Tryphon give evidence for two or more generations of weavers each; and although there usually is very little evidence for what happens between generations, here at least we can point to intergenerational persistence ensuring the next generation's entry into the weaving trade.

Freeborn female apprentices

Slave apprentices concern both boys and girls, in roughly equal numbers.[201] Most of the freeborn apprentices, however, were boys. But not all. Bradley's often-cited conclusion that there were no freeborn female apprentices should therefore be qualified, as Van Minnen attempted to do in 1998.[202] At the time, Van Minnen's publication failed to convince many scholars, but the publication of a new papyrus from Oxyrhynchus has added another persuasive example of a freeborn female apprentice.

In *P. Heid.* 4.326 (AD 98), included by Van Minnen, the girl Syairûs is apprenticed out by her parents Ischyras and Didyme to another married couple, Isidorus and Apollonarion.[203] The document is extraordinary in many ways. The text does not state explicitly that we are dealing with an apprenticeship contract, nor does it say anything about wages, or about what exactly the girl is to be taught. The information we need comes from another contract, dating to a year later: AD 99. In this contract, *P. Heid.* 4.327, the son of Ischyras' deceased (?) brother Nikanor is apprenticed out by Ischyras (this time without mention of Didyme) to Apollonarion (the wife)

[199] Brewster (1927) 140 suggests that it is because of his incapacitation. However, Biscottini (1966) 64–65 points out that Tryphon can nevertheless be seen actively involved in the weaver's trade, as his purchase of a new loom dates still later than the accident. Freu (2011) 36–37 suggests that Tryphon might therefore have been more of a large-scale businessman than a weaver himself at this point.

[200] According to Brewster (1927) 138, Tryphon's other brother (Thoonis) left the district "without trade and without means" in AD 44 – with reference to *P. Oxy.* 2.251.

[201] Laes (2015b) counts 12 slave contracts of whom six were girls; Appendix 2 below has 11 (five girls).

[202] Voiced by Bradley (1991) 108–9. Van Minnen (1998).

[203] This text and its connection to *P. Heid.* 4.327 is also explained in Van Minnen (1998).

to learn the *somfiake techne*, an unknown art which appears to be the work of an undertaker. In lines 35 to 39 they refer to their previous arrangement.

P. Heid. 4.327, 33–40

ἐ̣πὶ δὲ τούτοις καὶ τὴν Ἀπο\λ/
λ̣[ωνά]ριον μη[δ]ὲν παραβῆν[α]ι
ἢ ἔ[νοχ]ο̣ς̣ ἔ̣σται τῷ̣ [ἴ]σῳ̣ ἐπιτίμῳ̣, με-
νο̣[ύ]σ̣η̣ς κυ̣ρί[ας ἧ]ς ἔχει ἡ Ἀπολλω-
νά[ρ]ιο̣ν τοῦ [Ἰσχυ]ρᾶδος ἑτέρας
συ[γχω]ρή[σεως] διδεσκ̣α̣λείας
[τῆς θυγ]α̣τ̣ρὸς α̣[ὐτ]οῦ Συαιρ[ο]ῦ̣δος.

Unter these terms, Apollonarion will be bound not to trespass or she will be subject to the same penalty, while the other teaching agreement remains applicable, [the one] Apollonarion holds from Ischyras, concerning his [i.e. Ischyras'] daughter Syairûs.

The connection between 326 and 327 seems to be a safe one: Syairûs is a name that we hear of more often, but it is only spelled like this twice – in our documents. Therefore we may presume that *P. Heid.* 4.326 was indeed a *synchoresis didaskaleias*, the term used in *P. Heid.* 4.327 (line 38) to refer to the earlier text: an apprenticeship contract for a freeborn girl.

Another girl is now also securely attested in *P.Oxy.* 67.4596 (AD 264):[204] Aurelia Aphrodite is the daughter of Aurelios Polydeukes (line 7) and apprenticed out to learn the weaving trade. Their name (Aurelius, -a) is a clear indication of citizen status, so there is no doubt that Aphrodite was born free.[205]

In addition to female apprentices, there are a few female master artisans. That fact also suggests some form of job training for women.[206] The woman Apollonarion was already referred to in my description of two apprenticeship contracts (*P. Heid.* 4.326–27). A master weaver, Aurelia Libouke, features in

204 *P. Oxy.* 67.4596 was already briefly referred to above in the context of loans and apprenticeship.

205 I hesitate to include the fragmentary example of *P. Ross. Georg.* II. 18.450 (AD 140), which merely hints at an apprenticeship contract for a girl; it has the occurrence of some form of the verb *manthanein* in connection with the accusative *auten*. Nor am I inclined to bring in the late example of *P. Aberd.* 59 (late fifth–early sixth centuries), which is also very fragmentary. Van Minnen names two others besides *P. Mich.* 4.326: at 202–3 he suggests a conjecture through which *P. Mich. Inv.* 5191a = *SB* 8.13305 would also include a freeborn girl, but the suggestion has not been widely accepted; he also refers to an eighth-century Coptic text far outside the scope of my research (*KSB* 1.045).

206 Van Minnen (1998) 201 pointed me to the existence of female artisans in the contracts as evidence of job training for women, though again he did not have all the texts we have now and has to resort to a late example.

the apprenticeship contract *P. Mich. Inv.* 5191a = *SB* 8.13305. Finally Aria, a master of unknown trade, writes a letter (*P. Mich. Inv.* 337) to her son about the financial problems she has supporting her (male) apprentice.[207]

The scarce attestation of freeborn females in the apprenticeship contracts is likely not coincidental. That does not mean that women necessarily were without an occupation, however. Van Minnen suggested that girls were more likely to learn a job at home to preserve their chastity: "That was safer".[208] Obviously it would not strengthen girls' chances at a job training if they were to be married in their early teens, at an age when apprentices started their education.[209] The age of most apprentices is unfortunately lost to us, but apprenticeships seem to commence shortly before age 14.[210] The marriage pattern of Roman Egypt was perhaps not all that different from that of Roman Italy: non-elite girls are attested to have been married from age 12 onwards, but with a similar peak in the (mid- and) late teens as their counterparts in Roman Italy. The theoretical possibility of an apprenticeship therefore may have been open to some, but it was clearly not always taken up.

Human-capital theory also suggests that investment in human capital for girls was less extensive than in boys, based on the expectation that women's future earnings were lower than could be expected in the case of men. That is not just because of the expectation that a girl would be married soon, and that she could therefore spend less time in the labour market. There was a strong gender bias on the labour market as well. Women had fewer job opportunities and because of that they probably earned less, as was the case in many historical periods. Though Roman women are sporadically attested in virtually all types of jobs, there seems to have been a limit to female labour participation, and the apprenticeship contracts suggest that this may have curbed investment in their human capital through formal apprenticeships.[211]

Family matters: economic strategies

All business was family business, if not always in the literal sense. There were, of course, family businesses in a literal sense: they were mostly entrepreneurial families working together in a workshop. Other, wage-earning,

207 On *P. Mich. Inv.* 337 = *SB* 11588, see Bergamasco (2006b).

208 Van Minnen (1998) 203 and *passim*.

209 For the Egyptian marriage pattern, Hübner (2013) 48–50; Bagnall and Frier (2006) 111–16.

210 Bradley (1991) 107–8; Van Minnen (1998) 201.

211 See Introduction s.v. human capital and Chapter 20 s.v. gender. Cf. Saller (2007) 106: "the effect of the ideology may have been to limit the training or human capital of freeborn women".

families hired out their labour in a necessarily more diversified approach to the labour market.

The urban population of Rome was dense, hence unskilled labour was probably in ample supply in the Roman cities and wages were accordingly low; and though skilled labour was more exclusive and the work paid good money, securing a job as a skilled wage labourer may have proven difficult. In most non-elite households, therefore, it is likely that all family members – men, women, and children – were required to contribute their labour power merely to maintain, or to rise above, subsistence level.[212] Skilled work was the most important differentiating factor that had the potential to lift the family up from the poorer masses. Even for skilled artisans and craftsmen, however, fluctuating demand in the urban economy necessitated the availability of a flexible workforce.[213] The most flexible workforce, and the cheapest place to find additional labourers when business was good, was one's family. Conversely, when demand was low, family members were also the labourers whose time was most easily redirected towards the more rudimentary tasks in and around the house.[214] Labour allocation among family members, and between domestic work and the labour market, therefore, is the most basic form of family adaptive strategy.

Male labour: occupational pluralism and seasonal labour

It is interesting to note that the ideology surrounding male labourers has received little scholarly attention, certainly when compared to studies into contemporary views about Roman women. That presumably has to do with the fact that literary sources were written from a male perspective in a patriarchal society, by elite men who concerned themselves with putting women in their place.[215] The elite views about artisans and craftsmen outlined in the Introduction to this book, for example, are implicitly about male labourers. There is very little material in terms of an ancient discourse about labour allocation between husband and wife. In a passage of Xenophon's *Oeconomicus* a farmer called Ischomachos recaps at length a conversation with his wife on how the gods as well as the law viewed

[212] See Chapter 2 above on living standards and skilled labour; Groen-Vallinga and Tacoma (2017) Section 4; Scheidel (2010b) 454: "Since wages for adult male workers were often so modest, labor force participation by both adult women and minors must have been high in order to fend off starvation".

[213] Hawkins (2021) 192–95.

[214] Cf. Hawkins (2017); Hawkins (forthcoming) who names this as an advantage of slaves in the permanent workforce. In my view, this holds equally well for non-slave family members. Knotter (1994) 68 on the sudden growth of the cloth production in the Dutch Republic of the nineteenth century: "Gezinsarbeid is een voor de hand liggende oplossing voor gebrek aan arbeidskrachten".

[215] See Chapter 2 above.

the tasks of husband and wife. He concludes, "for to the woman it is more admirable to stay in the house than to be in the open air, but to the man it is more shameful to stay in the house than to attend to the work outside".[216] In other words, male labour was allocated to the non-domestic sphere 100 per cent, be it on the farm – as in the case of Ischomachos – in the workshop, or in the form of wage labour; the women, conversely, were allocated to the domestic sphere.

This extreme labour division between husband and wife is still common, even if it is no longer the only option available. The ideal has prevailed for a long time and has blended into reality, even if adhering to a labour division was regularly impossible, because of the vital contribution of women's income to the family finances. I suspect that the prevalence of this labour pattern until the later twentieth century is one of the reasons why scholars never felt the need to explicate it for ancient Rome. Economic theory even predicts that it is often economically rational, on the assumption that women have a comparative advantage in the home.[217] It may be safely concluded that Roman men were expected to be the breadwinners of the family, as head of a workshop, as merchant, wholesaler, or wage labourer. Male wage labourers were expected to find an income through a job, or, when there was none, through other means. The unfortunate *faber* from Apuleius' *Metamorphoses* discussed earlier, for example, found himself without work and without pay unexpectedly one day, and decided to sell a *dolium* so that he could afford a meal in the evening.[218] Apuleius' carpenter seems to have had a relatively steady job with his boss for the time being. As a result of the male–female labour division, adaptive strategies for men were not concerned with the division of their time between home and work, but they were aimed particularly at battling unemployment and economic insecurity.

An interesting historical example of adaptive strategy is my grandfather. Born in 1920, my grandfather Wim was a house painter, before he was drafted to serve in the Royal Netherlands Navy during the Second World War. After the war, he found work in a butcher's shop, and then as an overseer in the mines of Limburg. Two things are relevant about this historical case. The first is that as one of twelve children to a farmer, Wim only received a relatively basic education. Work as a house painter and butcher are both jobs that we might consider (semi-)skilled, but he

216 Xen. *Oec.* 7.30–31: "τῇ μὲν γὰρ γυναικὶ κάλλιον ἔνδον μένειν ἢ θυραυλεῖν, τῷ δὲ ἀνδρὶ αἴσχιον ἔνδον μένειν ἢ τῶν ἔξω ἐπιμελεῖσθαι."

217 See introductory chapter above s.v. male and female labour for this ideal of separate domains, with reference to Hemelrijk (2015) 9–12; in economic theory with reference to Cigno (1991) Part I, e.g., 24, 41–42; cf. De Vries (2008) 186–237 on the 'breadwinner–homemaker household'.

218 Apul. *Met.* 9.5–6, cf. Chapter 2 above.

was self-taught (the navy and the mining corporation provided additional training). Although this is just one modern case, it puts into perspective the ways in which much of the human capital may have been accumulated in the Roman world. Strategic adaptations like these must have been a general occurrence in the Roman world as well, but they are virtually impossible to trace. Perhaps the fact that there are relatively few occupational inscriptions also has to do with the fact that there were few Romans who identified with only one particular job. Specializing too far makes for less flexibility. Of course the circumstances were highly specific after the Second World War, the ruins of which increased labour demand and decreased labour supply. My grandfather's career switches were responses to that demand. But the Roman world was not devoid of stochastic shocks either.

A certain flexibility was necessary to find employment. The seasonal and cyclical changes in demand for labour in the Roman world were considered in the previous chapter. The agricultural calendar, the building trades, and the shipping trades all contributed to seasonal labour migration flows between town and country, and it was pointed out that recurring circumstantial factors such as the political calendar at Rome, religious festivals, and even the weather also influenced a cyclical demand for luxury and other goods in the urban market.[219] Seasonal fluctuations in labour-intensive trades are most likely to have impacted larger numbers of unskilled labourers. As a result, many unskilled male wage labourers performed more than one different job during the year: an adaptive strategy termed occupational pluralism. Similarly, in the nineteenth century the shipyard workers of Nova Scotia were often part-time farmers or lumberjacks.[220] If a worker was unemployed for part of the year, however, the alternative historical example of early twentieth-century Dutch dockworkers shows wives (or children) going out to find temporary work instead.[221] This is a useful reminder that the contribution of the other family members should also be considered. It should be kept in mind that in a high-mortality regime like Rome, there may not have been an adult male in the home to be the breadwinner, and even if there was, he may not have earned enough money to sustain the family.

Female labour

A persistent traditional view of the woman in the household envisages her movements as limited to domestic work and raising children. That was the Roman ideal as well, and the larger the home, the greater the unpaid

219 Chapter 2 above. See especially Erdkamp (2016); Erdkamp (2008) for seasonal labour migration; Hawkins (2021) for unstable demand.

220 McCann (1999).

221 Knotter (2004) 222.

task of managing it.[222] In practice, however, women must have contributed much more than unremunerated domestic work.[223] Women stepped in when the family income was insufficient, or when labour demands were high. In the family life cycle, women's monetary contribution from labour was greatest in the year(s) before the birth of any children. Presumably their input went up again from the moment older children started looking out for their younger siblings. Perhaps, then, Roman women should no longer be defined by this life cycle dip in their working life, but by their otherwise active labour participation.

The ancient evidence itself seems to be struggling with this inherent duality in women's socio-economic position as well. There were no serious legal restrictions on doing business with female shop owners, saleswomen, or artisans, nor were there any legal obstructions to hiring women. Verboven adduces intriguing evidence from the Pompeian graffiti for a number of small-scale loans, for example, that were executed by women.[224] Having said that, a perception of female weakness did uphold the system of *tutela*, or legal guardianship.[225] In practice, it is questionable whether the male guardian had anything to do with business transactions, unless they were related to a woman's patrimony, which is true only for a restricted number of goods, such as land, houses, and slaves.[226] A woman was equal to a man in the labour market, at least according to the law.

In practice, when Roman women entered the labour market, their options were nevertheless restricted by the prevailing gender biases.[227] Looking at the occupational inscriptions, the range of jobs open to women was far less wide than that for men: my catalogue of job titles contains 556 entries for jobs for men, and 78 for women, of which 54 are attested for men and women alike. There are a mere 24 solely for women.[228] Again, it should be stressed that these precise numbers are deceptive. On occasion, the female version of a job is attested, for example, but not (yet?) in Italy, and it is therefore not included here.[229] The figures do illustrate a clear pattern, though the biases in the material should caution us not to take them at

[222] Berg (2016).

[223] Cf. Scheidel (1995) for an extensive argument about women's contribution in agricultural (wage) labour.

[224] Verboven (2017a) 375; Hemelrijk (2020) 178–82 for other examples of financial transactions.

[225] Dixon (1984).

[226] Gardner (1995) 378.

[227] See Chapter 2 above on engendered dual labour markets.

[228] See Appendix 1 below. Cf. Treggiari (1979a) 66; Varga (2020) Graph 1 for a similar patter in the western provinces; similarly Harris (2002) for classical Athens.

[229] Hemelrijk (2020) 175 records a *plumbaria* (no. 119) and at 176–77 several *vilicae* (nos 121–23), for example.

face value. Historically, women's work was (and is) sometimes recorded in broader terms than men's. A lack of differentiation in the (census) records therefore need not mean that women's jobs were less differentiated than men's to the same extent in reality; although for all the reasons mentioned above, a more restricted range of occupational possibilities might be assumed. Epitaphs for Roman women in general were less numerous than those for men.[230] Women were perhaps also even less likely to have a stable job – with a specific job title to record – than were men. Moreover, it was common to give prevalence to family relations in the image constructed on the epitaph for a woman, to the exclusion of occupational titles. When occupation is mentioned alongside family relations, however, it is generally placed *before* familial bonds, as in *CIL* 6.9616:

> ***CIL* 6.9616**
>
> D(is) M(anibus) / Terentiae / Niceni Terentiae / Primaes(!) medicas li/bertae fecerunt / Mussius Antiochus / et Mussia Dionysia / fil(ii) m(atri) b(ene) m(erenti)
>
> To the divine spirits. To Terentia of Nicaea, doctor and freedwoman of Terentia Prima. Mussius Antiochus and Mussia Dionysia her children set up (this monument) to their well-deserving mother.

As this epitaph demonstrates, Roman women and their next of kin were not always devoid of a sense of female occupational pride.[231]

In line with Roman views of femininity, most of the professions recorded for women in occupational inscriptions are 'feminine' jobs, in the service sector or otherwise in the domestic sphere. The one occupation that is most frequently attested is ***nutrix***, wet nurse; second is ***ornatrix***, or hairdresser; not surprisingly a broad spectrum of wool work, spinning and weaving in particular, is also well-attested.[232] In other pre-industrial

230 Hopkins (1966); Hopkins (1987).

231 Cf. Dixon (2001a) 9 for two examples where the women of the family seem to be identified primarily by their familial role and the men by occupation.

232 E.g. Günther (1987) 40–137 discusses occupations by sector (only for freedwomen). The job of *ornatrix* took (at least) two months of training, which can be inferred from *Dig.* 32.65.3 (Celsus apud Marcianum), but cf. Forbes (1955) n. 50: "Other jurists disagreed with this". Barber's 1994 monograph on wool working has the telling title *Women's Work: The First 20 000 Years: Women, Cloth and Society in Early Times.* Larsson Lovén (1998) correctly demonstrated that wool work in Rome could be a byword for the virtuous matron, though there is very little epigraphic evidence for the use of *lanifica* or *lanam fecit* solely in praise of domestic virtue (in *CIL* 6 I can think only of *CIL* 6.10230, 11602, 15346, and 37053). In most instances the text strongly suggests that wool work was a money-earning activity, like *CIL* 6.6339, which simply reads *Acte quasillaria*: "Acte, spinner". Cf. Dixon (2001b) 117.

periods, the domestic and service sector, particularly working flexible hours as a cleaning lady, laundry lady, or seamstress, is where women turned for unskilled casual work. In Rome, however, many of the occupational inscriptions in this line of work attest to female slaves and ex-slaves. If the predominance of servile women is a reflection of reality, the chances of a freeborn woman finding work in the service sector were severely limited. But since we know that occupational inscriptions over-represent the servile population by a wide margin, the dominance in this sector need not have been as pronounced as the epigraphic record suggests. Moreover, there is every reason to believe that women were not exclusively engaged in the service sector. Charting the possible family strategies and checking them against the evidence makes it possible to paint a much broader spectrum of women's work in Roman society.

Women involved in family business

Cooperation of husband and wife in a business is an obvious efficiency drive.[233] Actual attestations of informal cooperation between spouses, however, are difficult to identify in the Roman world. Women working with their husbands are easily obscured. There are historical examples of the fact that when husband and wife shared the same occupation, it was only recorded for the man, for instance.[234] Within the sample of occupational inscriptions, if husband and wife are both named, and the husband is recorded with a job, his wife generally is not.[235] In the rare inscriptions that record an occupation for both partners in a marriage or *contubernium*, husband and wife usually do not share the same job and one or both are engaged with gendered work (see below). On a number of funerary monuments, a trade is only represented through an image of tools of the trade.[236] The deceased are then referred to by means of a portrait bust and/or the accompanying inscription. Although it is tempting to interpret the tools as the husband's in these cases, the possibility that a family business is indicated should at least be left open.[237]

[233] Well-attested also in pre-industrial Europe: Holderness (1984) 425. Cf. Van den Heuvel (2008) 218 on commerce in the Dutch Republic: "Scholars generally assume that in commerce wives helped their husbands in the shop, doing the necessary business administration or filling in during their absence"; Van den Heuvel goes on to nuance that view by illuminating various forms of spousal cooperation in retail.

[234] This problem pervades sources for early modern England; see Erickson (2008) 282–83 on the lists of women taking apprentices from Christ's Hospital in eighteenth-century London: "The wife's occupation was not recorded in addition to her husband's if the two were identical".

[235] Broekaert (2012) 18.

[236] See introduction above.

[237] Zimmer consistently interprets the tools of the trade as referring to a man's profession. Zimmer (1982) 13.

Two reliefs in particular have been adduced to illustrate the probability of an 'unequal' division of labour between men and women within the household business. One funerary relief shows a butcher at work, while his wife sits on a chair holding what looks like a stylus and wax tablet, perhaps doing the administration.[238] It has been suggested that the attributes refer to the wife's education, proudly advertising that she did not have to work.[239] The consensus now seems to be that in this relief we are indeed seeing a family business. The second example of this is even more convincing. It is a funerary relief from the Isola Sacra necropolis showing a husband and wife in a smithy: he is hammering away at the anvil to the right, and the woman on the left appears to be engaged in selling the products.[240] Holleran has argued that, since retail requires little skill or training and is compatible with child care, "For unskilled women who married skilled artisans, retailing the products produced by their husbands may have been the easiest way for them to contribute to the household income".[241] Two or three reliefs from Ostia support the idea of Roman women in retail, and the epigraphic evidence also attests to the non-negligible presence of saleswomen.[242] This type of labour division between men and women may well be true for many historical cases, and there is no doubt in my mind that it was a common feature of Roman society. But it does not account for all the evidence, so we must look at the possibility of other strategies as well.

There is evidence to suggest that some women developed skills in arts or crafts equal to those of their husbands. A few women gained their expertise through formal apprenticeships, as we have seen, but a wife could presumably also acquire skills as an informal apprentice first to her parents, then to her husband, learning by doing.[243] Through ongoing practical engagement with the trade, a woman eventually created her own occupational identity.

238 A cast of the relief is on display in the Ashmolean Museum, Oxford; Zimmer (1982) cat. no. 2, at 94–95; Berg (2016) 187 adduces this as an example of women as household managers; similarly Broekaert (2012) 47; and Kampen (1981) cat. no. 53, at 157.

239 Zimmer (1982) 63; cf. Dixon (2001b) 9.

240 Isola sacra, tomb 29; Zimmer (1982) cat. no. 123, at 185–86; D'Ambra (1988) discusses the funerary monument and the artistic program on the reliefs and sarcophagus.

241 Holleran (2013) 321.

242 Kampen (1981) cat. no. 2–4, at 138–39. I deliberately write "two or three" because the vegetable seller (no. 4) is not always identified as female; Herfst (1922) 36 suggests that women in classical Athens also must have played a large part in commerce.

243 Hawkins (2021) 252–55 with doubts about its frequency; cf. practices in eighteenth-century London: Erickson (2008) 288.

A few inscriptions stress the professional equality of both partners by the explicit use of both the male and the female form of their profession.[244] This is the case for Venusta, who married a freeborn nailsmith:

> *CIL* 5.7023
>
> V(iva) f(ecit) / Cornelia L(uci) l(iberta) / Venusta / clavaria sibi et / P(ublio) Aebutio M(arci) f(ilio) Stel(latina) / clavario Aug(ustali) vir(o) / et Crescenti libertae et / Muroni delicatae
>
> While she was still alive Cornelia Venusta, freedwoman of Lucius, nailsmith, set up [this monument] for herself and for Publius Aebutius of the Stellatine tribe, nailsmith, Augustalis, and for Crescens her freedwoman and Muron her *delicata*.

As a freedwoman, Venusta may, of course, have picked up the tricks of the trade earlier in her life during slavery in the service of a certain Lucius Cornelius, in which case her trade might have made her an attractive match for P. Aebutius. It is also possible, however, that she became a nailsmith under her husband's guidance.[245] The *conditarii* in *CIL* 6.9277 provide another telling example:[246]

> *CIL* 6.9277
>
> [Aul(ia)] Mercurian{e}<a> fecit paren/[tibu]s su{bu}<i>s Aul(io) Maximus(!) / [con]ditarius de castris pra/[etor]i{bu} <i>s Aul(iae) Hilaritas(!) condita/ria(e) e{o}<i>s in pace //]unt / [
>
> Aulia Mercuriane set this up for her parents Aulius Maximus, dealer in preserved foods at the *castra praetoria*, and Aulia Hilaritas dealer in preserved foods. May they rest in peace.

Maximus and Hilaritas were freedmen, but the inscription suggests to me that they had subsequently set up their own independent family. Hilaritas, too, probably learnt her profession as a slave. Most examples of men and

[244] Contrary to inscriptions such as *CIL* 6.37781, where a man and freedman, but not the female dedicator, are explicitly indicated as *aurifices*, even though she is likely to have had the skills; with Hawkins (2021) 252–53.

[245] Contra Broekaert's (2012) 47 unfounded assumption: "as the profession of a smith seems to be better suited for male laborers, it seems plausible that Venusta was only organizing sales in a shop, while Abutius was responsible for the production of merchandize [*sic*]".

[246] Other couples in the same trade: *CIL* 6.9211 (*brattiarii*); 6963 (*brattiarii*); 9934 (*turarii*); 370820 (*purpurarii*); 370826 (*vestiarii tenuarii*, quoted below); with Holleran (2013) 315–16; Groen-Vallinga (2013) 306.

women working in the same business concern freedmen, but we shall see shortly that the same holds true for couples with distinct job titles: most of the occupational inscriptions represent ex-slaves, and the evidence for conjugal couples conforms to this pattern.[247]

Work within the family business was the most acceptable alternative to domestic work in line with gender ideals of domesticity and feminine jobs. Whereas it is probable that many women did help out in the family business – in line with the model of the family economy, in which the family is the unit of production – the examples just presented demonstrate that caution is necessary towards the often implicit assumption that they did so "on unequal terms".[248] Moreover, such an assumption fails to explain attestations of independent women; that is, women with a job different from that of their husband, or women without a husband, but with a profession.

Independent women

Women who are attested with a job different from that of their husband must have been engaged in the Roman equivalent of a double-business household, or have worked as independent wage labourers hiring out their labour. Such scenarios go beyond the family economy, or even the family wage economy, and represent a wider range of adaptive family strategies.

The occupational inscriptions show a noticeable pattern for non-slave couples belonging to this category. Many couples with distinct job titles appear to have been independent freedmen. It is significant that both husband and wife can generally be traced back to an elite household *columbarium*: they were ex-slaves, who either were still part of the elite household after manumission or subsequently established a non-elite household of their own and are therefore integral to the current chapter.[249] The example of *CIL* 6.9824 shows a conjugal couple who probably were manumitted by members of the same family:

> ***CIL* 6.9824**
>
> Critonia Q(uinti) l(iberta) Philema / popa de insula / Q(uinti) Critoni |(mulieris) l(iberti) Dassi / scalptoris v(as)<cu=UC>lari(i) / sibi suisque poster(isque) / eor(um)
>
> Critonia Philema, freedwoman of Quintus, cookshop owner, [set up this monument] for Quintus Dassus, freedman of a woman, carver of vessels, for herself, and for their dependants and their descendants.

[247] Similarly, Broekaert (2012) 46.

[248] Saller (2007) 105–6.

[249] E.g. *CIL* 6.33794, 6342 cited in Chapter 4 below; cf. Broekaert (2012) 45–48.

Philema was set free by a Quintus Critonius, and Dassus was manumitted by a woman; that woman must have been related to Q. Critonius to give Dassus his *nomen*.[250] Even if there is some discussion as to what *popa* may mean, as well as about the correct reading of *vascularii*, it is clear that these two people did not share the same business.[251] It is very well possible that, in slavery, both Philema and Dassus had been employed in an elite family in very different activities. They may well have formed a family there, and retained their separate jobs after their manumission upon forming their own family unit. A similar insight explains an altar with three inscriptions collected as *CIL* 6.37469:[252]

CIL 6.37469

Nostia /(mulieris) l(iberta) / Daphne / ornatrix de / vico Longo //
M(arcus) Nerius M(arci) l(ibertus) / Quadratus / aurifex de / vico Longo //
Nostia / Daphnidis l(iberta) / Cleopatra / ornatrix de vico / Longo

Nostia Daphne, freedwoman of a woman, hairdresser from the Vicus Longus.
Marcus Nerius Quadratus, freedman of Marcus, goldsmith from the Vicus Longus.
Nostia Cleopatra, freedwoman of Daphne, hairdresser from the Vicus Longus.

Nostia Daphne and M. Nerius Quadratus, judging by their names, are freedmen who probably originate from two different households. The monument does not state explicitly that Daphne and Quadratus are husband and wife, but it is a distinct possibility. Slave unions crossing household boundaries are not unheard of; alternatively the marriage may have been formed only after manumission.[253] Husband and wife have very different jobs, but the shared monument suggests that the newly formed

250 Alternatively, one may have freed the other (either way around is possible, judging from their nomenclature). Manacorda (2005) suggests that Philema's patron may be the Cretonius from Juvenal's 14th Satire (vv. 86–95); Richardson (1992) 209 hazards a suggestion on the identity of Dassus as the owner of an *insula Q. Critoni*.

251 For *popa* = *popinaria*, cf. *CIL* 14.3709 (Tivoli); *vascularii* has been supplemented as *vir clarissimi* in *CIL* 6, which I would think unlikely because of his libertine status. The variant reading *ocularius* has also been proffered. *Scalptor* has not been doubted, however, so it is clear that Dassus was a carver of some kind.

252 *CIL* 6.37469 combines *ILS* 9426 with *CIL* 6.9736 and 3895; see Di Giacomo (2010) for the text edition with *CIL* 6.9736. Contra Solin (2000) 168, who argues that Daphnidis does not refer to Daphne. Treggiari (1979a) 75 already suggested the connection with *CIL* 6.9736.

253 See Chapter 4 below; cf. also *CIL* 6.9732; 9775.

family set up shop together in the Vicus Longus. Cleopatra is Daphne's freedwoman, of the same occupation.

Virtually all rare instances from outside the *columbaria* of a conjugal couple holding different occupations can be similarly explained by their maintaining a job learnt in their former household or households.[254] Having said that, it should also be noted that as a general rule one or both of the spouses held an exclusively female or exclusively male job, which may also have prompted the commemoration of both professions: there is no male equivalent to the *ornatrix* or *popinaria*, for example, and no female *aurifex* or *scalptor* is attested. In such instances this may help to explain why both professions were recorded. Even in the case of spouses holding gender-specific jobs, however, a joint enterprise is possible. *CIL* 6.37811 shows a couple of freedmen who ran what looks like a barbershop together:[255]

> *CIL* 6.37811
>
> Pollia C(ai)/ (mulieris) l(iberta) / Urbana ornat(rix) de / Aemilianis ollas II/ M(arcus) Calidius M(arci) l(ibertus) to(n)sor/ Apoloni(us) de Aemilianis
>
> Pollia Urbana, freedwoman of a woman, hairdresser from the Aemiliani, two urns. Marcus Calidius Apolonius, freedman of Marcus, barber from the Aemilian district.

Widows

Roman Italy, particularly its cities, suffered from high mortality rates. It was argued above that most women got married at a relatively early age, and that there was probably a significant age gap between spouses. These factors predict the existence of a relatively large group of young widows in Roman society.[256] Even without an age gap, women who survived might expect to be widowed at some point in their lives.

The loss of a husband did not just have an emotional impact, but also had economic consequences. In some instances this was solved by the dissolution of the nuclear family: Hübner illustrates that in Roman Egypt where the extended family predominated, the widow generally went back to her natal family, while the children remained in the house of their father's family.[257] Because it is likely that the nuclear family was the prevailing

[254] Same household: *CIL* 6.8958; 8711 (imperial); 8554 (imperial); other households: *CIL* 6.37811, perhaps also 9792.

[255] A "unisex establishment" was suggested by Treggiari (1979a) 75 n. 47.

[256] Pudsey (2011) 61; Hübner (2013) 94–95 for a similar pattern in Roman Egypt. Saller's micro-simulation is not helpful for percentages of surviving husbands, since he presupposes universal marriage and universal remarriage until the age of 50 for women and 60 for men in accordance with Augustan marriage legislation. Saller (1994) 46.

[257] Hübner (2013) 99, 103.

family form in an urban environment, however, the situation may have been different in cities. The widow had become the new household head, who had to deal with the life cycle squeeze that was the structural loss of the family's main income, and who now carried sole responsibility for possible children. The widow may therefore have needed to find additional income, and if she was not already employed in a money-earning occupation, this was the time to start looking for a job.[258]

Widowed female household heads were freed of male supervision and freed from the 'stigma' attached to the maiden, and had greater liberty in society and implicitly also in the economy. Widows' economic endeavours were probably based on their employment during marriage. Widows could, of course, continue their independent jobs or work as wage labourers; an artisan's widow may have taken over from her husband.[259] It should be stated that a widow would not inherit the household or the business in intestate succession: in the common variant of *sine manu* marriage the wife was not legally part of the family, and was thereby excluded from a share of the inheritance. What survives of Roman testamentary practice indicates, however, that spouses were generally accounted for in wills.[260] It is therefore not unlikely that widows would have access to a workshop or other property.

Whether a widow could step in or not, however, may have differed according to individual circumstances. Broekaert points to papyri concerning Berenice, a second-century Roman Egyptian wine merchant, who continues the business seamlessly after her husband's demise.[261] Similarly, an elderly beer seller from Philadephia perpetuated the trade until her daughter's elopement:

> But Demetrios the vine-dresser, having deceived my daughter, has carried her off and conceals her saying he will set up house with her without my consent. And she helped me to manage the shop and supported me in my old age. Now therefore since she has gone away I am making a loss and I do not have the necessities of life.[262]

[258] Cf. Tilly and Scott (1978) 51; Wall (2007); Pudsey (2012) 167 has five examples in Roman Egypt of a male adult lodger living in with a single woman (widows?).

[259] There were no guild restrictions to taking over. In early modern times, a widow was not always a full member of the guild, although she was often allowed to continue the workshop and take on apprentices of her own: Erickson (2008) 290; Prior (1985) 103, 105 for early modern England; the 'widow's right' in the Dutch Republic ensured that she could continue the business if there was a master journeyman to accompany her. Schmidt (2001) 146–54; Schmidt (2007) 273.

[260] Champlin (1991) 112–13, 120–26, esp. 124.

[261] Broekaert (2012) 47–48 with *P. Oxy.* 3.493, 6.985, 22.2342.

[262] *P. Lond.* 7.1976 (253 BC), lines 6–17. Translation Rowlandson (1998) via papyri.info.

And other fates were possible: Lucian's fictional character Crobyle explains to her daughter, now a courtesan, what happened when her father passed away:

> He worked metal and had a great name in Piraeus [...] When he died, first of all I sold his fire-tongs and his anvil and his hammer for two minae, and we managed to live off of that for seven months. Then I earned our daily bread with difficulty, sometimes by weaving, sometimes by spinning the two kinds of thread, for woof and warp. I was feeding you, daughter, waiting for you to fulfill my expectations [...][263]

It is difficult to find epigraphic attestations of working widows. Treggiari suggests that because a husband was also the prime commemorator, a young widow who had taken over her husband's shop or workshop was perhaps less likely to receive commemoration in an epitaph.[264] Occupational inscriptions include only a few women with job title who may have been widows. Claudia Trophime in *CIL* 6.9720 was a midwife who died aged 75, and is commemorated by her son and grandson. Her age, the fact that she has a son and grandson, and the absence of a husband among the dedicators make widowhood the most plausible hypothesis for Claudia Trophime. The example of *CIL* 6.9498 is a little less straightforward:

> *CIL* 6.9498
>
> D(is) M(anibus) / Iuliae Soteridi / lanipendae v(ixit) a(nnos) LXXX / fecerunt / M(arcus) Iulius Primus /Iulia Musa Iulia Thisbe / Iulia Ampliata Iulia Roman(a)
>
> To the divine spirits. For Iulia Soteris, wool weigher, who lived eighty years. Marcus Iulius Primus, Iulia Musa, Iulia Thisbe, Iulia Ampliata and Iulia Romana set this up.

The inscription is open to various interpretations. It specifies names, but not the relationship between the recorded individuals. The epitaph may have been set up by five children of Iulia Soteris. It is also possible that M. Iulius Primus was not a son, but her husband. If the four Iuliae were daughters of Soteris, their father must after all have been a Iulius, too. Iulia Soteris' advanced age makes it implausible, though not impossible, that the father of her children was still alive, however. Finally, the epitaph could also be interpreted as a monument set up by her freedman and -women. Based on

263 *DMeretr.* 6.1. Translation from Strong (2012).

264 Treggiari (1979a) 77.

these scenarios, it is highly likely that this wool weigher who died at the respectable age of 80 was a widow.

Two final examples are a *resinaria* (*CIL* 6.9855) and a shoemaker (*sutrix*, *CIL* 14.4698); both inscriptions are accompanied by a relief that depicts the profession. From the fragmentary image we gather that Iulia Agele, the *resinaria*, not only was a dealer in resin, but also seems to have performed beauty treatments with it.[265] The inscription was set up by her freedwoman. The inscription for Septimia Stratonice, *sutrix*, was set up by a friend "because of her benefactions towards him", "ob benefacta ab ea in se". In these last two cases, it appears that there was no family (left) to commemorate these women. They appear to be truly independent, and relatively well off at that. Treggiari is right to point out that "[w]omen who appear on epitaphs alone may of course be in trade in their own right. But they may also be carrying on the business of a dead husband."[266] However, carrying on the business of a dead husband is not very likely in the case of the midwife, the wool weigher, or even the *resinaria*,[267] and the shoemaker at least shows no evidence of it. These examples incidentally illustrate the various social networks that a widow could depend on: the bond with her children, her freedmen, or a 'friend'.[268]

"The chaste widow who refrains from remarriage after her first husband's death is a nearly universal paradigm of female virtue across societies".[269] We saw that Rome, too, subscribed to the ideal of the one-husband woman, the *univira*. It is equally universal across societies that the non-elite could not afford to keep up with this ideal and that of economic necessity many widows remarried sooner or later. Despite marriage ideals, the emperor Augustus implanted a law stating that all Roman women were to be married, and it stipulates explicitly how long a widow could, or should, mourn before remarriage.[270] We can therefore expect remarriage to have been a fairly common economic strategy, especially for younger widows.[271]

265 Zimmer (1982) 204–5.

266 Treggiari (1979a) 76.

267 The male equivalent for *obstetrix* and *resinaria* is, to my knowledge, not attested. There are several male *lanipendi* from elite *domus*: *CIL* 6.3976; 3977; 6300; 8870; 9495; 37755; Herfst (1922) 53 notes a similar preference for the assistance of midwives rather than male medics in classical Athens.

268 Cf. Müller (2010).

269 Hübner (2013) 92.

270 Even though this law is thought to have been most effective in the upper classes, it is saying something that the period of ten months is based on the period in which a child of the deceased husband could still be born – the suggestion is that if it were not for a possible pregnancy, a quicker remarriage was better.

271 Goody (1990) 202; in Roman Egypt the clear pattern is of young widows until age 30–35 remarrying: Bagnall and Frier (2006) 126–27, more extensively Hübner (2013) Chapter 6.

The benefits of marriage ties to the family economy have been outlined above. The widow of an artisan who had access to his workshop may have been a particularly well-desired match. In early modern England a widow's new spouse, if he had the proper training, was allowed entry into the profession and the guild; hence the stereotypical image of the widow marrying an apprentice.[272] Even if the guild restriction was not an issue in the Roman period, widows with substantial capital must have been desirable marriage partners, and if she inherited a workshop, that certainly qualified as substantial capital. It may also have been in the widow's interest to remarry within the business. Widows were not always able to continue the business on their own because they lacked either the skills or the resources, or both.[273] By analogy with the stereotype of a widow marrying an apprentice, Roman widows may have married their freed slaves, particularly if they themselves did not have the skills to continue the family firm.[274]

This is not to say that all widows remarried. Especially in the case of wealthy widows, it was in the interest of their birth family to keep them from remarrying and to preserve their property, including a workshop, or tools, within the family – witness the lawsuit filed against Apuleius by the children of his new wealthy wife Aemilia Pudentilla.[275] Moreover, at all social levels, increasing financial security and family networks surely contributed to the higher incidence of single women from the age of 30 to 35 onwards attested in Roman Egypt.[276] The pattern is suggestive.

To sum up: women evidently contributed to the family economy in various ways, despite the existence of pervasive gender biases. Gender ideals confirm that it was considered appropriate for women to engage in housework and childcare, which economic theory considers a profitable form of labour differentiation. This particular division of labour, however, was strongly connected with the female life cycle. In addition, therefore, most women will have had paid work at some point in their lives. Women who engaged in the labour market were employed chiefly in so-called 'feminine' jobs, which is a deceptive commonplace because in these sectors, as in all specified occupations, men are more frequently attested than women. Women also participated in the family business in various ways – in administration, retail, or the arts and crafts – working together with their husbands. With advancing age, women's legal and economic independence

[272] E.g. Brodsky (1986) 142 (London), contra Todd (1985) 70–71 (Abingdon).

[273] Cf. Hawkins (2021) 254.

[274] This is suggested by Temin (2004) 529 with reference to Garnsey (1998) 30–37; cf. Broekaert (2012); and Treggiari (1979a), tentatively suggesting marriage to men in the same business.

[275] Fantham (1995). This story is but one example of the Romans' fear of inheritance hunters; general pattern: Goody (1990) 205.

[276] Hübner (2019).

increased, and seems to have become more accepted, whereby more economic opportunities opened up. On the death of their husband they would sometimes take over as household head, which illustrates that in such instances the wife's skills were probably no less than the husband's. Freedwomen (and freedmen) sometimes continued their earlier job, as shown by the various examples of double-business households. The demographic life cycle was thus particularly influential for women's economic life.

Child labour

The Romans did not have a clear concept of child labour: it appears to have been self-evident that children would contribute to the family economy to the best of their abilities. As a consequence, child labourers are seldom explicitly mentioned. This may be the reason why scholarship on child labour in antiquity is relatively limited.[277] Child labour must nevertheless have been commonplace, for the simple reason that it often was economically indispensable.

If the Romans did not have a clear concept of child labour, they did display a general awareness of 'childhood'. I believe that this was recognized for all children, regardless of social status.[278] For many, both slave and free, childhood jobs thus were probably more like chores. This is reflected in the fact that responsibilities assigned to children appear to have been adjusted to what they could do at their age. Columella, for example, signals bird keeping and weeding as children's work (*puerilis opera*).[279] Herding chickens and other animals, and taking care of younger siblings, are all known activities for children. Even if they could not make a full contribution to the household income yet, the children will have ensured that the adults had more time on their hands for productive work. "Child labor was a function of people's basic struggle for survival, a means of acclimatizing children to the common realities of material life around them".[280]

[277] The 2013 *Oxford Handbook on Childhood and Education in the Roman World*, for example, includes no chapter focusing on child labour, although it does feature in some of the chapters. For child labour, see Porena (2016); Laes (2011a) 148–221; Petermandl (1997), Kleijwegt (1991); Bradley (1991) 103–24 ("Child Labor in the Roman World") focuses on apprenticeship contracts. For late antiquity, see Laes (2015a).

[278] Contra Porena (2016) 664 and *passim*, on the assumption that 'childhood' was an elite prerogative; e.g. Evans Grubbs and Parkin (2013) on the historiography of the concept of childhood in antiquity.

[279] Petermandl (1997) 119 with reference to Colum. *RR* 2.2.13 (weeding, *quod vel puerile opus*, "work that is surely child's play"); 8.2.7 (for bird keeping as suitable for old ladies or children (*unus sedula vel puer*)), among other examples.

[280] Bradley (1991) 118. This sentiments resonates in Porena's (2016) 667 suggestion that slave as well as freeborn children were working towards their predetermined positions as adults.

The economic contribution of children to the family economy could take various forms. An artisan with his own workshop, as we have seen, may have instructed his children in the trade or apprenticed them out. Holleran has argued that children (like women) may also have taken to retailing the products from the workshop, a job that required little training.[281] Gaius notes that many (*plerique*) left boys and girls in charge of *tabernae*.[282] Children from poorer families could also turn to vending, if they were not scavenging the streets begging and searching for food. In nineteenth-century London, "child sellers tended to hawk cheap products that required little capital outlay, such as oranges, apples, or watercress; girls also sold flowers", and child hawkers are still common among the poor in many places today.[283]

Children were also judged on their individual merits, being singled out for a number of individual occupations. They were popular performers, and are attested as actors, mimes, dancers, acrobats, and musicians; there were also child athletes who competed in agonistic festivals. In the mines, too, collecting rubble from the narrow mineshafts was specifically reserved for children, who were relatively small and agile.[284] Children might also end up in prostitution. Crobyle's daughter Corinna is a good fictional example of this.[285] A late antique legal case from Hermopolis also suggests that prostitution provided a necessary income for some: mother Theodora sues a councillor involved in the death of her (adult) daughter, a prostitute. The prefect assigns to her a substantial sum of money, for the sole reason that with the death of her daughter, she had lost her main source of income.[286] It is perhaps not a coincidence that these two instances concern daughters supporting their single mothers.

Only a small number of young children with a job title can be identified in funerary epigraphy. In large part that is a result of the nature of the evidence. It is not very often that age is commemorated, and it is not very often that a profession is recorded: as a result, children are especially unlikely to be represented with an occupation. Moreover, children were not always

281 Holleran (2012) 224; Holleran (2013) 316.

282 *Dig.* 14.3.8, "Nam et plerique pueros puellasque tabernis praeponunt."

283 Holleran (2012) 220. The number of children hawking on the street in contemporary Nigeria, to name but one example, is increasing. See e.g. Ojo (2013); George (2011); Umar (2009); Oyefara (2005). In this research there is a particular focus on the risks involved for girls.

284 Laes (2011a) performers 195–97, sports 197–200, the poor 200–6; for the mines, 212–16; and Porena (2016) 683–84.

285 Above, Luc. *Dial. Mer.* 6; with Strong (2012).

286 *BGU* 4.1024.6–8 exc. G; discussed by Bagnall (1996) 196–98, with n. 87 refuting the comment that the text may be fictional. Cf. Crobyle sending her daughter Corinna to become a courtersan in Luc. *DMeretr.* 6.

assigned a particular occupation, when they were too young to have picked up a trade. And especially in the case of very young children, it is likely that familial bonds preceded ties of labour in their epitaphs. Nevertheless some of the occupational inscriptions were set up for young children. Their jobs range from unskilled to highly specialized occupations. A boy of four years old was commemorated as a tailor of fine clothing (*vestiarius tenuarius*); in this case I am inclined to think that it was the job he was expected to take up later in life rather than a current occupation, although he may well have participated in the labour process in some small way.[287] Another boy, 12 years old, is commemorated by his sister as a shoemaker (*sutor*); he, too, was probably a shoemaker in training.[288] In other cases, however, it is likely that the (semi-)skilled work was actually performed by the young employees themselves. Nine-year-old Viccentia was a gold spinner (*auri netrix*), for example, and we know of a few hairdressers (*ornatrices*) who were still quite young.[289] A boy named Pagus was commemorated for his skills as a jeweller or goldsmith (*gemmarius*) in an elaborate epitaph:

CIL 6.9437

D(is) M(anibus) / quicumque es puero lacrimas effunde viator / bis tulit hic senos primaevi germinis annos / deliciumque fuit domini spes grata parentum / quos male deseruit longo post fata dolori / noverat hic docta fabricare monilia dextra / et molle in varias aurum disponere gemmas / nomen erat puero pagus at nunc funus acerbum / et cinis in tumulis iacet et sine nomine corpus / qui vixit annis XII / mensibus VIIII diebus XIII ho(ris) VIII

To the divine spirits. Whoever you are, traveller, shed your tears for this boy. Two times six years he carried the years of budding youth. He was the love of his master, the thankful hope of his parents, who did not deserve to mourn long after the end. He knew how to make intricate bracelets and to gently set various gems in gold. The name of this boy was Pagus, but now his ashes lie in a tomb, after a premature demise, a corpse with no name. He lived for 12 years, 9 months, 13 days and 8 hours.

It is evident that the labour input of children was of vital importance to the family. Their contribution started at an early age, with simple tasks. Like Pagus, however, young children with an actual job title generally appear to be of servile descent. The four-year-old boy tailor mentioned above,

[287] *CIL* 6.6852.

[288] *CIL* 6.10546; cf. *Dig.* 9.2.5.3 quoted earlier in this chapter for an unlucky apprentice cobbler.

[289] *Aurinetrix*: *CIL* 6.9213; *ornatrices CIL* 6.9726 (12 years old), 9728 (13 and 19 years old), and 9731 (nine years old).

too, was commemorated as a freedman.[290] Viccentia, the gold spinner, is likely to have been a slave girl because of her single name, though this is not stated explicitly. Many of these young slaves would have been trained within wealthy elite households, which seem to have catered to their own slaves' education.[291] As we have seen, however, there are clear indications that freeborn boys and girls also had access to job training, and that children adapted their labour power to the family economy in whatever way they could.

The hereditary nature of jobs

Based on the foregoing discussion, many Roman children may be expected to have followed their parents in their choice of career. Informal learning in the household was identified as one of the most cost-effective solutions to build up human capital. That strategy automatically confers the family trade on the next generation. The examples of formal apprenticeship also showed continuity of profession within the family, even if children were sometimes apprenticed out rather than taught by their father, as illustrated by the weaver families of Pausiris and Tryphon. Indeed, family ties occasionally are proudly stated in occupational inscriptions, as in that of the two brother carpenters of *CIL* 6.9411 ("duo fratres tignuarii"), or that of the brother painters of *CIL* 6.9796 ("fratres pigmentarii"). Presumably the brothers were involved in a family trade. At other times a family business is not stated, but can fairly securely be inferred.[292]

Continuing in the line of work of one's parents does not equal working in the household of birth. In his analysis of 'commemorative links' in the occupational epitaphs from the city of Rome, Hawkins found that artisans and retailers were rarely commemorated by their sons or daughters – ties of dependency between patrons and slaves or freedmen are much more common.[293] On the plausible assumption that the commemorator frequently was also heir to the deceased, Hawkins concludes from these findings that few Romans stood to inherit a (household) business from their parents, which seems to have fallen to freedmen instead, and that this may well have been a deliberate strategy. Hawkins deserves credit for

[290] This is probably a case of deathbed manumission; see Chapter 4 below.

[291] See Chapter 4 below. Saller (2013); Laes (2011a) 184–89.

[292] As in *CIL* 6.33809, discussion in Groen-Vallinga (2013) 307. A spectacular instance of family continuity that falls outside the scope of my current research is the mention of a *bapheus* from Thyatira, "the sixth of his line to head the shop", "ἐπιοτησάμενον τοῦ ἔργου ἀπὸ γένους τὸ ἕκτον", *IGR* 4.1265. Translation MacMullen (1974) 98, with n. 23 at 188. Camodeca (2016) 25 states confidently that the office of *unguentarius* and *thurarius* was often transmitted within the same *gens*.

[293] Hawkins (2021) 203–27. The percentages are somewhat higher for other occupational categories. Ibid., 215, Table 4.3.

stressing the importance of freedmen as heirs to the household business. This finding might well be related to the predominance of freedmen in the arts and crafts: combined with the fact that the freed had relatively few freeborn children, their own freedmen became the natural successors.[294] But Hawkins's conclusion that children who did not inherit invariably had a different occupation from their parents does not hold; he himself points out that when fathers and sons were demonstrably active in the same trade, they were often working in separate workshops. That observation actually sits nicely with the outcome of my discussion of family form above, which suggests that in an urban context sons as well as daughters as a rule moved out to constitute their own economic household unit upon marriage.

Thus Hawkins's analysis should not be taken to mean that children generally did not follow in their parents' footsteps, or that family labour was inconsequential when compared to servile labour in the household.[295] The evidence for family ties in occupational inscriptions, in my view, is inconclusive about the frequency of inherited occupations. Occupational inscriptions are rare, and rarer still among those with family ties to commemorate: a general preference for recording familial bonds rather than profession is the main reason why freedmen and slaves are over-represented in the occupational inscriptions to such a high degree.[296] Family labour is therefore easily obscured. Likewise, the theory of intergenerational persistence does not require that persistence to be in the same job, but it would have been the obvious choice. It is reasonable to presume that inherited jobs were more frequent than the sources suggest, even if their actual share must remain unknown.

There is evidence both for continuity and diversification of occupation. Both are often implicit in the same source. Thus Saller adduces as evidence for informal learning at home Vitruvius' remark that architects used to train their own children on the job.[297] Vitruvius' reference to past practice may still have been valid during the Principate, but he could also be reminiscing about times long gone in a silent complaint that sons were not trained as architects any more.[298] Legal texts attest to fullers who engaged both sons and apprentices in their workshop.[299] The census documents from Roman Egypt provide a handful of examples of extended households that record the employment of adult males from different generations, where

[294] De Ligt and Garnsey (2012) 85–90; Hawkins (2021) 212–14 addresses this bias explicitly.

[295] As Laes (2015a); Laes (2015b) seem to suggest.

[296] Joshel (1992).

[297] Saller (2013) 75; Vitruvius 6 pr 6.

[298] Cf. Hawkins (2021) 200.

[299] Flohr (2013) Chapter 2.

some sons hold the same occupation as their father, and others have a different job.[300] Lucian initially started out in the family trade of sculpting, before he made a career switch to writing. Pausiris and his sons were all weavers, but Tryphon is known to have also had a brother who was not a weaver. The son of a veteran and the grandson of an *agoranomos*, too, were apprentice weavers.[301] Finally, there are some indications of family bonds within professional associations, but the evidence is scanty and very rarely indicates more than one generation.[302]

In an urban context, as we have seen, the Romans needed to be flexible enough to adapt to market instability, which is one explanation for some children not following an inherited vocation.[303] Successful entrepreneurs will have continued their business, though, and some will have done so through their children. The adaptive family strategies of continuity or diversification both evidently were possible during the Principate, and both strategies were actively employed. Market forces seem to have functioned well to fulfil labour demands for a long time: it was only in the fifth century that the emperor Honorius felt the need to coordinate the process of continuity of trades: he made membership of the professional organizations hereditary, in what reads like an attempt to tie artisans' families to their job.[304]

Patrons and freedmen: the freedman economy[305]

The Romans had a wide spectrum of options available for continuing the family name, and the family business. Biological children could not always, or did not always, take over, for various reasons. Adoption of an heir presented the Romans with an alternative, but to find the preferred choice of an adult (male) relative who was of the right age, as well as educated in the right trade (see above), may have been more complicated than looking to the trusted and experienced slave labourers of the household and setting them free. A manumitted slave became quasi-family, and was family in name because the ***nomen gentilicium*** of the patron was bestowed on the freed slave.[306] Manumission thus seems to have been at the heart of a particularly Roman form of family firm, made up of patron and one or more freedmen, or of *colliberti*.[307] This phenomenon is well attested in epigraphy, and it

[300] Bagnall and Frier (2006) 72–74, with some discussion by Hawkins (2021) 196–97.
[301] Freu (2011) 30.
[302] See Chapter 5 below; Venticinque (2010) 279–82; Liu (2009) 181–83.
[303] Briefly touched upon by MacMullen (1974) 98–99.
[304] *Cod. Theod.* 14.3.21, 403 AD; Waltzing (1896) vol. 2, 306–7.
[305] This refers to the title of Verboven (2012b).
[306] Mouritsen (2011b) 36–51.
[307] Mouritsen (2011b) 218–19.

is noteworthy that the patron when recorded regularly was a freedman himself, which led to a pattern with multiple generations of freedmen. If, as has been argued, freedmen had few children of their own, that explains their choice for this inheritance strategy.[308]

Verboven would go so far as to say that "slavery was a passing phase necessary to produce [skilled] freedmen".[309] The number of freedmen with skilled jobs and responsible positions recorded in occupational inscriptions does suggest that the presence of such freedmen in the family business was fairly common. Their role in the family firm could vary: "Probably some freedmen [...] were branch-managers, some had separated from the parent firm, some may have inherited businesses from their patrons".[310] Others will have stayed with their patron under the same roof.

Many of the separate non-elite, freedmen households must have originated from larger elite *domus*. Other homes were set up by the freed slaves of non-elite patrons. The connection between patrons and freedmen could take various forms, but they have in common that the bond was never completely severed. It has been argued that the entire institution of manumission in fact depended on the continued guidance of freedmen by their former master. Patrons (or their heirs) could rely on a number of informal and formal ways to ensure their freedmen's loyalty.[311]

In terms of labour economics there was a distinction between slaves who bought their own freedom, and slaves who were freed: those who were granted their freedom remained in the debt of their patron. This moral deference (specified in terms of *obsequium*, *reverentia* or *pietas*) towards a patron could consist in part of labour input, called *operae libertorum*. *Operae* were a legal obligation that was generally specified as a number of working days, for which a patron could call on his or her freedmen (who, in turn, could subcontract these working hours). Hawkins stresses the importance of these *operae*, particularly in the case of skilled work. In his view, manumission was a powerful tool to battle the risks of fluctuating demand that was characteristic of Roman society. The labour of freedmen could be called upon whenever the patron chose; such a flexible workforce of freedmen saved much in transaction costs in times of high labour demand.[312] This interpretation of freedmanship as a solution in times of fluctuating

308 Notably in the demographic model for Herculaneum by De Ligt and Garnsey (2012) 85–90; cf. Garnsey and De Ligt (2016) 83 n. 38.

309 Verboven (2012b) 88.

310 Treggiari (1979a) 72; cf. Verboven (2012b) 93.

311 "[D]efined in vague terms of *obsequium*, *reverentia*, and pietas", Mouritsen (2011b) 51–65 ('controlling freedmen'), at 57. In this chapter Mouritsen stresses the importance of social discourse, and the (limited) options in Roman law, for keeping freedmen 'in their place'; cf. Hawkins (forthcoming).

312 Hawkins (forthcoming); Hawkins (2021) 146–57.

demand is based on a majority of freedmen moving out: they would no longer require sustenance, but could still be drawn upon as a labour force.[313] The subject of *operae* looms large in the juristic literature, although it remains to be seen how widespread *operae* were.[314] However, *operae* were not the only method of economic cooperation between patron and freedmen.

The bonds between patrons and freedmen may be envisaged, following Verboven, as 'trust networks', where freedmen benefited from the funds and economic advocacy of their patron; they in turn promoted their patron's interests, as agents or business partners, for example.[315] The importance of trust networks in Roman society cannot be overstated, as Chapter 5 will illustrate in more detail. At the very least, economic benefits for both sides will have resulted from the connection between patrons and freedmen.

Funerary monuments set up by freedmen to their patron provide convincing evidence for economic cooperation after manumission, as in this example of two axle makers from Rome:[316]

CIL 6.9215

M(arcus) Sergius M(arci) l(ibertus) / Eutychus / axearius sibi et / M(arco) Sergio M(arci) l(iberto) / Philocalo / axeario patron(o).

M. Sergius Eutychus, freedman of Marcus, axle maker [set up this monument] for himself and for M. Sergius Philocalus, freedman of Marcus, axle maker, his patron.

There is no doubt about their relative positions or occupations. Another example is a little more complex, but illustrates a similar situation:

CIL 14.2721 = 2722

P(ublius) Licinius P(ubli) l(ibertus) / Philonic[us] // P(ublius) Licinius P(ubli) l(ibertus) / Demetrius patrono fecit[317]

[313] Hawkins (forthcoming). He acknowledges that some freedmen could and did remain in the household, for which cf. Chapter 4 below.

[314] On the possible marginality of *operae*, see Mouritsen (2011b) 224–26. When slaves bought their own freedom, they were not liable for *operae*; Hopkins (1978) 128–29 believed this was the majority of freedmen.

[315] Verboven (2012b) 98–100; see also Mouritsen (2011b) 213 on the "practical economic opportunities for the new freedman". For associations as trust networks, see Chapter 5 below.

[316] *CIL* 6.9215. Joshel (1992) 128–45, specifically 136–37 for the example of the axle makers.

[317] *CIL* 14.2721 = *CIL* 14.2722. I have added the square brackets for Philonic[us], and the word *fecit* in accordance with the text in George (2006) n. 24, though they are lacking

> [For] Publius Licinius Philonicus, freedman of Publius. Publius Licinius Demetrius, freedman of Publius set up [this monument] for his patron.

This text is inscribed on a relief with two portrait busts, now in the British Museum: presumably Philonicus is the younger man on the left, and Demetrius the older man on the right, as their names are written under their portraits. In its shape it conforms to the well-known type of family portrait groups of *liberti*, signalling that Demetrius meant to represent their bond as a family unit. The portraits are lined by prominent motifs: *fasces* on the left, the tools of a carpenter on the right and on the tympanon. In my view, this must mean that Demetrius set up this relief for his patron Philonicus, and that they were bound by a shared occupation as carpenters.[318]

CIL 6.37826, finally, records no less than four 'generations' of freedmen in one epitaph:

> *CIL* 6.37826
>
> [Camer]ia L(uci) l(iberta) Iarine fecit / [L(ucio)] [Cam]erio L(uci) l(iberto) Thrasoni patrono / [et] L(ucio) Camerio L(uci) l(iberto) Alexandro / patrono eius et / [L(ucio) C]amerio Onesimo lib(erto) et / [vi]ro suo posterisque omnibus / [vest]iariis tenuariis de vico Tusc(o)
>
> Cameria Iarine, freedwoman of Lucius, set this up to Lucius Camerius Thrasonus her patron, freedman of Lucius, and to Lucius Camerius Alexander, freedman of Lucius, his [i.e. Thrasonus'] patron, and to her own freedman and husband Lucius Camerius Onesimus and all their descendants, fine tailors from the Vicus Tuscus.

The text indicates the freedmen's working relationship in a workshop (or workshops – plural?) located in the Vicus Tuscus in Rome. The text records that Lucius Camerius Alexander was the one who freed Thrasonus, who in turn manumitted Iarine, who freed (and married) Onesimus. Because L. Camerius Alexander, who is at the top of the pyramid in this epitaph, was himself a freedman, we know that there was in fact at least one more L. Camerius [...]. Their shared profession and shared location suggest that they were probably working closely together. Trying to maximize

in the Clauss-Slaby transcription. Photographs clearly show that this is justified. The meaning of the text or even the names of the Licinii were never in doubt, however.

318 George (2006) 22–23 believes that they are *colliberti* and that Demetrius set up this or another monument for their (common) patron. It is my contention that *patrono fecit* here must refer to the monument itself, and that therefore the younger man on the left, Philonicus, also a freedman (not coincidentally the one with the *fasces* by his side, hence possibly a *sevir augustalis*), is the patron of Demetrius on the right. The structure of the text incidentally is an exact parallel of *CIL* 6.9215 above.

the information from this text, it could be argued that even the marriage between Cameria Iarine and L. Camerius Onesimus was part of an economic strategy.[319]

If economic ties between master and slave were regularly maintained after manumission, then what about the 'independent freedman'? Garnsey has argued persuasively for the economic independence of the rich freedman: with wealth came autonomy.[320] In this view, the freedmen made up a new class of self-made men who fulfilled a particular, prominent position as traders and craftsmen in the Roman economy. Garnsey's views have been widespread in the historiography of freedmen as the nouveaux riches and explorations of a Roman middle class. That there was some competition between the new freedman and the established patron is evident from the fact that the jurists consider extensively the possibility that a patron would object to his freedman exercising the same trade as himself, in the same place. If a patron should object, the law prevented the patron from doing anything about it.[321] In response, however, Mouritsen has postulated that it generally was the economic support of a patron, and thus dependence rather than independence, that brought forth the wealthy freedman.[322] The rent of a *taberna* may well have been part of that financial support, and this profitable relationship between both parties has been adduced by Ellis to explain freedman prominence in retail, as well as the tantalizing question why *tabernae* were regularly annexed into elite houses: believing built-in shops to be economically irrational, Ellis suggests that a patron allowing freedmen the use of built-in *tabernae* aimed at maintaining their sociopolitical backing.[323]

Independence of freedmen thus appears to have been subject to restrictions, not necessarily for the worse. Even if the death of the patron

[319] Cf. Broekaert (2012) 46: "We can therefore imagine that Roman businessmen tried to encourage inner-family marriages between freedmen with the same specialization as some kind of guarantee for prolonged cooperation."

[320] Garnsey (1998) 28–44 = Garnsey (1981); with d'Arms (1981) 144–48, specifically on Augustales in Ostia and Puteoli.

[321] *Dig.* 37.15.11 (Papinian) for a freedwoman(!); *Dig.* 37.14.2 (Ulpian); *Dig.* 37.14.18 (Scaevola). The jurists are quite resolute in their protection of freedmen rights, but see *Dig.* 38.1.45 (Scaevola), "'Can a freedman of a cloth merchant exercise the same trade in the same society and the same place as his patron – who does not want this?' He responded: 'I can proffer nothing, why he should not, if the patron experiences no damage from it'". "Libertus negotiatoris vestiarii an eandem negotiationem in eadem civitate et eodem loco invito patrono exercere possit? Respondit nihil proponi, cur non possit, si nullam laesionem ex hoc sentiet patronus." Cf. Verboven (2012b) 96; Mouritsen (2011b) 212 n.28.

[322] Mouritsen (2011b) 228–47, e.g. at 234: "Since the one advantage which the freedmen enjoyed was their familial background and patronal connection, an 'independent' freedman would generally have been a disadvantaged freedman".

[323] Ellis (2018) 108 ff.

de facto secured a freedman's independence, the legacy of having worked for that patron may have remained influential. The *familia* Veturia, for example, appears to have brought forth many freedmen who had mastered the art of purple-dying: *purpurarii*.[324] Doubtlessly these freedmen learnt the trade as slaves in the household. They were rewarded with manumission and the opportunity to set up shop themselves, presumably aided by the financial support as well as the name of their patron(s), which appears to have become a distinguished purple-dyers' brand: Veturius.

In sum, the occupational inscriptions suggest that freedmen constituted "extended *familiae*".[325] Economic family ties, it should be added, ran horizontally between *colliberti* as well as vertically between patron and freedman.[326]

Conclusion

The family lay at the heart of Roman society. It was crucial in determining the life course of an individual in every way, ranging from their birth to investment in education and participation in the labour market. This chapter has attempted to show the importance of the family in economic decisions.

The Roman family was ubiquitous. It was constituted upon marriage, and for freeborn Romans, women in particular, marriage was virtually universal. A largely neo-local marriage pattern has been identified in the cities, which means that every marriage constituted a new economic family unit. The family itself was characterized by the dynamics of demographic and cultural determinants: the prevailing cultural norms were that the couple would have children; the prevailing high-mortality regime predicted that the marriage would not necessarily last very long. The urban family generally started out as a conjugal couple and expanded with children, with the possible addition of slaves or freedmen. In an urban context, it appears that the dominant family structure was the simple family, with extensions of slaves, freedmen and/or relatives. That should not obscure the fact that the family changed quickly over time as it fell apart, and was subsequently reconstituted through remarriage, or through taking in widowed or orphaned relatives, apprentices, lodgers, and various others.

The family changed over time in a natural life cycle as well. The demographic life cycle presented restrictions to the economic contribution

[324] Dixon (2001b) collects the evidence: *CIL* 6.9498 and 37820; *CIL* 14.2433; *NS* 1922, 144.

[325] Extended *familiae*: Verboven (2012b) 99.

[326] *Dig.* 17.2.71.1 (Paul) mentions a *colliberti societas*. For more examples of inscriptions with *colliberti*, see Chapter 4 below.

of individual family members: a mother's labour opportunities in particular were restricted by childbirth and the care of young children; very young children were not yet able to contribute (much), even if they were put to work from a very early age. This chapter has underlined the fact that the money-earning activities of women and children were vital to the family, and heavily dependent on their individual life cycles. The economic benefits of family cooperation are clear. In this context it is significant that in the Roman empire, the family included servile labour. Servile labour is not restricted by demographic restrictions to the same extent as free labour of family members is. Where the adaptive element of the early modern family largely consisted of women and children, therefore, the slave component made the Roman family more versatile and capable of adapting to the market. Slaves could be bought, educated, hired out, sold, or manumitted, all according to need. Children could only be educated or hired out. Even in the continuity of the family business, substitutes for biological children in the form of foundlings, adoptive children and freedmen were not uncommon.

An interpretation of Roman society on the basis of the family economy model would expect to find predominantly small workshops or artisans and craftsmen in the city: family businesses with one or two slaves and/or apprentices. That does not explain all of the sources, however. There were variations to the theme of 'family business', notably because of the significant role that freedmen played in the economy: freedmen were considered family and were therefore included in family ties. Sometimes they even made up an economic unit of *colliberti*, with or without their patron. The evidence attests to a complex web of labour relations that extended beyond the household. Household businesses are most likely to explain the situation of artisans and craftsmen – not surprisingly also the group that is best attested in the occupational inscriptions – but not everyone was an artisan or craftsman. The pull of the city must have attracted large numbers of unskilled workers as well, seasonal workers as well as permanent migrants. Particularly in the cities the importance of skilled and unskilled wage labour should therefore not be underestimated.

Chapter 4

Family Economics

The Elite *Domus*

Introduction

The occupational inscriptions include a striking number of working individuals who can be connected to a larger elite household. Slaves and ex-slaves in the epigraphy from the city of Rome are especially likely to reveal a connection with one of the aristocratic houses. A correlation between the presence of aristocratic households and urban slavery will have had a significant impact on employment opportunities for the free urban population. It will be argued that the elite *domus* were a non-negligible presence in the larger cities of Roman Italy, and that this had important consequences for the urban economy. The elite *domus* and their role in the labour market might be termed the '*domus* economy'.[1]

The elite *domus* of this chapter should be offset against the smaller family units of the preceding chapter. Whereas it is difficult to present a clear-cut definition, I take elite *domus* to be wealthy families, who could afford to have most of the required work and labour carried out by subordinates rather than by their own hands. Although some of these dependent workers were freeborn, it must be presumed that in practice this characterization implied a significant servile presence in the household. Smaller families may, of course, have included a modest number of dependent labourers, including apprentices, slaves, and/or freedmen, but, in contrast with the elite, in smaller families the household head and his or her direct relatives would actively contribute their own labour power. It was argued that non-elite families' labour strategies were largely governed by economic motivations. Financial restrictions can be expected to have been less decisive in the more wealthy households of this chapter. Throughout the text I refer to the elite *domus* indiscriminately as upper-class *familiae*, aristocratic households, large domestic households, or other synonyms.

1 The insightful term '*domus* economy' was suggested to me by Rens Tacoma.

A large servile presence certainly was characteristic of the Roman aristocratic family. Examples abound. Cicero's household staff, for instance, has been charted from his literary output; this revealed that most of his live-in staff, as well as hired labourers, were slaves or ex-slaves.[2] Part of the newly found riches of Petronius' fictional character Trimalchio was that he could boast a substantial number of personnel, and plenty of his slaves, many of them with highly specialized occupations, feature in the *Satyricon*.[3] The consul of AD 43, L. Pedanius Secundus, was said to have owned 400 slaves.[4] Sizeable elite households are attested epigraphically as well: several large *columbarium* tombs provided collective burial space for the domestic staff of aristocratic families.

The reasons for having numerous slaves were not just economic, regardless of the fact that many of them were put to work. *Noblesse oblige*: for the elite, the number of slaves owned was a significant status indicator. It could be argued that slaves were more important to their aristocratic owners as a visible token of wealth and status than as labourers. In that scenario, slaves did not need to work to perform their primary, ideological function as a status symbol.[5] Slave-holding for appearance's sake may be classified as conspicuous consumption, honour, or prestige creation.[6] And the Romans were not alone in their traditional value judgements of slavery:

> in a great many slaveholding societies masters were not interested in what their slaves produced. Indeed, in many of the most important slaveholding societies [...] slaves produced nothing and were economically dependent on their masters or their master's nonslave dependents.[7]

This particular form of conspicuous consumption must have been a great stimulus to the presence of slaves within cities. Honour and prestige did not preclude economic motivations for slave-holding, however.[8]

It follows from the above that aristocratic households probably were among the most important employers of the slave part of the urban population. If adaptive strategies of the non-elite family were mostly

[2] Park (1918) 55–79. Largely slaves and ex-slaves: concluding remarks, ibid., 88–89. See also Treggiari (1969a).

[3] Cf. Baldwin (1978).

[4] Tac. *Ann.* 14.42–45.

[5] Harper and Scheidel (2018) 99–100; Mouritsen (2011b) 194–95; Bradley (1994) 15–16; cf. Joshel (1992) 150 and *passim*.

[6] Vlassopoulos (2021) 64–65 on prestige creation; Patterson (1982) on honour (for masters) and dishonour (for the enslaved).

[7] Patterson (1982) 11.

[8] Vlassopoulos (2021) 60 on "co-existence and entanglement of various slaving strategies"; Patterson (1982) 11.

implemented by means of the labour participation of women and children, for the elite *domus* they were probably largely concentrated in the management of slaves and ex-slaves. Wealthy Romans could easily respond to changes in their situation, chiefly through buying, selling, and manumitting slaves. Conversely, elite expenditure was crucial to urban production as a whole, which will have provided employment for the urban freeborn as well. The freeborn population was engaged both directly and indirectly with the elite: as employers, as landlords, and as market consumers. All of these processes to some extent must have contributed to the reality of urban labour systems. Elite households made up a very specific sector of the urban labour market that to date has not received proper analysis as such.[9] The aim of this chapter is to illuminate the ways in which the aristocratic household shaped and influenced the workings of urban labour relations in Roman Italy.[10]

Chapter outline

This chapter starts off with an attempt to attach a rough sense of magnitude to the *domus* economy, trying to determine the share of the labour force that the large *domus* stood for. Once the market share of larger *familiae* has been established, we can take a closer look at their workforce. It is apparent at the outset that marked differences in size and make-up between non-elite and elite families are likely to come up. In line with this structural divergence, we may also expect to find distinct cultural or economic considerations and strategies concerning the labour participation of the (members of) elite *domus*. It is likely that the elite *domus* engaged in labour for the market to some extent, in addition to work efforts for the maintenance of the household itself.

The larger household was subjected to a family life cycle of its own. The family life cycle predicts that labour supply and demand within the family change over time, because of the dynamics of demography, notably mortality and fertility, but also because of fluctuations in economic circumstances. Like the non-elite family, therefore, the aristocratic household workforce was not a static entity. Quite the opposite is likely to be true: because of its greater size, the elite family can be expected to have been even more dynamic than the non-elite family, because there were more

[9] Cf. Ellis (2018); Robinson (2017) for elite investment.

[10] The ultimate elite household, the *familia Caesaris*, features in this chapter only through the personal, domestic households of members of the imperial family. The *familia Caesaris* has received excellent coverage in Schumacher (2001); Boulvert (1974); Weaver (1972); and Chantraine (1967). Penner (2013) 9, correctly points out that in the early empire, "the boundaries between public civil service and private domestic service were porous and undefined". Much of her dissertation on the imperial households of the Julio-Claudians therefore is also relevant here.

variables to consider – it concerns more individuals, and even whole families within the *familia*, or surpassing the boundaries of the household in a wider *domus* network. Size may also have allowed for more flexibility in economic strategy and risk absorption.[11]

The slave component of the elite *domus* stands out. It will become clear that the purchase, sale, procreation, and manumission of slaves played a significant part in the adaptive labour strategies of the elite household. Another economically strategic opportunity for the elite was investment in human capital. It was illustrated above that the freeborn, artisans and craftsmen in particular, regularly invested in some kind of job training for their family. Slave-holders invested in training, too, to such an extent that it has been assumed that much of the available education in the Roman empire actually took place within the elite household.[12] Slave and ex-slave labourers from the aristocratic *domus* are attested in a wide variety of jobs that range from unskilled to highly skilled. With regard to the more skilled labourers, this raises the question how and where they learnt their trade. The answer reflects economic strategies of investing in human capital. It is commonly suggested that slaves in the larger household had exceptionally good opportunities to acquire skills, and that (as a result?) skilled work was the prerogative of slaves and ex-slaves. This chapter shows that possibilities for the education of slaves were indeed extensive, and that investment in human capital was high on the household agenda. But the question to what extent this imposed limitations on the free population's labour opportunities, and consequently to what extent we can speak of an integrated labour market, demands a more differentiated and intricate answer.

The final section of this chapter is concerned with *columbarium* tombs. The so-called *columbaria* are large-scale funerary monuments that are exclusive to the city of Rome under the Principate. Their importance for this chapter lies in the fact that the *columbarium* tomb population has generally been equated with elite households, in the sense of the elite *domus* which are the topic of this chapter. *Columbaria*, moreover, are exceptional in that they provide us with a relatively well-defined context for the inscriptions they hold. Many of the epitaphs from these tombs also record the profession of the deceased, and occasionally that of the commemorator. The sample thus makes for a perfect case study of the labourers from the elite *domus*. It is readily admitted that the equation of the tomb population with an aristocratic household is not entirely warranted for most samples:

[11] Cf. De Vries (2008) 17.

[12] This is voiced among others by Mohler (1940) esp. 262–63. Mohler (1940); Forbes (1955); and Booth (1979) all focus on slave education because of this presumption. Schooling as a slave prerogative is still implicit in Saller (2013).

it will become clear that such direct overlap between *columbarium* and *domus* is limited to a handful of 'single-family tombs'. It will be argued that the equation is helpful to the current analysis, however, because in most instances the tomb occupants can indeed be related to elite families, even if they are not necessarily from the same household unit.

Demography: the servile presence in elite households and free hired labour

This section considers the demographic context for elite households in terms of the larger urban population, or, more specifically, in the context of the available workforce in the cities of Roman Italy. On the reasonable assumption that most of the labourers of the *domus* were slaves and ex-slaves, it deals with the concept of urban slavery first, and tries to establish whether there is any correlation between urban slavery and the presence of elite households. The free labourers in the service of elite *domus* are investigated subsequently. On the basis of the ancient evidence it remains difficult to find out just how prominent the elite households were within Roman society; this section on demography is a modest attempt to situate the elite household as an employer in the labour market, in terms of its market share.

Slave labour and the city

The elite tended to cluster together in towns. This is both a contributing factor to, and a result of, high urbanization rates.[13] A strong elite presence in cities should therefore certainly hold for Italy, the heavily urbanized political heart of the Roman empire, which attracted the upper classes from all over the empire. The elite invariably employed slaves, to underline their status. With the consistent presence of the elite in the cities, it can be surmised that there were relatively many slaves in the cities too. It has indeed been estimated that the percentage of slaves in the city was higher than the percentage of slaves in the countryside,[14] even if many upper-class Romans owned a rural estate with its own staff in addition to their property in the city.[15] With the exception of Rome, with its large population of urban

[13] De Ligt (2012) 196–97; based on the work of Jongman (1988) 192–98, esp. 196.

[14] See also Jongman (2003); Scheidel (2005a) 66; Scheidel (2011b) 289. Conversely, Bradley (1994) 71 apparently does not feel a need to substantiate his claim that "most slaves were *rustici*".

[15] Bradley (1994) 58 for the distinction between the urban and rural staff of a slave-owner, the *familia urbana* as opposed to the *familia rustica*; Rosafio (2016) 102 for a distinction between the *familia rustica* as the site of production versus the *familia urbana* as the locus for trade in Plautus.

freeborn, many urban settlements may have had a slave population of no less than 40 per cent.[16]

A correlation between urban slavery and wealthy households matches the pattern that is evident in the occupational inscriptions. No less than 73.8 per cent of slaves with job titles were connected to a wealthy household in Joshel's calculations for the capital. This pattern of employment has prompted Joshel to suggest that many of the other occupational epitaphs of slaves also belonged to aristocratic households, even if we cannot now trace them confidently to a known household.[17] Based on Joshel's findings, equally 73.8 per cent of the occupational inscriptions that are connected to an elite *domus* concerns slave workers.[18] Borbonus's analysis of the combined *columbarium* tomb population, however, results in a significantly smaller estimate of 25.5 per cent slaves.[19] There should be an explanation for the difference in these two estimates. Criteria for which inscriptions belonged to a larger household, and which did not, are not easy to define. Most inscriptions lack context, and with the limited information they record, the relation to an elite *domus* often cannot be identified. With that in mind, what do these numbers really tell us?

It is clear that slaves and ex-slaves make up a large majority of the occupational inscriptions, and it is also clear that for many of them a connection to an elite *domus* is likely: this in itself underlines the hypothesis of a correlation between slavery and elite presence. But biases in the material evidence may also partly account for the apparent connection between slaves and aristocratic households. For one thing, the well-preserved *columbarium* tombs from the city of Rome are likely to have swelled the relative numbers attested for slaves in an aristocratic household. It is particularly noteworthy that those in the category 'slaves in a *columbarium*' are the ones most likely to mention their profession: 44 per cent of all slaves

16 Cf. De Ligt (2012) 190, Table 4.3; De Ligt and Garnsey (2012) for Herculaneum.

17 Joshel (1992) 74, 98 and Table 4.2 at 99 for the percentage, and at 103 she writes, "Further, I believe that many of the slaves and possible slaves whose epitaphs lack signs of social context did in fact belong to large households. The pattern of their employments resembles that of slaves whose epitaphs confirm their membership in upper-class *familiae*". Moreover, Borbonus (2014) 119 notes a strong similarity in general of status distribution in the *columbaria*-inscriptions, and other *CIL* samples, and remarks, "A factor that probably contributes to this similarity is the provenience of inscriptions that are listed in the CIL without context: many of them may stem from now-destroyed columbaria".

18 Joshel (1992) Table 4.2 at 99 provides the numbers from which I calculated the slave percentage in the elite household (slaves in a private context (346)/all inscriptions from a private context (469) × 100). It appears to be a mere coincidence that the percentage is exactly the same.

19 Borbonus (2014) 121, Table 5.

in *columbaria* do so.[20] The discrepancy between Borbonus's lower count of 25.5 per cent slaves in the elite household and Joshel's higher finding of 73.8 per cent slaves recording an occupational title in a private context is thus explained in part by the difference in a sample of 'occupational inscriptions from *columbaria*' on the one hand and '*columbaria* inscriptions in general' on the other.

Slaves and ex-slaves in an aristocratic family were perhaps also more likely to be commemorated than others of the same legal status; servile labourers may have received a proper burial in a smaller household, in the family tomb even, but it was not always a named burial – implicit in the common use of the formula *libertis libertabusque posterisque eorum*. There is no doubt in my mind that servile labourers from elite *domus* are over-represented in the epigraphic evidence. For all these reasons, an estimate placing 73.8 per cent of the urban slave workforce in elite households, in accordance with Joshel's results, is likely to be too high.

To put the epigraphic evidence into perspective, we may compare another way to quantify the slave presence in elite *domus*. Although few scholars have taken up the challenge, Scheidel touches upon the number of slaves in aristocratic *domus* in an attempt to quantify the slave population of Roman Italy.[21] His model provides us with a very tentative sense of scale. There is no hard evidence for these numbers, but they should be read as informed guesses that are good to think with.[22]

Scheidel's understanding of elite, for calculating purposes, is the total of all senators, knights (*equites*), and councillors (*decuriones*). The number of senators is set at 600, knights at 5,000, and councillors at 20,000. Scheidel takes every senator to have owned 80 slaves, every knight 20 slaves, and every decurion five slaves, which makes for a total of 248,000 elite household slaves. This working definition of the elite is, of course, substantially less inclusive than my definition of the larger household, and Scheidel acknowledges that there are more elite *domus* beyond the three *ordines* that may have owned quite a number of slaves.[23] The resulting figures should therefore be read as a minimum estimate.

20 Borbonus (2014) 126. Cf. the numbers for the *monumentum Liviae* in Treggiari (1975a) 59, Table D: only five out of 41 slaves do not record a job. It is interesting that in Treggiari's account of Livia's household, almost 50 per cent of the freedmen also record a job there.

21 The following paragraphs are based on the model for "non-agricultural slavery" in Scheidel (2005a) 66–67.

22 Cf. Scheidel (2005a) 66 n.15.

23 Senators, *equites* and *decuriones* add up to 25,600 households. Scheidel (2006) argues for 40,000 elite households. It is reassuring that 40,000 times six provides a similar number – six being Flory's (1978) 85 educated guess for the average number of slaves in a household.

Scheidel's numbers can be used to calculate the percentage of elite household slaves. In order to do so, we need to know the total of all slaves in the city as well. Smaller households may also have owned a slave or two, who should be added to the number of urban slaves.[24] Scheidel does so by analogy with the census data from Roman Egypt (one slave to 5.8 freeborn). For an urban population of 1.4 million to 1.6 million non-slave and sub-elite urban residents in Roman Italy, that means adding another 240,000–275,000 slaves living in non-elite households. The calculation leads to a total of approximately 500,000 slaves in the cities of Roman Italy. Since most of the numbers fed into the model are likely to be too low, Scheidel doubles the minimum estimates in "controlled speculation". He goes on to say, "If we schematically place all senatorial slaves, half of the equestrian slaves and half of all sub-élite slaves in the capital, we arrive at approximately 220,000 to 440,000 slaves in Rome and 280,000 to 560,000 in the other cities".[25] I tabulated the lower range of these numbers to calculate the percentage of slaves in elite households in Table 4.1 – doubling all estimates leads to exactly the same percentages, of course.

Table 4.1. Urban slavery and the percentage of slaves in elite households. Numbers derived from Scheidel (2005a).

	Rome	Other cities in Roman Italy	Totals
Slaves in urban elite households	100,000	150,000	250,000
All urban slaves	220,000	280,000	500,000
Slaves in urban elite households (%)	45.4	53.6	50.0

What can be gathered from Scheidel's model, therefore, is that approximately 50 per cent of urban slaves should be located in elite households. This number is likely to be too low, because of Scheidel's limited working definition of the elite.[26]

24 See Chapter 3 above on slaves in smaller households.

25 Scheidel (2005a) 67; compare De Ligt (2012) 190 for 700,000 urban slaves in 28 BC, which suggests that Scheidel's doubling of the estimates was perhaps too crude.

26 Scheidel (2005a) 67 himself notes that "a more pronounced [...] concentration of slave-ownership in the top ranks of Roman society would help redress the apparent imbalance between centre and periphery". Cf. Harper (2011) 38–60, esp. 58–60, with Table 1.1, who proffers a similar model for rural and urban households combined to conclude that "the wealthiest 1.365 percent of Roman society owned 49 percent of slaves". Harper's focus is on the later empire, but the numbers fed into this model are equally relevant for the Principate.

If we offset the epigraphic evidence against the model of Scheidel, a plausible range can be established for how many urban slaves were employed in elite *domus*. Scheidel's theoretical 50 per cent for Roman Italy is likely to be too low, whereas the 73.8 per cent extracted from Joshel's sample for the city of Rome is likely to be too high. That leaves me with the hypothesis that most urban slaves, between 50 and 74 per cent, were employed in large domestic households. This finding seems to endorse the proposed correlation between urban slavery and elite presence in the cities. However, Scheidel's model cannot shed light on the question what proportion of the workforce in the elite *domus* was made up of slaves. The widely differing results from Joshel (73.8 per cent of occupational inscriptions for slaves originate from a private context) and Borbonus (25.5 per cent of the *columbarium* population were slaves) leave us with something of a conundrum – but perhaps balancing these findings with the data for freedmen can shed some light on the matter.

Freedmen

The connection between elite *domus* and urban slavery prompts the related question how the elite households tied in with freedmanship. If somewhere between 50 and 74 per cent of urban slaves were employed in the aristocratic household, it is not too far-fetched to presume that many freedmen were closely related to those households too; the previous chapter illustrated the fact that ex-slaves often maintained a close relationship with their patrons, and it will become clear that this was no less true for freedmen of wealthy patrons. It is generally presumed that proximity to the master increased the chances of manumission, and such proximity was perhaps most likely in the personal service of a wealthy family – the elite had plenty of employment for slaves in their personal vicinity, which should be understood quite literally in the case of, for example, bedchamber servants (*cubicularii*).[27]

Most of the freedmen in *columbaria* are relatively easy to identify as such, since their full names – when recorded – reflect their owner's names.[28] Joshel attributes only 25.9 per cent of the freedmen with occupational title securely to domestic service.[29] Her numbers suggest that, conversely, around 21.3 per cent of work 'in a private context' was filled in by freedmen.[30] The elite *columbaria* attest to many freedmen who were buried there,

[27] Mouritsen (2011b) 196–200.

[28] There are exceptions to the rule: some whom we know were free(d) chose not to sport the *tria nomina*, especially in 'homogeneous' tombs; see Borbonus (2014) 123. There were also 'unrelated freedmen' with a distinct *nomen*; see below.

[29] Joshel (1992) 98.

[30] Joshel (1992) Table 4.2 at 99, from which I calculated the freedmen percentage in the elite household (freedmen in a private context (109)/all inscriptions from a private context (469), × 100).

22 per cent in Borbonus's calculation.[31] The fact that these numbers sit much closer together than the numbers for slaves, however, should not trick us into believing that they mean the same. According to Borbonus, only 11 per cent of the freedmen in *columbaria* recorded an occupation.[32] More than half of the individuals with named burial in a *columbarium* belong to the uncertain category of those who carry the *tria nomina*, but for whom there is no other indication of whether they were free or freed: surely some of them were freedmen, too.[33] On the sole basis of these percentages, we should therefore probably attribute more than 21.3 per cent to freedmen labourers.

A brief exercise may confirm a rough order of magnitude for the number of freedmen. If the 2:1 ratio for slaves to freedmen in the general urban population is applied, as postulated by Garnsey and De Ligt, the percentages for slaves mentioned above (25.5–73.8 per cent) would lead to somewhere between 12.7 and 37 per cent for freedmen.[34] Since it is impossible to go above 100 per cent, however, the maximum cannot go beyond 33.3 per cent. Joshel's finding of 21.3 per cent does sit nicely in the middle, and would imply a highly plausible 42.6 per cent for slaves. Since there were few, if any, freeborn in the household (see below), however, to get to 100 per cent we can tentatively place the percentage of freedmen at a third, which leaves two-thirds.

Freedmen, however, may have stayed in the *domus*, but may also have left after manumission to set up their own workshop and family. The nature of the evidence of *columbaria*-inscriptions is such that it only accounts for freedmen who were buried in the household tomb. The previous chapter expanded in more detail on how economic bonds between patrons and freedmen continued, with or without the formal *operae libertorum*, because freedmen were considered as quasi-extended family. In other words, freedmen could be linked to the elite household in more than one way, not all of which meant that they would be buried in a *columbarium*. We may therefore estimate the contribution of freed labour to the elite *domus* to be less than a third, but more than Joshel's 21.3 per cent. Joshel's tally admittedly does go beyond the *columbaria*, but her text indicates that her definition does not include freedmen "in the public world" – bankers, salespeople, and artisans, for example – a group that is likely to have been non-negligible.[35] This finding of

31 Borbonus (2014) 121, Table 5, records 50.9 per cent free(d).

32 Borbonus (2014) 126.

33 Borbonus (2014) 121, Table 5.

34 De Ligt and Garnsey (2012); Garnsey and De Ligt (2016). Incidentally the ratios of slaves to freedmen in the Statilian household tomb shows something like 68 per cent to 32 per cent – though not the Volusian tomb, which has 54 per cent to 46 per cent; see Mouritsen (2013) 46–47.

35 Joshel (1992) 98.

somewhere between 21.3 and 33.3 per cent freedman labour in the *domus* also further specifies the numbers for slaves, at more than 66.7 per cent.

An explanation for some of the freedmen buried in *columbaria* could be that manumission was a deathbed gift. This is particularly plausible for those who died as freedmen under the legal minimum age of 30. Underage freedmen may have been informally manumitted and become Iunian Latins, free without Roman citizenship, a status that could serve as a kind of safeguard to the influx of new citizens.[36] Underage deathbed manumission, however, was also tolerated for obvious reasons. A freedman manumitted in the face of death was never truly free and remained a slave their entire life. Examples of very young freedmen in the *columbarium* tombs are not hard to come by.[37] Age is not a common feature to record, however.[38] One could therefore plausibly argue that age is recorded particularly to underline special circumstances, such as an early demise and, potentially, deathbed manumission. Significantly, of those recorded with age, most under 30 were slaves, and "most slaves were not freed until after the age of twenty".[39] To my mind, therefore, deathbed manumission accounts for no more than a small proportion of the evidence.

In addition to potential deathbed manumissions, there is also the theoretical possibility that freedmen maintained the right to be buried in the household *columbarium* after leaving the household – and some ostensibly unrelated freedmen gained their burial rights because they were related to one of the tomb's 'inhabitants'.[40] There is thus always a possibility that the freedmen in the *columbaria* were not, or were no longer, working for an elite *domus*. All these arrangements are virtually impossible to trace and come to the fore only occasionally.

There is, however, compelling evidence for the fact that at least some of the freedmen did remain within the household after manumission – which suggests that they kept working there too.[41] Such a pattern was perhaps more common in some households than in others.[42] The reasons for freedmen to

36 Lopez Barja de Quiroga (1998).

37 The example of the four-year-old *vestiarius tenuarius*, L. Anicius Felix (*CIL* 6.6852 cited above) springs to mind.

38 Hopkins (1966) remains the *locus classicus*; for other problems with age such as age rounding, Scheidel (1996).

39 Mouritsen (2013) 52–53 for both the Volusii and Statilii.

40 See the example of *CIL* 6.7290 = *CIL* 6.27557 from the columbarium of the Volusii, discussed below.

41 Cf. Edmondson (2011) 343: "manumitted slaves (i.e. freedmen and freedwomen) quite frequently remained part of the household even after manumission, as in the household of the Statilii Tauri".

42 As suggested by Penner (2012) 147, who suggests that the percentages of slave–freed–free of the *monumentum Marcellae* could indicate that this tomb encouraged

stay are not difficult to think of. Especially in larger households, it is likely that the newly freed had previously engaged in personal relationships with other household members.[43] Joshel points out the simple truth that service occupations like that of a footservant (*pedisequus, -a*) were rather difficult to carry out in the absence of someone to escort.[44] A good example of a resident freedwoman is Iulia Elate in *CIL* 6.4002, *pedisequa* to Livia, whose husband M. Iulius Carisius (for whom no occupation is recorded) is also from the same household – the bond with her husband and her service job in the household would be two compelling reasons for her to stay.[45] The category of service occupations includes mainly 'work', geared towards the maintenance and self-sufficiency of the household. Even if their labour was more 'marketable', however, freedmen may have stayed. Thus we know that Cicero's gifted and well-educated freedman Tiro did not leave Cicero's side until after his patron's death.[46] A passage in the *Digest* likewise records a case of a slave who continued his employment as a banker after manumission.[47] Examples like these suggest that many of the *columbaria*-inscriptions do indeed commemorate privileged, freed slaves who still lived and worked in the elite *domus*. Mouritsen has even argued that the high manumission rates from the *columbarium* inscriptions of the Statilian and the Volusian tombs could indicate that, in these two households, slaves were freed on the assumption that they remained in the household.[48]

The evidence can only securely attest to continued burial rights of freedmen, however, not to continued residence patterns. Whereas Mouritsen may well be correct about the Statilii and the Volusii, the previous chapter has illustrated that many occupational inscriptions from outside the *columbarium* tombs attest to ex-slaves who set up their own household. This regularly concerns conjugal couples originating from the same *domus*, and they principally record job titles that could be promoted as labour for the market. It is known that the bulk of all epitaphs were set up by freedmen. This phenomenon is generally attributed to the wish of the freedmen population

continued bonds after manumission, in contrast to the Statilian tomb; the latter finding at least sits well with Mouritsen (2013) 58–61. See below.

[43] The classic article is Flory (1978); more recently, see Mouritsen (2013) 55 on the mixed status of nuclear families in the households of the Volusii and Statilii; Mouritsen (2011a); and Edmondson (2011). See also below.

[44] Joshel (1992) 101.

[45] Libertinization and marriage are not explicitly mentioned in this epitaph, but the context is strongly suggestive.

[46] Park (1918) 63 for a very brief summary (with references) of Tiro's services to Cicero, including those after manumission; more elaborately, McDermott (1972).

[47] *Dig.* 14.3.19.1 (Papinian). To be precise, the slave was an *institor* "apud mensam pecuniis accipiendis".

[48] Cf. Mouritsen (2013) 58, 61.

to display their lifetime achievements in public, more than any other social group in the empire.[49] Considering this prominence of freedmen in funerary epigraphy, combined with the significant percentage of slaves who were working for aristocrats, it is highly likely that many of these 'independent freedmen' originally came from elite families. *CIL* 10.3957 from Capua is an unambiguous example of this: the inscription clearly refers to a separate family tomb for a cabinetmaker and his wife, both freedmen by the same principal and therefore probably from the same *domus*:

> *CIL* 10.3957
>
> M(arcus) Avidius M(arci) l(ibertus) Aesopus sibi et / Avidiae M(arci) l(ibertae) Zosimae coniugi / fab(e)r intestin(arius) / h(oc) m(onumentum) s(ive) s(epulcrum) e(st) hh(eredes) n(on) s(equetur)
>
> Marcus Avidius Aesopus, freedman of Marcus, [set up this monument] for himself and for Avidia Zosima, freedwoman of Marcus, his wife. He was a cabinetmaker. This monument or tomb will not go to the heirs.

This is a clear example of independent freedmen who had left the *domus*, which underlines once more that the attested *columbarium* tomb population can only provide a minimum for the freedmen percentage in the elite *domus*.

It can be gathered from the above that the elite market share in servile labour was very large by any account. Adding Borbonus's numbers for the slave and freed presence in the *columbarium* tombs totals 47.5 per cent of the household, which is a bare minimum that could potentially be as high as 98.4 per cent – 100 per cent minus the 1.6 that Borbonus securely identified as freeborn.[50] That leaves some room for freeborn labourers in elite employment, but it was not necessarily very much.

Free hired labour

In 53 BC Cicero writes to Tiro, "make sure that the doctor is promised whatever wage he demands".[51] Apparently, at the time of the letter in 53 BC, Tiro is unwell and a doctor is hired. Imported products, perishables, and custom-made luxury items could not all be produced within the elite *domus*. If out shopping for exclusive jewellery or other luxury items, the elite might parade the porticoes of the Saepta Iulia; if in need of first-quality meat, the *macellum* was the place to be.[52] The aristocratic houses must have hired labour and bought commodities from free labourers, in addition to

49 Mouritsen (2011b) 127–28.

50 Borbonus (2014) 121, Table 5.

51 Cic. *Fam.* 6.14.1–2; "Medico, mercedis quantum poscet, promitti iubeto".

52 Holleran (2012) 232–57 on elite consumption.

the labour or goods provided or produced by their own servile staff and freed labour relations.[53] This pool of free labourers significantly includes independent freedmen, a term that is here taken to refer to those unrelated to the particular elite *domus* looking to do business with them. I have strived here to avoid confusion between these independent freedmen and the freedmen labourers who were associated with the household through burial in the following discussion on free hired labour.

Free hired labourers in ancient Rome were not very likely to become a part of the elite family, *familia*, or household. From a broader historical perspective, this statement is not necessarily as obvious as it may sound: even today, there are families with a live-in au pair, for example. In early modern times, certainly, it was common for a free servant to move into the house and be considered as family for the time of their appointment. Young girls from the countryside regularly moved to the city to work as maids for a few years, and then returned and settled in a marriage. The early modern live-in household staff could be substantial, and included maids, butlers, doorkeepers, child attendants, cooks, and others.[54] In the Roman world, however, most of these service professions were practised by slaves or ex-slaves. Hired free artisans or craftsmen, conversely, would not be prone to moving in – in either time period.[55] Taking in freeborn apprentices or the Roman equivalent of journeymen also was much more likely to be confined to the non-elite household, because the elite *domus* included slave children and youngsters who took this place.

If there were freeborn workers in the elite household, they are hard to trace. The epigraphic record does not include many instances of freeborn domestic workers. For the city of Rome, Joshel found that only one individual who is certainly of free birth can be related to a wealthy household. If we include those she has identified as uncertain freeborn, there are a few more attestations ($n = 10$). These *incerti* of elite households were mostly "architects, doctors, or teachers".[56] This enumeration corresponds exactly with the jobs that Cicero holds to be "respectable for those whose status they befit", and this might be one of the reasons why Joshel prefers to see them as freeborn

[53] Park (1918) 78–79 lists tradesmen "from whom Cicero himself bought", among whom some *ingenui*, and mostly *liberti*.

[54] Cf., to name but one example, the well-attested household of Joyce Jeffreys in seventeenth-century Hereford: Spicksley (2012).

[55] Park (1918) 61 finds that Cicero's *familia* "did not supply skilled artisans", nor "regular artisans". The household of Joyce Jeffreys (Spicksley (2012)) only supported a jack of all trades.

[56] Joshel (1992) 99–100. She suggests that many more *incerti* may have been connected to an elite household, as many *incerti* from an unknown context (public or private) were engaged in "the most typical household jobs", such as the nurse and childminder cited above, or as a personal servant. Joshel (1992) 205 n. 19.

rather than freedmen.[57] In reality, identification of these *incerti* as freeborn workers remains entirely hypothetical.

Borbonus's analysis of the *columbarium* tomb population confirms that the freeborn make up only a minority there, 1.6 per cent.[58] Because such people are unlikely to have lived in the household in the first place, this should not come as a surprise. It is rather more noteworthy that *ingenui* are attested in the *columbaria* at all. A closer look at Borbonus's results brings out once more the significant group of 50.9 per cent 'free(d)', who carry the *tria nomina* but who cannot otherwise be identified as either *libertus* or *ingenuus*.[59] An estimate of 1.6 per cent may therefore be considered low. Having said that, with Borbonus, I do believe that the majority of this group of 'free(d)' were in fact freed.

Ingenui were less inclined to record their profession than slaves or ex-slaves; indeed the freeborn tended to put up fewer inscriptions altogether. It has been suggested that freeborn employees were more likely to be commemorated by their family than by the *collegia* that in many cases were responsible for the collective *columbarium* tombs.[60] On this basis one would expect to find a modest freeborn presence in the *columbaria*. Not all of the funerary monuments for the freeborn urban population were inscribed, and not all of those that were graced with an inscription have survived. The more humble grave monuments were probably also the more common, such as amphorae or small markers in the ground that are likely to have been lost over the centuries – that is, if a funerary monument was erected for the burial at all, because not everyone could afford one.[61] These biases in the ancient evidence are another part of the explanation why so few freeborn workers are attested, and why even fewer can be linked to aristocratic *domus*. Still, the pattern is remarkably consistent and suggests that freeborn town dwellers working and living in the elite household were indeed scarce.

That at least the possibility of working in an elite household existed for the freeborn is proven by Lucianus' satirical piece *On Salaried Posts in Great Houses*.[62] It does not become clear exactly what kind of posts are

[57] "Quibus autem artibus aut prudentia maior inest aut non mediocris utilitas quaeritur ut medicina, ut architectura, ut doctrina rerum honestarum, eae sunt iis, quorum ordini conveniunt, honestae": Cic. *Off.* 1.151. Translation Finley (1973) 41–42.

[58] Borbonus (2014) 121.

[59] Borbonus (2014) 121. This group was already referred to above, under 'freedmen'.

[60] Hasegawa (2005) 81–88. Patterson (1992) 23 emphasizes the likelihood of the family and *collegia* working together for an individual burial, which would also facilitate the creation of burials outside the *columbaria*.

[61] E.g. Hope (2009) 159–66 on the variation in funerary markers.

[62] *De mercede conductis*, which in the Loeb edition is characterized by Harmon (1921) 411 as "[a] Hogarthian sketch of the life led by educated Greeks who attached themselves to the households of great Roman lords – and ladies".

meant, but Lucian talks of educated men in a position of what I would describe as a 'glorified footservant'; in terms of an actual task, the text merely hints at the possibility of teaching the master's children (19). The existence of other, unskilled positions in the household that were filled by the freeborn poor, however, are also mentioned in passing. Even if Lucian's words are hardly a recommendation for the job – which he sees as selling oneself for wages into the service of an elite employer – the hundreds of thousands looking for a job in the city must have been happy to take up a position in the domestic service of a wealthy master. Lucian acknowledges that for unskilled labourers domestic service is no worse than other jobs (4, underlining his sentiments against 'wage slavery' once more). Apart from the income earned, such labourers perhaps hoped to benefit from the master's patronage. Lucian's second-century satire obviously is not the most factual account, but other literary references are in short supply.

A passage from the jurist Marcian has been adduced as evidence for free *mercennarii* living in their employer's house:[63]

> *Dig.* 48.19.11.1
>
> Furta domestica si viliora sunt, publice vindicanda non sunt, nec admittenda est huiusmodi accusatio, cum servus a domino vel libertus a patrono, in cuius domo moratur, vel mercennarius ab eo, cui operas suas locaverat, offeratur questioni: nam domestica furta vocantur quae servi dominis vel liberti patronis vel mercennarii apud quos degunt subripiunt.
>
> If domestic thefts are relatively minor, they are not to be punished publicly, nor is an accusation of this sort to be granted, when a slave shall be brought to question by the master, or a freedman by the patron in whose house he is staying, or a contract worker by him, to whom he hired his labour: because those thefts are called domestic that slaves steal from their masters, or freedmen from their patrons, or contract labourers from those with whom they live.

Although there has been some debate about the term *mercennarius*, it is now commonly accepted that it generally refers to free labourers – it is certain that there were slave *mercennarii*, too, but whenever reference is made to them it says so explicitly in the texts.[64] This passage from the *Digest*, therefore, presents the possibility that free hired labourers would sometimes

[63] *Dig.* 48.19.11.1 (Marcian); Brunt (1980) 100; Treggiari (1980) 50: "this does not amount to a declaration that all *mercennarii* (or all *liberti*) lived in, nor does it put them on a par with slaves".

[64] Brunt (1980) 100 ff. Bürge (1990) has argued at length that the term *mercenarii* refers exclusively to slaves unless explicitly stated otherwise: *mercennarius* in his opinion must refer to another man's slave (renting himself out) living in the employer's *domus*.

(temporarily) move in with their employer. Free *mercennarii* living in the house were not legally part of the family, but that does not mean that they were not considered as such by the outside world.[65] Marcian explicitly indicates that free hired labourers were subject to the 'justice' of the employer. Brunt points out that the *mercenarii* from this particular text are likely to have been engaged in occupations other than domestic service.[66] That suggests that there was at least some opportunity for the freeborn to work in the elite *domus*, outside the domestic sector. Incidentally, the passage also confirms the existence of freedmen living in their patron's house.

We might expect to find some additional evidence for live-in freeborn workers in sectors such as childcare. It seems natural that wet nurses and pedagogues would have lived in with their charges, just as a governess, nanny, or au pair did in later periods. Scholars have indeed emphasized the strong and often lifelong ties maintained between childminders and the family. The bond is evident from the epigraphic record, where nurses and others are frequently linked with the family who employed them.[67] The following texts may illustrate this.

> *CIL* 6.6686
>
> Dis Manibus sacru[m] / Ti(berio) Claudio Neothyrso / qui vix(it) annis XXIIII dies XI[3] / Ti(berius) Claudius Stephanus / patrono bene merito de / se et Cacia Restituta nutrix / eius et sibi et suis po(s)terisq(ue) / eoru(m) ita uti cippi fine / fecit libe(n)s animo / [
>
> Sacred to the divine spirits. To Tiberius Claudius Neothyrsus who lived 24 years and 11(?) days. Tiberius Claudius Stephanus to his well-deserving patron from his own funds and Cacia Restituta, his [i.e. Neothyrsus'] nurse, set this up willingly; also to himself, his [family] and their descendants; as far as the boundary stone.[68]

His claim is convincingly refuted by Möller (1993), however. See also the comments of Scheidel (1994) throughout 153–202.

[65] To my knowledge it is only when the law states that *publicani* are liable for wrongful acts committed by their subordinates that it includes the freeborn in their *familiae*, and then only "if they were similarly employed", i.e. in tax farming. This situation would not be very common: *Dig.* 39.4.1.5 (Ulpian).

[66] Brunt (1980) 100: "It is interesting that some *mercennarii* might actually live in the employer's house; we might perhaps think of craftsmen employed in a business, which was carried on in the employer's home; it seems unlikely that free *mercennarii* were used as domestic servants".

[67] Günther (1987) 86, 96 adds that nurses' own families are notably absent from the epigraphic record.

[68] The Latin here is difficult to translate, though the meaning of the words is perfectly clear; I have taken *sibi* etc. to refer to Stephanus and his family; *ita uti cippi fine* is meant to confirm what has been said before: the monument is open to them, on this burial

***CIL* 6.10766**

D(is) M(anibus) / P(ublius) Aeeius(!) Placentius / nutritori filiorum suorum / dignissimo / M(arco) Aurelio Liberali / b(ene) m(erenti) f(ecit)

To the divine spirits. Publius Aelius Placentius set this up to the carer of his sons, the most honourable and well-deserving Marcus Aurelius Liberalis.

Restituta the nurse and the childminder Liberalis both probably were freeborn workers, considering the fact that they sport the *tria nomina*, while their *praenomen* and *nomina* are different from that of the families they worked with. The majority of child minders, however, were of servile origins.[69] Moreover, even if a nurse were freeborn, we know that nurses did not always move in with their charges. In wet-nursing contracts from Roman Egypt it is regularly specified that the infant will reside in the home of the freeborn nurse.[70] Although that points to labour demand for freeborn women in this sector, it does not make them part of the elite *domus*.

The aristocratic families are more likely to have made extensive use of the services of free hired labourers living elsewhere than of free live-in staff. As stated above, the elite presence in the city generated ample demand for the (luxury) products and the expertise of free artisans and craftsmen, and so provided a livelihood for many. The doctor hired for Tiro is one example, the architect in *CIL* 10.8093 is another:[71]

***CIL* 10.8093**

T(itus) Vettius Q(uinti) f(ilius) / Ser(gia) architectus / porticus de peq(unia) / pagan(ica) faciund(as) / coer(avit) / A(ulo) Hirtio C(aio) Vibio / co(n)s(ulibus)

Titus Vettius Sergia, son of Quintus, architect, arranged for the colonnade to be built, paid for by communal funds, in the year when Aulus Hirtius and Caius Vibius were consuls [43 BC].

It is widely believed that, as a rule, free artisans and craftsmen were independent labourers and many business encounters with the elite will indeed have been of a temporary nature, be it a single transaction to

plot, as far as (in a rare use of *fine* with genitive, Lewis and Short s.v. *finis* I.B2) the *cippus* (which may carry both the meaning of boundary stone and grave marker here).

69 Bradley (1991) 19–20 for nurses, all of servile background, but that finding is outdated. Restituta is not on the list, for example; ibid., 82 for *tatae* and *mammae*. Tacitus, *Dial.* 28.4, writes of an *emptae nutricis*, a "bought nurse", and therefore a slave. Aulus Gellius, *NA* 12.1.1–5, however, writes *adhibendas nutrices*, where *adhibendas* leaves open whether the nurses-to-be-acquired were bought or hired.

70 See, e.g., *P. Reinach* 2.103, a wet-nursing contract from Oxyrhynchus, AD 26.

71 *CIL* 10.8093 = *AE* 2006, 356 (Grumentum). Architects were mostly freeborn.

buy bread or cater to a dinner, or a contract for the construction of a tomb complex that would take a certain period of time to complete. Rens Tacoma and I have argued elsewhere that the most important document for prices in ancient Rome, Diocletian's Prices Edict of 301 AD, underlines the importance of hired labour in the market: it presents daily wages for all kinds of jobs, including those for which we might rather expect priced items, such as a baker, or a gold- or silversmith.[72] What the Edict cannot tell us, however, is who were hired: free, freed, or slave labourers. Nor does it tell us whether they lived in with the contractor for the duration of a contract. And although this section has presented some evidence for free hired labour, like Cicero's doctor, Park demonstrated almost a century ago that Cicero in fact, insofar as he mentions it in his writings, hired chiefly (someone else's) slaves and ex-slaves.[73]

The evidence taken together suggests that occasionally the freeborn will have worked in elite households. The epigraphic evidence implies that when they did, they were unlikely to be remembered for it. The scarcity of the evidence is thus likely to reflect reality, indicating that the freeborn employees living in the elite *domus* were not numerous. If correct, this implies that the freeborn poor could not find long-term employment within the elite *domus* easily. The market for commodities they shared with independent freed labourers, leaving them only a small niche in the urban economy.

This crude demographic analysis of the live-in workers in elite households confirms the suggestion that urban slave labour centred around upper-class *familiae*. The aristocratic *domus* was an important employer in the city, particularly for its numerous slaves and ex-slaves: the resulting lack of vacancies in the household will have restricted labour opportunities in domestic service for the freeborn, and indeed very few free domestic workers are attested.

The dynamics of demography within large slave-owning households

The composition of the aristocratic household, like that of a non-elite family, was always changing. The marriages and remarriages of the nobility are relatively well documented, and Bradley aptly refers to their "matrimonial careers".[74] It is certain that many of these marriages concerned strategies, meant to form or strengthen political alliances,

[72] Groen-Vallinga and Tacoma (2017); the *Edict* includes some prices for piecework, too, but the prevalence of hired labour is significant.

[73] Park (1918) 71–77.

[74] Bradley (1991) 156.

because they often reflect contemporary politics.[75] It is not unthinkable that economic aspects also played a part in the marriage practices of the elite, as they did for the non-elite family.[76] In fact, all of the basic demographic 'strategies' that were identified for the non-elite will also have been practised by the elite to a certain extent. Children, and the number of children, mattered to the elite family, too: ideally, the family fortune was split up as little as possible.[77] Although the discussion in the previous chapter showed that the extent to which the Romans acted upon such ideals by means of infanticide or exposure is difficult to grasp, the wish for an heir or a son may have induced a form of family planning. Adoption to preserve the family line and the family fortune is one strategy that was perhaps more common among the elite than among the (supposedly) more prolific and (certainly) less affluent non-elite; the evidence for elite adoption at least is more abundant, though that is partly the result of the fact that the elite is better documented overall. Within the aristocratic family, then, the available demographic strategies were broadly similar to those for non-elite families.

The main difference between elite *domus* and non-elite households in terms of demographic changes over the life cycle is that many of the structural changes to the larger family took place in the servile segment of the family, precisely because slaves and ex-slaves made up such a large part of the household. On the one hand, slaves and ex-slaves were passively subjected to the events in their principal's life, such as death or divorce: because 'his' slaves were legally distinct from 'her' slaves, they were separated into two *familiae* if the marriage was broken up.[78] The life course of individual slaves, on the other hand, also contributed to the family life cycle. Slaves were regularly replaced upon death, disease, sale, and manumission, and slaves could procreate. Slaves could buy slaves of their own, again increasing the number of slaves in the *familia*. These sub-slaves or *vicarii* are not uncommonly attested. Structural change of the family was therefore based on somewhat different demographic factors than the factors influencing the demographic life cycle of smaller families.

An additional slave in the house increases family expenditure through the cost of maintenance, but he or she would also add to the family's

75 Corbier (1991) 49–63; Bradley (1991) 156–76.

76 Broekaert (2012); and Chapter 3 above.

77 Champlin (1991) 114–17 illustrates a pattern where sons tended to receive a substantially larger share of the inheritance than daughters. They were clearly favoured over their sisters, who held a smaller share that was often in the form of their dowry. Champlin says nothing about shares for brothers. In my view, such wills were effectively keeping (landed) property together as much as possible.

78 Cf. *Dig.* 29.5.1.15.

collective productivity, or maintain it in case of a replacement. If a slave fell in value because he or she was elderly or unwell, this might prompt the decision to sell.[79] A slave could also be 'removed' from the household through manumission. The motivations underlying manumission are rather more complex than those concerning sale. The question then becomes, to what extent did economic considerations shape these deliberate changes in the slave labour force of the aristocratic household? The process of structural change in the large family is impossible to follow, because we simply do not have the data to do so. Following a similar approach to that of the previous chapter, however, we can analyse the ways in which new slaves were added and other slaves removed from the household.

The sources of slaves

Where did elite families get their slaves from? It is not too difficult to come up with various possible sources of slaves in the Roman empire, but it has proven far more complicated to decide on the relative importance of such sources during the Principate.[80] It has been argued that the slave market gradually transformed into a system of predominantly home-born slaves under the high empire.[81] During the expansion of the empire, numerous captives of war were put up on the stands.[82] Initially, this will have been the most important source of slaves for sale. In the period under consideration, however, the slave influx from war and conquest dwindled, for lack of war and conquest. To maintain slave numbers, other sources, such as natural reproduction among slaves, must have played an ever more important part. Distinct evidence like the album of Herculaneum, however, suggests that at least in this particular context natural reproduction of slaves was

[79] Cato *RR* 2.7 encourages the sale of everything that is superfluous: e.g. surplus produce, but also old tools or deadbeat oxen – and old or sick slaves.

[80] Much has been said in the pioneering work of Jones (1956); and Bradley (1994) 31–56; Finley (1980) 128 is still to the point; the 'grand debate' took place between Harris (1980) (repr. 2011) 57–87; Harris (1994); Harris (1999) (repr. 2011) 88–109; and Scheidel (1997); Scheidel (2005a); Scheidel (2011b).

[81] Still maintained by Vlassopoulos (2021) 89; see Jones (1956) 193; and especially Scheidel (1997); Scheidel (2005a), with critique from Harris (1999), who contends that the slave population would have become stable only after the high empire (ibid., 75): "Something like Scheidel's model [...] must in the end have imposed itself. When?"

[82] Scheidel (2011b) 295: "The scale of enslavement was primarily a function of the geographical reach of Roman imperialism"; Rosafio (2016); and Welwei (2000) for captive slaves under the Republic; cf. Finley (1983) 174 on the continuity of "the army as a slave-supplying instrument"; similarly, Finley (1980) 128 notes that although the massive expansion ended, "war did not".

not sufficient to maintain the town's population, which therefore had to be supplemented by other means.[83]

The means of acquiring slaves was not just a response to the available supply: it also reflects economic considerations. We can say that new additions to the slave population of the elite *domus* conformed to one of three categories: slaves were bought, inherited, or born and raised within the household.[84] It will be argued here that the purchase of slaves remained the most important source of enslaved labour for elite households, which had an impact on the demographic make-up of the household, and on the balance between investment in slave education and buying skilled slaves. Home-born *vernae* nevertheless filled many of the most coveted positions in the occupational hierarchy.

Buying and selling slaves

Evidence for the slave trade under the empire is unmistakable, even if the specifics, such as the identity of actual slave-traders, are sometimes difficult to identify.[85]

The (unnamed) *mango* or *venalicius/venalicarius* (both mean slave-trader) is a familiar stock figure in literature, which suggests that he was a familiar figure in the streets of Roman Italy too. Think of Martial's complaint when a slave boy he wants, excessively priced by the *mango* at 100,000 sesterces, is bought instead by the equally excessively wealthy Phoebus, in Epigram 1.58. Although Phoebus' conduct is mocked by the satirist, the passage does suggest that slaves did not come cheap.

This clue from Martial is corroborated by other, scattered indications of slave prices.[86] Slaves are listed as a commodity in Diocletian's Prices Edict of AD 301.[87] In the Edict, the maximum price is set at 25,000 denarii for an adult female slave, and 30,000 for a male of the same age category. The

[83] De Ligt and Garnsey (2019); Mouritsen (2019); Garnsey and De Ligt (2016); De Ligt and Garnsey (2012).

[84] Mouritsen (2013) 67 n. 53 with reference to ps-Quintilian, *Decl. Min.* 311.7 – "aut natus aut relictus hereditate aut emptus."

[85] Bodel (2005); Bradley (1994) 42–43 offers some compelling evidence for the continued importance of the independent slave trade, which was drawing on "a combination of sources"; Finley (1983) on continuous trade in enslaved people, especially from the Danubian and Black Sea regions, from the late seventh century BC to the sixth century AD; Harris (1980) 129–31 notes on at 129 "the reticence which surrounded an occupation that was naturally despised by the elite". *CIL* 10.8222 (Capua – the slave trade can only be inferred from the accompanying relief) nevertheless suggests that they sometimes took pride in their trade.

[86] For slave prices, see Scheidel (1996); Scheidel (2005b) esp. 2–8; Ruffing and Drexhage (2008); and Harper (2010) on late antiquity.

[87] Prices Edict, Chapter 29; with Scheidel (1996); and Salway (2010).

prices for a skilled slave could add up to double that amount.[88] To get a sense of real slave prices, we can compare these sums with the average daily wage in the Edict of 50 denarii a day for skilled labour and 25 for unskilled work. It means that the cost of buying an unskilled slave amounted to the equivalent of 500 to 600 days of work for a skilled labourer, and twice as long if that slave was paid for by unskilled work.[89] The Edict is a late source, but it is reassuring that scattered price data from Roman Italy for the high empire fall in the same order of magnitude.[90] It is clear that, even for the well-to-do, buying a slave was costly. It is also clear that slaves were being bought and sold regardless.

"Where did the merchandise itself come from when slaveowners were ready to buy?"[91] The attestation of foreign slaves is indicative of a continuous influx of enslaved persons who in all probability were not born into slavery. For some of the slaves in aristocratic households, a foreign background can be inferred from their nomenclature: some have foreign names, and in rare instances their origins have been explicitly recorded.[92] Thus the couple in *CIL* 6.6343 are referred to as *Dardana* and *Dardanus*, which suggests that they both came from the province of Moesia (Superior – modern Serbia).

CIL 6.6343

Messia Dardana / quasillaria / fecit Iacinthus / unctor Dardanus

To Dardanian Messia, spinning woman. Dardanian Iacinthus masseur set up [this monument].

The epitaph, which was recovered from the Statilian household tomb, clearly stresses a common background for this pair, which may be the reason it is included in their epitaph. If not in the case of this particular example, however, the onomastics of slavery are generally difficult to interpret. Greek names predominate for slaves and ex-slaves in the first two centuries AD. The explanation of this undeniable pattern is rather complex. Greek names are generally considered to be an indication of servile status, even if such names do not necessarily point to specifically Greek or even more

88 29.8: "Pro mancipio arte instructo pro genere et aetate et qualitate artium inter emptorem vel venditorem de praetio placere conveniet ita ut duplum praetium statutum in mancipium minime excedere."

89 The daily wage is taken here excluding the food allowance. On prices and wages in the Edict, and on the validity of relating these price data to each other and to the world outside the Prices Edict, see Groen-Vallinga and Tacoma (2017).

90 Scheidel (2005b) 5 on Roman Egypt, 8 on Roman Italy; slaves remained an expensive good into late antiquity; Harper (2010) 230.

91 Bradley (1994) 31.

92 Mouritsen (2013) 58; Hasegawa (2005) 75–79.

generally foreign origins.[93] Those with Greek names as a rule are therefore deemed (children of) slaves and ex-slaves. In a re-evaluation of epigraphic evidence from Pompeii, however, Penelope Allison demonstrates that the correlation is not always straightforward.[94] She argues that the presence of freeborn inhabitants with ancient or more recent Greek origins, expressed also through Greek names, is to be expected in settlements with Greek historical influences such as Pompeii, and in southern Italy more generally. This calls for more differentiated research into onomastics. With due attention to context, though, the popularity of Greek names for slaves might indicate a continuing presence of bought slaves: Christer Bruun analysed the names of home-born slaves (*vernae*) in inscriptions from Rome, for whom he finds demonstrably more Latin *cognomina* than for the slave population at large.[95] As Bruun himself points out, the implication is that many individuals on the slave market were not home-born slaves, but ended up there through different channels: if *vernae* had been in the majority, we should expect to find mostly Latin *cognomina* among the servile population, rather than the attested pattern of mainly Greek names for slaves and freedmen.[96]

Many of the slaves in Italy came from within the empire, and often they were locals.[97] This suggests that at least some of them were born as *vernae*. An unknown number may have been enslaved only later in life, through various means. Thus piracy and kidnapping were known, but are difficult to quantify. Roman society was also familiar with a form of penal slavery, although this was probably a marginal phenomenon, if only because of its often temporary nature.[98] The extent of self-sale and enslavement of freeborn children is also hard to estimate.[99] Since many Romans lived at or under subsistence levels, as we have seen, it would make sense that for some Romans self-enslavement became a reasonable economic strategy to

93 Solin (1971) demonstrated the earlier supposition that Greek *cognomina* denote a servile status or servile background (at 121–45), and added the finding that Greek names do not generally refer to Greek or foreign origins (at 146–58). Silver (2011) 87–88, conversely, hypothesizes that the name pattern indicates that foreigners from the Greek east of the empire voluntarily sold themselves into slavery to finance migration to the Italian heartland. In his view, their presence in turn inspired a taste for giving slaves Greek names.

94 Allison (2001).

95 Bruun (2013).

96 Bruun (2013) 33. Either that, "or they were born in conditions where they never encountered their master and the names were given by a *vilicus* or someone else who routinely chose typical slave names, which mostly were Greek".

97 Silver (2011) 84 with references; cf. Scheidel (1997) 164; Finley (1980) 128.

98 On penal slavery: Groen-Vallinga and Tacoma (2015); Millar (1984).

99 Harris (1999); Ramin and Veyne (1981). Both maintain that self-sale was a major source of slaves, or at least "commonplace" (Harris (1999) 73).

avert chronic poverty and destitution.[100] If certain jobs, and job training, were more easily accessible to slaves and freedmen, as I believe it to have been the case, this strategy becomes all the more rational. Considering the fact that economic behaviour is *not* strictly rational, however, the prospect of slavery would in my view always remain a last resort.[101]

From the viewpoint of the buyer, there were a number of practical concerns, which created a continuous demand for slaves. In the words of Mouritsen,

> Elite households would have seen a steady influx of newly purchased slaves, who supplemented existing staff members who had died. Slave functions were often highly specialized and vacancies might occur unpredictably before home-born apprentices had been fully trained. Slaves from the market were therefore a natural supplement to the self-regeneration of the *familia*.[102]

Moreover, owning and training skilled slaves of every type may have been exceedingly expensive for all but the wealthiest households. Varro remarks that for the farm, at least, there were occasions when hiring the services of doctors, fullers, and builders (if available) from a nearby city could be wiser than training its own slaves, "for sometimes the death of one artisan wipes out the profit of the farm".[103]

Buying slaves at great expense in itself was a form of conspicuous consumption: because domestic slaves were something of a luxury product,

[100] Silver (2011).

[101] Cf. also the comments in Tacoma (2016) 68 n. 95, and 182–83 n. 64. Texts that might be interpreted as referring to voluntary slavery are often ambiguous: Sen. *De ben.* 4.13.3, "mango venalibus prodest", "the slave-trader benefits those for sale", might indicate that those for sale actually want to be sold. Harris (1999) 73 n. 84 records legal references to self-sale. I believe both references to Ulpian are flawed: *Dig.* 21.1.17.12 does not refer to self-sale but to fugitive slaves who seek refuge with a statue of Caesar. *Dig.* 28.3.6.5–6 casually refers to penal slavery, not self-sale.

[102] Mouritsen (2013) 58; Treggiari (1979b) 188–89: "A young Roman considering how to encourage the production of children by the slaves he had inherited from his father might not be able to foresee that he would marry a woman whose dotal estates would unexpectedly involve him in, say, marble-quarrying for which he would need a special staff, or that he would have eight daughters who would need an unusually large complement of maids, or that his only son would be a scholar who needed research assistants with expertise in Etruscan".

[103] *RR* 1.16.4, "quorum non numquam unius artificis mors tollit fundi fructum". Translation Hooper and Ash (1934, Loeb Classical Library). The passage was brought to my attention by Silver (2011) 100. It is interesting that in this context Varro speaks of a "yearly contract" (*anniversarios*) for doctors, fullers, and builders (*medicos*, *fullones*, *fabros*).

buying slaves – particularly male slaves – was a means of showing off. Scheidel contends that the continued existence of slavery can only be explained by accepting that ideology and tradition, not economic rationality, lay at the heart of ancient slavery.[104] The cultural expectation that an elite *domus* should entertain numerous slaves was real.[105] As noted in the citation by Mouritsen, however, economic considerations also played a part. Even elite owners must therefore have sought to strike a balance between the quantity and the quality of their slave retinue; that is, between slaves who largely conferred status through their mere presence and others who were also meant to be economically productive. The question whether slave-holding was economically viable has not been answered decisively.[106] Nevertheless, it was definitely possible to reap a substantial profit by selling or hiring out slaves. The value of slaves and (skilled) slave labour will be explored further in the section on human capital below.

It seems reasonable to conclude that the slave trade continued under the high empire, but also that a demonstrable shift in the sources of slaves occurred from mainly war captives under the Republic, to a variety of sources in the Principate, including foreigners and home-born slaves.

Home-born slaves

An increasing number of slaves must have been born into slavery. Home-born slaves were called *vernae* or, more matter-of-factly in a legal context, *partus ancillarum* (literally the 'offspring of slave women').[107] They had a firm reputation for trustworthiness, for which they were valued highly by their masters.[108] The particular status is proudly advertised in inscriptions by both *vernae* and masters.[109] *Vernae* sometimes record it even after manumission, like Anicetus, for example, an imperial freedman architect and *verna* we meet in *CIL* 6.5738, the epitaph for his wife Aurelia Fortunata. More commonly it is used as a term of endearment for a slave

[104] Scheidel (2005b); Scheidel (2008). White (2008) is unhelpful for a purely economic comparison from the perspective of the owner's investment, because his argument focuses on welfare economics and allocative efficiency, which is an ethical approach that includes the value of freedom (immeasurable).

[105] Cf. Vlassopoulos (2021) 64–65.

[106] See the introductory chapter.

[107] Sigismund-Nielsen (2013) 293 writes on *vernae*, "But it is not under this term that we meet them in the *Digest*. We know them only as the *filii* of a male, high-status slave and his *contubernalis*". The *Digest* also refers to *partus ancillarum*.

[108] Rawson (2013); Bradley (1994) 33 remarks that *vernae* had "a certain *cachet*" (his italics). On *vernae*, see especially Hermann-Otto (1994). Sigismund-Nielsen (2013) 293 seems not to have been able to substantiate her earlier doubts about the special position of *vernae* on the basis of the literary material. Sigismund-Nielsen (1991) 226.

[109] Sigismund-Nielsen (1991) analyses inscriptions from *CIL* 6.

child by his or her master, suggesting ties of affection; although presumably the mention of a home-born slave also advertised the fact that the master possessed the resources to raise one. *CIL* 14.472 is an elaborate example:

> *CIL* 14.472
>
> D(is) M(anibus) / Melioris calculatoris / vixit ann(os) XIII hic tantae memoriae et scientiae / fuit ut ab antiquorum memori[a] usque in diem / finis suae omnium titulos superaverit / singula autem quae sciebat volumin[e] potius / quam titulo scribi potuerunt nam / commentarios artis suae quos reliq(u)it / primus fecit et solus posset imitari si eum / iniq(u)a fata rebus humanis non invidissent / Sex(tus) Aufustius Agreus vernae / suo praeceptor [i]nfelicissimus / fecit / in f(ronte) p(edes) II in ag(ro) p(edes) VI / excessit anno urbis condita / DCCCXCVII
>
> [Sacred] to the divine spirits. To Melior, *calculator*, who lived 13 years. He was of such wisdom and knowledge that he surpassed the renown of all from the memory of the ancients until the day of his passing. The singular things (*singula quae*) that he knew were more voluminous than they could inscribe on his headstone; for the commentaries that he left behind of his art, he was the first to make, and only he could duplicate them, if the hostile fates had not begrudged him the human realm. Sextus Aufustius Agreas to his *verna*, [his] most unhappy instructor, set up this monument. Two feet wide, six feet long. He passed away in the year 897 from the founding of the city [AD 145].

A child born to a slave mother was a slave and belonged to the mother's owner. This was of obvious benefit to the master, and it must have been one of the reasons why slave unions were allowed. If women were kept in slavery longer than men, as can plausibly be argued, this is probably no coincidence and it should be explained in part by the fact that the women were still of child-bearing age.[110] It is a commonplace that at least some slaves, of either sex, were sexually exploited.[111] As a result of sexual exploitation of slave women by their owner, it is conceivable that an unknown number of slave children were in fact the biological offspring of the master himself. It is also possible that in some instances the sexual relations of a slave with another slave were forced: Bradley suggests that slave offspring was "so convenient" to owners, that for slave unions "perhaps more than approval

[110] Drawing on the data for Roman Egypt: Scheidel (1997) 160–62; Bagnall and Frier (2006) 94 n. 10 and the age-table (D) at 356–57.

[111] Both male and female slaves, though for obvious reasons the emphasis is on slave women here; Scheidel (2009) 284–99; repeated in Scheidel (2011a) 113–14; cf. Treggiari (1979b) 192–94, who in addition references the possibility that owners fell in love with slaves, or protected their female slaves from prostitution by contract.

was involved".[112] To my knowledge there is no hard evidence for this. As Matthew Perry points out, however, "Although not always the primary concern of Roman slaveholders, reproduction consistently shaped how they assessed the worth and ideal behavior of enslaved people – even if they did not attempt to directly manipulate slaves' sexual activity".[113]

There are certainly clues that the ability to beget children was valued in a slave woman. A female slave was priced highest at the time when her reproductive capacity was highest, between 16 and 40 years of age.[114] It should be noted, however, that this was also the age when male slaves were most expensive. The *Digest* offers more compelling evidence that slave-owners took an interest in their slave women's offspring. Women who had given birth to several children could apparently be rewarded by manumission, which indicates that there was some encouragement, or at least appreciation, of the fact.[115] Moreover, one could go back on the purchase of a slave woman who was sold "with her offspring added", if she turned out to be infertile or over fifty – which was really the same thing in Roman law.[116] Conversely, it is spelled out that the sale of a woman was considered valid also when she was pregnant – Ulpian continues, "after all, the first and foremost task of women is to conceive and to take care of the child".[117] Elsewhere, however, the same Ulpian notes that "slave women were not simply purchased for that reason that they bear children".[118] That is to say, women's childbearing potential was definitely a consideration, but it was not the sole reason for purchase.[119]

Relationships between male and female slaves, ideally, could, of course, also be voluntary. Many epitaphs of slave partners suggest that their unions not uncommonly developed out of affection. Slaves were

[112] Bradley (1994) 50–51; see also Bradley (1987b) on 'slave-breeding'.

[113] Perry (2021) 255.

[114] Cf. Bradley (1987a) 55 on 30 Egyptian contracts of sale that demonstrate a correlation "between the age of adult female slaves at the time of sale and the period of expected reproductivity".

[115] *Dig.* 1.5.15 (Ulpian); *Dig.* 34.5.10.1 (Ulpian); cf. also Colum. *RR* 1.8, 19.

[116] *Dig* 19.1.21 pr: "Si sterilis ancilla sit, cuius partus venit, vel maior annis quinquaginta, cum id emptor ignoraverit, ex empto tenetur venditor".

[117] *Dig.* 21.1.14.1 (Ulpian): "maximum enim ac praecipuum munus feminarum est accipere ac tueri conceptum".

[118] *Dig.* 5.3.27 pr. (Ulpian). In context: "slave women's children and their children's children should not be considered proceeds (*fructus*), since slave women were not simply purchased for that reason that they bear children, though their offspring does add to an inheritance" – "ancillarum etiam partus et partum partus quamquam fructus non existimantur, quia non temere ancillae eius rei causa comparantur ut pariant, augent tamen hereditatem".

[119] Cf. Treggiari (1979b) 186–88.

regularly allowed to engage in *contubernium*, a de facto marriage bond that was recognized by all but the law, since slaves did not have the legal capacity to marry.[120] Whereas it cannot be excluded that some slave-owners allowed such unions out of the sheer goodness of their hearts, it will not have been easy to establish a slave family.[121] There is some evidence to suggest that consent to *contubernia* was part of a reward system to increase labour productivity, which would make it a strategic move on the part of the master(s).[122] Moreover, we should consider the fact that the dynamics of the slave population simply came with the phenomenon of slave family formation and slave infants. That process may not necessarily have been easy to control within a large household, even if the owners had wanted to. Perry emphasizes that slaves' sexuality and reproduction must have been a delicate balancing act of control and resistance between the master and the enslaved.[123]

When slaves engaged in a partnership, more often than not they found a partner within the same *familia*.[124] The following examples are of such *contubernia* between (ex-)slaves from the same household.

CIL 6.33794

Maritimi / Antoniae Drusi l(iberti) / rogatoris // Quintiae / Antoniae Drusi l(ibertae) / cantricis

[Grave] of Maritimus, freedman of Antonia wife of Drusus, questioner.
[Grave] of Quintia, freedwoman of Antonia wife of Drusus, singer.

120 On the legalities and practicalities of *contubernium*, see Treggiari (1991) 52–54, 410–11, and more through her index s.v. *contubernium* and *contubernales*; see also Flory (1978), "Family within *familia*".

121 Broekaert (2019).

122 Bradley (1987a) 50, 51: "permitting marital and familial associations among their slaves could contribute positively to the preservation of social and economic order". Varro *RR* 1.17.5 mentions marriage as a reward for the *vilicus*: "The foremen are to be made more zealous by rewards, and care must be taken that they have a bit of property of their own, and mates from among their fellow-slaves (*coniunctas conservas, e quibus habeant filios*) to bear them children; for by this means they are made more steady and more attached to the place". Translation Hooper and Ash (1934, Loeb Classical Library).

123 Perry (2021) 269 and *passim*.

124 Mouritsen (2013) 54, Table 8, for marriages within the Statilian (and Volusian) households; Edmondson (2011) 347; Flory (1978) 82; Treggiari (1973) on the household of the Volusii (and, in passing, on that of the Statilii). With the approval of both masters, however, a relation could also be maintained over two households – presumably the owner of the male partner would be compensated for the benefit of children resulting from the union, who would automatically be assigned to the *familia* and possessions of the woman's owner; for examples see Rawson (1966).

Maritimus and Quintia both served Antonia Minor, one of the women of the Julio-Claudian family. The juxtaposition of both epitaphs on one memorial plaque suggests that Maritimus and Quintia were partners in a *contubernium*, even if the stone does not record it explicitly. Even if the questioner and singer were not *contubernales*, the existence of other, similar marble plaques juxtaposing husband and wife suggests that they might have been. Leaving no doubts about the nature of the recorded relationship, for example, is *CIL* 6.6342 from the tomb of the Statilii:

> *CIL* 6.6342
>
> Italia quasillaria / vixit ann(os) XX / Scaeva tabellarius Tauri / coniugi suae fecit
>
> Italia, spinning woman. She lived 20 years. Scaeva, *tabellarius* of Taurus set this up to his wife.

Scaeva refers to his deceased partner with the word for a lawful wife, *coniux*, which can only be a reflection of sentiment, not of the status of their relationship.[125] The union of the Dardanians in *CIL* 6.6343 cited earlier is a *contubernium*, too; in their case it is one that may have pre-dated their enslavement, since they were both from the same region. If so, it is an interesting detail that the continuity of their union was allowed for by their masters, again the Statilii.

Accommodating family formation among slaves led to valuable slave offspring and slave families also were a contributing factor tying the freed to their former master's household.[126] There are thus very few reasons why aristocratic masters would be opposed to their slaves and ex-slaves forming families of their own. Especially where it concerns domestic urban slavery rather than chattel slavery, the sources indicate that there was no lack of opportunity for slaves to form a family. This, therefore, cannot have been a limiting factor on slave fertility.[127] *Contubernia* effectually brought an extra demographic factor into play for the household, and could lead to families branching out widely among the servile population of the *domus*.[128]

[125] *CIL* 10.3957 quoted above is another example. Treggiari (1979b) 195 (with refs.) points out that even the jurists sometimes use *uxor* rather than the correct *contubernalis*.
[126] This chapter, above; Mouritsen (2013) 55 also suggested as much.
[127] Harris (1980) proffers this as one of the main arguments that would lower slave fertility (according to the addenda to the reprint (Harris (2011) 108), he still agrees with his earlier argument).
[128] Edmondson (2011) 347 notes that "house-bred slaves (*vernae*) might well have had a number of aunts, uncles and cousins", with examples at 348: a maternal uncle (*avunculus*, commemorated in *CIL* 6.6469), and a paternal uncle (*patruus*, commemorator in *CIL* 6.6619) whose niece and nephew were with them in the household of the Statilii.

Slave families and *vernae* were therefore a common phenomenon, certainly within elite *domus* of the city. However, this does not mean that slave reproduction alone was enough to fulfil the demand for slaves – the previous section already underlined the evidence for other sources of slaves.

Those inclined to tone down the importance of home-born slaves as a source of slaves have adduced skewed sex ratios as a major limiting factor on slave reproduction: there were too few slave women.[129] More male than female slave labourers are attested; it is not unlikely that the slaves who were bought in the slave market were chiefly young adult males; and it has been argued that although foundlings perhaps were more likely to be girls, the boys were more likely to be brought up.[130] It becomes difficult to discard entirely the suggestion that men were in the majority among the slave population. Scheidel forcefully advocates that there were as many slave women as there were men, however, and that the sex ratios will have balanced out by the time of the early empire.[131]

I would argue that the solution to maintaining slave fertility, despite a slight misbalance in sex ratio, lies predominantly in the distinctive life course of men and women. By analogy with the general marriage pattern, female slaves undoubtedly 'married' earlier than men, and were more likely to remarry and balance out the marriage market; 'marriage' here always meaning the quasi-marital form of *contubernium*.[132] Add to that the fact that women probably were manumitted later than men (see below) and that, as a result, most of their children were in effect born as slaves, and the sex ratio becomes less of a 'problem'. And there were other solutions that would support fertility rates. Mouritsen's analysis of the households of the Statilii and the Volusii demonstrates a skewed sex ratio for both *domus*. Importantly, it also shows that the 'surplus' of males – slave, freed, and free – was not necessarily celibate, because not infrequently they were married to women from outside the household.[133] The incidence of inscriptions that attest to unions between freed slaves with distinct *gentilicia* also supports the suggestion that there were slaves who maintained their 'marriage bond' over two different households.[134] It will also become clear (below) that a large number of individuals were employed in childcare, which underlines

129 Especially Harris (1980); and Harris (1999) 69–72.

130 Male slaves predominating in the market, e.g. Mouritsen (2013) 58; De Ligt and Garnsey (2012) 86. Helpfully contextualizing the gender of *expositi* with references: Evans Grubbs (2013) 90–92.

131 Scheidel (2005a) 71–73; Scheidel (2011b) 307–8.

132 The general marriage pattern is discussed in Chapter 3 above.

133 Mouritsen (2013) 53–55 – the pattern is especially clear for the Volusii, where marriages are better documented: 21 per cent (N = 54) of males married an outsider.

134 Rawson (1966) offers some examples.

a significant presence of infants and older children in the household. In sum, there is no evidence for systematic slave breeding, but procreation was accommodated and perhaps encouraged, because slave children were a welcome side effect of a larger slave *familia*.

The slave members of the family faced considerable insecurity regarding their own biological families; slave parents, spouses, or children could be sold off. The owner need not take the personal lives of his or her slaves into account, dislocating familial bonds. But the slaves' story may not always have been as grim as some scholars would have it.[135] Edmondson notes that there is evidence that now and then the choice was made to sell a nuclear slave family, or a mother and child, together rather than to separate them; presumably this was better for morale than selling off slave children separately.[136] The latter scenario is nevertheless more commonly attested. Upon the death of the master, too, it is likely that the slaves of the household were scattered among heirs, again not necessarily taking into consideration the slave family. Yet there is evidence that slave parents were allowed to keep in touch with their children over two or sometimes more households.[137] Moreover, there are clues that slave-owners who expected their slaves to be sold off or split up upon their death or, like Cicero, for example, upon their exile, were inclined to free more of their slaves in advance.[138] Apparently slave-owners did not always let their personal economic gain preside over more humane considerations. And the slaves of the elite *domus* may well have been the more privileged group in this respect, because of the proximity to their masters.

Foundlings or the purchase of infants

Child slaves were not always born in the household: foundlings and bought infant slaves should also be considered in this context. Most foundlings who were taken up were raised as slaves.[139] Harris has suggested that provincial foundlings – born where life was cheap – were regularly raised to be sold

[135] Harper (2011) 77; and especially Bradley (1987a) 47–80 emphasize implicit insecurity; cf. Flory (1978) 87.

[136] Edmondson (2011) 349–50 n. 44 for references to contracts of sale on papyri; cf. Treggiari (1979b) 196–201, who considers "the legal attitude to slave families [which] became gradually more humane under the empire" (at 196), respecting slave's family bonds.

[137] Rawson (1966) 78–81 for examples of such 'broken' slave families, since, paradoxically, the evidence for broken families itself is proof offor a continued bond. Sigismund-Nielsen (2013) 292–93 adds some useful primary references.

[138] Mouritsen (2011b) 184-85 with references.

[139] Corbier (2001) 66–67; Harris (1980), especially, argues for the importance of abandoned children as a source of slaves.

on the slave market in the city of Rome.[140] Children could be bought at reduced prices: slaves up to the age of eight were available at half the price of an adult slave or less.[141] These children were not always born into slavery. Parallel to self-enslavement, there may also have been parents who sold their free children into slavery, out of practicality perhaps, out of necessity, or in hope of a better future for their newborn than they had to offer.[142] The legal sources are ambiguous towards the practice, as freedom was absolute in Roman law – but every legal obstacle to child (or self-)sale seems to have had a way around it, including a fictional 'exposure' of the infant so that the buyer could claim not to have been aware of its free status.[143] It presumably was a profitable arrangement for both seller and buyer.

Raising a foundling or buying a slave infant may well have been an attractive investment, not just for slave-traders but also for an individual household. An infant was much less costly than an adult slave, both in price of purchase and in cost of maintenance. As with home-born slaves, the cost of raising an infant is more gradual than buying an older slave for a substantial sum to be covered all at once. The possibility that some preferred such gradual payment should not be underestimated. The total cost of raising a foundling seems to have been roughly similar to the price of a young adult slave; moreover, these very young individuals would be raised in the household, and they could perhaps reach the same informal status that was awarded to the *vernae* who were lauded for their alleged loyalty.[144]

There was a risk to the investment, as infant mortality in particular was notoriously high in ancient Rome.[145] A one-year-old had already lived through the most hazardous times, however, and at the age of five the original life expectancy of around 25 years at birth may have been raised to 40. Perhaps, then, it was smarter to buy a slightly older slave child. Apparently, however, the life of a child slave and his or her prospective earnings were worth the gamble to many. Although it would be a while before labour output would reach its maximum potential, children did put

140 Harris (2011) 87.

141 E.g. Diocletian's Prices Edict of AD 301, 29.1–7 lists 15,000 for a male or 10,000 denarii for a female slave up to the age of eight, compared to 30,000 (male) or 25,000 (female) for slaves aged 16–40; cf. Scheidel (1996); Scheidel (2005b).

142 Scheidel's (1997) 164–65 model for the slave population predicts that one mother in five (in one scenario even one in three) bore a child that would become a slave through exposition, a number he then dismisses as unrealistic; Scheidel works with an attrition rate among *expositi* of 33 per cent.

143 Silver (2011) 80–81, 83, 107–8, with references to various legal sources.

144 Saller (2013) 73 n. 5 offers a very rough calculation of investment in a female foundling in Roman Egypt, compared to buying an older female slave.

145 Parkin (2013) 46–50 provides a sophisticated account of the available models and numbers, and forms the reference for the numbers in this paragraph.

in their labour from a very early age onwards.[146] Raising children as slaves was economically rational.

Inheritance

Relocating slaves or acquiring slaves through an inheritance, finally, should probably not be considered as a conscious policy, even if we allow for the possibility that a few masterminds or inheritance hunters did make plans for when their rich aunt, or they themselves, passed away.[147] Although not technically the result of economic strategizing, this way of acquiring slaves may well have been quite common in a high-mortality regime.[148] With the passing of an aristocrat, the number of slaves to be relocated could be substantial. It is unlikely that this posed much of a problem: a son or daughter already made use of that very slave *familia* living in the same *domus*, and if that did not work out slaves could be freed or sold if they were unwelcome in the household – with all due considerations of the factors already discussed above under the heading of buying and selling.

Alternatively, testamentary manumission could provide the heir with a freedman, rather than a slave. From the perspective of the deceased master, this had the benefit of not missing out on the slave's services during his lifetime. Making up a will required a delicate balance between benefiting the heir on the one hand and the (ex-)slave on the other, which is why testamentary manumission often specified certain obligations of the freedman to the heir, sometimes including economic contributions such as *operae*.[149] The *lex Fufia Caninia* of 2 BC specified a maximum for the number or percentage of slaves that could be manumitted by will, which could conceivably also be understood as a contribution to help maintain the balance. It should be recalled also that the patron often was heir to a substantial part of a freedman's property, particularly when the freedman had no (freeborn) children.[150] Moreover, since there is sufficient evidence for the continued bonds between patrons and freedmen – in non-elite and elite

146 *Dig.* 7.7.6.1 (Ulpian) notes that slaves counted as productive from age five onwards; cf. Laes (2011a) 165 for this and other references to the value of slave child labour.

147 Or those wanting to win imperial favour, Penner (2012) 128.

148 Penner (2012) 125–30 offers a very interesting analysis tracing the origins and circulation of inherited slaves in the Julio-Claudian *domus* through *agnomina*; cf. Mouritsen (2013) 60 n. 53.

149 Because of this delicate balancing act, Mouritsen (2011b) 180–85, esp. 182, argues that testamentary manumission was probably fairly limited.

150 Mouritsen (2011b) 238: "Freedmen were expected to consider their patrons in their wills, and if they failed to do so and died without direct natural heirs, the patron could claim half the estate (from Augustus onwards)". The converse – freedmen as heirs to their patron – was not uncommon either, see ibid 240–42 and Chapter 3 above.

families alike – it can safely be said that inheriting a freedman was in many ways as desirable as inheriting a slave.

That on occasion an inheritance of slaves and freedmen did result in economic strategizing, and that there were economic advantages involved, is suggested by Appian. One of the strategizing masterminds who was not certain of his inheritance of freedmen, because he was not a biological son of the deceased he was to inherit from, was Octavian Augustus. In an interesting passage Appian suggests why Octavian would have wanted the people to confirm his adoption by Caesar in accordance with the *lex curiata*:[151]

> Appian. *BC.* 3.13 (94)
>
> Γαΐῳ δ' ἦν τά τε ἄλλα λαμπρὰ καὶ ἐξελεύθεροι πολλοί τε καὶ πλούσιοι, καὶ διὰ τόδ' ἴσως μάλιστα ὁ Καῖσαρ ἐπὶ τῇ προτέρᾳ θέσει, κατὰ διαθήκας οἱ γενομένῃ, καὶ τῆσδε ἐδεήθη.
>
> Among the other splendid accessories of Caesar was a large number of freedmen, many of them rich, and this was perhaps the principal reason why Octavian wanted the adoption by a vote of the people in addition to the former adoption which came to him by Caesar's will.

Octavian wanted to be absolutely certain that his (testamentary) adoption by Caesar was publicly accepted, because – according to Appian – he wanted to profit from the large and, so it is poignantly added, wealthy freed entourage of Caesar. Even though political legitimacy was obviously the most important factor in the reconfirmation of Octavian's adoption, it is striking that Appian singles out this very point.

In sum, it is clear that the decision to acquire new slaves or to sell them was based on economic as well as cultural considerations. The same is true for manumission, which has been the subject of incessant debate among historians and which, because of the complexity of the matter, deserves to be dealt with in a separate section.

Changing slaves to freedmen: manumission

> Why did Roman masters free so many slaves? At first sight, it seems amazing. Slaves cost money. Skilled or talented slaves apparently stood the best chance of securing their freedom, and they cost a lot of money.[152]

Hopkins sought to explain the economic rationality behind manumission and came up with an answer that was as elegant as it was plausible: he

[151] Appian. *BC* 3.13 (94). Translation H. White (1913 Loeb Classical Library).
[152] Hopkins (1978) 117.

argued that slaves generally bought their own freedom, which allowed the owner to buy a replacement.[153] A spectacular first-century inscription from Asisi would seem to support this view:

> ***CIL*** **11, 5400 = *ILS* 7812**
>
> P(ublius) Decimius P(ubli) l(ibertus) Eros / Merula medicus clinicus chirurgus / ocularius VIvir / hic pro libertate dedit HS L(milia) / hic pro seviratu in rem p(ublicam) / dedit HS II(milia) / hic in statuas ponendas in / aedem Herculis dedit HS XXX(milia) / hic in vias sternendas in / publicum dedit HS XXXVII(milia) / hic pridie quam mortuus est / reliquit patromoni(i) / HS DCCC(milia?)
>
> Publius Decimius Eros Merula, freedman of Publius, clinical ophthalmologist, septemvir. For his freedom he gave 50,000 HS; for his sevirate he gave 2,000 HS to the commonwealth; for the placement of a statue in the temple of Hercules he donated 30,000 HS; for the paving of roads he gave 37,000 HS into the public treasury; on the day that he dies he will bequeath 800,000(?) HS from his patrimony.

The price Merula paid for his freedom would be more than enough to buy a new slave – but would it be enough to purchase an experienced ophthalmologist?

Such rare incidences aside, Hopkins's view has only limited support in the evidence. Mouritsen concluded that, in the end, there is no simple economic explanation.[154] This sums up the difficulty of understanding the economics of manumission in twenty-first-century terms: manumission does not appear to adhere to any economic rule. Even if the motivations for freeing slaves were not, were not entirely, or were not even predominantly economically rational, however, freedmanship certainly was an important factor in Roman labour relations.

Freedom is considered to have been the ultimate reward for slaves. In terms of economics, manumission was a positive incentive for slaves, particularly, or so it was argued, for those in "care-intensive" jobs: occupations that required initiative and responsibility from the slave, and that were difficult to supervise.[155] A reward system built around the prospect of freedom can only have functioned if manumission was not granted

[153] Hopkins (1978) 126–31.

[154] Mouritsen (2011b) 202: "The Roman system of manumission gave owners considerable scope for rewarding slaves irrespective of their age, gender, and occupation. The result is a picture that does not conform to any narrow economic logic".

[155] Scheidel (2008) with reference to the work of Fenoaltea (1984); Hawkins (forthcoming). Frequent manumission is also crucial to Temin's (2004) 522 understanding of an integrated labour market.

indiscriminately, which means either that slaves working in these positions stood a better chance of being freed than others, or that they were freed at an earlier age, or both. The evidence, however, is not systematic enough to be able to support either of these scenarios. There are a few attestations of very young freedmen: Lucius Anicius Felix, a fine tailor (*vestiarius tenuarius*) only four years old, was freed – though this was probably a case of deathbed manumission. There is also evidence to the contrary. Seventy-year-old Oriens, a tailor (*sarcinator*) from Tarentum, was probably still a slave, judging from his single name.[156]

The fragmentary nature of the ancient evidence, and the biases that it entails, do not allow modern scholars to establish the frequency of manumission with any certainty. With Mouritsen I hold that manumission was probably "both very common and very selective".[157] Manumission was not for everyone.[158] It remains to be seen whether manumission was frequent enough to be a strong incentive for self-sale.[159] There does not appear to be a clear pattern as to which slaves were freed and which were not.[160] One of the more convincing selection criteria, however, appears to have been the opportunity to stand out in the eyes of the master – which provided an advantage for slaves in the domestic context of large urban families in comparison with those working on a rural estate.[161] That particular criterion leveled the chances of manumission, which could potentially have functioned as an added labour incentive: "all had a chance and no one was formally beyond hope".[162]

Mouritsen postulated that manumission of the domestic staff of the Volusii and Statilii was granted on the assumption that the new freedman did not leave the household. By implication, as the author points out, manumission became a nominal gesture of very little practical consequence to the slaves, which would take away much of its economic function as a positive labour incentive.[163] The household *columbaria* of the Volusii and the

156 *CIL* 6.6852 (Felix) and *AE* 1972, 111 (Oriens).

157 Mouritsen (2011b) 140. Mouritsen provides a useful survey of past scholarship on the frequency of manumission at 120–41. At 131 he complains, "Given the state of our evidence, most scholars have remained cautious about the rate of manumission, merely suggesting that many slaves had a 'good chance', *vel sim.*".

158 Interestingly, manumission in Roman Egypt *was* virtually universal. Tacoma (2006) 257 with reference to the data in Bagnall and Frier (2006).

159 As Silver (2011) 92–93 would have it.

160 Mouritsen (2011b) Chapter 5 on manumission, at 120–205.

161 E.g. Mouritsen (2013) 59–60.

162 Mouritsen (2011b) 200.

163 Mouritsen (2013) 58–61, at 58: "The high rate of manumission, the commemoration of freedmen alongside other family servants, and the extensive use of *vicarii* all point in that direction", and at 61: "Manumission was 'rational' in the sense that it

Statilii show a freed population of 32 per cent and 46 per cent respectively, suggesting that "between a quarter and a third of the household may have been freed at any time". This matches with an overall manumission rate of more than 50 per cent for slaves over the age of 30. Considering the limited practical effect of manumission if freed slaves did indeed maintain their own jobs in the household, Mouritsen suggests that the chances of manumission for the Volusian and Statilian slave staff may well have been better than for others.[164] High manumission rates, however, should also be postulated for Herculaneum, judging from the album, though the exact numbers are still subject to debate.[165] Mouritsen suggests a 'life stage' model in which slave-born children took the place of parents who could subsequently be freed – thus strengthening continuing ties with their patron.[166] Such a strategy would turn a potential loss of labour power into a double gain.

From an elite owner's perspective, manumission as a strategy to battle the risks of a fluctuating market or to create a flexible workforce is unlikely to have played the part it may have done for the non-elite households of Chapter 3.[167] The manumission tax of 5 per cent will not have posed an obstacle to a wealthy master either.[168] In the context of the elite *domus*, cultural considerations were just as important as strictly monetary concerns, if not more so. There was social capital in having freedmen. Freedmen brought name recognition, for example, and throngs of dependent freedmen at one's door for the morning *salutatio* can only have been an impressive sight.[169] Even the manumission of a slave on his or her deathbed was perhaps not merely a humanitarian and emotional act, but potentially also an opportunity for "social ostentation".[170] Ancient authors also make a number of (disapproving) references to the idea that slaves sometimes were freed by will only to ensure a good following in the funerary procession.[171] Whereas we should be careful not to caricaturize this solely as spendthrift of the elite, we may safely concur that "[t]he notion

involved limited losses for the owner, but that does not entail it was therefore part of a logical system of rewards and incentives for slaves performing particularly responsible economic roles".

164 Mouritsen (2013) 46–47, quote at 53; cf. Garnsey and De Ligt (2016) 80 n. 29 for the implications of Mouritsen's numbers on general manumission rates.

165 De Ligt and Garnsey (2019); Mouritsen (2019).

166 Mouritsen (2019) 228.

167 With reference to the work of Hawkins (forthcoming); and Hawkins (2021) Chapter 3.

168 The tax would not apply in case of informal manumission, Lopez Barja de Quiroga (1998) 160.

169 The possibility of Veturius as a brand name was explored above.

170 Suggested by Mouritsen (2011b) 187, with references to some literary sources of deathbed manumission.

171 Mouritsen (2011b) 184 with references in n. 295.

of 'profitable' manumission would have been out of tune with the ideology of the Roman elite".[172]

Human capital

The high degree of specialization and job differentiation in Roman Italy suggests significant investment in human capital. Scholars have argued that opportunities for job training were particularly good for slaves, especially so for the slaves in elite households. Indeed, skilled professions are attested chiefly for slaves and for ex-slaves. Skilled slaves and ex-slaves are a logical result of slave education: because human capital is not transferable, skills remain with the slave upon manumission. This is why the supposedly widespread access to education during slavery is considered to be one of the economic advantages of being a freedman.[173] It is an open question whether it was so expedient that a freeborn pauper should want to sell himself into slavery in the hope of a better life.[174] Temin takes these notions one step further and states that self-sale was "like the process of apprenticeship in early modern Europe".[175] To my mind, however, that is pushing the argument too far.

The interpretation of job training as a slave prerogative has given rise to the idea that skilled labour can be equated with slave labour:

> The demand for skilled workers was met by the importation of slaves from abroad or the training of slaves bred in the household (*vernae*). *Ingenui* who were not born into a craft had little prospect of acquiring the skills necessary to compete with slaves.[176]

Although Garnsey explicitly mentions the possibility of free artisans who were "born into a craft", in this quotation he emphasizes the point that skilled labourers were often captives who were already experienced in a trade, or home-born slaves who were taught in the household.[177]

To what extent were schooling and job training really the prerogative of slaves? Did the freeborn have "little prospect of acquiring skills necessary to compete" with them? Surely the evidence for freeborn artisans, and

172 Mouritsen (2011b) 196. On testamentary manumission: Gai. *Inst.* 1.42–43 specifies that no more than 100 slaves may be freed in one will.

173 Treggiari (1969b) 87; Mouritsen (2011b) 219; Verboven (2012b) 94.

174 Cf. Silver (2011); Ramin and Veyne (1981).

175 Temin (2004) 526.

176 Garnsey (1980) 44; cf. Mouritsen (2011b) 219, esp. n. 63: "There is little evidence that more responsible or specialist functions were filled with hired labour".

177 Burford (1972); cf. Park (1918) 49, 88–89, who seems to adhere to this scenario also for unskilled labourers.

the representation of freeborn children in apprenticeships in the previous chapter, count for something. Nevertheless, investment in the human capital of slaves deserves close examination in its own right.[178]

Investing in slaves' education seems to have made economic sense, since skilled slaves apparently were a precious commodity. The product they were responsible for was worth more, and they would typically command higher prices in the market.[179] The jurist Paul refers to a case in which a skilled workman was commissioned by a friend to buy a slave apprentice, who was afterwards sold for double the original price.[180] Likewise, the slave chapter in Diocletian's Prices Edict includes a clause that a skilled slave could be sold for up to twice the standard price for a slave of the same age and gender.[181] According to Plutarch, the elder Cato allowed his slaves to buy slaves and train them for a year, with the specific goal of selling them at a profit.[182] Conversely, Crassus personally invested heavily in the education of his slaves and benefited from their labour himself, again going by Plutarch's account.[183] Moreover, it is unlikely that elite *domus* were capable of replacing all of their skilled personnel with home-taught individuals. Death, illness, and various other factors that necessitated replacement could not always have been planned for, so there was no way to ensure that a replacement was at the ready.[184] Hence there must have been quite a market for skilled labour, which meant that there was also a demand for skilled slaves.

Household schools and household schooling

The argument for the training of slaves within larger *domus* comes mainly from various references to the so-called *paedagogium*.[185] A *paedagogium* seems to have been an in-house school for slave boys that was part of some larger households. It is best described as a 'page-school', something Columella refers to as "training-schools for the most contemptible vices – the seasoning of food to promote gluttony and the more extravagant serving of courses".[186]

178 The articles by Booth (1979); Forbes (1955); and Mohler (1940) are still relevant.

179 Saller (2013) 78; Mouritsen (2011b) 219: "The slaves' status as property meant their value could be improved".

180 *Dig.* 17.1.26.8.

181 Edict 29.8, cited above; cf. Col. *RR.* 3.3.8 (first century AD), estimating the price of a skilled vine dresser at 6,000–8,000 sesterces, roughly three or four times the price of an adult slave.

182 Plut. *Cato* 21.7.

183 Plut. *Crass.* 2.4–6; cf. Saller (2013) 78: "Plutarch's phrase *organa empsucha* might be translated, with some license, as 'human capital'".

184 Mouritsen (2013) 58, 60, quoted above.

185 Mohler (1940); Forbes (1955); Keegan (2013) 73–75.

186 Forbes (1955) 335; Columella 1 praef. 5: "contemptissimorum vitiorum officinae,

These boys were pretty and well-dressed 'pet' slaves, home-born *vernae* in particular.

The evidence on these page-schools is not so straightforward, however. A reference to the *paedagogium* in the *Letters* of Pliny the Younger is exemplary in the lack of information it provides:

> Plin. *Ep.* 7.27.13
>
> Puer in paedagogio mixtus pluribus dormiebat: venerunt per fenestras (ita narrat) in tunicis albis duo cubantemque detonderunt, et qua venerunt recesserunt. Hunc quoque tonsum sparsosque circa capillos dies ostendit.
>
> A boy slept in the *paedagogium*, in among many others: two figures in white tunics came through the windows (so he says) and shaved the sleeping boy, and went back the way they came. The day shows this boy bald and amidst scattered locks of hair.[187]

We are informed that many boys slept over in the *paedagogium*, which is why Mohler takes it to be a kind of boarding school.[188] Unfortunately Pliny offers no further details as to what goes on in the *paedagogia*.

The remains of two archaeological structures in Rome have been nominated as a possible locus for the imperial *paedagogium*: one on the Caelian Hill, one on the Palatine Hill. In an analysis of graffiti from the Palatine *paedagogium*, Keegan attempts to demonstrate that slave boys were educated in reading and writing.[189] It is the only evidence that suggests that the *paedagogium* is "where urban slave children were taught the elements of letters and numbers, as well as the finer arts of elegant domestic service".[190] Keegan's tentative suggestion is that the *paedagogiani* may even have had the opportunity to learn a job,[191] because a *custos*, *ianitor* (both doorkeepers), *opifer* (helper),[192] and *perfusor*

gulosius condiendi cibos et luxuriosius fericula struendi". Translation Ash, Loeb Classical Library.

187 Plin. *Ep.* 7.27.13; I translated *ostendit* as a *praesens historicum*, in accordance with the analysis of the narrative modes in Pliny 7.27 by Kroon (2002). See ibid., 196, for the probability of reading *ostendit* as historical present rather than perfect.

188 Mohler (1940) 270.

189 Keegan (2013) 75–78. Keegan brings out the "educational heterogeneity" of the graffiti about 10 per cent exhibits "a certain grade of instruction corresponding suggestively to the use of the building as a *paedagogium*". Ibid., 76. This educational heterogeneity is then interpreted as a reflection of "the process of learning to write".

190 Saller (2013) 78. The assumption that language and arithmetic were also taught in the *paedagogium* is widespread: Mohler (1940); Forbes (1955).

191 Keegan (2013) 79–81.

192 Keegan (2013) 81 thinks that this is a slave who provided medical aid, which would make it a highly skilled job. At ibid. n. 40 he admits that literally the word

(bath servant)[193] are identified in the scribbles. Whereas I am willing to accept that some or even most boys obtained a very basic literacy, I do not think that this necessarily happened in the *paedagogium* (see below). Moreover, the occupations mentioned are few and unskilled, and so I remain unconvinced that any systematic job training took place in the *paedagogium*. Having said that, Keegan is, of course, right in his more general observation that the boys were prepared for "personal service at close quarters to the emperor, his family, and the imperial retinue of aristocratic and equestrian retainers".[194] In my opinion, the remainder of Keegan's article reads mostly like a confirmation of Columella's prejudices towards the *paedagogium* as a "training school for the most contemptible vices" – such as they were in Columella's interpretation.

The foregoing discussion raises the question how widespread and how influential the *paedagogium* as an educational institution really was. If this was indeed "antiquity's most systematic and durable plan for educating slave children",[195] then Roman plans for slave education in general do not appear to have been either systematic or durable. Students from the *paedagogium* are attested almost exclusively for the imperial household.[196] The archaeological evidence is for the imperial *paedagogia*, and it should be underlined that the identification of these structures as a *paedagogium* is less than secure.

Many of the elite households included a so-called *paedagogus* (male or female), and it is of course tempting to connect *paedagogi* as teachers to a *paedogogium* – in the sense of school. There is, however, no indication for *paedagogi* in a *paedagogium*, or for a *paedagogium* in the households where a *paedagogus/-a* is attested. Moreover, the occupation of *paedagogus* is not so easy to define.

Apuleius records a *paedagogus* "in the classic role of escorting a boy to and from school".[197] Lucius the Ass recalls the story of the wife of a town councillor, who is mother to an older stepson, and her own boy (of whom it is said that he is over 12 years old). She tries to seduce her stepson and – when the young man does not give in – plans to poison him with the help of her slave:

means 'aid-bringer'. I should like to add it also means 'helper', which may be no more than a generic term for a trusted slave. I know of no other attestation of *opifer* as a job title.

193 A slave who pours water over bathers.

194 Keegan (2013) 81.

195 Forbes (1955) 336.

196 Keegan (2013) 73–75.

197 Bradley (2012) 85, talking about Ap. *Met.* 10.5.1–4. The reference in Bradley is erroneous (he writes 10.4.5).

Apul. *Met.* 10.5.1–4

Ac dum de oblationis opportunitate secum noxii deliberant homines, forte fortuna puer ille iunior, proprius pessimae feminae filius, post matutinum laborem studiorum domum se recipiens, prandio iam capto sitiens repertum vini poculum, in quo venenum latebat inclusum, nescius fraudis occultae continuo perduxit haustu. Atque ubi fratri suo paratam mortem ebibit, examinis terrae procumbit, ilicoque repentina pueri pernicie paedagogus commotus ululabili clamore matrem totamque ciet familiam.

But while those two were conferring as to when to offer him the wine, fate chanced to intervene. The younger boy, the stepmother's own son, came home from morning school for his lunch, and feeling thirsty found the wine, already imbued with poison. Ignorant of the danger lurking there, he drank it in one great gulp, and swallowing the venom destined for his brother fell lifeless to the ground. His servant [*paedagogus*], terrified at this sudden collapse, raised a cry of horror that brought the mother running along with the whole household.[198]

The boy survives and the stepmother and her slave are punished (*Met.* 10.11–12). For our purposes we may focus on the fact that the younger son, not actually that young any more, apparently was accompanied to school by his ***paedagogus***, which surely means that the ***paedagogus*** was not the boy's teacher.[199] Indeed the frequent occurrence of ***paedagogi*** in the epigraphs suggests that they were the more common childminders. The same story does contain an earlier mention of the elder brother's 'old teacher' (*educator senex, Met.* 10.4.5), however, which indicates that this family had access to a teacher, who may or may not have lived in with them. The linguistic connection between ***paedagogium*** and ***paedagogi*** is thus misleading.

Attending to children is, in fact, one of the most common professions attested overall for both men and women. The household of the Statilii included five ***paedagogi***; the household of the Volusii employed three – plus an additional four nurses and two *grammatici*.[200] Thamyris, slave footservant

[198] Translation A.S. Kline, poetryintranslation.com.

[199] A witty reference to this escort function of the paedagogue can be found in Terence's *Phormio*: a young man called Phaedria falls in love with a slave girl he cannot have and can therefore only follow her around, v. 86: "in ludum ducere et redducere"; later one of the characters jokingly refers back to this when asking about Phaedria: "What of the pedagogue of that lute-girl?" ("quid paedagogus ille qui citharistriam …?", v. 144).

[200] Hasegawa (2005) 36, Table 3.4, lists childminders for the households of the Statilii, Volusii, Livia, and Iunii. In this context it is perhaps interesting to note that Mouritsen (2013) considers the Volusian tomb to be the most complete *columbarium*, and therefore the most representative.

of Livia, "gives an urn" (*dat ollam*) to his *magister* Cnismus.[201] Although the exact functions of the various childminders are not always clear, their considerable presence in the aristocratic *domus* demonstrates that the resources for in-house schooling were present. Childminders themselves proudly advertised that they looked after elite children – although the epigraphic evidence suggests that both the children of their elite owners and home-born slave boys and girls were left in their care.[202] A single name for pedagogue and charge, for example, suggests servile status for both, as in *CIL* 6.9748 and *CIL* 6.33894:

> ***CIL* 6.9748**
>
> Hilario / paed(agogo) / Celeris
>
> To Hilarius, pedagogue of Celer.
>
> ***CIL* 6.33894**
>
> D(is) M(anibus) / Rufi qui / vixit an(nos) XIIX / m(enses) VII d(ies) X / Nicepiorus / paedag(ogus) b(ene) m(erenti) f(ecit)
>
> To the divine spirits. (Grave of) Rufus. He lived 18 years, 7 months and 10 days. Nicepiorus his pedagogue set this up for him, for he was worthy.

This scattered evidence appears to support the assumption that young urban slaves – both male and female – may have been taught the basics of reading, writing, and perhaps arithmetic.[203] Their primary education need not have taken place within a *paedagogium* or even within the household: Booth adduces literary evidence that makes it plausible that slaves also attended the ordinary street schools of the *ludi magister* alongside freeborn boys and girls.[204] Schooling could be expensive, but it was probably well within the means of the elite: Diocletian's Price Edict lists a price of 75 denarii per pupil per month for a *grammaticus*. At a daily wage of 25 denarii a day for unskilled and 50 for skilled work, the investment would soon pay itself back.

A basic education therefore appears to have been regularly available to slaves, but even though it is clear that there were virtually no practical obstacles, it is impossible to say how many actually received such an education.

201 *CIL* 6.4006.

202 Bradley (1991) 37–75 on (male) child attendants of slave children as well as aristocratic children, with appendix of inscriptions from Rome.

203 Most extensively: Mohler (1940).

204 Booth (1979) refers specifically to Martial and Petronius, of which Martial *Epig.* 10.62 is most convincing; on the *ludi magister* see e.g. Laes and Strubbe (2008) 75.

Arts and crafts

It is clear from the evidence that some slaves were skilled beyond a basic education, and were trained in the arts or crafts. From the perspective of the wealthy owner, one option was, of course, simply to buy skilled slaves on the market – this has already been discussed. All specialized slave artisans nevertheless must have learnt their trade in one of two ways: informally within the household itself, or through an apprenticeship. The following sections deal with both options for investing in the education of artisans.

Informal job-training

Although there is no direct evidence for slaves learning their trade within the aristocratic household, it can be made plausible.[205] From Cicero's correspondence we know of his friend Atticus' sophisticated copy shop. Nepos addresses what was exceptional in Atticus' business, however, and that had everything to do with his slaves:

> **Nep. *Att.* 13.3–4**
>
> Usus est familia, si utilitate iudicandum est, optima; si forma, vix mediocri. Namque in ea erant pueri litteratissimi, anagnostae optimi et plurimi librarii, ut ne pedissequus quidem quisquam esset, qui non utrumque horum pulchre facere posset, pari modo artifices ceteri, quos cultus domesticus desiderat, apprime boni. (4) Neque tamen horum quemquam nisi domi natum domique factum habuit; quod est signum non solum continentiae, sed etiam diligentiae.
>
> He kept an establishment of slaves [*familia*] of the best kind, if we were to judge of it by its utility, but if by its external show, scarcely coming up to mediocrity; for there were in it well-taught youths, excellent readers, and numerous transcribers of books, insomuch that there was not even a footman [*pedisequus*] that could not act in either of those capacities extremely well. Other kinds of artificers [*artifices ceteri*], also, such as domestic necessities require, were very good there (4) yet he had no one among them that was not born and instructed [*factum*] in his house; all which particulars are proofs, not only of his self-restraint, but of his attention to his affairs.[206]

The slave *familia* of Atticus is praised in all but its beauty (*forma*). Their excellence is explained as a direct result of the fact that they were born, raised, and trained in the household – a token of Atticus' *continentia* and *diligentia*, presented by Nepos as the qualities that set Atticus apart in a

[205] Mouritsen (2011b) 212.
[206] Translation Rev. J.S. Watson (1853).

positive way. The passage thus underlines the existence of job training within the household, but it also points to the fact that this was not necessarily the standard.

While Nepos' account of Atticus' raising and educating his own slaves in his household might be viewed as recording a laudable exception, the epigraphic evidence supports the practice of home-schooling artisans as well. The family of the Statilii, for example, clearly focused on textile production.[207] Their household included, among others, no less than eight wool spinners (all female), five seamstresses, four fullers, and three weavers (male and female).[208] This can plausibly be read as relatively direct evidence of specialized job training within the elite household. Epigraphic evidence from the *columbaria* is scanty, but the following inscription from the *monumentum Liviae* is suggestive:

> ***CIL*** 6.6376 = ***ILS*** 7416a
>
> Antiocho / magistro / unctores
>
> The masseurs (set up this monument) for their instructor Antiochus

It is not difficult to come up with reasons why a family of aristocrats, or a family of entrepreneurs, should have wanted to train their slaves within the *domus*. The students would soon be able to contribute substantially to the working process, even during the learning process when they had not fully mastered the trade. Their continuous labour contribution would therefore limit the cost of forgone earnings during the time of education, making this type of on-the-job training a more profitable, or at least less costly, way to invest in human capital.

Occupational inscriptions offer additional evidence for informal training, or at least evidence for the education of slaves in the household and of the wide-ranging effects of the *domus* economy. Every job title for a freedman is an indication of his or her job training as a slave. The ties between patrons and freedmen were never completely severed. The overwhelming numbers adduced in this chapter above indicate that many freedmen used to be part of a larger aristocratic household when enslaved.

The continued economic bonds between patron and freedman are unambiguously recorded in an inscription as often as they can be postulated. When fellow freedmen are explicitly ascribed the same occupation, the assumption that it reflects learning on the job in the household of one's

[207] On the Statilii and cloth production, Hasegawa (2005) 39–44.

[208] Most likely to be contemporaneous: the inscriptions are all dated between AD 20 and 97; see Buonocore (1984) 44.

master is surely not too far-fetched.[209] Small groups of three or more *colliberti* commemorated together are a recurrent phenomenon in the occupational inscriptions.[210] The freedmen of the Veturii who worked in the business of purple-dying together were already mentioned in the previous chapter.[211] Similarly, fellow freedmen who were also co-workers are attested for the profession of *thurarius* (incense dealer, *CIL* 6.9934), *gemmarius* (jeweller, *CIL* 6.9435), *ferrarius* (ironsmith, *CIL* 6.9398), *aerarius vascularius* (tableware bronze maker, *CIL* 6.9138), and *vestiarius tenuarius* (fine tailor, *CIL* 6.37826) – and these are just attestations from *CIL* Volume 6. The additional example of the tailors in *CIL* 6.33920 deserves a closer look.[212]

CIL 6.33920

P(ublio) Avillio P(ubli) l(iberto) Menandro patrono / post mortem liberti fecerunt et / sibi {i}<et> qui infra scripti sunt / Avillia P(ubli) l(iberta) Philusa / P(ublius) Avillius P(ubli) l(ibertus) Hilarus / P(ublius) Avillius P(ubli) l(ibertus) Anteros / P(ublius) Avillius P(ubli) l(ibertus) Felix / vest{e}<i>[a]ri(i) de Cermalo minusculo a [3] / sobe[

To Publius Avilius Menander, freedman of Publius, patron. His freedmen set this up after his death, also for themselves, [c.q.] those who are recorded below. Avilia Philusa, freedwoman of Publius; Publius Avilius Hilarus, freedman of Publius; Publius Avilius Anteros, freedman of Publius; Publius Avilius Felix, freedman of Publius. Tailors from the smaller Germalus …

It should be noted that the patron mentioned in this inscription, Menander, was a freedman himself. The other four – three men and a woman – commemorate him in death, while referring to their current workplace on the Germalus.[213] This epitaph is evidence for the continued bonds between patron and freedmen on a somewhat larger scale than the examples in Chapter 3 above. There can be no doubt that all of these freedmen gained their skills in slavery; we may infer that P. Avilius Menander set up his own independent workshop sometime after manumission, or that he became independent upon the death of his master. He continued the business with his own slaves, whom he subsequently freed. Even if Menander's master were still alive, there was no law to prevent competition between freedmen and their former masters: indeed, in this context the law protects

[209] The example of *CIL* 6.9215 discussed in Chapter 3 above is unique in that it designates both freedman and patron (himself a freedman) as axle makers.

[210] Joshel (1992) 128–45 has much to offer on the occupational inscriptions of freedmen artisans and their relations with patron and *colliberti*.

[211] P. 136 with reference to Dixon (2001b).

[212] Also singled out by Joshel (1992) 131–33.

[213] 'Germalus' refers to a part of the Palatine hill.

freedmen's interests.[214] Alternatively, Menander could have continued to work for, or with, his former master after manumission, in which case this example would reflect cooperation and continuation of the family business rather than competition.

A different category of inscriptions records *liberti* – husband and wife – with distinct job titles. Identical *nomina* suggest that they came from the same *familia*; some carry different *nomina*, which illustrates a shared servile history but not in the same household. In most instances couples remained within the shared elite household of origin, as the example of Maritimus and Quintia shows – *CIL* 6.33794 quoted above. Others set up their own household, or at least their own epitaph. The fact that husband and wife had distinct occupations was explained in Chapter 3 by the fact that both had already learnt a trade as slaves in their master's household.[215] This type of epitaph therefore also presents indirect evidence of the *domus* economy.

Apprenticeships

Members of the slave *familia* in a wealthy household could also be apprenticed out rather than home-schooled, just like the slaves from a non-elite family. Twelve out of 50 apprenticeship contracts from Roman Egypt were concluded for slave children.[216] The numbers are too small to base strong arguments on, and it should be noted that slavery in Roman Egypt may have been of a different nature than slavery in the cities of Roman Italy: in Egypt slaves only made up 5 to 10 per cent of the urbanized population, and they are likely to have been mostly household slaves.[217] Seen in that light, 12 slaves out of 50 artisan apprentices is perhaps more than expected.

Within these 12 documents for slave children, there is no apparent discrimination regarding the gender of the child. Their equal representation in apprenticeship contracts notably sets slave girls apart from their freeborn counterparts. It is also remarkable that the documents for slave children are more consistent in terms of the investment than those for freeborn children: slave apprentices generally are paid for their work, save for those in the luxury trades. As a result, the direct and indirect costs of investment in human capital through apprenticeship were mitigated somewhat.

The cost of apprenticing out many slaves could add up, but even so monetary considerations were, or so it must be presumed, less of a problem from the perspective of a wealthy owner than for the non-elite. Therefore

214 Chapter 3 above; Verboven (2012b) 96; Mouritsen (2011b) 212 n. 28.

215 The category is also discussed under the heading of 'independent women' in Chapter 3 above.

216 See Appendix 2 below; Strauss (2017) focuses on slave apprenticeships.

217 Scheidel (2011b) 289–90.

the decision must have rested on more practical considerations. If a household essentially was a textile production unit in itself, it would make no sense to apprentice out another weaver when it was so easily taught at home. More importantly, the point of having a slave entourage in the city for the elite was that the slaves would be conspicuously present in the *domus*, in large numbers and at all times. It was also the most pragmatic way to have slaves multitasking and/or working after hours, both of which appear to have been normal procedure. Whatever the reasons, most lines of reasoning suggest that learning on the job within the aristocratic household production unit apparently took precedence over apprenticeships. I would go so far as to tentatively suggest that the slave apprentices we know of conceivably originated from non-elite households – though this cannot be more than speculation.

Investment in education of slaves

Despite the limited quantity of the surviving sources, it seems possible to conclude that elite slave-owners were prone to investing in slaves who showed potential. In-house schools, on-the-job training, and apprenticeships were all very real options. The direct cost of investing in schooling appears to have been relatively modest, tempered by in-house schooling or job training, so all it took was time and effort; a slave apprentice was regularly – if not always – paid for his or her efforts. Both constructions helped to mitigate the indirect cost of forgone earnings.

In the long run, an educated slave brought many advantages. Education or job training will have exponentially increased the slave's lifetime earnings. Contrary to the freeborn, slaves could not run away with their human capital.[218] Even the human capital of those slaves who were freed remained available to their former owners through various forms of dependence. Saller argues that the elite households were in need of trustworthy managers and overseers in particular: "The large *domus* (households) were the largest private productive units in the early empire, requiring coordination, monitoring and record-keeping".[219] This, according to Saller, will have encouraged them to educate their own future administrators, to make sure that these key positions were filled by individuals who could be trusted because of their strong link with the household. If it were merely a matter of training sufficient numbers of managers and overseers, however, as Saller seems to imply, the education of slaves in the elite *domus* arguably would not have left such a clear record. Quite apart from such considerations of reliability, economic opportunism was probably also an important incentive: this chapter has pointed out

218 Saller (2013) 78.
219 Saller (2013) 78.

that in the market a skilled slave brought in twice the wages, or twice the price, of an unskilled slave. And there certainly was a market for skilled slaves because, as we have seen, the need for a replacement often arose unexpectedly.

To sum up, household slaves were in a good position to receive a basic education and/or some form of job training. That means that in terms of skilled work, the freeborn workforce faced some serious competition from the servile population. At the same time, we have seen that Varro advised farmers on hiring skilled services rather than educating slaves – advice that the non-elite will have followed more broadly and which must have left opportunities for the free skilled worker.[220]

The evidence from *columbarium* tombs

In terms of the occupational inscriptions, the larger household is reflected specifically in the epigraphic material from elite *columbaria*. *Columbaria* are "closed, collective funerary monuments that deposit cremation ashes in urns and niches on their interior walls".[221] 'Elite *columbaria*' more specifically refers to subterranean *columbaria* only. *Columbarium* tombs built above ground form a more diverse tomb type of a later date. Above-ground *columbarium* tombs were geographically more widespread than the subterranean ones, but the above-ground monuments that I know of as a rule were considerably smaller, raising the suspicion that they were perhaps also rather less likely to concern elite households.[222]

The construction of subterranean *columbaria* was a relatively short-lived phenomenon of the first century AD. Many of the tomb chambers were used for only a generation or two, which adds to a coherent picture of the tomb population; some tomb populations are more difficult to analyse in their entirety, however, because the *columbarium* remained in use until the second and third centuries. It is also significant that the existence of *columbarium* tombs was restricted mainly to the capital and its environs.[223]

220 *RR* 1.16.4, cited in Chapter 2 above.

221 Borbonus (2014) 20. Borbonus provides the most extensive study of subterranean *columbaria* to date. Much of the general information that follows was taken from (or corroborated by) his work. At ibid., 18, Borbonus points out that, strictly speaking, *columbarium* refers to one niche only. Technically the tomb should therefore be called '*columbarium* tomb' or '*columbarium* monument', and this I will do. However, *columbarium* has become accepted usage and will be applied here as well. Cf. Bodel (2008) 195–96.

222 To my knowledge there is no comprehensive study of this type of tomb, let alone its epigraphic heritage.

223 Borbonus (2014) 146 ff. for scarce attestations of *columbaria* outside Rome; they do not quite match the definition provided.

This points to urban elite households as part of the specific nature of the city of Rome, which should not come as a surprise: the elite may have clustered in towns more generally, but for the wealthiest senators, there was no place like Rome – so that is where their slave *familiae* resided, and were buried.[224]

It is a fortunate characteristic of the *columbarium* tomb type that many of the deceased who found their final resting place in them received individual commemoration in an epitaph.[225] The inscriptions reveal that these monuments contained the remains chiefly of slaves and ex-slaves from elite households.[226] That is why this material offers an excellent opportunity to study the composition of aristocratic *domus*.

Epigraphic evidence for elite domus *from the columbaria*

Columbarium tomb inscriptions in Joshel's sample make up 21.4 per cent of the occupational inscriptions from the city of Rome (including slave, freed, and free).[227] Because the *columbaria* are exclusive to Rome, that percentage is lower for Roman Italy as a whole. It is likely that the *columbaria* we know of do not encompass all (occupational) inscriptions that originate from an elite household. Ex-slaves in particular, but also slaves, may have been buried outside the household *columbarium*, as the following epitaph seems to illustrate:

> *CIL* 6.9775
>
> Doris Statiliae Mino[ris] / pediseq(ua) / Erotis ad i{m}[n]pediment[a] / vixit an(nos) XXIIII
>
> For Doris, footservant of Statilia the Younger, (companion) of Eros, caretaker of baggage. She lived 24 years.

Even if it was not actually found in the Statilian tomb, there is no doubt in my mind about the affiliations of Doris and Eros. And if the text itself were not clear enough, the editors of *CIL* add that the inscription also appears to have been found near the monument of the Statilii. But not all of the epitaphs for household members buried outside the *columbarium* can be identified as such as easily as this.[228]

224 Rens Tacoma pointed out that there is also the practical matter of tufa, which allowed the building of columbaria in the vicinity of Rome.

225 Cf. Borbonus (2014) 106–9.

226 Borbonus (2014) 1.

227 Joshel (1992) 73.

228 Penner (2013) 27 notes that "of all Livia's slaves and freed slaves attested in the inscriptional evidence, slightly more than half come from the Monumentum Liviae, while the remainder were found elsewhere".

There must also have been several other *domus* of a considerable size that were somewhat less extravagant than the ones we know of. The unique text of *CIL* 14.5306 from Ostia is interesting in this respect.

CIL 14.5306

Agathemeris Manliae ser(va) / [Ac]hulea Fabiae ser(va) ornatrix / [C]aletuche Vergiliae ser(va) ornatrix / Hilara Liciniae [ser(va) orn]atrix / Crheste(!) Corn[eliae] ser(va) ornatrix / Hilara Seiae ser(va) ornatrix / Moscis ornatrix / Rufa Apeiliae ser(va) ornatrix / Chila ornatrix

This is a lead tablet with a list of nine hairdressers. Seven of them are designated *ser(va)*, 'enslaved', and their single, Greek names may suggest slave status for all nine individuals. Although the document is obscure in many other respects, the list suggests to me that all of these women served aristocratic women.[229] For seven of nine *ornatrices* an aristocratic owner is mentioned; only for Moscis and Chila is no mistress recorded and the designation *serva* missing, which may indicate that their status was different somehow.

It is clear that many inscriptions of slaves connected to elite households were also found outside the *columbaria*. Therefore inscriptions connected to elite households are likely to have made up a larger percentage of the occupational inscriptions from the city of Rome than the 21.4 per cent mentioned above. Indeed, Joshel connects 31.6 per cent of all occupational inscriptions from Rome to a private context.[230] Although Joshel's definition of a 'private context' is nowhere made explicit, the pattern in the occupational inscriptions is clear and can be supported even if we just take into account the more secure evidence of the *columbaria* inscriptions. It must be concluded that many Romans were employed in the service of wealthy elite *domus* – particularly, but not exclusively, slaves. These findings match up well with the more general pattern outlined above connecting urban slavery with elite households.

A word of caution is in order, however. The epitaphs from elite household *columbarium* tombs from the city of Rome represent a change in epigraphic habit, a localized "early peak of epigraphic output", that was established because the particular form of a *columbarium* tomb meant that virtually every

229 The lead indicates that it is a curse tablet, also noted by Meiggs (1960) 226 n. 1; in my view this makes Treggiari's (1979a) n. 47 suggestion that the inscription is evidence of a school for hairdressers highly unlikely. The inclusion of Agathemeris in this list indicates to me that she was a hairdresser, too, even if this is not stated explicitly.

230 Joshel (1992) 74.

tomb occupant received an inscription.[231] That peak of epigraphic output and the additional fact that the *columbaria* have been relatively well preserved are reflected in the data. In other words, *columbarium* tombs, and therefore elite households, are over-represented in the epigraphic data. Moreover, it was apparently more common to record professions in *columbaria* inscriptions than in other epitaphs, increasing the prominence of elite staff labourers among the occupational inscriptions.[232] In the monument of the Statilii, for example, no less than 28 per cent of all individuals recorded an occupation. For all *columbaria* combined the percentage is much lower, but still significant at 15.9 per cent.[233] In contrast, it may be recalled that profession was generally recorded in less than 5 per cent of inscriptions. The question how representative the numbers are is ultimately insoluble.

Single-family tombs

If the *columbaria* reflect elite households, the assumption that they were set up by aristocratic heads of family follows naturally: they were viewed as monuments *libertis libertabusque*, so to speak. Contrary to earlier and still influential interpretations along these lines, it has now convincingly been argued that the tombs were most likely set up, or at least organized, by household associations (*collegia*).[234] Emphasis on the agency of *collegia* does not preclude the possibility of (financial) support from an elite patron, just as the earlier interpretations left room for the practical responsibilities of

[231] Borbonus (2014) 108. Borbonus mentions one columbarium near the Sepulcrum Scipionum (his cat. no. 1) where this niche-by-niche identification was planned (there are painted *tabula ansata* under the niches), but this was not executed (they are not filled in); similarly, I noticed that in the smaller columbarium 'of Pomponius Hylas' (nearby) the burials are more numerous than the individuals identified in inscriptions, with coffins under the floor, loose urns added, and so on. The general 'early peak in epigraphic habit' is nevertheless not in doubt.

[232] The various households have been said to demonstrate different preferences for what was recorded on the epitaphs, and so occupation may not be as prominent in every tomb: Treggiari's (1976) 98 observation that "fashions vary from *columbarium* to *columbarium*: job data are prominent in the Statilian tomb and family data in the Volusian. There was little room for both on the standard plaque" is corroborated by Penner (2012). Whereas there may well have been such a thing as *columbarium* fashions, the mention of occupation was relatively prominent in most of them; Borbonus (2014) 128, Table 9; Penner (2012) 157, Figure 10.10; Hasegawa (2005) 32.

[233] Hasegawa (2005) 4, 32, Table 3.1 for 28 per cent of the individuals in the *columbarium* of the Statilii (Chambers N, O, and P combined); cf. Borbonus (2014) 128, Table 9: 28.8 per cent for the Statilii (chamber N), 15.9 per cent on average.

[234] Borbonus (2014) 136 ff.; contra Hasegawa (2005); Patterson (1992) 18; and Purcell (1987), who all stress the importance of patronage. Note that a (household) association may provide for burial, but that does not necessarily imply the existence of *collegia funeraticia*; see Chapter 5 below.

the associations, but I embrace the shift in perspective.[235] That the initiative rested with a burial association rather than with the wealthy patrons would explain why the aristocratic family itself was not included in the tombs, why the monuments were of a relatively modest nature, and, most significantly, why the tombs cannot always be connected to a single elite family, but regularly include slaves and freedmen of several elite masters in one chamber.[236]

The best means of identifying the household(s) represented in a *columbarium* is the nomenclature of the deceased. Borbonus devised a cluster index ("C") of *nomina* for all *columbaria* to analyse this aspect: in the *columbarium* 'of the Statilii' for example, one would expect to find a clustering of the *nomen* 'Statilius'. By measuring the clustering of *nomina* in each tomb, Borbonus ascertains four 'single-household *columbaria*' (with C > 40): the *columbarium* of the Statilii does indeed qualify, and in addition so do the *columbarium* of the Volusii, that of the Iunii Silani, and that of the Arruntii.[237] The case of the Volusii is exceptional because no *columbarium* structure was ever found, but the collection of epitaphs suggests a similar collective household burial arrangement.[238]

Clustering of *nomina* is somewhat less strong in the *columbarium* known as that of Livia (C = 20/21), yet Treggiari feels that "[t]he individual slave-owner whose household staff can be most fully reconstructed is Augustus' widow Livia".[239] In my view it is highly likely that the monument does represent the household of the empress. In this case, however, the cluster index presumably signals the monument's continued use into the third century, which is why it contains imperial slaves and freedmen of later emperors, for example, in addition to members of Livia's domestic staff – thereby lowering the cluster index.[240] Moreover, the larger the monument, the more likely it was to contain 'outsiders', since slaves and freedmen

[235] Cf. Treggiari (1975a) 63 n. 148, who points to the apparent permission of Lucius Noster in some of the Statilian inscriptions, such as *CIL* 6.7370.

[236] Patterson (1992) 18 seems to think that the patron's natural family was buried in the *columbarium* tomb, too, but I know of no evidence for this.

[237] Borbonus (2014) 122: "the values exceeding a 'c' of forty [...] are 'single family columbaria' that accommodated, wholly or predominantly, slaves and freedmen of a single aristocratic household". The monument 'of the Carvilii' has C = 53, but the ten inscriptions also mention others from various families, which is presumably why it is not classified as a single family tomb. The formula for the cluster index is at 248 n. 53.

[238] The same is true for the 'monument' "of the gens Abuccia": Borbonus (2014) 28, cat. no. 17; Hasegawa (2005) 4.

[239] Treggiari (1975a) 48. For an analysis of Livia's domestic staff see especially Treggiari (1975a); but also Treggiari (1973); Treggiari (1975b); Treggiari (1976); Hasegawa (2005).

[240] Borbonus (2014) 175–76. Conversely, there are also servants of Livia in tombs with other imperial servants. Treggiari (1975a) 65 n. 4; Hasegawa (2005) 22.

did not always marry within the household. Even so, their families were regularly included.[241] The following example from the Volusian tomb shows that the family connections could branch out far:

> ***CIL* 6.7290 = *CIL* 6.27557**
>
> [Dis] / Manibus [sacru]m / Primigenius L(uci) Volusi / Saturnini ser(vus) ab hospiti(i)s et / paedagog(us) pueror(um) Charidi cont(ubernali) s(uae) b(ene) m(erenti) / T(itus) Iulius Antigonus gener eius / Spurinniae Niceni Torquatianae / nutrici suae bene merenti / sanctae piae amantissimae / fecerunt sibi et suis posterisq(ue) eor(um)
>
> Sacred to the divine spirits. Primigenius, slave of Lucius Volusius Saturninus, in charge of guests and teacher of the [slave?] children, for Charis, his well-deserving *contubernalis*. Titus Iulius Antigonus his brother-in-law, for Spurinnia Nice Torquatiana, his nurse, a well-deserving, loyal, most amiable woman. They set this up for themselves, their [family] and their descendants.

Apart from two slaves of the household, Primigenius and Charis, the text also includes Antigonus and Torquatiana, who carry the *tria nomina* but were not freedmen of the Volusii. Apparently, Primigenius' right to use the household tomb extended to his wider family, if it could accommodate his brother-in-law Antigonus, and Antigonus' (freeborn?) nurse.

There are thus only five single-family *columbaria* that could potentially give us an indication of the occupational structure of a single household staff.[242] Even single-household tombs do not reflect the occupational structure of a household accurately, however, because the boundaries of who were buried in it and who were not are so blurry. Moreover, it is not certain at all that the epigraphic collection from any one tomb is complete, nor is it always easy to distinguish whether the inscriptions – and therefore the recorded jobs – were contemporaneous or not.

The nomenclature of those buried in single-family *columbaria* indicates that the large majority were part of the dominant household. There

[241] See above for *contubernia* and marriages crossing household boundaries; Mouritsen (2013) 54, Table 8, includes his count of outsider marriages for the *columbaria* of the Volusii and Statilii, for example. It would not be unusual if some of the husband's slaves had relations with some of the wife's slaves and thereby ended up in 'her' columbarium, a practice Treggiari (1975a) 48 identifies for Livia's monument.

[242] It is no coincidence that Sandra Joshel (1992) 194 n. 47 singles out precisely these five single family *columbaria* in her sample: "Only *columbaria* that include individuals predominantly from one *familia* are considered". The five single-family *columbaria* are only mentioned as an example, however, so she probably includes more of the *columbaria* inscriptions.

are many other plausible single-family households, however;[243] even in multi-family tombs, a large group of individuals can often be connected to a larger household.[244] In her study of the *familia urbana*, for example, Kinuko Hasegawa distinguishes 15 groups of *columbaria* inscriptions that can be connected with a known aristocratic family or individual owner.[245] In all likelihood, all *columbarium* inscriptions are representative of the domestic staff of elite households, regardless of whether the 'inhabitants' originate from one household or several households. In order to maintain a clear sense of context, however, it is important to keep in mind that there is a difference between single-family tombs, multi-family tombs, and unconnected attestations of household servants, when discussing the particulars of the large domestic household. Having said that, unrelated individuals were probably a minority.

Occupational differentiation

Many of the occupations recorded for slaves in the *columbaria* are so specific that they make us wonder whether they would have taken up all of the slave's time: Bradley cites the examples of the *ostiarius* (doorkeeper) and *scoparius* (sweeper), but one might also speculate what is the purpose of the nine footservants in the household of Livia.[246] Despite their obvious function as an indication of status, it is unlikely that they were left idle when their work was done, so they will have been engaged in other activities now and then.[247] Some household slaves who are not recorded with a specific job title may have been working for the household itself rather than labouring for the market. Others were perhaps employed in multiple tasks, like jacks of all trades. There are two interesting parallel inscriptions of 'multitasking' slaves, but they are the only such occupational epitaphs I know of.[248] The first inscription is written on an altar from the

[243] Penner (2012) analyses epigraphic data from the five largest columbaria, including not only the Statilii, Volusii, and Livia, but also the *monumentum Marcellae* and the *monumentum filiorum Drusi*.

[244] E.g. the columbarium 'of the Carvilii', or that of the Stertinii. Borbonus (2014) cat. nos 10, 27.

[245] Hasegawa (2005) 5, Table 2.1, lists 16 households, but that of Iunius Silanus is a duplicate entry.

[246] Bradley (1994) 60. For *pedisequi* (male and female) in the household of Livia, see Hasegawa (2005) 33; Treggiari (1973) 75–76, who only lists seven.

[247] Bodel (2011) 326 n. 25 for references. Harper (2011) 103–5, at 103, sees domestic service as "a way of utilizing the extra time and labor of otherwise productive slaves".

[248] But compare also *P. Wisc.* 1.5 (Oxyrhynchus, AD 185), which is the contract of lease for a slave woman, who is leased out to help a weaver with his craft, but who can contractually be called back by her owner to bake bread during the night. There is some evidence of moving from one job to another, for which see elsewhere in this book.

columbarium of the Volusii, and records a freed *capsarius* (carrier of scroll holders) who apparently served also (*idem*) as an *a cubiculo* (bedchamber servant) to "our Lucius". The second is for a freed *a cubiculo et procurator* (bedchamber servant and manager), again to "our Lucius".[249] *Lucius noster* freed both of them.

The fact remains that a great variety of jobs is attested for the slaves of elite households.[250] Harper correctly notes that household "scale and specialization were correlated": certainly, elite households were more wealthy and populous, which enabled specialization.[251] One could also imagine that it would be helpful to distinguish between individuals with the same name, such as Hilarus the doorkeeper, Hilarus the surgeon, and Hilarus the cashier, who were all part of Livia's household.[252] There could be various other reasons for the fact that job titles are prominent in the *columbaria*, however.

Bradley quotes the following passage from Columella to argue that there was a practical side to job specialization, encouraging a slave's pride in the assignment as well as conferring the responsibility for it onto him or her.[253]

Col. *RR* 1.9.5–6

[...] ne confundantur opera familiae, sic ut omnes omnia exsequantur. (6) Nam id minime conducit agricolae, seu quia cum enisus est, non suo sed communi officio proficit, ideoque labori multum se subtrahit; nec tamen viritim malefactum deprehenditur, quod fit a multis.

[...] the duties of the slaves should not be confused to the point where all take a hand in every task. (6) For this is by no means to the advantage of

[249] *CIL* 6.7368: "Di{i}s Manibus / sacrum / L(ucio) Volusio Heraclae / capsario idem / a cubiculo L(uci) n(ostri) / Volusia Prima patron(o) / suo piissimo idem / coniugi bene merent(i) fecit / et sibi p(ermissu) L(uci) n(ostri) / Thyrso a cel(l)a / v(ixit) a(nnos) XXXV"; and *CIL* 6.7370: "Dis Manibus / L(ucio) Volusio / Paridi a cubiculo / et procuratori L(uci) n(ostri) / Claudia Helpis cum / Volusia Hamilla et / Volusio Paride / fili(i)s suis coniugi suo / bene merenti / permissu L(uci) n(ostri) / s(ua) p(ecunia) f(ecerunt)". It is difficult to establish to which Lucius Volusius Saturninus the inscriptions refer, see Hasegawa (2005) 20–21.

[250] Emphasized by e.g. Treggiari (1975a); and Bradley (1994) for the household of Livia.

[251] Harper (2011) 102.

[252] The *ostiarius urbanus* (doorkeeper) of *CIL* 6.8964, the *medicus chirurgus* (surgeon) of *CIL* 6.3986; and Hilarus Gugetianus *ad argentum* (cashier) of *CIL* 6.3941. There was at least one other Hilarus, a freedman of Livia, commemorated without profession in *CIL* 6.8722.

[253] Bradley (1994) 73; Col. *RR* 1.9.5–6. Translation Ash (1941, Loeb Classical Library).

> the husbandman, either because no one regards any particular task as his own or because, when he does make an effort, he is performing a service that is not his own but common to all, and therefore shirks his work to a great extent; and yet the fault cannot be fastened upon any one man because many have a hand in it.

Presumably the motivations of a dependent freedman or even of hired labourers would be similar.

Occupational titles of slaves could be considered also as a means of cataloguing material goods. In the words of Bodel, "one may reasonably question whether studies of the phenomenon are not more revealing of the Roman mania for classifying property than of the varieties of tasks that Roman slaves actually performed".[254] The jurists, for one, were indeed much concerned with the job specification of slaves, at least when they were part of a bequest.[255] The following excerpt from Marcian, however, is illuminating in various ways. The passage is placed in the context of bequests concerning slaves:

> ***Dig.*** 32.65.1–2
>
> 1. Si ex officio quis ad artificium transierit, quidam recte putant legatum exstingui, quia officium artificio mutatur: non idem e contrario cum lecticarius cocus postea factus est.
>
> 1. If someone proceeds from a job to a craft, one would rightly think to exclude him from the bequest, because the job changed into a craft: that does not hold, conversely, if a litter-bearer is later made a cook.
>
> 2. Si unus servus plura artificia sciat et alii coci legati fuerunt, alii textores, alii lecticarii, ei cedere servum dicendum est, cui legati sunt in quo artificio plerumque versabatur.
>
> 2. If one slave knows multiple arts and the cooks were bequeathed to one, the weavers to another, the litter-bearers to another, the slave should be ceded to him, to whom are bequeathed those in the craft in which he [the slave] is most often engaged.

The text illustrates not only that it was possible for slaves to proceed in a career, but also that a slave potentially did exercise more than one occupation: the latter theoretical example works with three different engagements for one slave, of which two are perhaps (semi-)skilled. At the same time it highlights the use of highly specialized slaves as a form of conspicuous consumption.

[254] Bodel (2011) 321. Similarly, Bradley (1994) 57: "It was a habit reflecting the Roman's [*sic*] fixation with categorisation and hierarchy".

[255] Bodel (2011) 326–27 n. 26.

A brief reference in Tacitus' *Germania* indicates that household specialization was deemed a sign of civilization, one that the Germans did not exhibit:

> Tac. *Germ.* 25.1
>
> Ceteris servis non in nostrum morem, descriptis per familiam ministeriis, utuntur: suam quisque sedem, suos penates regit.
>
> The other slaves they do not use as we do, with designated duties throughout the household; each one controls his own holding and home.[256]

Tacitus is not without implied criticism of Roman sumptuousness as opposed to Germanic simplicity;[257] nevertheless there are other indications that in Roman thought ideally it was not advisable for an aristocrat to have one slave perform more than one job – regardless of how realistic that scenario may have been.[258]

The care with which the manifold occupations are specified in the often brief and modest epitaphs from the *columbarium* tombs, however, suggests to me that such household specialization was deemed important beyond mere legalities in the early Roman empire. While job differentiation on *columbaria* inscriptions partly stems from the owners' interest in it, the fact that the resulting plethora of job titles was subsequently recorded in such high numbers reflects that, to the workers of the servile staff their job title was a distinctive source of pride.[259]

Occupational structure

For reasons set out above, no single one *columbarium* tomb can be expected to provide the material to allow an accurate outline of the occupational structure of the associated aristocratic house. Even if the full collection of inscriptions from one tomb had survived – and it most certainly has not – there were individuals who were excluded or buried outside the tomb for various reasons; there were also jobs that were not recorded or were under-represented; in addition, an epitaph generated around the moment of death generally does not inform the twenty-first-century reader about possible previous careers of the deceased in more humble lines of work. That said, the body of *columbaria* inscriptions offers what is arguably the best opportunity to reconstruct the basic outlines of occupational structure

256 Tac. *Germ.* 25.1. Translation Rives (1999).

257 Rives (1999) 61–62 on Tacitus' portrait of the Germani as "moral exemplars" reflecting an idealized past, devoid of the vices that civilization brings.

258 Cic. *Pis.* 67; Ael. Arist. *Rom Or.* 71b; Treggiari (1975a) 61.

259 Joshel (1992) esp. 145–61.

in an important segment of the urban labour market of early imperial Rome.

The organization of labour in an urban elite *domus*, if anything, does not appear to follow any ideal of self-sufficiency. But a single household should not merely be looked at in isolation: spouses had their own separate slave *familiae* and his and her households were – and were expected to be – used in a complementary way.[260] Penner's research on the Julio-Claudian households has illustrated that labour interdependence between aristocratic households could extend to wider family bonds, between siblings or in-laws.[261] An argument about the self-sufficiency of the household should therefore be made on the basis of an analysis of the overarching network of two or more elite *familiae* rather than a single household; moreover, the collaboration and overlap between the *familia urbana* and the *familia rustica* should also be taken into account.[262] Even then it appears that autarchy was probably never achieved.

The complementary nature of these '*domus* networks' has implications for an understanding of the occupational structure of the elite household. All individual households appear to follow the same blueprint, however. Every single household had a nucleus of domestic servants and personal attendants serving the master or mistress. In line with the legal independence of *familiae*, perhaps, each *domus* also seems to have had an administrative section. Both categories include chiefly the staff members necessary to run a *domus*. The remainder of the employees were employed in a multitude of professions that occasionally seem to suggest a kind of labour specialization for the market.[263]

In terms of the organization of work, the attested job specialization within the *domus* also reflected an internal occupational hierarchy.[264] The household was generally led by a steward (*dispensator*). After that, however, the situation could become rather more complex. A division into *decuriae* of workers with accompanying supervisors (*decuriones*) is attested with any credibility only for the enormous household of an emperor or the imperial family.[265] *Praepositi*, too – superintendents of one group or another – were

260 Penner (2012); cf. Treggiari (1975a) 54, who also suggests that Livia "relied on the vaster resources of the ruling Caesar".

261 Penner (2013), expressed also in Penner (2012); Rawson (2005) offers an epigraphic case study of a wet nurse who can be traced 'circulating households'.

262 Mouritsen (2019) 227 remarks on overlap in terms of labour; Rosafio (2016) 102 emphasizes a more traditional production/consumption differentiation.

263 Cf. Penner (2012) 148; Hasegawa (2005) Chapter 3.

264 In very general terms: Bradley (1994) 70, cf. Rosafio (2016) 102.

265 Not so credible by contrast: the *decuriae* in Petr. *Sat.* 47.12; Treggiari (1975a) 60 n. 131 for references. Compare, however, the dedication of the mon. Marcellae, *CIL* 6.4421, which also mentions decuriae: "C(aius) Claudius Marcellae / Minoris l(ibertus)

an imperial exclusive.[266] But where the emperor Claudius had a *decurio cubiculariorum*, other elite households nevertheless sported a *supra cubicularios* to supervise the bedchamber servants – which surely still points to a staff of significant size.[267] There are few, if any, other supervisory roles that come to the fore: the *supra cocos* was master chef, one may presume, but the *supra iumenta* (person in charge of pack and draft animals) did not necessarily have something to say about the *iumentarii* (drivers of those animals).[268] Examples that are similar in wording, like the *supra/ad valetudinarium* 'in charge of' health (presumably the sickbay *vel sim*), and the *a speculum*, 'in charge of' the mirror, abound, but they were really not overseers of staff.

The phenomenon of slaves or ex-slaves owning – and presumably supervising – 'under-slaves' (*vicarii*) is a much more prominent feature in the epigraphic data.[269] The following epitaph is a particularly beautiful illustration:

> *CIL* 6.6275
>
> Hic est ille situs / qui qualis amicus / amico quaque fide / fuerit mors euit (= fuit) indicio / f(unus) f(ecit) / Faustus Erotis / dispensatoris vicarius
>
> Here he is buried, he who was such a great friend and who died through such loyalty to his friend as an indicator of which this burial was set up. Faustus, *vicarius* of Eros the steward.

This epitaph, written on an altar found in the Statilian tomb, is exceptional in form, length and wording: the *amicitia*, friendship, between Faustus and Eros the *dispensator* is stressed. *Vicarii* in general, however, were not so exceptional. Eros owned another slave (Suavis, *CIL* 6.6276), yet he himself may in fact have been the slave of one T. Statilius Posidippus: *CIL* 6.6274 mentions an "Eros T(iti) Statili / Posidippi ser(vi) / disp(ensator)". T. Statilius Posidippus, freedman to the Statilii and

Phasis decurio / monumentum dedicavit et / decuriae epulum dedit d(e) s(ua) p(ecunia) huic / decuria ex aere conlato imaginem / decreverunt".

266 E.g. *Praepositus cellariorum*, *CIL* 6.8746; *praepositus cocorum*, 8752; *praepositus velariorum*, 9086. A few late antique, Christian inscriptions for *praepositi* commemorate clergy.

267 *Scriba cubiculariorum item decurio*: *AE* 1946, 99; similarly *CIL* 6.8773 (also imperial); *supra cubicularios*: *CIL* 6.4439 (mon. Marcellae), 6645 and 9287 (col. Statilii), 8766 (mon. Livia), and 33842 (unknown origin).

268 *Supra cocos*: *CIL* 6.9261.

269 It is well known for the imperial family (Weaver (1972)), or in *columbaria* (Penner (2013)); Baba (1990) also notes a number of *opus doliare* stamps that indicate the presence of some slave-owning slaves in the *familia rustica*, too.

himself apparently not buried in the tomb, had a *familia* of 19 (!) that can be reconstructed from the *columbarium*.[270]

One text on *vicarii* stands out from the rest and deserves quoting in full:

> *CIL* 6.5197
>
> Musico Ti(beri) Caesaris Augusti / Scurrano disp(ensatori) ad fiscum Gallicum / provinciae Lugudunensis / ex vicariis eius qui cum eo Romae cum / decessit {e}<f>uerunt bene merito / Venustus negot(iator) / Decimianus sump(tuarius) / Dicaeus a manu / Mutatus a manu / Creticus a manu // Agathopus medic(us) / Epaphra ab argent(o) / Primio ab veste / Communis a cubic(ularius) / Pothus pediseq(uus) / Tiasus cocus // Facilis pediseq(uus) / Anthus ab arg(ento) / Hedylus cubicu(larius) / Firmus cocus / Secunda
>
> To the deserving Musicus Scurranus, slave of Tiberius Caesar Augustus, accountant of the Gallic treasury in the province of Gallia Lugdunensis, from those of his slaves [*vicarii*] who were with him when he died at Rome: Venustus, tradesman; Decimianus, cashier; Dicaeus, secretary; Mutatus, secretary; Creticus, secretary; Agathopus, medic; Epaphra, in charge of silver; Primio, in charge of clothes; Communis, bedchamber servant; Pothus, footservant; Tiasus, cook; Facilis, footservant; Anthus, in charge of silver; Hedylus, bedchamber servant; Firmus, cook; Secunda.

This is the epitaph of Musicus Scurranus, slave to the emperor Tiberius. It was set up by his 16 *vicarii* – that in itself makes the text unique. In addition, the *vicarii* are virtually all mentioned with their occupational title, and that makes it the only inscription known to me in which *vicarii* specify their job.[271]

The complexity of these *familiae* in *familiae* has not yet received proper treatment in itself.[272] The slaves of a slave were legally the property of that slave's owner (thus Musicus and his *vicarii* were all the property of the emperor Tiberius), but that was not true for the slaves of a freedman. The case of Musicus Scurranus suggests that there may have been individuals who did have a distinct household-within-a-household catering to their needs – but they were exceptional, universally high-placed, and, most likely, imperial slaves and freedmen. The common inclusion of *vicarii* (especially

[270] Mouritsen (2013) 57 discusses both Eros and T. Statilius Posidippus.

[271] Could it be significant that the woman, Secunda, both is mentioned last and has no job title? Günther (1987) 131, 135, suggests that *vicariae* like Secunda were only owned by men, with the regular aim of 'marrying' them. Sometimes they were married, e.g. *ILS* 7981a, 7981b.

[272] With the exception perhaps of Di Porto (1984), who sees the *vicarius* as a kind of *servus communis* functioning as a go-between in economic partnerships or joint enterprises; but see the critique of Andreau (1999) 68–70.

those of freedmen) in the household *columbaria* strongly suggests that these sub-slaves or under-slaves should be considered a part of the social nucleus of the household. But the fact that these hierarchies are so meticulously inscribed suggests that analysis should go beyond "a strong possibility that such servants actually worked for their owner's *domina* or *patrona*".[273]

Domestic service and personal attendance

All elite *domus* had a core staff of domestic servants and personal attendants.[274] Joshel has plausibly explained the predominance of the service sector among the *columbarium* inscriptions in terms of the elite's need to be surrounded by servants to demonstrate their wealth and social standing:[275] it is perhaps predominantly in the large number of service jobs that we see reflected the concept of conspicuous consumption. The elite *domus* formed the locus of domestic service in the cities: virtually all employment in this sector can be traced to an aristocratic home.

Personal attendance

Personal care was all-pervasive, for example, in the case of Cn. Domitius Tullus, who according to Pliny had become so infirm that, to his own despair, he had to have his teeth brushed by servants.[276] Nothing similar to the home care that Tullus required is attested in the inscriptions, though it is plausible that servants were employed for such personal care when necessary. The epitaphs highlight instead that the elite certainly liked to have around a large throng of what could be termed 'luxury' carers, personal servants with a certain skill set. Masseurs and masseuses (*unctores*), hairdressers (*ornatrices*), barbers (*tonsores*), and perfumers (*unguentarii*) are ubiquitous. The job of hairdresser is for women only: in fact it is the single most common occupation attested for women in the city of Rome save one – for which see below – and virtually all hairdressers come from elite households.[277] The willingness to record this type of employment illustrates that these personal attendants took pride in their proximity to the masters,

[273] Treggiari (1975a) 51.

[274] Joshel (1992) 75, Table 3.2 ("Service occupations in the large domestic household"). Ibid., 145–61, discusses the domestic servant in the context of the large domestic household.

[275] Joshel (1992) 73–76; cf. Vlassopoulos (2021) 65.

[276] Plin. *Ep.* 8.18.9.

[277] Günther (1987) 45–53 on *ornatrices* confirms this pattern, though Günther's sample is limited to freedwomen. At ibid. 50–51 she has a few examples of freedwomen who apparently continued their business outside the household – regardless, I should like to emphasize that these women, too, originally came from an elite *domus*; see also Chapter 3 above.

as well as in their own skills. Unskilled personal attendance is not recorded. One cannot perhaps get much closer to a master than washing him or her, but the servants of Tullus and others who performed such daily care remain anonymous when we hear of them – as in Pliny – or are entirely obscured from us, since their job titles do not appear in the *columbaria*.

The *cubicularii* or bedchamber servants referred to earlier deserve separate mention in this context. Despite the fact that *cubicularii* are well attested, it is unclear what it was exactly that they did, in or regarding the bedchamber (*cubicularium*). However, the frequent recordings of *cubicularii* and their regular manumission suggests to me that their position was highly valued; therefore their tasks probably had less to do with securing clean sheets than with personal attendance in a wider sense, as informal advisor or confidant. *Cubicularii* of highly placed persons could become men of significant power and wealth.[278] Cleander, a notorious freedman of the emperor Commodus, is an extreme example who, according to Cassius Dio, could profitably control general access to consulships and senatorial status – among other things.[279]

The rather large group of *pedisequi* were personal attendants or footservants to their individual elite masters. It is interesting that they regularly include in their epitaph whose servant they were, like "Doris Statiliae Mino[ris] / pediseq(ua)" of *CIL* 6.9775 quoted above.[280] Other examples of footservants have already been referred to in various contexts. There are both male and female footservants, and from Livia's monument we also know of a boy (*puer a pedibus*).[281] It is generally assumed that this group is the entourage that accompanied a nobleman or -woman wherever they went. The concentration of *pedisequi* in the city of Rome may perhaps underline the significant presence of elite households there.[282] The relative frequency with which such a 'low' position is inscribed underlines Joshel's important point that occupation within elite households often designates a feeling of community and one's place within the household – not so much through pride in a job as through collegiality.[283] Collegiality and belonging certainly speak in the following example:

278 Men of wealth, since they were overwhelmingly male, though there are a few *cubiculariae*: *CIL* 6.5748, 5942, 33750, and potentially 9315 (fragm).

279 On Cleander's influence see esp. Cass. Dio 73.12. Under Diocletian the imperial '*cubicularius*' officially became one of the four major ministers, overseer of the "palace staff", see e.g. Potter (2009) 184.

280 Or Iulia Elate of *CIL* 6.4002.

281 *CIL* 6.4001.

282 Outside Rome there is only a concentration of *pedisequi* in imperial service from Africa proconsularis (*CIL* 8). The alleged skills of the *pedisequi* in Atticus' household are mentioned in Nep. *Att.* 13.3; cf. above.

283 Joshel (1992) 87–91.

CIL 6.4355

Philusa Andraei / liberti uxor / ollam et titulum / datum ab conservas / pedisequas

Philusa wife of Andraeus the freedman (lies here). The urn and plaque were given by her fellow slaves and footservants.

Childcare

A very large part of domestic service and caring for other people within the elite *domus* was devoted to childcare.[284] It is unlikely that these childcarers were all engaged only with the master's child(ren); their presence thus supports the earlier supposition that the elite household included a significant number of home-born slaves.[285] Penner identifies no less than 11 per cent of the Volusian staff as engaged in childcare, which has led her to tentatively suggest that the Volusii actually specialized in this domain.[286] But it seems to me that childcare was integral to the *domus* rather than aimed at the outside world as a business. The high percentage is unsurprising, however, considering the likelihood that children were ubiquitous, and taking into account the real possibility that the Volusian tomb represents one of the best-documented *domus*.[287]

Caring for children starts within the womb, up to and including birth. The Romans must have felt the same way, as a number of elite households attest to an in-house *obstetrix* (midwife) – Livia's substantial monument includes two.[288] Again, if babies were not a common phenomenon of the *familia*, having an in-house midwife would not make sense.[289]

The newborn infant then required breastfeeding, which in ancient Rome was not necessarily done by the birth mother, for various reasons that

[284] Cf. Laes (2016) for the interesting finding that in late antiquity these educators were no longer predominantly servile 'professionals' like these, but rather freeborn and family members.

[285] Hasegawa (2005) 36 does seem to assume that the childminders took care of the master's children only. Admittedly, it is not impossible.

[286] Penner (2012) 148; they also specialized in entertainers, who make up an equal 11 per cent.

[287] Mouritsen (2013) 44.

[288] Among others, the Volusii *CIL* 6.9725 = 27558; Statilii *CIL* 6.6325; Antonia Augusta *CIL* 6.8947; Marcella *CIL* 6.4458; Livia *CIL* 6.8948, 8949. Unsurprisingly, these slave women and freedwomen are all connected with female mistresses. See also Laes (2010) esp. 271–73 with appendix for the full Roman epigraphical dossier on midwives, at 272 with the remark that 'large families could employ their own midwives', because 13 out of 31 attestations, he finds, come from elite families in Rome.

[289] It also contradicts the interesting suggestion that women were regularly sent to the rural *familia* to give birth. Treggiari (1979b) 189–90.

do not need to be repeated here.[290] Many children were therefore suckled by a *nutrix*, a wet nurse, who generally was meant to breastfeed the child for a much longer period than the current Western average of three to six months. It is thus to be expected that the elite *domus* also included one or more *nutrices* at any one time, and indeed Livia has one, the Statilii have two, the Volusii have four.[291] It is not unlikely that often the *nutrix*'s care for the child continued after the weaning period, certainly within the context of the *familia*.[292] Naturally, the actual wet-nursing can only be done by women: this is, in fact, the most commonly attested occupation for Roman women, counting slave, freed, and free women, in and outside the elite *domus*.[293] It is the overwhelming number one on the list of jobs for women.

As they grew up, the children were cared for by various other childminders. In the context of the elite *domus*, noteworthy are the *paedagogi*, *educatores*, and *grammatici* also encountered earlier in this chapter. *Paedagogi*, as we have seen, provided a more general sort of childcare than the specific educational tasks of the *educator* or *grammaticus*. This is probably one of the reasons why the *paedagogi* are by far the largest group of childminders. Though female *paedagogae* are not uncommon, it is noteworthy that men outnumber them by a wide margin.[294]

Domestic service in larger households is where most women are attested, the majority of them in childcare, but also in other jobs.[295] The nine footservants of Livia are supplemented by various hairdressers and

[290] E.g. Harper (2011) 110–12, at 111–12, notes a "correlation between the practices of child exposure and wet-nursing"; and Bradley (1991) 26.

[291] According to Hasegawa (2005) 36. It is obvious that the male equivalent, the *nutritor*, also known epigraphically albeit in far smaller numbers, did not perform the same job. Or did he? Infants in Rome very occasionally were raised on animal milk – despite the considerable risks of giving them non-pasteurized animal milk. So did *nutrix* and *nutritor* perform the same job after all? It is unlikely. The frequent epigraphic connection of *nutritor* with their *alumnus*, and esp. the text of *CIL* 6.9967 ("Mem(o)riam ex origine vestiariorum in quo [sunt(?)] / nutritores mei ..."), suggests to me that the *nutritor* could be any kind of mentor, also in crafts.

[292] Continued service of nurses, e.g. Bradley (1991) 20, 25–28; Günther (1987) 100.

[293] Günther (1987) 98, 100, for her Roman sample. It was already stated above that most nurses were of a servile background, with reference to Bradley (1991) 19–20; see also Harper (2011) 109–12 on the continuance of this practice into late antiquity.

[294] Günther (1987) 76 records 70 men and four women.

[295] Cf. above; and Joshel (1992) 98 in her wider discussion of Roman labour indeed notes that large households provide "the setting in which women were most likely to name their work, usually as domestic servants of various kinds (especially nurses) and skilled service workers (especially *ornatrices*, hairdressers and maids)." That said, note that the large proportion of freedwomen in child care (42.6 per cent, or 20 out of 47 women) are left out of Joshel's discussion, "Because gender and status differentiate those in child care from domestic servants as such". Ibid., 145.

masseuses, but also by female doctors and midwives.[296] Domestic service matches well with the Roman ideal of women's domestic nature and their 'natural' place in the house. The incidence of women commemorated with occupation is higher in the *columbaria* than in any other category of inscriptions, and female jobs mentioned are usually service jobs.[297] Female owners were more likely to own female staff,[298] but whereas a female *pedisequa*, *cubicularia*, and so on was almost certain to work for a woman, a noblewoman could very well employ a male *pedisequus*, *cubicularius* and so on.[299] It is significant to highlight that there were more male than female childminders.[300] In sum, even here, the inscriptions still confirm the relatively restricted opportunities for female labourers. The question remains whether the skewed sex ratios that this suggests were a reality, because the demographic analysis above suggested that the gender balance is likely to have been more even in most households, when compared to the exceptional *domus* that provide our epigraphic evidence.

Other service occupations

The elite *domus* would often include a small medical staff, such as medics, midwives, or the *ad valetudinarium* (in charge of health), the latter of whom was probably more of a healer or nurse in case of less serious illnesses.

In addition to staff looking after people, there was a great variety of servants looking after (an equally wide variety of) possessions, such as an *ab argento* (silver), the *a speculum* ([*sic*] mirror), *ad imagines* (paintings, statues, (ancestor) portraits?), or the *ad margarita* (pearls). Those working with clothing are somewhat more common, as the *a veste*/*ad vestem*, or *vestispicae*/*vestiplica* (folders of clothes).

There are those service workers who are responsible for the running of the household in a practical sense, such as the *atriensis* (majordomo), *rogator* (questioner), *ab admissione* (usher), *nomenclator* (name teller), *ab hospitiis* (host).

Strikingly less visible in the epigraphic sources are those domestic servants who kept the household operational in a much more practical

296 "Nearly all these women work for women or for or with the children of the house". Treggiari (1979b) 190.

297 Some 41.3 per cent of women is engaged in domestic service; Joshel (1992) 69, Table 3.1.

298 Penner (2012); Penner (2013); Treggiari (1975a) 58: "A *domina* employed more women than did a bachelor". On the same page she notes a "low proportion" of women in the *monumentum Liviae*, while actually the 20 per cent is relatively high in comparison.

299 Günther (1987) 60.

300 Cf. Bradley (1991) 37–75, 'Child care at Rome: the role of men', at 38: "The appearance of female nurses in the service of aristocratic families is not really surprising, but the use of men is rather less predictable at first blush".

sense, by doing the cooking or cleaning, or by supplying water. In the premodern world it is very well possible that this category was in fact the largest.[301] A few job titles can be linked to acquiring and preparing food, though I wonder if the particular functions of the ***opsonator*** (caterer), ***ministrator*** (waiter), ***praegustator*** (taster), and ***a cyatho*** (cup-bearer), for example, were not more closely involved with elite dinner parties than with the household's food. There were few cooks – but cooks could be hired.[302] Interestingly, there appears to be no household that is truly fully staffed (or fully attested, of course); nor can this be solved by a *domus* network that we can trace.

Conclusion

The urban phenomenon of elite *domus* was restricted to the larger cities of Roman Italy where the elite tended to cluster together. Aristocratic households are particularly well attested for the city of Rome. It has become clear from the above that wherever the elite resided, this significantly changed the make-up of the population, and of the labour force. A large majority of all slaves lived in towns, and more than half of these urban slaves worked in aristocratic houses. Independent freedmen can also often be traced back to a servile history in elite households. The epigraphic sources exacerbate this focus on larger cities and on Rome in particular – which is precisely why it is so helpful to look at the uncharted territory of the *domus* economy as a whole.

It has long been known that slaves and ex-slaves predominate in pre-Christian inscriptions from the Roman empire. This is even more prominent in occupational inscriptions, and – as was illustrated in this chapter – the pattern is most explicit for the elite household epitaphs recording job title, originating from *columbaria* from Rome. On the one hand, the *columbaria* themselves make up such a large part of the material that it is difficult to draw firm conclusions about the servile labour population in relation to the free population. On the other hand, it has become clear that elite presence and aristocratic houses did provide substantial employment in the cities, which suggests that the predominance of household labourers in epigraphic data is at least partly a reflection of reality – at least in Rome and other large settlements. The over-representation of *columbaria* and elite households more generally, combined with a predilection for specialization

301 Harper (2011) 107.

302 Groen-Vallinga and Tacoma (2017); Hasegawa (2005) 45 has five *coci* for the four largest households, four of whom worked for the Statilii. Interestingly, Harper (2011) 108 observes, "It is notable how often the job of 'the cook' was a specialized occupation in late antique households".

of job titles among their staff, largely explains the strong occupational differentiation.

One of the main questions that lay at the heart of this chapter is whether the presence of elite *domus* restricted labour opportunities for the freeborn urban population. The study of occupational inscriptions, and of *columbarium* tombs in particular, confirms the predominance of slaves and ex-slaves within the labour force of elite *domus*, effectively closing off the domestic service sector for the freeborn (but not the freed). Then again, we should perhaps not expect to find freeborn labourers in elite *domus*, since other references indicate that the free working *in* elite households were probably the exception, whereas the free working *for* the aristocrats must have been quite common. The employment generated by the *domus* for the free, and particularly for the freeborn, remains difficult to grasp. The ways in which freedmen maintained and benefited from economic bonds with their families of origin (i.e. the *domus*) sometimes can be recovered from the evidence, whereas the singular bonds of *locatio conductio* with the freeborn remain largely unknown. But free hired labour did include both the freeborn and the freed, thereby increasing competition for the freeborn seeking to gain an income. The often sizeable and certainly numerous elite households must have been important employers for the free artisans and craftsmen represented within the material – many of whom worked in the more luxury trades and whose work might not be affordable by the masses.

The significant servile presence in occupational inscriptions and in elite households has also given rise to the assumption that education in the Roman world was a slave prerogative. My analysis of human capital suggests that slaves, at least in the context of labour in the cities of Roman Italy, were indeed in a good position to acquire some skills, varying from a basic education to becoming a fully trained craftsman. Investment in human capital of slaves was economically rational. Education at least doubled the value of a slave on the market, a market for skilled slaves in particular – and this market remained in operation long after the influx of captives had dwindled. A slave could not run off with accumulated knowledge and skills, thus ensuring that the income would go to the owner. Interestingly, the basic slave education did not take the form that scholars have long suggested; that is, through *paedagogia*. Instead, most elite *domus* included various levels of teachers, or alternatively sent their slaves to regular 'schools' with the *ludimagister.* Conversely, the arts and crafts were generally taught on the job, in the household, although occasionally both male and female slaves were apprenticed out, just like the freeborn. Competition between the servile population and the freeborn population therefore centred especially on skilled work. In Rome and other cities where elite households were prevalent, slave and free competed in domestic service as well, which by analogy with early modern patterns is most likely to have impacted women's job opportunities.

Teachers and childcarers in the home form indirect evidence of the ubiquity of children in the elite home. The majority of these young individuals presumably were slaves, often but certainly not always the offspring of slave unions. It is clear that slave families within households, and crossing household boundaries (within *domus* networks perhaps?) were a regular occurrence. The children of the household were not only *vernae*, however, but may have included foundlings, or individuals who were bought on the market. The slave market and the self-replacement hypothesis for the slave population therefore are not mutually exclusive. Servile families included biological ties, as well as the more complex and under-researched hierarchic bonds of (ex-)slaves owning under-slaves (*vicarii*), complicating the demographics of the aristocratic household.

The occupational structure of the upper-class household, large and not-so-large alike, nevertheless appears to follow a standard blueprint: a basis in domestic service, an administrative section, and a part that could specialize in the market. The concept of *domus* networks, derived from the interconnectedness of the Julio-Claudian households as indicated by Penner, fundamentally alters our understanding of the occupational structure of the individual *domus*.[303] A *domus* network could create more autarchy than one household could. If aristocratic households relied on *domus* networks to fulfil most of their labour demands, the need (and thus the opportunities) for free hired labour would lessen, and the demand for slave labourers on the market would be determined rather differently. Certainly not all aristocrats entertained a staff as sizeable as the manifest ones that dominate the evidence and the discussion (here as elsewhere), and because of this the influence of *domus* networks on the urban working population may have been limited in most settlements of Roman Italy. Though it is difficult to extrapolate these findings from the top aristocratic households to elite households more generally, it illustrates beautifully how even the largest elite *domus* were involved in larger interconnected social networks.

303 Penner (2013).

Chapter 5

Non-familial Labour Collectives

The Economics of Association

> The place of a Roman in society was a function of his position in the social hierarchy, membership of a family, and involvement in a web of personal relationships extending out from the household.[1]

Introduction

The social nucleus of the Roman family was interconnected with other, non-familial, socio-economic collectives, and needs to be considered as such. The focus so far has been on work and labour that was organized from the family-based household. But labour and labour market participation were also governed by labour relations between relative peers from outside the household. These horizontal labour relationships could be instrumental for the labour opportunities of an individual, not least because social and economic aspects of associating with others complemented or even substituted household negotiations in a number of situations. This chapter therefore concentrates on the economics of association and consider the topics of urban interconnectedness, occupational clustering, and the social network of the street within the close-knit urban communities of Roman Italy. It will do so through the lens of Roman associations.

Roman associations or *collegia* were patently not the only form of non-familial labour relations, but *collegia* both were prominent and are well attested. Add to this that every labour collective may be referred to as a *collegium* in Roman legal terminology and scholarly literature alike, and it follows that Roman labour associations may profitably be invoked to elucidate the economic features of associations in general. That implies taking into account the more general social and cultural integration of associations within Roman society. In what ways did such 'professional'

[1] Garnsey and Saller (1987) 148.

associations act as labour collectives influencing urban labour systems, and how did relationships between *collegiati* tie in with family bonds?

The integration of *collegia* into the debate on the Roman economy raises the question whether they were more economic than social, or more social than economic collectives (or whether they were chiefly funerary clubs, or religious, and so on).[2] Scholarly consensus has shifted towards the point of view that the question whether the *collegia* were a predominantly social or mostly economic phenomenon is irrelevant. It is clear that the *collegia* did function as an economic institution, and they should therefore be taken into account in a New Institutional Economics account of the Roman economy.[3] Social gatherings may well be used for economic benefit, and any kind of network is likely to be economically useful, or at least potentially so. *Collegia* were part of the urban social structure that helped define individual labour opportunities.

The balance between the social function of *collegia* on the one hand, and family on the other, was a decisive structural influence on individual participation in the economy. Moreover, economic associations are a distinctly urban phenomenon, whereas comparative evidence indicates that family ties tend to lose some of their influence in the city.[4] Family and association thus functioned as both complementary and overlapping informal networks, within "precisely that space between the individual and society which voluntary associations are commonly thought to inhabit".[5]

Chapter outline

The first section of this chapter deals with the place of associations in the urban community more generally. *Collegia* as a collective were a distinct part of the civic order. Paradoxically, they also provided a separate, symbolic order for those who were excluded from the civic order. Although the essential goals of forming an association appear to remain the same everywhere in Roman Italy, it will become clear that there was a difference in structure of the associative network of Rome and that of smaller urban centres. Who were part of the *collegia*, and what can the distribution pattern of the *collegia* tell us about their nature? Membership was open to virtually any Roman of some means, although options for women were severely limited. This theoretical openness of *collegia* challenges common presumptions that associations were mostly populated by freedmen.

The functional analysis of the *collegia* commences with their perceived social meaning and the way they structured the lives of individual Romans.

2 Verboven (2011a).
3 Cf. Venticinque (2016) 35–39.
4 Lucassen et al. (2008) 15–16.
5 Wilson (1996) 5.

Just as in the case of the Roman family and the elite household, the form and function of the social networks that associations helped to create and maintain had a bearing on the organization of work and especially labour in society. It will be considered to what extent they can usefully be seen as substitute families, as many scholars have hinted at in the past, when familial and collegial networks overlap and interact.

The next section looks into the economics of association: the choice to associate with others in itself quickly becomes an economic act. But is there any direct evidence to show the involvement of the Roman *collegia* with economic life? The occupational *collegia* have often been likened to medieval and early modern guilds. It will be argued here that the comparison remains a promising one. Roman *collegia* were not monopolists of the arts and crafts sector, but as it turns out the medieval guilds did not have such a monopoly either. The significant *comparandum* is that both guilds and *collegia* functioned as trust networks with so-called multiplex relationships, not merely social, but also religious, familial, and economic.

In the last part of this chapter, the lines will be drawn together to form a coherent story of the part *collegia* may have played in structuring the Roman urban labour market. *Collegia* and the family form two intersecting axes of reference.

Formal organization and variation

The impact of the expanding empire, notably a growing population and increasing urbanization rates, led to a proliferation of *collegia* and an improvement in their social standing over the second and third centuries AD. This development was outlined most extensively by John Patterson, and his views may be briefly summarized here.[6] Public benefactions and euergetism from the resident elite must have formed a substantial part of the city budget in the early Roman empire.[7] With the coming of the empire, local autonomy and political offices lost much of their significance. The traditional elite of senators and knights tended to move away from their home towns towards the seats of power, Rome in particular, where they hoped to find political advancement. Although instances are known of those who, when in Rome, still maintained a level of euergetism in their native towns (such as Pliny the Younger and his native Comum), it is likely that most would take their resources with them, to the detriment of that town.[8] Small settlements would have been particularly vulnerable to

[6] Patterson (2006) esp. Chapter 3. Cf. Patterson (1994).

[7] Cf. Brown (2012) 58 ff.: "an empire of gifts".

[8] *CIL* 5.5262 lists many of Pliny's benefactions in Comum. Pliny also mentions his gifts in his letters, e.g. Plin. *Ep.* 1.8 (donation of the library). Cf. Eck (2017).

this drain of resources and only those with a benevolent and sufficiently wealthy patron could survive. In larger cities, however, it is likely that enough people remained to step in. The gap was filled by members of associations (*collegiati*), local council members (*decuriones*), or wealthy freedmen (often in the role of Augustales). They were able to do so because, on the one hand, patterns of benefaction changed towards a preference for more affordable forms (banquets rather than buildings), and, on the other hand, the members of a *collegium* taken together were wealthy beyond their individual capacity.[9] Their contribution to the civic community in turn led to a rise in social status and prestige. This, in a nutshell, is the background to the growing cachet and numbers of associations in the first centuries AD. By the second century, the associations are so well attested in public inscriptions that "their presence in a town can reasonably be assumed even if it happens not to be directly proven".[10] The *collegia* had become a set and valued element of the civic order.[11]

The prior history of the *collegia* during the Republic and the early Empire, however, is one of unrest and political interference. It is telling that the *collegia* are included amongst MacMullen's *Enemies of the Roman Order.*[12] His narrative of the tensions between the *collegia* and the ruling powers emphasizes a history of politics, riots, and upheaval, versus anxious senators and emperors: a history that is well known from ancient literary accounts.[13] In response to the political involvement of the *collegia*, the Senate repeatedly took action against the associations.[14] Julius Caesar appears to have issued a *lex Iulia de collegiis* that prohibited virtually all associations.[15] A *senatus consultum* now commonly referred to as the *senatus consultum de collegiis tenuiorum* ("regarding associations of people of lesser means"), issued in the first or early second century, specified what categories of *collegia* were to be allowed, thereby restricting the possibility of starting new associations.[16] The unease of the authorities towards private associations may also be

[9] Wen (2018) on communal dining.

[10] MacMullen (1974) 73; cf. Liu (2013) 364; this chronological development is largely confirmed by the archaeological evidence for collegium buildings in Bollmann (1998), who at 169 notes a change not only in the number (more) but also in the nature (more elaborate) of the *scholae* in the second century. The second century also saw mostly professional *collegia* compared to the first century, which had more evidence for Augustales.

[11] Patterson (2006) 257–58.

[12] MacMullen (1966) esp. 173–79.

[13] A more detailed overview can be found in Cotter (1996); or De Ligt (2000); insightful as well is Venticinque (2016) Chapter 5, with a view from the provinces.

[14] Cotter (1996) 75–76.

[15] Cotter (1996) 76–77; Suet. *Div. Iul.* 42.3.

[16] *Dig.* 47.22.1 pr. (Marcian, third century), discussed by De Ligt (2000) 247–49.

illustrated by the emperor Trajan, voicing his concerns in a letter to Pliny the Younger:

> **Plin. *Ep.* 10.34**
>
> Tibi quidem secundum exempla complurium in mentem venit posse collegium fabrorum apud Nicomedenses constitui. Sed meminerimus provinciam istam et praecipue eas civitates eius modi factionibus esse vexatas. Quodcumque nomen ex quacumque causa dederimus iis, qui in idem contracti fuerint, hetaeriae eaeque brevi fient.
>
> You are of the opinion it would be proper to constitute a guild of *fabri* in Nicomedia, as has been done in several places. But it is to be remembered that societies of this sort have greatly disturbed the peace of the province [Bithynia] in general, and of those cities [Nicomedia] in particular. Whatever name we give them, and for whatever purposes they may be founded, they will not fail to form themselves into factions, assemblies, however short their meetings may be.[17]

The same emperor does allow the citizens of Amisus to form an association, however, which appears to be aimed at the protection of the lower classes.[18]

What was the effect of this friction on the nature and prevalence of associations up to the first century AD? There is relatively little epigraphic evidence of formal *collegia* before the second century.[19] But there certainly was a form of socio-economic association. In Pompeii, the goldsmiths united (*aurifices universi*) supported C. Cuspius Pansa's run for *aedile* in electoral graffiti.[20] Tacitus writes that after a fight between Pompeians and Nucerians at the amphitheatre in Pompeii got out of hand in AD 59, the illegitimate *collegia* of Pompeii were dissolved (among other things): the phrasing suggests that there were illegitimate *collegia* as well as legitimate ones at the time.[21] Moreover, the continuous apparent dissension between

[17] Translation Melmoth (1927, Loeb Classical Library), with minor modifications.

[18] Plin. *Ep.* 10.93; Venticinque (2016) 188–90 on Pliny and the *fabri*.

[19] Liu (2008b) 66 concludes that "in general, *collegia* were a sporadic phenomenon in the West before the late first century AD". Bollmann (1998) 163–69, at 169, finds evidence of *Vereinshäuser* in the first century mainly for the Augustales. She finds little to no evidence for the Republic.

[20] *CIL* 4.710. On the form of association in electoral graffiti, Liu (2008b) 57–60. She concludes correctly that they are not formal *collegia* – but they are a form of professional association, even if they sometimes refer to only "the workmen in a workshop" (ibid., 57). *Universi* in this example points to a larger group, though.

[21] Tac. *Ann.* 14.17: "et rursus re ad patres relata, prohibiti publice in decem annos eius modi coetu Pompeiani collegiaque, quae contra leges instituerant, dissoluta" ("And, the case brought again before the magistrates, the Pompeians were prohibited another public assembly of this type for ten years, and the associations that existed against the

authorities and associations could be interpreted as evidence of the fact that the *collegia* had always remained extant, and influential.[22] Indeed, the stumbling block that was the *lex Iulia* appears not to have been very long-lived, and De Ligt has convincingly argued that the implications of the *senatus consultum de collegiis tenuiorum* were not nearly as restrictive as some scholars have believed.[23] In my view, such rules and regulations are a reflection of a government attempting to impose a formal structure onto the already widespread habit of forming informal associations.

Collegia increasingly sought, and were granted, government recognition. With an imperial or senatorial grant of the *ius coeundi* (right to assemble) they became legal associations (*collegia legitima*), which underlines once more that the authorities were not entirely hostile towards private associations. Liu concludes that "the proliferation of all kinds of *collegia* in imperial Rome suggests that the official regulations may in fact have had a positive impact on the development of associations".[24] She points out that predictably the state was particularly prone to supporting *collegia* that were useful to the public good.[25] State recognition was justified since associations were more than a potentially disruptive factor. They were also an important structuring principle in society that reaffirmed the civic order. From the perspective of the association, the grant of the right to assemble was not only important in itself, but also the prerequisite for other rights and privileges.[26] The right of *corpus habere*, for example – that is, the right to act as a legal collective – would significantly facilitate the owning and receiving of property.[27] Legitimate *collegia* seem to have been a desirable option for government and members alike.

To sum up, the first century saw the development from informal to formally recognized and increasingly widespread associations. During the second and third centuries AD the *collegia* flourished as independent organizations, and this is reflected in their epigraphic output. Much of what follows, therefore, is based on evidence that stems mostly from the late first to late third centuries. From the late third century onwards, the role of the *collegia* changed significantly in nature, as private associations were

rule of law, were dissolved"). Liu (2008b) 60–62 does not see any evidence for legitimate *collegia* in this.

22 So Patterson (1992) 23.

23 De Ligt (2000); De Ligt (2001).

24 Liu (2013) 357. The duality in the connections between government and *collegium* is emphasized by Liu (2009) 97–111; Liu (2013) 355 ff. ("double-edged effect").

25 Liu (2009) 123.

26 Liu (2013) 355, "at least from the second century on".

27 Solely prestige, Van Nijf (1997). Legal advantages, De Ligt (2001); Liu (2009) 103–11. The right of *corpus habere* was not handed out indiscriminately; cf. *Dig.* 3.4.1 pr (Gaius ad ed.). It was granted to all legitimate *collegia* only under Marcus Aurelius.

increasingly employed for the public good in service to the state and the city of Rome, notably for the food supply.[28] But that development lies outside the scope of the current analysis.

Hierarchies and civic life

It has long been recognized that the Roman population below the elite was just as hierarchically organized as the elite – a hierarchy that was structured by voluntary associations.[29] The question is how the hierarchy of the non-elite was formed and how it interacted with the elite hierarchy. The Roman elite as reflected in our ancient sources does not seem to have taken much notice of the rest. Or did they, and is their anxiety towards associations a consequence of the existence of an alternative road to power?

Forming associations can be perceived as a quest for personal achievement, a way to create opportunities for advancement. The *collegia* had a strong internal hierarchy, with a wide range of magistracies that their members could aspire to.[30] This hierarchy extended to a ranking of the associations themselves: first came the three principal *collegia*, next those related to the imperial *annona*, and then interregional associations.[31] 'First class' *collegia* seem to have been favoured by benefactors as well, so their donations made the wealthy associations wealthier.[32] An exception to the rule are the *collegia domestica*. They were somewhere at the lower end of the scale in terms of status, but could generally count on the support of their aristocratic patrons.

The *cursus honorum* within a *collegium* was as a rule completely separate from that in the civic hierarchy. That was no reason for the officials not to be proud of their title, even in a *collegium domesticum*. *Collegium* magistrates noted their position within the association rather than their freeborn citizenship.[33] It is interesting to see that membership alone apparently was not often deemed worth mentioning in epitaphs. It was magistracies rather than occupations that people were proud of. Since holding office within a *collegium* regularly required a *summa honoraria*, recording the title on a tombstone is also a reflection of wealth.[34]

[28] Venticinque (2016) esp. Chapter 6; Gibbs (2013); cf. Liu (2013) 367; Liu (2009) 112–15; Ausbüttel (1982) 99–108.

[29] Verboven (2007) 870, "institutionalized through the numerous voluntary associations across the empire".

[30] Royden (1988) collects the material on *collegia* magistrates.

[31] Verboven (2007) 875–80.

[32] Liu (2008a) 239, although she cautions not to push the stratification of associations too far.

[33] Joshel (1992) 113–19, esp. 118.

[34] Joshel (1992) 115: "In general, therefore, most of the men with this form of occupational title would have been among the wealthier practitioners of their trades".

It has often been stated that the *collegia* offered their members a chance of social status and rank that was as a rule not open to them in the civic hierarchy.[35] Within the ranks of the *collegium*, slaves could rise to become magistrates.[36] It was "an avenue for the ambitious without subverting the basic organization of society".[37] MacMullen observed that *collegia* both "resembled the whole social context they found themselves in and imitated it as best they could", calling them "miniature cities".[38] The terminology of their magistracies mirrored those of the city: there was a board of councillors (*decuriones*), for example, and a *quaestor*.[39] It was a literal alternative to the civic order. Verboven has dubbed this phenomenon "the associative order".[40] He argues that the associative order provided a means for successful *collegiati* to gain the social and symbolic capital that was valued within the civic order – and it gave them, or at least their children, the chance to actually enter into that civic order. Venticinque demonstrates how the wealthier *collegiati* in Roman Egypt themselves were actively engaged in local politics, which seems to be a broader pattern in the rest of the empire.[41] On a local level at least, it appears that the associative order and the civic order overlapped.

The *collegia* themselves were an integral part of the community.[42] As a reflection of the close connection with the town, their names would sometimes include the town name, as in the case of the *collegium fabrum tignuariorum Ostiensum*.[43] The *collegiati* participated in civic life as benefactors as well as recipients of benefactions; they were conspicuously present during religious festivals and processions; they could have separate seating areas in the theatres and set up buildings, statues, and inscriptions in the public space.[44] Interaction with elite patrons was mutually beneficial and

[35] E.g. Tran (2006); Patterson (2006) 260; Kloppenborg (1996) 18; Ausbüttel (1982) 48.

[36] Liu (2009) 177 n. 56 points out the unambiguous examples of *CIL* 11.4771 (*fullones*) and *CIL* 14.2874 (*cisiarii*); Royden (1988) lists no slave magistrates, and does not include these two inscriptions.

[37] Patterson (2006) 262.

[38] MacMullen (1974) 77, 76.

[39] Patterson (2006) 255.

[40] Verboven (2007).

[41] Venticinque (2016) e.g. 140–41, 153.

[42] Verboven (2007) 881; cf. Van Nijf (1997); Van Nijf (2002). The ambivalence of the people of Tarsus towards the linen weavers (an association?), as sketched out by Dio Chrysostom 34.21–23 in detail (they were "as it were, outside the constitution", ὥσπερ ἔξοθεν τῆς πολιτείας; sometimes considered on the inside and sometimes on the out), is revealing and deserves more attention in this respect. Dio argues that they should be accepted as citizens.

[43] Cf. Patterson (2006) 256.

[44] Cf. Wen (2018) Chapter 4; Patterson (2006) 262–64 (benefactors); Patterson (1994) 232, 235: Augustales, *decuriones*, and *collegia* were the three groups important in civic life in the second and third centuries.

confirmed as well as shaped the community: "the *collegia* could be expected to reciprocate meaningfully through the grant of honorific titles and so on in a way impossible for the individual".[45]

Membership composition

> It is as if no principle of either inclusion or exclusion could meet all demands – as if clusters of every conceivable private sympathy required expression. Where two neighbors at a corner pub today will raise their glasses and at most exchange a friendly "Cheers!" the two in antiquity seem to have said, "Be it resolved, to call ourselves the society of …".[46]

There was significant variation in Roman associations. There were associations from a minimum of three to over a hundred members;[47] there were private, semi-public, and state associations. Membership of an association was not open to everyone, but still the *collegia* were open to many: it was available to slave, freed, free, male, and female. This was a matter of matching the right individual with the right *collegium*, because many associations catered for a specific group of people. Candidates for membership of a *collegium* therefore had to fulfil certain requirements of occupation, religion, wealth, gender, or other. If qualified, they had to be voted in, generally by the guild magistrates or by the democratic vote of all members. A kind of background check of prospective candidates could be part of the procedure.[48] For trained artisans or craftsmen, however, membership of the corresponding association does not appear to have been obligatory, hereditary, or self-evident in any other way.[49] There is thus every reason to assume that membership of (professional) associations was not universal.[50]

MacMullen once guesstimated that in the first century AD, one-third of the (male) urban population were members of an association.[51] This view has been challenged by Liu, who carefully calculates a maximum

[45] Patterson (1992) 22.

[46] MacMullen (1974) 82.

[47] For the legal minimum, *Dig.* 50.16.85 (Marcellus, attributed to Neratius Priscus): "Neratius Priscus tres facere existimat 'collegium', et hoc magis sequendum est".

[48] Broekaert (2011) 27–29 with reference to the *lex* of the *citrarii et eborarii*, *CIL* 6.33885, "debebunt utique curatores de eo / [que]m adlecturi fuerint ante ad quinq(uennales) re[fe]rre".

[49] Compulsion and inheritance of guild membership may have played a part from the fourth century onwards; see Gibbs (2013), with references.

[50] Verboven (2007) 883–84 on the proliferation of guild membership; see also Van Minnen (1987) 68–69, who illustrates for Roman Egypt that it could be difficult not to be part of a guild.

[51] MacMullen (1966) 174; cf. Ausbüttel (1982) 36–37.

of only 13 per cent of the male population of the city of Rome, using the combined data for the first four centuries AD.[52] Her problem with the earlier guesstimate is that it did not use a strict definition of formal *collegia* for the calculation: it was based on the numbers from Pompeii as representative of other cities, counting as associations all (occupational and other) identifiable 'groups' that were found in Pompeian inscriptions, including electoral graffiti. The current inclusive analysis of the associative phenomenon, however, would argue for the inclusion of such informal (or rather 'less formal') associations.[53] An inscription like that of "the fullers for Eumachia, daughter of Lucius, civic priestess", surely suggests that there was a collective of the fullers, even if no mention is made of a *collegium* per se.[54] In the broader picture, the distinction between formal and informal *collegia* in epigraphic evidence generally is not a problem: to my knowledge there are few instances of 'unspecified' associations whose status as such is ambivalent outside the Pompeian graffiti.

Even with a clear data set for the associative phenomenon, no certain numbers would come up; it is also likely that the percentage will lie somewhere between 10 and 30 per cent for the first century AD.[55] The epigraphic evidence shows unequivocally that *collegia* became both more numerous and more prosperous in the second and third centuries AD, though their numbers remain elusive. Having said that, *collegiati* probably remained a minority throughout, and it needs to be kept in mind that there always was a significant group of outsiders. Qualitative data can considerably further our understanding of who could join the *collegia* and who was excluded.

Wealth

The *senatus consultum de collegiis tenuiorum* could tentatively be read to suggest that *collegia* were particularly common among the 'poorer', depending on one's interpretation of *tenuiores*.[56] The *collegia* have been

[52] Liu presented these calculations in her paper for the Work, Labor and Professions conference, Ghent, 31 May 2013, but they were left out of the published version. Liu (2017). According to her calculations the real percentage was probably lower; extensive refutation of interpreting occupational or religious groups as formal *collegia* in Liu (2008b).

[53] Liu (2017), and elsewhere, is in favour of this new approach, and goes on to consider as *collegia* some debatable evidence that I would not necessarily include as such: for instance, the networks surrounding Tryphon and Pausiris, for which see Chapter 3 above.

[54] *CIL* 10.813: "Eumachiae L(uci) f(iliae) / sacerd(oti) publ(icae) / fullones".

[55] Some answers may come from the Ghent Database of Roman Guilds(+), still under construction. The (+) refers to the fact that it includes associations more generally.

[56] See above; *Dig.* 47.22.1 pr (Marcian).

referred to as a form of social security, "designed for lower class self-help".[57] This suggests they were 'mutual-aid societies' that catered to the needs of the poor, and of those who had no family to fall back on – interpreting *tenuiores* as the poor and destitute. In this view, they also provided the financial means by which a bereaved widow might take care of her children and could secure the funds for a decent burial, for her deceased husband and for herself and her children in the future.[58] But membership was probably out of the reach of that widow if she were truly poor and destitute.

The *collegium* charters that have come down to us suggest that membership was not free. Aspiring members were probably required to pay an entrance fee, as well as a regular monthly contribution.[59] The best-known charter of a Roman association reports that the worshippers (*cultores*) of Diana and Antinoos from Lanuvium owed the *collegium* 100 HS plus an amphora of good wine upon admission; their monthly contribution amounted to five *asses*.[60] This entrance fee was not negligible, and together with the continuous monthly contributions effectively makes money a selection criterion for membership.[61] *Collegia* also required their members' presence at meetings, banquets, and so on, and the time investment, too, was one that presumably not everyone could afford.[62] Burial arrangements through a *collegium* were costly by implication.[63] The idea that the associations functioned mainly as a burial insurance for the poor has long been refuted.[64] These considerations make clear that *collegia* did not provide social security to the poor in our sense of the word. One might say that they did so in the Roman sense of the word. "In the eyes of wealthy Roman

[57] The words are Van Nijf's (2002) 307, who then goes on to refute this interpretation. Social security: MacMullen (1966) 174.

[58] "Mutual-aid societies", Garnsey and Saller (1987) 156; the hypothetical widow was introduced by Hopkins (1983) 213.

[59] Cf. Liu (2009) 163, with n. 10 listing the evidence, who writes that it is plausible, but not very widely attested, that *collegia* commonly demanded an entrance fee.

[60] *CIL* 14.2112, now in the Museo Nazionale delle Terme Diocleziani in Rome; cf. Bendlin (2011), with updated text and translation.

[61] Patterson (1992) 21; cf. Venticinque (2010) 274 n. 4 for Roman Egypt.

[62] Liu (2017) 209. At ibid., 210, she cites a very interesting case of someone resigning from his association because he could not bring up the investment anymore: ἀσθενῶς ἔχων (*P. Mich.* 9.575, l. 4–5, Karanis 184 AD).

[63] Verboven (2007) 875: "Membership of an association was in itself relatively expensive. Indirectly burial by or with assistance of a *collegium*, was an expensive option. Rather, the *collegia* contributed to adding lustre to the funeral of their members, affirming for the last time their social status, reflecting favourably on their family and heirs".

[64] Contra Mommsen (1843), whose views have long been influential, e.g. Hopkins (1983) 214. See now Perry (2006) Chapter 1, esp. 29–32.

officials, most people must have appeared to be men of modest means".[65] *Tenuis* was thus a relative concept that distinguished a very wealthy elite from all the rest: when Augustine referred to himself and his father as *tenuis* or *pauper*, for example, we know that he certainly was not referring to any financial problems the family might have had.[66] In all likelihood the use of the word *tenuiores* in the *senatus consultum de collegiis tenuiorum*, therefore, did not so much refer to the poor, as to the non-elite or the 'not-wealthy'.[67]

It is certain that the professional *collegia* attracted a number of wealthier members, some of whom belonged to the senatorial or equestrian elite. A *collegium* with such upper-class membership did not conform to the general rule of the *senatus consultum de collegiis tenuiorum*. That would have made the *collegium* illegal, so it is likely that it would have had to apply to the authorities to gain official association status.[68] This practical drawback may not have been so severe in reality – it was argued above that many associations were granted the right of assembly – and one can imagine that the presence of elite members had its advantages. That there was such a wealthier group of members and associates, is evident from the amount of money circulating in substantial benefactions bestowed upon associations, as well as in the significant expenses incurred by the associations' involvement in burials and collective deeds of euergetism.[69] Their place in the urban community depended on it. Most of the occupational inscriptions relating to the *collegia* record *collegium* magistrates or benefactors, who cannot have been entirely without means.[70] *CIL* 6.1872 is found on an altar dedicated to Tiberius Claudius Severus by the association of fishermen and divers at Rome:

CIL 6.1872

Ti(berio) Claudio Esquil(ina) Severo / decuriali lictori patrono / corporis piscatorum et / urinator(um) q(uin)q(uennali) III eiusdem corporis / ob merita eius / quod hic primus statuas duas una / Antonini Aug(usti) domini n(ostri) aliam Iul(iae) / Augustae dominae nostr(ae) s(ua) p(ecunia)

65 Venticinque (2016) 182.

66 Brown (2012) 148–54; Aug. *Conf.* 2.3.5 for Patricius as a *tenuis municeps*; Aug. *Sermo* 356.13 referring to himself as "hominem pauperem, de pauperibus natum", "a poor man, born from poor parents"; cf. Woolf (2006); Shaw (1987b) 8–10 seems to have changed the mind of Peter Brown, who still took Augustine's word (*tenuis*) at face value in his biography – Brown (1967) 21.

67 Ausbüttel (1982) 25: "Mit dem Wort *tenuiores* wird die einfache, aber [...] keineswegs besitzlose Bevölkerung im Gegensatz zu den *honestiores* oder *divites* bezeichnet".

68 Cf. De Ligt (2000).

69 This is evident, for example, from Liu's discussion of membership in the *collegia centonariorum* – Liu (2009) 164–69; and Liu (2008a); more generally, see also Ausbüttel (1982) 43–48.

70 For Rome, Joshel (1992) 113.

> p(osuerit) / una cum Claudio Pontiano filio / suo eq(uite) Rom(ano) et hoc amplius eidem / corpori donaverit HS X mil(ia) n(ummum) / ut ex usuris eorum quodannis / natali suo XVII K(alendas) Febr(uarias) / sportulae viritim dividantur / praesertim cum navigatio sca/pharum diligentia eius adquisita / et confirmata sit ex decreto / ordinis corporis piscatorum / et urinatorum totius alv(ei) Tiber(is) / quibus ex s(enatus) c(onsulto) coire licet s(ua) p(ecunia) p(osuerunt)
>
> To Tiberius Claudius Severus of the Esquiline tribe, *decurialis*, *lictor*, patron of the associated fishermen and divers, threefold president (*quinquennalis*) of the same association, because of his benefactions, first among which two statues he placed out of his one funds, one of Antoninus Augustus our emperor [= Caracalla], the other of Julia Augusta our emperor-mother; one [statue] with Claudius Pontianus his son, a Roman knight; and on top of that he gave to the same association 10,000 sesterces so that out of the dividend of these on his birthday, the 17 Kalends of February, gifts can be handed out man by man; above all for the navigational rights (*navigatio scapharum*) gained through his diligence and confirmed by decree of the board (*ordo*) of the association of fishermen and divers of the entire Tiber-shore to whom it was allowed by senatorial decree to assemble [i.e. they had the *ius coeundi*].

This text gives a good overview of what such a man might be capable of in terms of money (and influence).[71]

The wealthier segment of the population thus took part in larger associations as well, and some associations, like the Iobacchoi, were even characterized by a largely upper-class membership.[72] There were real benefits to be gained from *collegium* membership, so the presence of the elite is unsurprising: it appears that by the third century some of the more affluent Romans joined a *collegium* to gain immunities from *munera publica* (public benefactions for which only the wealthy were eligible), or to get other privileges.[73]

Collegia were therefore not for the poor, and they did include some rich people. In line with this finding, the possibility that the professional *collegia* included only employers, not employees, has been stressed repeatedly.[74] In

[71] *CIL* 6.1872 = *ILS* 7266, AD 206. A different side of the altar adds consular dating and the corporate magistrates responsible for setting up the dedication.

[72] Remus (1996).

[73] Liu (2009) 109–11; Verboven (2007) 881. This led to legal measures to exclude from these privileges those who were too wealthy or who were not actually of the nominal occupation. *Dig.* 50.6.6.12 (Callistratus). Cf. also Liu (2009) 57–62.

[74] Recently voiced by Verboven (2007) 882; Patterson (2006) 255; and Van Nijf (2002) 308. See also the influential work of Ausbüttel (1982). This possibility was also emphasized by Brunt (1980) 87, 91, including the *collegia* inscriptions explicitly among

this view, the association of bakers would consist of wholesalers or large property owners in charge of those actually kneading the dough and baking the bread, which interestingly sounds rather like what we think we know of that famous *pistor*, M. Vergilius Eurysaces. Membership would have concerned master craftsmen and shop owners, rather than wage labourers, apprentices, or salesmen. Indeed we have seen that the truly poor were not among the *collegiati*. However, it is highly likely that a skilled labourer could afford to join an association.[75] And since not every skilled artisan was an entrepreneur, this means that the *collegiati* would – at least potentially – include employees as well as employers.[76] In some cases the *collegia* effectively were so large that it is quite unlikely that they only included the top echelon of master artisans and shop owners, to the exclusion of others.[77] Moreover, the inclusion of both employers and employees matches the hierarchical nature of the *collegia*, reflecting the relationships outside them. It would also make the associations a rather convenient platform for finding labourers to fill any vacancies.[78] I suspect that one of the reasons why the idea of associations of employers is still cited is that guild membership is one of the criteria scholars have used to try to distinguish between a manual labourer and a wholesaler, when an inconclusive job title was the only thing certain. It is true that there is nothing in the ancient evidence to suggest that affiliation with a *collegium* was close to universal, so there were restrictive factors at work.[79] However, I do not believe that the selection criterion for *collegium* membership was 'entrepreneurship'. They must have been restrictions of a different kind.

Legal status

Slaves, freed, and freeborn were equally welcome to join associations as long as they complied with the association's conditions for entry. It is difficult to say anything more about the respective proportion of the freeborn, freed, and slaves among the *collegiati*. Virtually everything we know about individual *collegiati* outside Roman Egypt comes from

"those [inscriptions] which might be held to mention manual workers at Rome, but in fact often relate to employers".

75 See, for example, the section on 'economic differentiation' in Groen-Vallinga and Tacoma (2017) 118–22; cf. Ausbüttel (1982) 46.

76 Skilled slaves in *collegia* are especially unlikely to have been entrepreneurs; for slave members in *collegia* see below.

77 Cf. Liu (2009) 169–71.

78 Even more directly than suggested by Holleran (2017) 99–100.

79 Unless the Pompeian graffito *CIL* 4.960 can be read as "all of the woodworkers": "Cuspium Pansam/ aedil(em) lignari(i) universi rog(ant)". There is no evidence that the Pompeian woodworkers formed a *collegium*, however. Compare also the *universi dendrofori* in *CIL* 8.23400 (quoted below, n. 95).

inscriptions and, like all epigraphic material, the *collegia* inscriptions are not without biases.[80] Private associations in Rome had the fortunate habit of keeping lists with the names of their members (and beneficiaries) and, more importantly, of inscribing them on stone. Some of these documents have survived, and are now known as the *alba collegiorum*. Unfortunately, however, for most members these *alba* do not explicitly record filiation, libertinization, or servile status. Perhaps they explicitly omitted legal status to emphasize the general equality of their members to the outside world. To complicate matters further, explicit mention of libertinization was omitted in the epigraphic record more generally from the second half of the first century onwards. It is interesting that in accordance with the lack of status indication in the *alba*, Joshel's study of the occupational inscriptions for individuals from *CIL* 6 finds that professional *collegiati* were particularly likely to leave out proper status indication in favour of stating their ties with a *collegium*.[81] This would also indicate a tendency among *collegium* members to emphasize collective identity and equality rather than individual status distinctions, although the significant proportion of *collegium* magistrates among them underlines that the associations in themselves were actually strongly hierarchical in nature.

Scholars who took up the challenge of studying the membership composition of associations, including status structures, resorted to onomastics. Onomastic analysis indicates that most members were free, but it cannot always say whether they were freed or freeborn.[82]

The majority of those known *collegium* members whose legal status we can identify with any certainty appear to have been freedmen.[83] A noticeable majority of office holders in the *collegia* were also of freed status.[84] These observations have led some scholars to believe that associations were chiefly or exclusively made up of freedmen.[85] However, since the evidence for *collegium* membership is largely epigraphic, and freedmen are relatively prominent in the epigraphic evidence from the Roman empire, it is to be expected that freedmen are relatively well represented among *collegiati* as

[80] Cf. Tran (2006); Venticinque (2016) 15–16 on the legal status of *collegiati* in Roman Egypt, where members were mostly male and freeborn.

[81] Joshel (1992) 117–19.

[82] For an onomastic approach see Tran (2006); and Huttunen (1974). These *incerti* were not necessarily *ingenui*, as Ausbüttel (1982) 39–40 concludes on the basis of some very questionable onomastics: he works with the assumption that freedmen are (all and only) those with a non-Latin cognomen. See Liu (2009) Chapter 5 for a systematic analysis of membership composition of the *collegia centonariorum*, the value of which is not limited to the *collegia centonariorum*.

[83] Cf. Joshel (1992) 117–19.

[84] Royden (1988) 230.

[85] E.g. Van Nijf (2002) 308.

well. But the predominance of freedmen in associations ostensibly was not always so pronounced: it is lacking in the numerically significant *collegia centonariorum*.[86] The conclusion that members of associations were mostly freedmen is not so straightforward.

I would suggest that the argument that *collegia* (and professional associations in particular) were a freedmen prerogative builds on a number of other presumptions regarding Roman freedmen. Freedmen were an elusive group of individuals who are highly visible in the ancient evidence, and therefore speak to the scholarly imagination. Freedmen have at various times been equated with successful businessmen, the nouveaux riches, or a version of the bourgeoisie or the middle class/*plebs media* – and so have the *collegiati*.

Conspicuous funerary monuments, and literary references to wealthy freedmen like Petronius' famous satirical character Trimalchio, all contributed to a picture of freedmen as rich upstarts: the nouveaux riches or, in more Marxist terms, the Roman counterpart of the 'bourgeoisie'. Their obvious wealth could not have run in the family because of their servile background. The money had to be earned through their economic enterprises. There were many sectors of the economy that the elite traditionally kept away from. The evidence at first seems to support the idea that (successful) businessmen invariably were freedmen. The occupational inscriptions taken at face value also suggest that manual labour was generally executed by freedmen, and artisans and craftsmen historically make up the 'middle class' in society. The associative order outlined by Verboven was the way through which Roman upstarts could convert economic capital into social and symbolic capital, and although Verboven, to his credit, does not explicitly talk about a middle class, this is how one presumably moved up from the *plebs media* to the upper class.[87]

A real middle class cannot be isolated in Roman society, let alone equated with freedmen. It is also clear that the group of freedmen in itself was decidedly heterogeneous. These observations are not new. Some of the old notions, however, still resonate in attempts to explain the function and membership composition of *collegia* through the freedman presence – a view not fully supported the evidence. Associations were not a freedman prerogative.

The participation of slaves and *ingenui* in Roman associations has not been studied with quite the same intensity as freedman participation. It is tacitly assumed that the freeborn were allowed to congregate into professional and other voluntary associations; Ausbüttel even assumed that most of the *collegiati* were freeborn.[88] The latter assumption cannot be supported

86 Liu (2009) 171–72.

87 Verboven (2007).

88 Ausbüttel (1982) 39–40, cf. n. 82 above.

by the evidence, but it is securely attested that the freeborn were part of the *collegia*. Publius Aufidius Fortus, son of Publius, for example, was prefect of the *fabri tignuarii* in Ostia, and patron as well as an honoured official (*quinquennalis perpetuus*) of the associated fruit sellers and divers in the same city.[89] Another example is Lucius Cincius Martialis, son of Lucius, who was affiliated with the *collegium* of *fabri tignuarii* at Rome.[90]

We know that at least in theory slaves, too, were eligible to join a *collegium*, even if not all associations were open to them. The few references we have to membership lists of a *collegium familiae publicae* naturally include many slaves (and freedmen).[91] The inscription of the *cultores* of Diana and Antinoos in Lanuvium specifically records prescriptions for the eventuality that a master should refuse to hand over the remains of a deceased slave to the *collegium*.[92] Slaves who were manumitted were expected to donate an amphora of wine to the association. The text therefore clearly reckons with slave membership among the *cultores*. The jurist Marcian also underlines that there was no reason why slaves could not join an association, provided they had their owner's permission.[93] As we have seen, slaves were even sometimes among the guild magistrates. This is a vivid illustration of how the collegial hierarchy would sometimes overturn the hierarchy of society. Looking at the named members, however, few *collegiati* can be securely identified as slaves.[94]

Gender

What has been said so far about membership in associations largely applies to the male population. The *collegia* may have been less inclusive when it comes to gender, however. Women are seldom recorded formally among the members listed in the *alba collegii*: they are not attested as members of the professional *collegia* at all, though their membership is sometimes confirmed for religious associations.[95] Yet, as we have just seen, the distinction between

[89] *CIL* 14.4620, "corpus mercatorum frumentariorum et urinatorum".

[90] *CIL* 6.9405.

[91] Bruun (2015) 613 for one in Venafrum, *CIL* 10.4856, and one *familia publica* in Ostia, *CIL* 14, 255.

[92] Implying that it was common practice (or at least desirable) that the *collegium* arrange a proper funeral for their slave members, *CIL* 14.2112, 2, 3–5.

[93] *Dig.* 47.22.3.2 (Marcian). Translation Cotter (1996): "Servos quoque licet in collegio tenuiorum recipi volentibus dominis", "It is also lawful for slaves to be admitted into associations of indigent persons, with the consent of their masters".

[94] Tran (2006) 49–65.

[95] Hemelrijk (2015) 200 for women and occupational *collegia*, ibid., 199–204 for female membership of associations in general. It is interesting to note that virtually all come from Italy. Ibid., 200, 224; cf. Waltzing (1895) 348; Ausbüttel (1982) 42: "Allerdings besassen einige, vor allem religiöse Kollegien, einen hohen Prozentsatz

professional and religious *collegia* may have been little more than an indication of two different sides of the same coin.[96] In addition to female membership of predominantly male associations, there are one or two references to all-female associations: the collective of female mimes (*sociae mimae*) from Rome is the best example.[97] Exclusively female collectives seem to have existed in Roman Italy on a limited scale but, parallel to the idea of a secondary labour market, we might call it a 'secondary associative phenomenon'.[98]

There is a difference between legal membership of associations on the one hand, and women's actual engagement with *collegia* on the other.[99] A famous example that always comes up in this context is Eumachia, commemorated for her benefactions by the fullers of Pompeii.[100] Hemelrijk has illuminated the position of women who come up as benefactress, patroness, or so-called 'mother' of a *collegium*. She argues that contrary to patronesses of associations, the title of 'mother' of the *collegium* (*mater collegii*) was bestowed upon women who in all likelihood were 'insiders', chosen from among the same social strata. The suggestion is that these women may have been associated members themselves.[101] It is tempting to read into this that as members of the occupational associations, women may have been recognized artisans. As Hemelrijk shows, however, few 'mothers' were recorded within professional associations. Moreover, there is no way of knowing whether their engagement with an association did not originate chiefly from their relationship with another (male) collegiate member.[102]

weiblicher Mitglieder" – he mentions an association from Mactar, Africa, with the telling title "universi dendrofori et sacrati utriusque sexus" (of both sexes), the reference must be *CIL* 8.23400; cf. North (2013) on variations in the relation between the gender of the worshippers and admission to religious cults; Dixon (2001b) 14.

96 An interesting background to the observation of Waltzing (1895) 348–49: "En ce point, les collèges d'artisans différaient donc des collèges funéraires qui admettaient les femmes et leur confaient même des fonctions collégiales". If a distinction between occupational and funerary associations is no longer valid, what is the significance of the observed difference?

97 *CIL* 6.10109 quoted in full below; noted by Hemelrijk (2015) 205; Ausbüttel (1982) 42; Waltzing (1895) 348.

98 Hemelrijk (2015) 205–21.

99 Hemelrijk (2015) Chapters 4, 5; Hirschmann (2004) 403–4, 412.

100 *CIL* 10.813 quoted in the text above; Hirschmann (2004) 409; Hemelrijk (2015) 198; Hemelrijk (2008) 119 n. 12 notes that Eumachia is not explicitly indicated as a patroness of the fullers.

101 Hemelrijk (2015) esp. Chapters 4, 5; earlier publication of findings in Hemelrijk (2012) on fictive motherhood; Hemelrijk (2010); Hemelrijk (2008) on female patronesses and 'mothers' of *collegia*; see also the discussion of Liu (2009) 178–80.

102 Hemelrijk (2015) e.g. 184–85; family was important in the choice for patronesses, too, ibid., 231–35; also Hemelrijk (2012); Hemelrijk (2008) 140: "as a rule, a 'mother'

Because there is very little evidence for female membership of professional *collegia*, the latter option seems to be the most likely explanation. This outcome is entirely in line with the engendered patterns of labour in Roman society: "fictive motherhood allowed women a position of authority within a city or *collegium*, a role which was cast in socially acceptable terms".[103] It seems that women could be, but usually were not, among the members of an association. As demonstrated in the previous chapters, this does not mean that they were not involved in a trade.

Ethnicity

The existence of a *corpus splendissimum mercatorum Cisalpinorum et Transalpinorum* at Mediolanum and Novara, or the epitaph of the president of the *corpus negotiantium Malacitorum* found in Rome – to name but a few examples – indicates that common ethnic background could be the organizing principle behind an association, for those who moved to or within Roman Italy.[104]

The port cities of Ostia and Puteoli were also home to many migrants, often merchants from abroad, and here they organized themselves into collectives that sporadically come up in the epigraphic sources.[105]

Clustering of migrants in larger cities more generally, however, is chiefly attested through trading stations (*stationes*) such as the Piazzale delle Corporazioni in Ostia and the famous Tyrians of Puteoli; but *stationes* were perhaps more like embassies (with a commercial function) than associations.[106] When Verboven writes that "*collegia* grouping foreigners are widely, but not abundantly, attested throughout the empire", it is significant that this includes *stationes* – and it is even more noteworthy that, with the exception of Ostia and Puteoli, much of the more substantial evidence comes from outside Roman Italy.[107] Likewise, there are no inscriptions for resident aliens in Roman Italy united in *collegii consistentes* or *peregrinorum*, as there are in other provinces. In Lugdunum there was a *collegium* of the

of a *collegium* was a female official who was probably recruited from among the female members of the association, or from the relatives of male officials".

103 Hemelrijk (2012) 212.

104 The *corpus splendissimum* is also attested at Aventicum, Lugdunum, and Trier. Verboven (2011b) n. 31 for references; this particular epitaph is *CIL* 6.9677.

105 Verboven (2011b) 337 lists Berytenses, Heliopolitanenses, Germellenses, Nabataenses, and individual foreigners. He writes, "Puteoli was an exceptional place. Like Ostia, the city was a commercial stronghold, where the number of outsiders rivaled the number of citizens. Both towns shared many features, but differed substantially from 'ordinary' cities".

106 Tacoma (2016) 236–37. For the *Piazzale* see *CIL* 14.4549; Terpstra (2013) 100–12. The Tyrians at Puteoli: *CIG* 3.5835 = *IG* 14.830, AD 174; Terpstra (2013) 70–84.

107 Verboven (2011b) 337.

fabri tignuarii consistentes as well as a *collegium fabrum tignuariorum* (of locals, we may presume). This leads Liu to signal exclusion of resident aliens from associations "in large port cities or commercial centres".[108] Whereas there are sporadic examples that seem to reflect this duality elsewhere in the empire,[109] a similar ban is not apparent in Italy. Foreigners may have been prevented from joining existing *collegia* sometimes, but if they were it is not traceable.

In sum, migrant associations in Roman Italy do not appear to have been common, even in the city of Rome. It must be assumed that migrants who wished to join a collective were quickly assimilated into the existing pluriform associative structure.[110]

Occupation

Gender thus far appears to be the best general indicator for inclusion in or exclusion from associations. Legal status or wealth does not seem to be a specific requirement for membership in the professional associations. More interestingly, however, occupation was not always a decisive prerequisite either.[111] Perhaps that curious fact should not come as a surprise, considering the functional overlap between associations that was emphasized earlier in this chapter. Nevertheless, surely the titular profession of an association must have meant something. After all, Roman history would have it that the associations first created in the time of the kings were occupational in nature.[112]

In professional associations, occupation took pride of place. The *lex* of the dealers in ivory and citrus wood (*negotiatores eborarii et citrarii*) is clear on the matter:

> ***CIL* 6.33885, 4–6**
>
> [item] placere ut si alius quam negotiator eborarius aut citrarius [p]er / [fr]audem curatorum in hoc collegium adlectus esset uti curatores eius / [cau]sa ex albo raderentur ab ordine…

[108] Liu (2017) 214, 214–16. She notes that the *consistentes* demonstrably accepted local members into their ranks, which mitigates a strict duality.

[109] Cf. Koestner (2017) on the linen weavers of Alexandria in *P. Giss.* 40 II.

[110] Tacoma (2016) 232–37, excluding the *stationes*, and ibid., 237–40 for the volatile nature and weak ties of many migrant networks.

[111] Ausbüttel (1982) 36, 74; Liu (2013) 360: "The link to a particular occupation, however, did not mean that all the practitioners of a trade had to become members of the corresponding association, or that each and every professional association admitted artisans and/or tradesmen of its titular trade only".

[112] The first *collegia* are said to have been created by Servius Tullius or Numa Pompilius, *Flor.* 1.6.3; Plin. *HN* 34.1.1; 35.46.159; Plut. *Num.* 17.1–2; cf. *Dig.* 47.22.4 for *collegia* in the Twelve Tables.

> if by a mistake of the curators someone other than an ivory dealer or a citrus wood dealer should have been admitted into this *collegium*, then the curators will be erased from the membership list by the *ordo* because of it ...[113]

Note that the curators are removed, but the text does not explicate what was done about the erroneously appointed *collegiatus*.[114]

It is probably significant that the *negotiatores eborarii et citrarii* were based in the city of Rome: larger cities like Rome and Ostia had a greater variation of associations, often connected with highly specialized trades such as the *faber soliarius baxiarius* (women's sandal maker).[115] With such a wide choice in associations it is difficult to see why, say, a *faber soliarius baxiarius* would even consider joining the *eborarii et citrarii* rather than the *collegium* of his own trade. There were obvious economic and social benefits to associating with those in the same trade. As a rule, therefore, professional *collegia* could indeed be defined by shared occupation. However, it appears to have been a recognized fact that various professions could also sometimes be assembled under the heading of one occupational *collegium*: the law acknowledged that this occurred, although it is difficult to find actual attestations of it.[116] It has been suggested that occupational plurality within a professional association was characteristic particularly of smaller settlements, in which case this scenario may have been the more common one throughout Italy.[117] This geographical differentiation is where I shall turn now.

Urbanism and association

There is a correlation between urbanism and association: generally speaking, *collegia* are attested in urban centres.[118] In part this is due to

[113] The *ordo* here probably refers to the guild or guild magistrates, cf. Tran (2007b) 124.

[114] Expulsion was a possibility, cf. Tran (2007b).

[115] *CIL* 6.9404.

[116] E.g. *Dig.* 50.6.6.6; 50.6.6.12; for an example see *AE* 1981, 387; cf. Liu (2009) 203–8 on 'outsiders' in the *collegium centonariorum*; Verboven (2007) 883–84 with other examples. The converse was also possible: there are those with multiple affiliations, despite the fact that it is forbidden by law (*Dig* 47.22.1.2, Marcian); see Liu (2009) 206–8.

[117] Liu (2009) 22.

[118] Liu (2008b) 65 notes that "the case of Pompeii implies that a high degree of urbanization, such as that found at Pompeii, or craft-related specialization does not automatically lead to the formation of *collegia*. It is my understanding that the relationship between urbanization and the formation of *collegia* is not always straightforward." This viewpoint is based on a strict definition of formal *collegia* which I have discussed under the heading 'Formal organization and variation' above, where I outlined the development of private associations into *collegia*, and of *collegia* into active organizations in the civic community. What follows is valid, too, if in the first century

the nature of the evidence: associations are chiefly attested epigraphically, and inscriptions on stone are an urban occurrence. Moreover, associations generally tend to form where people cluster together in large numbers, and that is in the cities. The more people, the more associations.[119] The perceived distribution pattern of *collegia* inscriptions is therefore not surprising. The precise nature of the correlation between urbanism and the associative phenomenon is, however, not immediately apparent. In order to get to the nature of this connection, the distribution of inscriptions recording *collegia* deserves somewhat closer scrutiny.

There was a wide variation in number, size, and prestige of associations, all of which was largely related to their location.[120] Some basic distinctions between *collegia* in large and small towns have already been noted in the scholarly literature. But there is a third category, both the largest and most obvious one: the associations of Rome. Rome cannot be equated with the other large cities, and conversely the material from the eternal city has a tendency to become an unwarranted model for all (large) cities. The tripartite distinction between the capital, large cities, and small settlements is not often explicitly recognized.[121]

Rome

Almost two-thirds of the epigraphic attestations of *collegia* come from Italy.[122] The majority of *collegia* inscriptions originate from the capital.[123] This pattern appears to be broadly consistent with the general pattern of epigraphic output. More significant is that the city of Rome also exhibits a greater differentiation in the 'occupational' associations attested than any other city.[124] The difference therefore is not just in number, but also in the nature of the inscriptions. In Rome, there appear to have been three *centuriae* of women's sandal makers alone.[125] In Rome, too, there are *collegia* for highly specialized professions like *caudicarii* (lightermen) and *specularii* (mirror makers?), or the *lenuncularii traiectus Luculli* (ferrymen working at

there were private associations (as I have argued above for Pompeii) rather than formal *collegia*.

119 This distribution pattern is corroborated by the results in Hanson et al. (2017).

120 Ausbüttel (1982) 33 pointed out that there probably were regional differences, but does not go into this.

121 Liu, especially (2013) and (2008b), is the positive exception. For a working definition of large, medium, or small settlements, see De Ligt (2012) 201.

122 Ausbüttel (1982) 32.

123 Roughly 700 according to Liu (2013) 352.

124 Liu (2013) 352 notes a total of around 500 different *collegia* at Rome. Cf. Royden (1988) 238; cf. Liu (2009) 22–23. Compare Harper (2011) 102, who finds that also household "scale and specialization were correlated".

125 *CIL* 6.9404.

the crossing of Lucullus), "and many, many other specialists quite untranslatably named according to what they did for a living".[126]

Rome stood at the apex of the urban network. Migration to Rome was substantial and included many young males, who migrated without any family or pre-existing networks.[127] The city may have had a million inhabitants, locals as well as immigrants. Because of the large number of people involved, all of whom were looking for a place to belong, as often as not without a family to fall back on, the structuring principle offered by *collegia* was more important in Rome than anywhere else in Roman Italy. As a result, there were many identifiable associations in the capital but, significantly, most of them did not enjoy the same social prestige as their counterparts in other settlements. Perhaps more than anywhere else, in Rome the 'associative order' presented an alternative for those who had no part in the civic order.[128]

In most cities *collegia* became part of the civic order, and as part of the civic order, *collegiati* gained certain privileges. The development was outlined in more detail above. Associations were included in public banquets and ceremonies, and together with the *decuriones* and Augustales, they were the core group of recipients of distributions and benefactions from wealthy patrons.[129] Taking over civic benefactions and duties in the absence of the traditional elite, *collegium* magistrates and *collegiati* enjoyed a certain prestige. By implication, so did their patrons and benefactors, as indicated by the fact that they proudly advertised their relationships of patronage and euergetism with the associations. This mutually beneficial system facilitated attracting high-ranking individuals as patrons and benefactors for the *collegia*. All of that was, however, not the case at Rome.[130]

The capital represented a unique civic landscape. The emperor resided at Rome, and so did the Senate – and many senators in addition. This was the seat of power that attracted the elite from all over the empire. With the emperor in the lead, all of these wealthy men were in constant competition for political power. The emperor took pains to affirm his position in relation to the *plebs*. Euergetism to the people and to the city of Rome, in the form of a building programme, games, and distributions of money or bread, was a prime method of doing so. The virtual monopoly over euergetism claimed

[126] *CIL* 6.1795, *CIL* 6.2206, and *CIL* 14.5320 respectively, all also attested in other inscriptions; quote MacMullen (1974) 73.

[127] Tacoma (2016) Chapter 4, esp. 107–23.

[128] For this symbolic associative order in Rome, Liu (2013) 362.

[129] Cf. Liu (2013) 362; Patterson (2006); Patterson (1994); Patterson (1992) 21–22; Van Nijf (1997) for the Roman East.

[130] Noted by Liu (2013) 362. Ausbüttel (1982) 48 predicts quite the opposite: "So werden in Rom und Ostia reichere Leute einem Verein angehört haben als z.B. in Britannien".

by the emperor left little space for the *collegia* to step in as civic benefactors. There was also no need to fulfil a desire for political influence among those who had very little, as in smaller cities. It was difficult for associations in Rome to secure wealthy patrons, both because of the associations' limited role in the community and in high-end politics, and because of the limited social capital that came with their position.[131]

There was a considerable variation in types of association. In Rome they ranged from the *collegia domestica* of the elite *domus* to the prominent *collegia apparitorum*.[132] *Collegia domestica* and others of a more private nature presumably did not compete for a more substantial role in the community, as their modest aims may have been fulfilled by their elite patron. Most of the professional collectives seem to have fallen somewhere in between these two, presenting social not merely but also economic networks that were of great value to their members but less so to elite patrons and the civic community.

There certainly were very large, influential, and prestigious associations in the city. An association like that of the *pistores* (bakers) or the *navicularii* (skippers) gained imperial recognition and the right of *corpus habere*, presumably because of their significant role in the *annona*.[133] The *collegia tria* or *collegia principalia*, the 'three associations' or 'principal associations', were among the ancient and respected guilds everywhere, including in Rome. These three principal associations commonly concern the *fabri* (often *fabri tignuarii* or *tignarii)*, *centonarii*, and *dendrophori*.[134] Tentatively

[131] Presumably one of the reasons why so many *collegia* are seen to have engaged in emperor worship in the hope of gaining this powerful patron's favour. Cf. Liu (2013) 364.

[132] Liu (2013) 356; The *collegia domestica* are more relevant to Chapter 4 on the elite *domus*, above, than here. The specific nature of the *collegia domestica* shows also, e.g., from the prominence of women in them. Hemelrijk (2015) 186–89.

[133] *Dig.* 3.4.1.pr (Gaius ad ed.); see also Verboven (2007) 875–78.

[134] Sometimes the *utriclarii* are also included. Liu (2009) 50–55 questions the value of studying these three *collegia* as a coherent group, stressing differences in origins and development. See also ibid., 393–94, on the epigraphic record of the *tria collegia/ collegia III*, urging caution in the equation of the *collegia tria* with these *collegia* when the sources do not specify which ones are meant. In what follows I use *collegia tria principalia* to refer to these particular three associations, as is common in scholarly literature. The prominence of these *collegia* has sometimes been linked to public utility as a fire brigade vel sim. That the *collegia centonariorum* and *fabrum* in particular were so widespread because they might have served as a fire brigade or were involved with maintaining public safety, as suggested by earlier scholars on the basis of Pliny, *Ep.* 10.33 and 34 (quoted above), has rightly been questioned. See Van Nijf (1997) 177–81, Perry (2006) 7–18; Liu (2009) Chapter 4, 125–60, with additional references. Contra Verboven (2007) 880, who still speaks of the "fire brigade associations". Callistratus, *Dig.* 50.6.6.12, does speak of the public utility of the *fabri* (passage quoted elsewhere). If

these translate into the builders, textile dealers, and worshippers of Magna Mater (literally 'tree-carriers'). The *fabri tignuarii* of Rome were one of the longest-lived and largest *collegia* in the capital that we know of.[135] There were *fabri*, *dendrophori*, and *centonarii* here, too.[136] Many other associations were also prominently present in the capital through their buildings, *scholae*, or temples, the majority of them of an occupational signature.[137] *Collegia* set up inscriptions and statues in public places, and dedicated them to deities and the imperial house.

Larger cities

The port city of Ostia is the one settlement that would conceivably resemble Rome most, because of the close connection between the two. Walking around what is left of the city today, commercial spaces catch the eye. Ostia as we know it was largely constructed or transformed in the second century AD, when *collegia* flourished.[138] The elaborate buildings or *scholae* of associations undeniably shape the urban landscape, and the Piazzale delle Corporazioni is unparalleled, with its rows of market stalls or offices for various collectives.[139] Like Rome, Ostia is known for its great variety of occupational *collegia* and, as in Rome, they are omnipresent both in the epigraphic record and in the material remains of the townscape. In both respects, however, it appears that Rome and Ostia were exceptional within Roman Italy.[140] This makes it all the more vexing that there were significant differences between the positions of the *collegia* in the capital and at Ostia.

Ostia was a city of commerce, not a political hub. The Isola Sacra necropolis holds the remains of traders and craftsmen, with few or no reported magistrates.[141] Professional associations at Ostia are disproportionately well

we compare the finding that in AD 1791 a third of all the wage workers in Paris were employed in the building trade (Brunt (1974) 87), the prominence and public utility of an actual builders' association is perhaps not so unlikely.

135 Largest: *CIL* 6.1060 points to at least 59 *decuriae*, of around 22 men each. Long-lived: *CIL* 6.9034 (lustrum XIIX) and *CIL* 6.9406 (lustrum XXVII). There are attestations from the first to fourth centuries.

136 Liu (2009) Appendix B, 384–90 .

137 Bollmann (1998) 169.

138 Meiggs (1960) 133 (133–45. 'the architectural revolution').

139 Commercial space: Meiggs (1960) 272–74; DeLaine (2005); *Piazzale delle corporazioni*: many corporations are named in the mosaics on the floor of the offices, documented as *CIL* 14.4549; *Scholae*: Bollmann (1998).

140 Bollmann (1998) 169–70 notes that the rich evidence for *Vereinshäuser* in the second century is largely restricted to Rome and Ostia. Her discussion of the "Vereinshäuser in städtischen context" is structured accordingly: in Rome, Ostia, and the rest.

141 Meiggs (1960) 455; Kampen (1981) 23.

attested epigraphically compared to other occupational inscriptions from the town (roughly two to one). Incidentally and unsurprisingly, the most prominent guild is that of the *fabri tignuariorum Ostiensum*. There are also *fabri* (without addition to the name), as well as *dendrophori*, but no known *centonarii*. Many of the associations here concern collectives of sailors and traders, which is to be expected in a port city. The visibility of associations both in the epigraphic record and in archaeological remains of the town plan seems to reflect their importance in the community of Ostia. As a result of their position, the *collegia* at Ostia do not seem to have had any problem engaging high-ranking and wealthy patrons.[142] Quite unlike Rome, therefore, Ostia perfectly illustrates Patterson's narrative of how the associations took their place in the civic community over the course of the second and third centuries.[143]

A town like Pompeii also accounts for 25 known different professional associations, if the election notices are included.[144] Besides these two examples, however, the epigraphic record for *collegia* in the larger towns of the Italian peninsula is limited. Half of these cities have no record of any associations; the other half have one, maybe two. Puteoli does not appear to have had many associations despite its obvious importance in commerce, though there are *dendrophori* here.[145] The city of Capua, which seems to have ranked second in size after Rome, has *centonarii* and two interesting references to unspecified *collegia*, where "the *collegia* have set up" (*collegia posuerunt*) a dedication to influential individuals. Similarly, *CIL* 11.5416 from Asisium commemorates a patron of the city and three associations (*municipii et collegiorum III*).[146] The scarce references to *collegia III*, like this one, have been taken to mean 'the three principal *collegia*', *in*

[142] E.g. L. Calpurnius Chius, *CIL* 14.309, mid- to late second century AD. His name suggests family ties (libertinization) with one of the known consuls of the name L. Calpurnius Piso, perhaps (closest in time) the consul of AD 175 whose light might have shone down on Chius. Chius became a central person in Ostia's civic community: his epitaph lists that he once was sevir and president of the Augustales, president and twice treasurer (*curator*) of the *corpus mensorum frumentariorum* at Ostia, treasurer of the Ostian *codicarii*, three times and honorary president of the *collegium* of Silvanus Augustus maior; and *magister* to Mars Ficanus Augustus in the *collegium dendroforum*.

[143] Patterson (2006), discussed above.

[144] Verboven (2007) 874, in 41 inscriptions; cf. Liu (2008b) for the notion that these were not formally recognized *collegia*, at 62: "the phenomenon of *collegia* had not developed in Pompeii by the time the city was destroyed".

[145] Other than these, there is a *collegium scabillariorum* (some sort of ritual musicians?); *Baulanorum* (ethnic); *Heliopolitanorum* (ethnic); see above.

[146] *Centonarii* in Capua: *AE* 2010, 325; *collegia posuerunt*, *AE* 1985, 273; *AE* 1972, 75; cf. also the *reparator collegiorum* of *CIL* 9.1596 (Beneventum).

casu the *fabri*, *centonarii*, and *dendrophori*.[147] Though one should be careful in the assumption, it is easy to see where it comes from and it may not be far beside the truth: with the exceptions of Ostia and Pompeii, an investigation into the associations of larger cities effectively coincides with mapping the principal associations.

The question becomes why Ostia and Pompeii show such a different picture, compared to other large cities. That said, Ostia and Pompeii are both relatively large within a rather broad category of settlements. Ostia could perhaps also be explained through its proximity to Rome, though important differences between Ostia and Rome were pointed out above. More importantly, the state of the evidence in Ostia and Pompeii is better than in many other cities, which accounts for some of the discrepancy. If that is the case, however, should the circumstances in Ostia and Pompeii be seen as representative of other commercial centres? Comparison with the situation in other provinces would suggest as much; comparison with the other settlements of Roman Italy, however, would indicate that perhaps Italy was exceptional.[148]

Small towns

The range of (professional) *collegia* predictably was small in minor urban centres: in these settlements, too, many of the (professional) associations belong to one of the *collegia principalia*.[149] The *fabri* are everywhere, but there appear to be some regional differences within this pattern: the *centonarii* are predominantly located in north and central Italy, and are almost absent from the south where the *dendrophori* are most common.[150] An analysis of the occupational inscriptions of Picenum by Cristofori offers an interesting case in point, as it has virtually no evidence for *collegia* other than the three principal ones.[151] There are exceptions. The modest settlement of Falerio is relatively well documented in the region, and it is evident that *collegia* played an important part in its community. An elaborate inscription offers evidence for the existence of the three *collegia principalia* in the town, but there is also an epitaph set up for a magistrate of the collective of the

147 Liu (2009) 393. In my view, *AE* 1985, 273 and *AE* 1972, 75 from Capua cited in the previous note very likely also relate to the *III collegia* – in both instances there is an illegible space on the stone before the word *collegia* that would accommodate 'III'.

148 Venticinque (2016) 17 writes that associations in Roman Egypt appear to have been "ubiquitous".

149 The Augustales remain the most common *collegium* throughout; *collegia* were certainly not limited to the *fabri tignuarii* outside Rome and Ostia, which is what Royden (1988) 238 writes.

150 Liu (2009) 29–36 with Appendix B, table at 384–90 listing *fabri*, *fabri tignuarii*, *centonarii*, *dendrophori*, *utriclarii*.

151 Cristofori (2004).

fullers, who was also a magistrate of the *fabri*; his wife was a 'mother' to the *fullones* as well.[152] Another inscription mentions unspecified but presumably commercial associations taking part in the construction of a road: these *collegia* are said to be 'contiguous to the *forum pecuarium* (cattle market)'.[153]

There may be a rationale behind this more limited array of associations in smaller settlements. Hawkins suggests that associations may bring together artisans of broadly related trades, enabling easier collaboration and subcontracting.[154] He cites a passage from the *Digest* where the jurist Gaius writes that the designation *faber tignuarius* refers "not only to those who hew timber, but to all who work as builders".[155] Theoretically the *collegium fabrum* could therefore accommodate a broad range of people working in construction. It has been argued that Hawkins's idea is particularly useful for understanding associations in the smaller urban centres, because of the attestation of these more general *collegia* in smaller centres, versus the highly specific occupations in the names of associations attested for larger cities.[156] As we have seen, however, the more complex differentiation of *collegia* was limited to Rome, Ostia, and, to a lesser extent, Pompeii.

Many of the prerequisites and stimuli for the proliferation of *collegia* in Rome and Ostia were not equally present, or not pressing enough, in smaller settlements. There were simply fewer artisans to unite into associations, which would have made the (enduring) existence of more than a few associations untenable. Settlements as large as Pompeii and Puteoli have been considered as close-knit communities that provided their own kind of collectivity.[157] It also reasonable to suppose that, a fortiori, many of the social advantages of the collegiate network were less urgent in a neighbourhood where everybody already knew one another. To anticipate the socio-economic function of the associations to be discussed below, therefore, Liu may be correct to hypothesize that the very existence of *collegia* as well as "the potential of associations in further reducing transaction costs among members may be in reverse proportion to the size of the city".[158]

[152] *Collegia principalia CIL* 9.5439; *fullones/fabri CIL* 9.5450, quoted in full below. Hemelrijk (2015) 251–69; Hemelrijk (2008) for 'mothers' of *collegia*.

[153] "Collegia quae attingunt ... foro". *CIL* 9.5438.

[154] Hawkins (2021) 112–15.

[155] *Dig.* 50.16.235.1 (Gaius): "'Fabros tignarios' dicimus non eos dumtaxat, qui tigna dolarent, sed omnes qui aedificarent". Translation Hawkins (2021) 112.

[156] Cf. Liu (2009) 22: "Hawkins is certainly correct in noting that the Roman occupational *collegium* often included a wide range of artisans that were related to a broadly defined trade. But that seems to be a phenomenon typical of smaller centers. Larger commercial centers such as Rome, Ostia and Lugdunum featured many *collegia* whose titles suggested highly specialized trades". Cf. Verboven (2007) 880.

[157] Broekaert (2017).

[158] Liu (2009) 22.

Hawkins's vertical subdivision of labour therefore may well be part of the explanation for the existence of associations in larger cities. The active presence of *collegia* in even some of the smallest towns, however, cannot be explained merely by their function as a trust network or private enforcement network, but rather by their importance in the civic community. Small towns in particular needed the support of a broader group of benefactors if they were going to remain extant, and an active *collegium* could play a part in this.[159]

The social phenomenon of substitute families

Since the final decades of the twentieth century, scholars have 'discovered' *collegia* as a social phenomenon: it was a natural reaction to the formal and juristic treatment that went before.[160] Joining a *collegium* was a voluntary choice that broadened an individual's social network beyond the family and other networks he or she may have been associated with. Like the family, the *collegium* became a part of the Romans' self-identification.[161]

The presence of associations in the early Roman empire has sometimes been explained by a need for a surrogate family. The association was expected to take care of various issues when the natural family could not, such as financial intermediation, religious dedications, and, above all, burial arrangements.[162] Consequently, the *collegia* have been referred to as *grandi familie* by De Robertis; Schultz-Falkenthal similarly writes that they were "so etwas wie eine grosse Familie". Associative life has been termed *la vie familiale*.[163] There are some indications that the *collegiati* themselves also appreciated each other this way, as they occasionally refer to the others as brothers (*fratres*). Surely, the 'brother builders' (*fabri fratres*) must refer to an association: the Romans were no strangers to the use of terms of fictive kinship as terms of endearment.[164] In a similar vain, the hypogeum of the Aurelii has been reinterpreted as a collegiate tomb of professional scribes, partly because of its mosaic inscription that reads "Aurelius Felicissimus made (this tomb) for (his) well-deserving brothers (*fratri*[*bu*]*s*) and fellow-freedmen".[165]

159 Patterson (2006), 271 ff. for his model of the small town, earlier in Patterson (1994) 236.

160 Perry (2006) Chapter 6; see particularly Tran (2006); Tran (2011)

161 Joshel (1992) 113–22; Van Nijf (1997) 111.

162 For fictive or substitute families, see e.g. Wilson (1996) 13; various issues, cf. Garnsey and Saller (1987) 157.

163 De Robertis (1946) 77; Schulz-Falkenthal (1972) 163, Waltzing (1895).

164 *CIL* 5.7487; cf. Hemelrijk (2015) Chapter 5, on 'mothers' (and 'sisters') of *collegia*; Harland (2005); Harland (2007) for this phenomenon in the Greek East.

165 Bradley (2018) 17, 27 with image, text, and translation.

In the absence of family, specifically in the absence of children, the Romans worried over a proper burial.[166] Anonymous graves marked by tiles or amphorae in the Isola Sacra necropolis were not necessarily appealing, and, what is more, Martial's *Epigram* 8.75, 9–10, suggests that many of the poor were simply cremated, their ashes scattered (into the Tiber perhaps), their memories forever erased:[167]

Mart. *Ep.* 8.75, 9–10

Quattuor inscripti portabant uile cadauer,
 accipit infelix qualia mille rogus

Four branded slaves were carrying a common corpse, of the kind that an unhappy pyre receives a thousand of.

Collegia habitually concerned themselves with funerary matters for their members. It follows from the nature of the ancient evidence on *collegia* – which consists of many epitaphs – that funerary activities are their best-attested pursuit.[168] The charter of the *collegium* of the *cultores* of Antinoos and Diana at Lanuvium stipulates that the association will pay out 300 HS for the purpose of burial.[169] Fellow *collegiati* mourned the deceased with all due ritual, participating in the funerary procession. The members of the *cultores* from Lanuvium received monetary compensation to attend the funeral; members of an unidentified association in Roman Egypt, conversely, were fined four drachmae if they did not go, and another four drachmae if they did not shave their heads in mourning.[170]

Collegia in their own right seem to have had access to burial space for their members. The monument of the *sociae mimae* in Rome measured 15 × 12 Roman feet; the *sodalici lanariorum carminatorum* (wool merchants and carders) from Brixellum sported a much larger plot of 100 × 55 feet.[171] In the city it would often be a *columbarium*, or a number of niches in a *columbarium* tomb, where members could be buried.[172] Also in the case

166 Hopkins (1983) 213; Patterson (1992); cf. Hübner (2013) 87 ff.

167 Bodel (2000); cf. Patterson (1992) 16 with ref. to Martial; Hopkins (1983) 205–11.

168 Patterson (1992) 20; Ausbüttel (1982) 70, 71: the funerary activities of *collegia* are only sporadically attested from the fourth century onwards and so they seem to have waned in favour of Christian rites.

169 *CIL* 14.2112.

170 *P. Mich.* 5.243, 9–12, cited by Venticinque (2016) 52–53.

171 *CIL* 6.10109: "Sociarum / mimarum / in fr(onte) p(edes) XV / in agr(o) p(edes) XII"; *CIL* 11.1031: "D(is) M(anibus) / haec loca sunt / lanariorum / carminator(um) / sodalici / quae faciunt / in agro p(edes) C / ad viam p(edes) LV".

172 Patterson (1992) 20–21, including an interesting reference to *CIL* 6.9405 where a number of niches appear to be given to specified members (and ten unassigned

of a single-family *columbarium* related to an elite *domus*, an overarching *collegium* is sometimes attested that ostensibly took care of the funerary arrangements.[173] Testamentary endowments to *collegia* often stipulated the continuation of commemorative rites.[174]

It is not unlikely that there were *collegiati* who did not have a family to provide their burial and therefore relied on a *collegium*. Many labour migrants to the city of Rome will have been unmarried young men who had left their birth families behind.[175] The same principle may have operated to a lesser extent in other urban centres. A number of migrant and local young men had some time before marriage when, because of the high mortality rates that were even higher in the city, there may not have been surviving parents to commemorate them. *CIL* 10.7039 from the Sicilian city of Catina could be an example of this:

CIL 10.7039

D(is) M(anibus) s(acrum) / L(ucius) Arrius / Secundus / vix(it) ann(os) XVII / marmorari(i) / convive fecer(unt)

Sacred to the divine spirits. Lucius Arrius Secundus. He lived 17 years. The marble workers sharing his life set up [this monument].

The marble workers appear to have financed the burial of the deceased, Lucius Arrius Secundus, and actively contributed to the arrangements (*fecerunt*).[176] Only 17 years of age, Secundus could fit the profile of a young man without family. Sigismund-Nielsen has shown that many 'anonymous' burials, meaning epitaphs without record of their dedicator, were set up for this demographic group, arguing on the basis of this and other criteria that they too were buried by a *collegium* for lack of family.[177]

places) of a *collegium*. There is no clear evidence for *collegia* setting up or owning a columbarium tomb; cf. Patterson (1992) 21, who points to the *cultores* of Hercules Victor of *CIL* 10.5386, who certainly owned a large burial plot (*loca sepulturae*); Liu (2013) 365–66 also notes *CIL* 6.9405, plus other examples.

173 Hasegawa (2005) 81–88 presents most of the direct and indirect evidence; e.g. *CIL* 6.6215 (Statilii), *CIL* 6.7282 (Volusii), *CIL* 6.9148–49 and 10260–64 (Sergia Paullina). See also Chapter 4 above.

174 Liu (2008a) 240.

175 Tacoma (2016) Chapter 4, esp. 107–23.

176 From Catina. This particular example was chosen because I did not want to leave unmentioned Perry's (2006) 1–5 telling reconstructions of the possible story behind it.

177 Sigismund-Nielsen (2006) 204 for "young males of the working classes"; ibid., 206 for unmarried men aged 15–30. I do not believe that all of these anonymous burials were set up by *collegia*.

But there were certainly members of associations who did have biological families. Not every member was necessarily buried in a collective burial place like a *columbarium*. The *collegium* did not take over primary responsibility from the family. Rather, in matters of death as in life, there seems to have been a delicate cooperation between the association and the relatives of the deceased.[178] Depending on the circumstances, the *collegium* could arrange everything, from retrieving the body of the deceased to a place in a communal tomb, but in other instances it would simply pay out to the next of kin.[179] Many members were buried by a *collegium*.[180] Associations would sometimes arrange a funeral for the biological family of their members, too.[181] When the family rather than the association set up the epitaph, or when family takes pride of place, the inscription often concerns *collegium* magistrates.[182]

The following is a clear example of how family and *collegium* may have operated together:

> ***AE* 2001, 879b**
>
> D(is) M(anibus) sacrum / L(ucio) Gavellio Felici Su/ellia Prisca coniu/gi b(ene) m(erenti) f(ecit) et collegi/um dendrofo/rorum
>
> Sacred to the divine spirits. To Lucius Gavellius Felix. Suellia Prisca set this up for her well-deserving husband, and the association of the tree-carriers (set this up).

The associations could also be burdened with the protection of the family tomb of one of their members.[183] In some instances, the *collegium* gained access to the tomb when the family line died out, as in the following example:[184]

178 Patterson (1992) 23; Van Nijf (1997) 32–33; and Venticinque (2010) 293: "Including provisions for burial in guild regulations or offering legal assistance does not need to imply a lack of reliance on one's kin or community as has often been suggested".

179 Cf. the Lanuvium inscription, *CIL* 14.2112, col. I.26–32: when a member has died more than 20 miles away and his death has been reported, three men will be sent to conduct the burial; when it has not been reported, the expenses of his burial will be compensated after the fact.

180 Joshel (1992) 113.

181 Cf. Hemelrijk (2015) 183–86.

182 Joshel (1992) 113–14. But she herself notes (ibid., 208 n. 45) that the evidence is skewed because these individuals are largely concentrated in two tombs – Joshel counts individuals, not inscriptions or monuments.

183 Ausbüttel (1982) 69–70. The *collegium* received money for this, as in *AE* 1951, 94 (1,000 HS to the *centonarii* of Comum).

184 Cf. also *AE* 2004, 210 (Ostia).

CIL 6.8750

Diis(!) Manibus / T(itus) Aelius Aug(usti) lib(ertus) Primitivus / archimagirus / fecit Aelia(e) Tyche et sibi et Aeliae / Tyrannidi coniugi et libertis li/bertabusq(ue) meis vel Aeliae Tyran/nydis / posterisque eorum / custodia mon{i}<u>menti inhabitandi ne quis inter/dicere velit quotsi nemo de n(ostra) memoria / exstiterit pertinebit ad collegium cocorum / Caesaris n(ostri) quot veniri donarive vetamus si ad/versus ea quis fecerit poenae nomine feret / arcae cocorum HS L m(ilia) n(ummum) / ate ex usuris eorum / celebretur suo quoq(ue) anno/ h(oc) m(onumentum) h(eredem) n(on) s(equetur)

To the divine spirits. Titus Aelius Primitivus, freedman of the emperor, head cook, set this up to Aelia Tyche and himself and to Aelia Tyrannis his wife and my freedmen and -women or those of Aelia Tyrannis, and to their descendants.
The care of the monument to be dwelt in (*inhabitandi*), so that no one may interfere, [we stipulate] that if no one of our memory [i.e. family] should exist, [the care] will fall to the association of the cooks of our Caesar. We forbid it [the monument] to be given or sold. If anyone should do these things in opposition [to these stipulations], he shall hand a nominal fine to the treasury of the cooks of 50,000 *nummi*, a yearly sacrifice from the revenues of this should be celebrated in his year. This monument does not go to the heirs.[185]

This is the inscription of the family tomb of T. Aelius Primitivus and his wife (both his first (Tyche) and second partner (Tyrannis)). His family, including freedmen, clearly takes precedence here. Primitivus apparently fulfilled a magistracy as *archimagirus* in the imperial association of cooks, which will take care that the tomb is not violated on the penalty of 50,000 *nummi* – to benefit the *collegium*.

The collaboration of family and association in matters of death and burial is illustrative of the way in which family and associative life overlapped. The *collegium* mourned the death of *collegiati* and their relatives, but there are indications that it was equally involved with the happier family life events of marriage and birth: the members of an unidentified association in Roman

[185] The translation of this text is more difficult than its meaning. Cf. Weaver, *Repertorium familiae Caesarum*, 276–77, for Aeliae Tyche (= dative) instead of Aelia, and for the meaning of *ate* [= ἄτη], as a penalty in the form of a yearly sacrifice. *CIL* 6.7458 has a remarkably similar text to this one; its contents are virtually identical to *CIL* 6.8750, but it does not mention Aelia Tyrannis, only Tyche as Primitivus' wife, and adds that the *collegium cocorum* "exists on the Palatine" and was "located in this place": "quod consistit in Palatio" and "corpori qui sunt in hac stationem". See for that text and the protection of tombs by a durable institution, Crook (1967) 136–37.

Egypt were required to pay two drachmae to the association on the occasion of their marriage or the birth of a son, and one drachma for the birth of a daughter. That same collective has it written in their charter, "If anyone neglects another in trouble and does not give aid to release him from his trouble, let him pay eight drachmas".[186] Eating, celebrating, and grieving together, *collegiati* can in many ways be usefully seen as extended family.

Collegia and family were not just intersecting and complementary networks, however: they could literally coincide. There is evidence for *collegiati* who were also related as family. This phenomenon is difficult to quantify, among other things because of the absence of explicit filiation and libertinization in the membership lists that was already noted above. Occupation and guild membership were not hereditary in the period under scrutiny, although it must be assumed that many did follow in their parents' footsteps.[187] It is therefore hard to say if we can speak of a "significant percentage" of kinship bonds among *collegiati*.[188] The membership lists occasionally contain identifications such as *sen(ior)*, *iun(ior)*, or *fil(ius)*, the son, in cases of homonymy.[189] Liu illustrates that in the case of the *collegium centonariorum*, there were family clusters within *collegia*, sometimes over two generations as in the case of the Octavii in the *collegium* at Rome.[190] Pearse reconstructs three generations among the *fabri tignuarii*, also at Rome.[191] Venticinque adds convincing material that shows blood relations between *collegiati*; his examples are largely from Roman Egypt, however, and the material is not abundant.[192]

Looking beyond the membership lists, it is clear that many *collegia* do indeed demonstrate kinship relations. In the following epitaph, interestingly, two sons chose to give precedence to official titles (including that of their mother) over kinship bonds and piety:

> ***CIL* 9.5450**
>
> D(is) M(anibus) / T(ito) Sillio T(iti) lib(erto) / Prisco / mag(istro) colleg(ii) / fabr(um) II et q(uaestori) II / mag(istro) et q(uaestori) sodal(icii) / fullonum / Claudiae Ti(beri) lib(ertae) / uxori eius matri / sodalic(ii) fullon(um) / T(itus)

[186] *P. Mich.* 5.243 (*BL* 9.160). Translation Venticinque (2010) 280–85, including full text and translation of the charter.

[187] Chapter 3 above on intergenerational persistence.

[188] Venticinque (2010) 279: "Persons united by at least one bond of kinship with a brother, father, or son account for a significant percentage of the overall membership."

[189] Ausbüttel (1982) 39. Unlike him I feel that the senior/junior distinction in case of homonymy probably is an indication of kinship as well as age.

[190] Liu (2009) 180–203, including patron freedmen or *colliberti*.

[191] Pearse (1976) 173; Liu (2009) 181–83.

[192] Venticinque (2010) 278–79.

> Sillius Karus et / Ti(berius) Claudius Phi/lippus mag(istri) et q(uaestores) / colleg(ii) fabr(um) / fili(i) parentib(us) / piissimis
>
> To the divine spirits. To Titus Sillius Priscus, freedman of Titus, twice magister of the *collegium fabrum* and twice *quaestor*, *magister* and *quaestor* of the *sodalicium fullonum*. To Claudia, freedwoman of Tiberius, his wife, 'mother' of the *sodalicium* of fullers, Titus Sillius Karus and Tiberius Claudius Philippus *magistri* and *quaestores* of the *collegium fabrum*, sons to their most revered parents.

Family clustering within *collegia* is also attested for forged family ties between freedmen and patrons, though not much research has been done on this.[193] Inscriptions of *colliberti* commemorating a patron already illustrated the continued bond with their patron, and their trade.[194] It is only natural that freedmen should proceed to join the *collegia* – it is known that associations accommodated many freedmen. Family ties within the *collegium* theoretically could occur for slaves, too, though this is difficult to trace. *Collegia domestica* of elite households largely seem to coincide with the *familia*, which means that for slaves and freedmen here the *collegium* may actually be equated with their 'family'.

In sum, the relationship between families and guilds seems to have been complementary.[195] Yet there is some truth in the idea of *collegia* as substitute families. The historical pattern predicts that a weakness of family ties influenced the emergence of associations.[196] Family ties were perhaps not less important, but they were not omnipresent in the city where the dominant family form was the nuclear family,[197] and where people often migrated without taking their family with them, because they had the intention to return one day. Many young men will also have migrated before they had formed a family of their own. For the numerous immigrants to Rome and other large Italian cities, therefore, the association must have been an important substitute for their native family. For locals, associative family might sometimes have been more durable than bloodlines in a high-mortality regime, and could even have incorporated biological family anyway. To slaves (and ex-slaves), finally, the *collegium* may have been the family they could not have.

193 Liu (2009) 180–203.

194 See Chapters 3, 4 above.

195 This is also the essence of Venticinque (2010) 277: "I argue that guilds, and in particular the ethical regulations dealing with relationships between members and their families, sought to create and maintain bonds of trust between members, rather than to compensate for any deficiency".

196 Lucassen et al. (2008) 15–16.

197 See Chapter 3 on family forms.

The economics of association: professional *collegia* as trade guilds, unions, or unique to Rome?

> *Collegia* were not constituted for economic purposes ... and this is reflected in the names they gave to their societies –'Mates and marble workers', 'Brother builders', 'the comrade smiths', 'the late drinkers'.[198]

There is an obvious social aspect to associating with others. Rather than proving that "*collegia* were not constituted for economic purposes", the titles of associations suggest that they were not constituted *solely* for economic purposes – the fact that they often include a profession surely indicates some economic engagement. In his important historiography of the Roman *collegia*, Jonathan Scott Perry wrote that "the dominant trend of contemporary collegial studies has been to explore the 'social' features of these organizations, to the exclusion of the other 'interests' that association may also have served".[199] Perry's work was published in 2006. The tide has now turned. Scholars emphasize the interaction between the various roles of the associations, and particularly the general involvement of *collegia* in the economy has again become a topic of research interest.[200]

Many of the *collegia* are professional in name. Accordingly they could be seen as economic associations. The comparison of occupational *collegia* with medieval and early modern trade guilds virtually imposes itself. But because of the absence of trade monopolies or universal membership in Roman society, the comparison invariably led to the conclusion that the *collegia* were no guilds, and that *collegiati* were nothing like the "economic masterminds of a medieval commercial revolution".[201] This view of *collegia* as 'not guilds' had a powerful protagonist in Moses Finley, who forcefully argued for their economic insignificance. In his *Ancient Economy* he writes on *collegia*,

> In no sense were they guilds trying to foster or protect the economic interests of their members, nor did they reveal a trace of the hierarchical pattern of apprentice, journeyman and master that characterized the mediaeval and early modern guilds.[202]

198 Walker-Ramisch (1996) 133; the names of the *collegia* she cites clearly were taken from MacMullen (1974) 77.

199 Perry (2006) 207.

200 See, e.g. Liu (2017); Verboven (2017b); Venticinque (2016).

201 Van Nijf (1997) 11–17, quote at 12.

202 Finley (1999) 81, cf. 138: "there were no guilds, no matter how often the Roman *collegia* and their differently named Greek and Hellenistic counterparts are thus mistranslated". See also MacMullen (1974) 19: "Any analogy with a medieval guild or modern labor union is wholly mistaken".

According to Finley, craftsmen, and craftsmen associations, were marginal factors in what he perceived as a largely agricultural economy. The comparison with trade guilds, and the 'mistranslation' of *collegia* as trade guilds, has nevertheless remained.[203] It is now known that the later trade guilds were not merely economic collectives, but fulfilled a score of other social functions too, not unlike the Roman associations.[204] Even the medieval guild monopolies probably were not as strict as has been thought. There is thus no reason not to refer to occupational associations as 'guilds'.

A perceived lack of evidence is another reason why the economics of association have been underexposed. Many studies into associations have focused on the funerary and dedicatory inscriptions that were set up by *collegia*, as well as on membership lists, and on legal evidence for state intervention in line with the story of rebellion and conflict that was understood from ancient literary evidence. The ancient evidence has not provided much incentive to emphasize the economic importance of associations.[205] Taking absence of evidence as evidence of absence underestimates the fact that the act of association in itself can be economically significant. Changing the questions may provide answers. How did the associative networks contribute to the economy? Are there any traces of economic zoning? Quite apart from inscribed monuments, there is documentary evidence for the economic involvement of *collegia*.[206] And then there is the fact that *collegiati* were a privileged group, in society, but also by law. With the hypothesis of economic significance rather than insignificance in mind, suddenly many of the existing sources from the western provinces, too, can be read as hinting at economic activity of the *collegia*, even if the evidence is not primarily economic in nature.

Occupational clustering

Professional associations generally were a local phenomenon. It has been argued that dealers and craftsmen working in related businesses were

[203] See Verboven (2017b); and e.g. Gibbs (2012); Gibbs (2011); Broekaert (2011); Van Nijf (1997); Van Minnen (1987).

[204] Cf. Liu (2009) 16–17; Van Nijf (1997) 11–18; Van Nijf (2002) usefully compares the *collegia* to yet another collective, the sixteenth- and seventeenth-century Dutch civic guards.

[205] Perhaps that is only to be expected, says Perry (2006) 207: "If, for example, a *collegium* were agitating for better working conditions, would it be likely to have inscribed a document demanding a resolution of their grievances by the power elite? And even more importantly, would they have chosen to share their most secretive deliberations with the larger society in an inscribed monument?"

[206] Mostly from Roman Egypt: see Venticinque (2016); Venticinque (2010); Gibbs (2011); Van Minnen (1987).

inclined to settle together in specific parts of a city.[207] This clustering or economic zoning subsequently could have led to the formation of the occupational *collegia*.[208]

For the city of Rome in particular, toponyms regularly suggest a connection with trades, such as the Forum Boarium ('cattle market'). Several districts and streets of Rome attest to a particular trade: the Via Sacra, for example, was the home of dealers in a number of luxury trades. Prostitutes were apparently found in the Subura.[209] Clustering of trades is historically well attested for pre-industrial cities, like London. This creates the clear economic advantage that buyer and seller can easily find each other. The idea is that if you needed a scythe, you went 'among the scythe makers', *inter falcarios*. Holleran suggests that clustering also made the sharing of information among workers in the same branch easier, and may have accommodated specialization because it makes for an easy network of subcontracting.[210] In theory, there could also be practical advantages in sharing access to raw materials and clustering noisy and smelly trades. There is a marble district in Emporion, to facilitate transport over water, and bricks were produced outside Rome where there were clay beds.[211]

As a result, the existence of clustering in Roman cities is widely accepted.[212] The problem with the evidence from Rome, however, is that it is inconclusive. Holleran concedes that the presence of a *Vicus Lorarius* (harness makers), for example, is attested in an inscription that records a *pigmentarius* (dealer in paints) and not a *lorarius*; similarly there is an *argentarius* (silversmith) attested *inter aerarios* (among coppersmiths); there is also an *argentarius* from the blacksmiths' alley (*Vicus* [...]*ionum ferrariarum*). By the second century, the *Vicus Sandalarius* (sandal makers) was more famous for its booksellers than for its sandal makers.[213] Conversely, it is quite likely that not all sandal makers were located in the *Vicus Sandalarius*. Most *vici* were not named after an occupation. And even what is potentially the most smelly of trades, fulling, was not clustered in one part of the city.[214] The list could be expanded.

The economic benefits of clustering are obvious, and there is just enough evidence to maintain the fable of economically rational clustering

207 For occupational clustering in Rome, Tacoma (2013) 139–42; Holleran (2012) 53–60; MacMullen (1974) 70–79, with appendix at 129–35.

208 MacMullen (1974) 73.

209 Cf. Mart. *Ep.* 6.66.

210 Holleran (2012) 57.

211 Tacoma (2013) 140.

212 Goodman (2016); Ellis (2018) 94 ff.

213 Holleran (2012) 54–55 with reference to *CIL* 6.9796 (*pigmentarius*), 9186 (*inter aerarios*), and 9185 (*Vicus* [...]*ionum Ferrariarum*).

214 Flohr (2013).

for particular groups of workers, such as the *thurarii* (incense dealers) in Puteoli, or of economic zoning in the *Vicus Saliniensis* in Pompeii.[215] In his exploration of elite motivation for investing in retail and *tabernae* adjacent to, and "veritably within", their homes, Ellis seems to suggest that this was formative of a self-evident process of clustering.[216] His theory that patrons positioned their own freedmen in these shops might at first glance seem to corroborate nicely my views on the continuation of family firms through freedmen. But it should rather be interpreted as a disruptive force leading not to clustering, but to a more random placement of divergent crafts instead, once we reconsider the diversity of job titles within the upper-class households it concerns. In addition, Chapter 3 above showed that intergenerational persistence indicated continuity within a family of the workshop, not necessarily of a trade – which would conceivably explain a *pigmentarius* in the *Vicus Lorarius*.

In my view, therefore, there must have been some clustering when opportunity arose, but I would concur that the "dominant pattern is one of random scatter, with a modest degree of clusters of specific shops and industries".[217] Economic zoning was simply not the foremost way in which the Romans battled an inadequate information supply.

Trust networks

Accurate, up-to-date information probably was a scarce good in the Roman world.[218] Transport of information and goods was slow and precarious.[219] Market demand was volatile; finding dependable workers was not always easy.[220] All of these factors led to a high degree of market insecurity and economic uncertainty: transaction costs were high.[221]

Successfully matching labour supply and demand only works if there is an institutional framework to enforce labour relations and to secure the rights of both parties. Roman law supplies some of the necessary provisions, including contracts and the possibility for a lawsuit.[222] It remains to be seen whether they were adequate. The legal framework was certainly biased towards "connections and money", which diminishes the chances of success for the non-elite in a court of law.[223] Status distinctions could distort the

215 Camodeca (2016) 26; Ellis (2018) 95.
216 Ellis (2018) Chapter 3, there 101.
217 Tacoma (2013) 142; similarly, Schoevaert (2018) on Ostia.
218 Broekaert (2011) 242–55; Bang (2008).
219 Broekaert (2011) 221; Terpstra (2008) esp. 352–54.
220 Holleran (2017); Hawkins (2021).
221 Cf. also Temin (2013a) 97–99 with the example of grain merchants.
222 Terpstra (2008) 351.
223 Terpstra (2008) 365.

outcome of a legal action against a well-connected opponent of high status; an opponent of lesser means may not have been able to compensate for a monetary loss, even when the case was won – if, that is, the defendant had appeared in court at all, for which the plaintiff perhaps needed the help of powerful patrons; in case of a no-show they needed to pay an auctioneer to be able to procure justice, seizing and selling the defendant's property.[224] Costly and protracted legal actions like these must have provided only a last resort. One can imagine that artisans who mostly conducted smaller transactions would try and avoid the hassle if at all possible, and that they were in need of a simpler, less expensive, and less time-consuming way to gain some economic security and lower transaction costs.[225]

Against this background, the economic importance of a network of people you knew and trusted and who worked in related positions was even higher than it is today, in a world where information travels faster than we can manage it.[226] Clearly it was important to find out as much as possible about the trustworthiness and creditworthiness of a potential business partner or employee.[227] The trust networks of the family or the neighbourhood therefore may not have been sufficient for all business undertakings. Within a *collegium*, there was plenty of opportunity to share information or to contract out work among fellow associates, reducing transaction costs. Moreover, the formal, hierarchic nature of the *collegia* made them suitable for enforcement and control.

The *collegia* therefore were an important addition to the Romans' institutional framework. Hawkins contends that associations functioned as reputation-based private order enforcement networks, and his view is beginning to be accepted more widely.[228] The argument may briefly be summarized as follows. The network of *collegiati* provided a basis of trust. There was a strong distinction between insiders and outsiders, making possible long-term cooperation. Not just anyone could join.[229] The formal organization of *collegia* was well suited to maintaining the bonds of trust between their members on the one hand, and to protecting the reputation of the *collegium* in the outside world on the other. Surviving guild charters and regulations regularly include a set of communal sanctions that the *collegium* could resort to should a member harm another *collegiatus* in any way: their

224 Terpstra (2008) 365; more extensively in Kelly (1966).

225 Hawkins (2021) 103–8.

226 Varga (2020) Chapter 4; Broekaert (2017); Terpstra (2008) 353: "Most business will have taken place in networks and between known associates". For some objections to these ideas, see Moatti (2017).

227 Verboven (2017a) on credit; cf. Temin (2013a) 100 on merchant networks.

228 Hawkins (2021) 101–24; Broekaert (2011) for a similar argument on "the potential advantages of being a *collegiatus*".

229 Cf. Broekaert (2011) 227–28.

interference was not limited to economic wrongdoing.[230] Penalties ranged from a warning or a monetary fine to expulsion; the wrongdoer would lose face and become an untrustworthy economic partner, thereby losing valuable connections and opportunities.[231]

The efficiency of associations as private enforcement networks can, of course, be questioned.[232] It should be noted that with guild by-laws, too, the relation between what was written and what was practised is not always clear. Decrease in membership, insufficient finances and defaulters could all be a problem. Because of their hierarchical nature, there is a chance of internal rivalry among members that could slowly erode the association.[233] Enforcement becomes difficult when the durability and stability of the *collegium* was not secure.[234] If membership became non-committal like this, and if (as Liu suggests) many alternatives existed, then the *collegium* as private order enforcement network would disintegrate.[235]

Not only does membership appear to have been highly valued; also the specific nature of *collegia* in Rome and Ostia and the scarce number of associations in the other cities suggest that there were not, in fact, many alternatives. Within the *collegia* that were sustainable enough for us to know of them, networks of trust were strong. It seems to me that the network provided by an active *collegium* as an institution must have been a powerful tool. The social and religious aspects of collegial life add to so-called multiplex relationships: "The more ties, the closer the connection between the members and the more likely they are to help and protect each other".[236] The integration within *collegia* would be even stronger if there was some overlap with biological or forged family ties, as sometimes was the case; moreover, it is not impossible that family ties were expanded by marriage bonds that were formed through the guild.[237] Apprentices may have been

[230] Cf. Venticinque (2010) 285–88.

[231] Cf. Broekaert (2011) 221: "Commercial networks created by the *collegiati* hence offered protection against various risks and uncertainties in a volatile trading world."

[232] This paragraph deals with the critique written up in Liu (2017).

[233] Liu (2009) 23 points to the strong hierarchy within the *collegia*, so that a member may still find himself in a dispute with an opponent of higher status which could potentially influence the outcome.

[234] E.g. Liu (2013) on durability.

[235] Liu (2017) 206–12; at 216 she argues that because of the lack of alternatives, "*collegia* as reputation-based, private-order enforcement mechanisms may have been best applicable to the organizations of the resident aliens".

[236] Broekaert (2011) 227 on multiplex relationships, see also 229–30. Similarly, Venticinque (2010) 288: "What began in the guild hall continued and extended beyond it in the form of closer business partnerships and social and economic connections".

[237] Cf. Broekaert (2012); Liu (2017) 216.

contracted out among fellow *collegiati*.[238] In my view, even the existence of clusters of trust and competition between them within a larger *collegium* could strengthen ties, albeit within a subgroup of the association.

Apart from building trust and ensuing business networks among the members themselves, membership of a *collegium* can tentatively be said to have increased the trustworthiness of each individual member in the eyes of potential customers, clients, or business partners from outside the association.[239] And it is no wonder that *collegiati* were a preferred choice, because there are some indications that the *collegium* may even have accepted liability in case of debts or adverse business outcomes for their members.[240] Moreover, it appears that the *collegium* as a collective, too, was viewed as a trustworthy business partner by external principals, and that the authorities may have preferred to hand out the contract for public works and distributions to a recognized association.[241]

In sum, whereas the membership of a professional *collegium* was not compulsory for Roman artisans and craftsmen, it seems that not joining an association may have made professional life rather difficult. The happy few on the inside may have made economic life more difficult for those on the outside.[242]

Financial benefits

Collegia were recognized legal actors: associations with the right to *corpus habere* could own property and engage in contracts with 'outsiders'; they could sue, and be sued, collectively.[243] There is strength in financial partnership.

If collectives could own property, it follows that they could own slaves and freedmen – even if these were also among their ranks. Collective slaves

[238] This is actually the main body of Liu (2017) 217–24. Whereas I think that *collegiati* certainly may have used this method to find a master artisan to teach, I do not believe that her examples of family networks of masters and apprentices (Tryphon and Pausiris, discussed at length in Chapter 3 above) provide enough evidence to indicate the existence of an association of weavers; Venticinque (2010) 289–91 likewise sees apprenticeship as a tie between households – via guilds.

[239] Cf. Ray (2017) 105–6 on building consumer trust.

[240] Broekaert (2011) 237–38 with reference to evidence from Roman Egypt: *P. Mich. Inv.* 1277 ("If any one of the undersigned men is held for debt up to the amount of one hundred drachmai in silver, security will be given for him for a period of sixty days by the association") and the very similar *P. Mich. Inv.* 720 (thirty days). Venticinque (2010) 282–83 also has these examples and adds *P. Ryl.* 2.94 = *Sel. Pap.* 2.255, first century, where an actual dispute has arisen and the weavers' guild steps in.

[241] For Roman Egypt, Venticinque (2016) 71–74; Liu (2009) 23 notes the difficulty in investigating the 'radius of trust' for *collegia*.

[242] "The dark side of particularized social capital", Ogilvie (2011); cf. Van Minnen (1987) 68–69 for Roman Egypt.

[243] *Dig.* 3.4.1. pr.-1 (Gaius).

of *collegia* are not widely known or studied, because there is very little evidence: Ulpian writes that Marcus Aurelius explicitly gave *collegia* with the *ius coeundi* the right to manumit. As a consequence, he goes on, associations could also claim the inheritance of their freedmen.[244] In other words: *collegia* had slaves to manumit. If there was common property, such slaves would be useful to manage it.

Other forms of collective ownership are also attested. An association of merchants set up an altar to the *genius* of the *horrea Agrippiana* in Rome:[245]

> ***AE*** **1927, 97**
>
> pro] salut(e) geni{um} <i> horreor(um) / [A]grippianorum negotiantib(us) / L(ucius) Arrius Hermes / C(aius) Varius Polycarpus / C(aius) Paconius Chrysanthus / immunes s(ua) p(ecunia) d(onum) d(ederunt)
>
> To the well-being of the genius of the *horrea Agrippiana* by the merchants. L. Arrius Hermes, Caius Varius Polycarpus and Gaius Paconius Chrysanthus, *immunes*, donated this votive from their own funds.

The mention of *immunes* (honorary members with exemption from fees) and, on another side of the monument, *curatores* indicates that this text concerns merchants in the formal structure of a *collegium*. It would seem that they shared storage space in the *horrea*, which could for obvious reasons be useful for merchants. In a similar vein, the *corpus Heliopolitanorum* in Puteoli owned seven *iugera* of land with a cistern and shops (*tabernae*), for the use of members present and future ("eorum possessorum / iuris est qui in cultu corporis Heliopolita/norum sunt eruntve").[246] If Ellis is correct in suggesting that investment in property like *tabernae* was more valuable for maintaining social networks than it was for making a profit, their common property underlines the association's aims of social cohesion and trust.[247]

The most important common property may have been the treasury.[248] The *collegium* received admission money and monthly fees, as well as the

[244] *Dig.* 40.3.1 (Ulpian, Sabinus book 5); and *Dig.* 40.3.2 (Ulpian, Sabinus book 14).

[245] An altar, or a statue base? The photograph available in the Clauss-Slaby database allows both. *AE* 1915, 97 = *AE* 1923, 57 = *AE* 1927, 97; the other sides of the altar are also inscribed: "Posit(um) dedic(atum) V Idus Iun(ias) / Cn(aeo) Cossutio Eustropho / L(ucio) Manlio Philadelpho // Cur(atores) ann(i) III". Example from Broekaert (2011) 236.

[246] *CIL* 10.1579, with Verboven (2011b) 343. In Roman Egypt there is additional evidence for a sixth-century *collegium* of linen weavers renting out workshops to its associated members. Broekaert (2011) 233 with reference to *SB* 14.12282.

[247] Ellis (2018) 107 ff.

[248] Liu (2008a) 242 for the unique *arca Titiana* that belonged to the *centonarii* and *fabri* in Milan jointly. *CIL* 5.5578; 5738; 5612; 5869; cf. Venticinque (2016) 43–45.

summa honoraria of their magistrates. Endowments to *collegia* are relatively well attested and could concern substantial sums.[249] Add to this that many guilds also had properties that generated revenue: there probably was money. The common treasury could potentially be a valuable tool in an insecure market, if only because many professional undertakings required a capital investment at the outset. The problem is that we do not know what associations did with their funds. It is possible that they extended loans to members and associates from the common treasury at a favourable rate of interest, or that they encouraged loans between members, in which case the formal framework of the association functioned as a guarantee that the money would eventually be paid off.[250]

There were other economic advantages to being a *collegiatus* that have already come to the fore in a different context, but they may be briefly recalled here. *Collegia* were regularly included as beneficiaries of distributions of food or money, in which case members invariably received a larger share than the *plebs*. Often this was a specific *collegium* which, we may safely conclude in line with what has been said above, was probably the single or most important local *collegium*. *CIL* 11.6053 is exemplary, in its generosity first and foremost towards the councillors (20 HS), then the Augustales (12 HS), the *collegium* of *mercuriales* (ten HS), and finally the people (seven HS).[251] This pattern recurs throughout Italy and the Empire.[252]

Finally, membership of a legitimate *collegium* could come with governmental grants of immunity from public benefactions (*munera*) or other *privilegia*.[253] This is an advantage of *collegium* membership that probably was not widespread in the period under scrutiny. It appears to be connected to the increasing reliance of the state on *collegia* for public services connected to the grain and other supplies over the third and fourth centuries.[254]

Trade unions?

Thus far the focus has been on 'internal' economic benefits, and I have dealt chiefly with relations of trust and enforcement mechanisms for dealings between *collegiati*. It is perhaps to be expected that the *collegia* also

249 Hawkins (2021) 116–17; Liu (2008a). *CIL* 6.1872 = *ILS* 7266, AD 206, quoted above, is an example of an endowment, of 10,000 HS in this case.

250 Venticinque (2016) e.g. 81–85; Broekaert (2011) 237; Liu (2008a) 245, who suggest in addition that the *collegia* may also have extended credit to outsiders, with reference to *P. Strasb.* 4.287 (sixth-century Hermopolis) recording a loan between members of the same association of tow workers.

251 Verboven (2007) 882 with this and other examples; Wen (2018); Patterson (2006) 256.

252 Wen (2018); but probably not in the city of Rome, Liu (2013) 362.

253 Liu (2009) 109–11; Verboven (2007) 881; *Dig.* 50.6.6.12; and see above.

254 Liu (2009) 113–14.

pursued external economic benefits by promoting their common interests, regulating a trade like the medieval guilds or demanding more pay or fiscal privileges like a modern trade union.[255] There were no legal formalities to stop them from taking economic action. Still, Tacoma felt that he could write,

> Professional associations are best known for what they did not do: they did not interfere in the urban economy, at least not before late antiquity. No price-setting occurred, they had no intermediary role in assigning apprenticeships, they offered no control of the quality of products, they did not monopolize labour.[256]

The evidence for economic action by *collegia* in Roman Italy has really not been researched thoroughly. The reason is simple: much of the evidence we have is from Roman Egypt, it all concerns highly specific cases, and it is difficult to draw a general picture from it. Gibbs is highly optimistic about the abilities of associations to take collective action.[257] But the evidence deserves a closer look.

There is one unique document that shows a form of price regulation and parcelling out the areas of work among the members of an association of salt dealers, basically doing exactly what we would expect a professional *collegium* to do. It is a first-century papyrus from Tebtunis that has no parallel, although Venticinque can point to other associations in Roman Egypt also collecting and sharing price information.[258] Actual price fixing by guilds, to my knowledge, is not attested.[259] Likewise guild monopolies were a phenomenon of the later empire only, such as a fourth-century deal for the *saccarii* (porters) unloading goods at the gates of Rome.[260]

There are sporadic attestations of collective action, though most of them are late and from outside Roman Italy: there was a riot concerning the bakers at Ephesus in the late second century AD, which we know from a state decree urging the bakers to comply; five *corpora* of seagoing *navicularii* in third-century Arles put a complaint before the *praefectus annonae*, Claudius

255 Ausbüttel (1982) 100 argues that the *collegia* did not act as an economic collective, because to his mind *collegia* were not a collective of a single professional group, as I believe they were.

256 Tacoma (2016) 233.

257 Gibbs (2013).

258 *P. Mich.* 5.245; Hawkins (2021) 73; Venticinque (2016) 45–49; Van Nijf (1997) 13–14.

259 Van Nijf (1997) 14–15 refers to what was apparently a price war in Smyrna, first/second century AD.

260 Liu (2009) 110, with reference to *CTh* 14.22.1 (AD 364); cf. De Robertis (1971) Volume II 192; Sirks (1991) 258.

Iulianus, about the supply of grain, and obtained assistance from him, as documented in a beautiful bronze plate found in Beirut.[261] The *nautae Rhodanici* may have succeeded in gaining fiscal privileges from the emperor Hadrian, in return for which they put up an honorary inscription, found in Valencia.[262] The one example from the city of Rome would be the rebellion of *monetarii* working in the imperial mint against the emperor Aurelianus. They allegedly went to war out of fear of punishment, presumably for fraud.[263] The rebels were evidently defeated cruelly, as it is Aurelian's cruelty that is emphasized by various antique writers.[264] The mint was dissolved for several years. This was not an association arguing for better terms. The possible involvement of several senators and the amount of attention paid to the revolt in the antique literature suggest that perhaps this was more than a conflict between the emperor and the *monetarii* trying to save their own skin, and that it had developed into a general uprising against the emperor.[265] Nevertheless it is clear that guilds could and did work together in the event of problems with the state or city council – or in case of public assignments from that city council.[266] Conflicts and contracts could also occur with a less lofty employer, of course.[267]

Patrons of the association were likely to intervene on behalf of the *collegium* or an individual member.[268] The political network of highly placed patrons was presumably the most efficient way for the collegium to achieve their goals. The inscription for Tiberius Claudius Severus cited above is actually not only an example of a wealthy benefactor and his gift to the association, but it is also an example of an individual's negotiation for navigational rights for the *corpus piscatorum et urinatorum*.[269]

The associations as institutions were steadily incorporated into the imperial bureaucracy, which appears to have made clever use of all available organizational structures. In Roman Egypt, many associations paid their taxes collectively and thereby had become part of the imperial

[261] Bakers *IEph.* 215 = *SEG* 4, 512 – the nature of the disturbance is unclear but it may have been a strike. Buckler (1923); pace Harland, http://www.philipharland.com/greco-roman-associations/?p=6299 (accessed 4 May 2022); *navicularii CIL* 3.14165,08 = ILS 6987, for a brief account of what happened Broekaert (2011) 248.

[262] Tran (2011) with reference to *CIL* 12.1797.

[263] Aur. Vict. *Caes.* 35.6 *poenae metu*. He also refers to fraud; cf. Eutropius *Brev.* 14.1.

[264] Aur. Vict. *Caes.* 35.6; HA *Aur.* 38.2; ibid. 21.5–6; *Epit. De Caes.* 35.4; Eutropius *Brev.* 9.14.

[265] Cf. Dey (2011) 112–13, with n. 7 for extra literature.

[266] *P.Tebt.* 2.287 = *W.Chr.* 251; *P.Oxy.* 12.1414 with Venticinque (2016) 45, 71–74.

[267] *P. Oxy* 1668 = *Sel. Pap.* 1.150 – in my opinion, this does not concern a guild, but cf. Broekaert (2011) 248.

[268] Broekaert (2011) 249–51 discusses this at various levels.

[269] *CIL* 6.1872 = *ILS* 7266. cf. Liu (2013) 364.

bureaucracy.[270] It remains to be seen what the actual benefits to the state were, and to the *collegiati* – paying taxes collectively was not at all universal, nor was membership of an association. Moreover, there does not appear to be any evidence for this outside Roman Egypt. It was only in the later empire that the state began to go through *collegia* for specific public services on a larger scale.[271]

For Roman Italy during the first three centuries AD, then, it is highly likely that *collegia* could defend their interests more easily than individual craftsmen or traders. Collegiate members could, and did, take economic action, from within trust networks that were broader than merely their associations. But as a collective, too, they were at the mercy of the governing bodies in the empire.

Conclusion: intersecting axes of reference

The first three centuries AD witnessed rapid change in the position of voluntary associations: their numbers and prestige grew to reach a peak in the second and third centuries, after which they became increasingly absorbed into the structure of empire. The increase of *collegia* was paired with an increase of governmental rules and recognition of legitimate associations: both developments seem to have reinforced one another. Despite their growing numbers in this period, however, *collegiati* always remained a minority.

Members of associations can be characterized perhaps as a sub-elite. They filled a niche in the urban community that came with a certain prestige. *Collegia* were a highly visible subsection of the population that engaged in benefactions to the community and in turn received backing from powerful patrons. The collective was prominent and influential in urban society and its esteem and combined power rubbed off on individual members. The internal hierarchy of *collegia* created the associative order, a *cursus honorum* similar but opposed to the civic order, which presented an alternative road to power, as well as a road to alternative power, for those who were for reasons of (mainly) legal status, origin, and/or gender not part of the traditional competition for civic influence.

Collegiate membership had the appearance of openness: slave, freed, and free could join, and so could men and women. The analysis in this chapter has demonstrated that membership was actually highly selective, because each association had its own demands and restrictions: not just anyone could join. Exclusive membership was perhaps also a prerequisite

[270] Venticinque (2016) 44–45; Van Minnen (1987) 49. The aforementioned salt dealers of *P. Mich.* 5.245 did the same.

[271] Venticinque (2016) 199–237 is insightful for more than Roman Egypt.

for the way associations seem to have meddled in all areas of life as dense trust networks. It is no wonder that those on the inside were always a minority.

Members of associations cannot have been the truly poor, who would not have been able to fulfil the financial minimum requirements of many *collegia*. The associations' place in the civic order and the continuation of the *collegia* demanded a substantial income. It is also clear, however, that membership was not restricted to employers and wholesalers. The assumption that membership of associations was a prerogative of (wealthy) freedmen turns out to be equally problematic. Although there is little concrete evidence for slaves and freeborn in the associations, it is evident that membership was decidedly heterogeneous, even within the group of freedmen. Women were least likely to join, yet female members of the *collegia* are attested, which suggests that even for them associations presented a road to alternative power and influence.

Looking at the distribution of various professional *collegia*, it is unsurprising that Rome and Ostia stand out: this is where a plethora of associations can be found. This finding is a reflection of a difference in the position of *collegia* in the civic community. Rome was, of course, one of a kind. In the seat of imperial power, associations had to make way for the emperor and his court, and embrace a more modest role in the civic community. Ostia was tightly linked to the capital, though it is interesting to see that here the *collegia* flourished, reflecting the commercial nature of the port city; stepping up and out of the imperial shadows of Rome, in Ostia associations were at the heart of the civic and political community. In Roman Italy as a whole, conversely, the types of associations are limited. The so-called three principal *collegia* are respected and well reputed everywhere. In larger towns their existence as an umbrella association (including various sub-types of occupation) may be explained in part by the need for vertical subdivision of labour. In smaller towns, however, this need was not as pressing, and their presence is perhaps defined more by their role in the community.

The limited range of associations has consequences for an understanding of their possible role as surrogate families. In this line of thought, *collegia* were thought to fill a need for burial provisions for the poor. It can now safely be said that this was incorrect. As it turns out, however, funerary evidence is a good reflection of the range of overlap between family bonds and *collegia*, ranging from burial solely by the *collegium* to only the family and everything in between. Some Romans will have been without family at the time of their death, which is predicted by high mortality, urban family forms, and the problems of family formation of migrants in the city. In some cases, family and association were literally the same thing, including biological relations or extended family of (fellow) slaves and freedmen. Both collegial and familial relationships fostered trust networks that lay at the heart of most business partnerships. It should not come as a surprise that sometimes they were one and the same.

The recognition of combined social and economic functions in *collegia* reintroduces the comparison with medieval and early modern guilds. The multiplex ties of social, religious, familial, *and* economic nature provided a valuable and efficient means of battling economic insecurity and transaction costs in a world where information was scarce. The formal organizational structure of the associations aided enforcement of business partnerships and other labour agreements, provided of course that the *collegia* were stable and durable. There is, therefore, quite enough common ground to incorporate the Roman *collegia* in a global history of the guilds in pre-industrial times.[272] The collective was a business partner to the outside world, its importance was reflected in legal state benefits, collective property aided in battling economic risks, and the association could take collective action to defend the rights of individuals and the group.

[272] Lucassen et al. (2008) 10. Their article is entitled "The Return of the Guilds: Towards a Global History of the Guilds in Pre-industrial Times".

Chapter 6

Conclusion

Social Structures and Urban Labour in Roman Italy

Introduction

Earlier research on Roman labour has done an excellent job of unlocking the ancient evidence on the Roman world of work; it incorporates a wealth of occupational inscriptions and juridical texts, as well as literary references. The material remains of artifacts, tools, and *tabernae* are increasingly well documented. Because of the abundance of the evidence, it is easy to lose track of the fact that the majority of Romans were engaged in agriculture, which is less well represented in the sources. In agriculture, much of the produce was destined for personal consumption, not for the market. Urbanization and agriculture are nevertheless intrinsically linked. The nature of urban labour, however, is different from labour in agriculture. The particular nature of labour in the city versus agriculture is one of the reasons why this study has focused on the cities of Roman Italy. The chiefly urban origin of the sources is another.

The ancient sources are biased towards the group of urban free male skilled labourers: the urban poor are significantly under-represented, and so are women. The 'ordinary' Roman of earlier accounts was a free male artisan or craftsman who lived in the city. But the working population contained many others, too, who have largely remained unseen. My aim has been to present an integrated analysis of the economic activities of the urban working population, including freeborn wage labourers and entrepreneurs, as well as the unremunerated domestic efforts of mainly women and children, and the dependent labour of slaves and ex-slaves, in accordance with a broad definition of 'work' which includes "any human effort adding use value to goods and services".[1] The integrated account of work and labour that was offered here started out from epigraphy, but was supported by a wide variety of sources, and by methodological considerations from other fields of history.

[1] Tilly and Tilly (1998) 22–23, Introduction.

The foregoing chapters have tried to strike a balance between social and economic factors to outline a new coherent picture. This composite view impinges heavily on larger debates concerning both the Roman economy and Roman society. It is worth drawing up at some length the broader implications of my findings for those fields. In what ways has the current investigation of urban work and labour in Roman Italy furthered an understanding of labour and labourers in Roman society under the early empire? How can the ideas that have been developed here be incorporated in forthcoming scholarship? Every suggested answer raises new questions, and I should like to take the opportunity to make some suggestions for future research that go beyond the scope of this work.

One of the reasons why the debate on Roman labour is steadily moving forward, in my view, is an increasing incorporation of modern theories of labour economics among ancient historians. My approach has been shaped by this trend and owes much to the field of neo-institutional (ancient) economics. The field of labour history has an equally rich tradition to connect with, and I want to stress the significant contribution that ancient history can make to the larger historical debate notwithstanding, or precisely because of, the particularities of Rome.

Early modern labour historians for their part have tentatively started to turn their attention to pre-industrial societies like the Roman empire, partly as a result perhaps of the new economic approaches to the Roman economy.[2] Converging trends of global history on the one hand, and opening up the Roman economy to general economic approaches on the other, have made possible the development of an inclusive global labour history. Against this background, this chapter not only summarizes the argument of the book, but also aims to place my findings on Roman labour explicitly in the broader context of the global history of work, where antiquity is still under-represented. It is worth exploring the intersection between ancient and modern explicitly from the side of the Roman historian, because the case study of Roman society can be a valuable addition to global labour history, and because the dialogue between ancient historians and historians of other periods is important. Larger patterns that may shed light on the past sometimes can only be perceived from the present, and conversely there are valuable lessons for an understanding of the present to be learnt from the past.

2 E.g. J. Lucassen (2013) 11; Lis and Soly (2012).

The general argument

Labour and labour market theories

The prevailing consensus among ancient historians would seem to be that although market forces and local markets may be identified in the evidence, the sources cannot support the hypothesis of an empire-wide integrated market, and to speak of 'the Roman market economy' therefore is overstating the matter.[3]

As a production factor, labour was more readily available in Roman antiquity than either land or capital. Investment in human capital preceded (investment in) technological development and was therefore of paramount importance to sustained economic growth.[4] That is why the existence of a functioning market for labour and labourers was vital to the Roman economy. The explicit question whether market forces were present in a market for labour, to the extent that we can speak of a Roman labour market, was not posed explicitly until recently.[5] The answer is not straightforward, since labour is an elusive good. Recent socio-economic approaches have shown that a labour market generally does not function according to any straightforward application of economic price theory. Labour market segmentation theory acknowledges that historical labour markets are rarely perfectly integrated, but are segmented along various lines. Such a multidimensional approach fits the evidence for urban labour in Roman Italy well. The Roman market for labour stands out because it did not just deal in labour, but also in labourers.

Roman slavery was essential to both the social structure and the economic development of Roman society. Analyses of the phenomenon of historical slavery have generally included Rome as one of the main 'slave societies'.[6] The history of Roman slavery is an established subdiscipline of labour history with a remarkably 'global' historiography, although Roman slavery has not often been considered specifically within the broader context of labour.[7] My approach to the urban working population has tried to fill that lacuna. Slaves and ex-slaves predominate in the occupational inscriptions, but it was argued above that the majority of the working

3 Cf. Temin (2013a).

4 Saller (2002) 261.

5 Temin (2001); Temin (2004).

6 Vlassopoulos (2021) 14–38 for recent historiography; with Harper and Scheidel (2018) on the concept of a 'slave society'; Bradley and Cartledge eds (2011); Patterson (1982); Finley (1998).

7 Despite Van der Linden (2006) 27–28, who introduces it among the relevant "historical sub-disciplines" of global labour history: slavery, family history, gender history, and migration history.

population must have been free. Moreover, slave and free labourers were largely eligible for the same vacancies. For these reasons I have adopted an integrated approach of forced and voluntary labour in my analysis. It was argued that there was a functioning labour market in the cities of Roman Italy. The question that was dealt with next was, in what ways did it function?

Labourers in Rome had the opportunity to respond to market incentives, in accordance with the principles of a labour market. Geographical mobility was possible, and migration to the city is likely to have occurred in substantial numbers. Movement between jobs was also an option for some, even for slaves. Migration, however, was most likely to occur over shorter distances. This is true for the mobility of people, but it also applies to the movement of information on prices, supply, and demand. Imperfections in information flows are an important reason why there was no single integrated market economy in Roman society: there were rather regional or local markets. The Roman urban labour market was similarly made up of a variety of more or less interconnected local markets. Within these local urban labour markets, other restrictions on labour market integration played a part. Skill levels, legal status, gender, and the availability of job training can be identified as the most influential ones, which led to segmentation into restricted groups with limited movement or competition between them. Fluctuations (both unpredictable and cyclical) in demand for goods and its derived labour demand are likely to have determined economic strategies for everyone, whereas seasonal patterns of high labour demand in the agricultural calendar, the building trade, and the sailing season were probably of great consequence especially for unskilled wage labourers.[8]

The importance of social and cultural determinants to the economy of Rome have correctly been emphasized in the past. The Romans could be said to have had a socially and culturally embedded or moral economy: they highly valued the insurance provided by family ties and bonds of friendship and dependency, reciprocity and trust, and relied on them for personal economic security.[9] More strictly economic approaches to the Roman economy left social structures largely out of consideration. However, the deep-seated economic functions of social networks like family and associations should not be underestimated: they were integral to what I believe to have been a sophisticated Roman economy. The lines of segmentation in the labour market were both reinforced and overturned by these institutions. In practice, then, the participation and the position

[8] Hawkins (2021); Hawkins (2013); Erdkamp (2016); Erdkamp (2008).

[9] Finley (1973); Verboven (2002) uses the term 'moral economy', borrowed from J.C. Scott (1976). Verboven's book sets out from a similar premise as this book, on the subject of *amicitia* among (mainly) the upper classes.

of an individual worker were not determined solely by his or her individual characteristics. He or she was embedded in the social structures of family and associations. 'Human resources' like these were even more important than they are today, where we have institutionalized employment agencies and other methods for creating weak ties, all to find the right person for the job. The importance of social structures, of course, did not preclude the existence of economic rationality and market forces, or of economic growth.

Work and the family

The Roman family has been high on the research agenda over the last five decades or so, and there are no signs that scholarly attention will be decreasing anytime soon. It is not just the scholarship on the Roman family in particular that has experienced a steady increase in the past half-century or so: the popularity of family history is a much wider phenomenon. The Roman family as an economic unit, however, has hardly received any attention at all, even though, in economics, the economics of the family is an established field. Similarly, in labour history the family and household are becoming increasingly central to the analysis.[10]

The pre-industrial family has often been explained by the model of the 'family economy'. The family economy explains the family as the unit of production and consumption; in my view, this is reflected in ancient Rome in the predominance of small-scale urban workshops. Small-scale workshops clearly were an important part of the urban landscape. The model of the family economy does not match completely what we know about ancient Rome, however. Families were crucial to the organization of Roman labour relations, but not necessarily, and not exclusively, as the unit of production and consumption. The evidence illustrates that there were also numerous wage-earning families, and families that included some wage labourers, for example. In order to accommodate this diversity this book started from the more inclusive model of the 'adaptive family economy', which has more explaining power for the Roman empire than the family economy model.[11] The adaptive family economy, and related concepts of adaptive family strategies, in the context of Roman family ideals, explains why women were found in domestic and subservient roles, but it can also explain their presence as artisans and entrepreneurs. Families consciously and unconsciously, allocated an individual's labour activities, taking both the individual and family life cycles into account, and differentiation was as much a strategy as engagement with the family business.

The demography of the family defined the parameters of supply and

[10] Hofmeester (2018) 319; Van der Linden (2013) 222 with references; J. Lucassen (2013) 7; De Vries (2008); cf. Van der Linden (2006) 27–28; Cigno (1991).

[11] Introduced by Wall (1986).

demand: it determined the amount of work and labour that was needed to support everyone, but also who was available to work. More than a demographic given, the demographic make-up of the family was subject to sociocultural conventions, such as contemporary ideals about family form and marriage ages. A neo-local marriage pattern in Roman Italy guided the decision to get married when resources were sufficient to set up a new separate household, which probably pushed the median marriage age towards the late teens for women and late twenties for men. In the urban context of Roman Italy, it is likely that the simple (nuclear) family was the dominant family form, although this regularly included slaves and freedmen. City dwellers appear to have lived in relatively small families – a relatively later marriage age will have curbed fertility to some extent. Several other ways to practise family planning were available, but none of them appear to have been reliable. Raising fewer children, or having fewer children that survived into adulthood, however, meant that there was more money to invest in the upbringing and education of remaining children. The economic opportunities and the resources of a family therefore will have influenced family formation and composition, just as much as the disease-ridden environment of the larger cities did.

The slave presence in the non-elite household is likely to have been limited. Slaves needed to be maintained, and it was expensive to keep a slave underemployed when demand fell. A small permanent slave workforce meant optimal flexibility in a volatile market.[12] A restricted number of slaves and ex-slaves ensured access to (skilled) labour, while it did not drain the household resources too much when business was slow. Such economic considerations are less likely to have played a part in wealthy elite households, where slaves could be found in large numbers: more than half of all urban slaves were probably linked to one of these large *domus*. Slaves were an indicator of wealth. Slaves were also economically active within the household, however, leaving few vacancies in the domestic sector open to freeborn labourers. The existence of a large elite household in the city, therefore, may have curbed job opportunities for the freeborn to some extent. The hypothesis was that this might be particularly limiting for women, whom we might expect to have worked mostly in this type of job, in line with gender ideals, which is what happened in early modern Europe. It is true that in occupational inscriptions women are commemorated chiefly in the 'female' role of *nutrix* (wet nurse), or *ornatrix* (hairdresser). In virtually all jobs, slave women and freedwomen outnumber freeborn women by a large margin, in line with my hypothesis. In all branches of work, however, including traditionally gendered occupations like childcare, women are also outnumbered by men. To some extent this is a reflection of biases in

[12] Hawkins (2017).

the evidence, but it also reveals the importance of the life cycle on female labour participation. Most women are likely to have engaged in work and labour at some point in their lives. It appears that Roman women found various ways to make a living: they were prominent in retail and family businesses, and are also attested in independent jobs.

The work of slaves was integral to the economics of the family, both in small households and in elite *domus*. The economic bond between the family and their slaves generally continued after manumission, and many ex-slaves maintained close connections with their former masters. Freedmen became 'extended family'; this extended family could be important for securing labour power whenever skilled labour or trustworthy labourers were in short supply; patrons and freedmen forged significant and potentially vast networks of trust of the kind that were so vital to the Roman economy.[13]

The Roman family was demonstrably significant as an economic entity. Economics therefore provides an additional criterion to define who should be included in the elusive Roman 'family', and a way to understand its structure and some of the organizing principles behind it. Economic considerations and strategies must have played a part even in the constitution of the nuclear family, through marriage alliances and measures for curbing or encouraging fertility, or its slave component. Conversely, family structure opens a valuable window onto urban labour in Roman Italy. Family form – the demography of the family – was not a stable factor, however. The family moved through a so-called family life cycle, driven forward by the standard life events of birth, marriage, and death that shape the structure of the family over time. With the addition or subtraction of family members, labour demand and labour supply change. At the birth of a child, for example, the family's needs go up (there is an extra mouth to feed), and the labour supply goes down (because the mother devotes time to childcare and the infant obviously cannot work). If, as in this example, the calculation leads to a net loss, we speak of a life cycle squeeze, a situation that calls for a change in the family's economic strategy.

The principle of the family life cycle also operated in elite households, only with a large slave population the demographic effects are potentially multiplied. Slaves, too, engaged in recognized, though illicit, 'marriages' (*contubernia*) and had families with a life cycle of their own. They had children, they sometimes also had slaves that – once they were freed themselves – they could manumit, and they passed away. The slave family life cycle of a household had an obvious effect on the need for additional slaves, or on the form of slave education. The slave *vernae* who were born, raised, and educated within the household were a preferred choice, but it is likely that home-born slaves were not enough to fulfil demand for slave

13 Verboven (2012b); Mouritsen (2011b).

labour. It was impossible to predict when a (skilled) slave would need a replacement, and it took time to raise and educate *vernae*. As a result, the market for forced labour probably remained substantial.

Human capital

The family determined the form of an individual's labour participation to a large extent. Investment in human capital was also a family decision. Skill paid off: skilled labour paid about twice as much as unskilled labour. There is enough evidence to suggest that job training in the form of a basic education or an apprenticeship was open to everyone: to slave and free, boy or girl. Apprenticeship contracts show that contrary to what is sometimes assumed, a number of freeborn girls could and did in fact receive formal job training, although admittedly not to the extent that boys or enslaved girls did. Despite the finding that the dominant marriage pattern left freeborn girls enough time to undertake an apprenticeship or learn from their birth families before they got married, both social expectations and the prospect of lower future earnings for women than for men evidently still limited an interest in women's education.

There were factors other than gender that governed investment in human capital as well. The high rate of mortality predicts lower investment, because it implied a risk that the returns on that investment might be short-lived. Education did not come cheap, and financial constraints are therefore also likely to have played a part. Not everyone could afford to miss out on the income a child could generate. In this respect it is interesting to note that since skilled labourers were better off than unskilled workers, they could more easily afford an education for their children: this phenomenon is called intergenerational persistence. Intergenerational persistence in Rome, however, did not imply that children always followed in their parents' footsteps. Job differentiation between the generations is well attested. The most significant implication here is that intergenerational persistence predicts a continuous presence of freeborn skilled as well as unskilled labourers in Roman society.

Elite households invested heavily in basic education and higher skill levels for slaves. There were (in-house and street) schools where slaves could learn the basics of reading and arithmetic, and some received additional training by learning on the job or through more formal apprenticeships. The master could cash in on this investment by employing the skills of slaves, or by selling them or their labour power. Under circumstances of highly fluctuating demand, freeborn skilled wage workers thus faced severe competition from the servile population. Having said that, there is also evidence to suggest that hiring a skilled labourer was on occasion considered to be more realistic than educating a slave; moreover, even *domus* networks could not account for (ex-)slaves with every conceivable skill set. That left options for the freeborn skilled worker.

In sum, in both small and large households, the family, or the head of the family, decided on collective labour participation and labour allocation, and the amount of investment in human capital for each family member. The Roman 'family business' could thus take various shapes and forms, from a household production unit to the cooperation between patron and freedmen.

Non-familial labour collectives

Labour opportunities were also decided by other, non-familial social structures. In small-scale settlements, the urban community may have been a social network in itself, more intricately so in the street or neighbourhood. The associative phenomenon provided the necessary networks of trust that went beyond the family. This was the topic of Chapter 5.

In the early modern world, craft unions or guilds are the prime example. In Rome, the most obvious equivalent of such labour collectives were voluntary associations or *collegia*. They may be seen to exemplify the economic functioning of all kinds of social networks. Whenever people get together there are economic benefits to be gained, a phenomenon which may be described as the economics of association. In the absence of a watertight legal framework for the enforcement of labour relations, the importance of mutual trust or personal security should not be underestimated. Market information, as we have seen, was hard to come by. Information travelled with people, but people are only as good as their word, and it takes a certain amount of trust to act on that information. Like the family, then, a *collegium* provided a trust network, a safety net that helped decide who to rely on. The ties among *collegiati* therefore were extended social ties, with clear economic consequences. The formal organization of *collegia* made them particularly useful for economic purposes. This is true even if outright collective economic action by the associations is rarely attested. It would thus be anachronistic to see them as Roman trade unions. The comparison with early modern guilds is helpful up to a point, because early modern guilds were not actually the monopolists they were once thought to have been. But *collegium* membership will have lessened transaction costs of finding business partners and employees, and perhaps the collective reputation of an association also made these *collegiati* the go-to place for consumers.

A Roman was therefore not entirely free in his or her choice of work, but had to deal with family and sometimes also with an association. This tension between social institutions is significant: it is what decided a labourer's working opportunities. To a certain extent family and *collegium* were complementary: family encouraged or precluded labour participation and paid for an education, whereas a *collegium* provided the business contacts. Yet there were some functional overlaps between the two. Job training was sometimes facilitated not by family, but by fellow *collegiati* who may have lent the money, or helped out in a more hands-on manner by taking in apprentices. Conversely, business contacts, for example, were also maintained through family, or a business partner became family by marriage. Sometimes family members were also members of the same *collegium*. Both institutions built one's reputation and social capital.

In an urban context perhaps the associations for some were more central than family: there are reasons to think that family ties were weaker in the city than in the countryside, thereby creating the need for associations complementary to the social network and the safety net that the family provided. This is a phenomenon that is historically well attested, and the evidence seems to indicate a similar pattern in ancient Rome. A predominance among labour migrants of young males, who could not and did not always bring their families with them, is suggestive. Insofar as can be ascertained, families in Roman cities were generally small. Under these circumstances, the advantage of joining a 'substitute family' in the form of a *collegium* must have been considerable.

Roman associations were relatively open institutions. This means that their social network was available to most: there are slave members attested as well as freedmen and freeborn, but membership was probably out of reach for the destitute, and we see few or no female *collegiati* – who were nevertheless included in the network by proxy. The *collegia* were selective in who they admitted, in order to protect their credibility and creditworthiness. It is perhaps their exclusivist character that explains why only a minority seem to have joined. However, for an honest worker with few prior connections in the city an association may well have provided a relatively easy point of entry into the urban labour network.

The contribution of the Roman case to the global history of work

> Global labour history is not conceived as a 'school', but rather as an 'area of interest'; it is not a vertical organization, but a network continuously assembling and breaking up in relation to specific research projects; it does not aim for a new 'grand narrative', but rather to partial syntheses based on multiple empirical research and various intellectual interpretations.[14]

The broader context for the history of Roman work and labour, is global labour history.[15] Pioneering studies of labour published before the Second

[14] De Vito (2013) 12.

[15] For the historiography of labour history and the development of the global history

World War provided important insights on labour history, including labour in ancient Rome, but they lacked theoretical and methodological sophistication. After the Second World War, particularly in the 1960s, 1970s and 1980s, labour history was taken up anew. A rapidly expanding body of research was devoted mainly to labour in Western Europe and North America, from the Industrial Revolution until present times. The wish to explain the so-called 'rise of the West' led to a limited field of research, focusing on wage labour in the context of early capitalism. The pre-industrial Roman empire did not fit that enterprise. Moreover, as a result of Finley's influential views, the Roman economy was long considered to be fundamentally different in nature from capitalist societies, and thus Rome was generally left out of labour history accounts. During the 'golden age of labour history', therefore, antiquity fell through the cracks.

In the final decades of the twentieth century, however, globalization gave rise to the academic field of 'global history'.[16] The globalizing trend soon extended itself to the (by that time) struggling field of labour history,[17] leading scholars to express the desire for a radically different approach to labour history. Van der Linden and Lucassen promulgated a global labour history, a kind of "universal history of work" that expanded the field geographically (notably to incorporate the Eastern world) and thematically, but also chronologically.[18] The first step has been to include the run-up to the Industrial Revolution from *c.*1500 onwards. Since 2018, the research field has become established with a *Handbook Global History of Work* – its title incidentally reflecting once more the shift from 'labour' to the more inclusive approach of 'work'.[19]

The global history of work acknowledges that not every labour effort since the Industrial Revolution concerned wage labour; various forms of commodified labour can coexist, even for one historical individual.[20] This understanding opened up the way to recognize that wage labour might be present in pre-industrial societies too, alongside other labour relations – including forced labour. Although this is not the place to present an

of work, see e.g. Hofmeester and Van der Linden (2018) Introduction; De Vito (2013); J. Lucassen (2013); Lucassen (2006); Van der Linden and Lucassen (1999).

[16] 'Global history' currently seems to be the favoured term, though alternatives such as 'world history' are sometimes attested. The first issue of the *Journal of Global History* was published in 2006; the Oxford Centre for Global History was established in 2011.

[17] Van der Linden ed. (1993).

[18] Van der Linden and Lucassen (1999); quote from Van der Linden (2006) 21; cf. Van der Linden (2012) 62–63, including both 'a universal history of work' and 'a history of globalized work'. See Winn (2012) for clear limits to its (current) reach.

[19] Hofmeester and Van der Linden eds (2018).

[20] Van der Linden (2012) 63–66.

extensive global labour history approach to the Roman urban labour market, some preliminary observations on the Roman case may be made.[21]

Rome was not exactly a capitalist society. However, the present book has underlined that besides an agricultural population living by self-subsistence, the evidence for more urbanized regions shows that market forces in labour were also present and influential. The Roman empire, moreover, clearly was familiar with wage labour. Lucassen argued that the volume of small coins that circulated in any given society is a sound indicator of the extent of wage labour and "small independent producers working for the market".[22] The widespread use of coins and, closely related, prices may also point to market forces and/or a market economy more generally.[23] The coin finds from the Roman empire are well known. The degree of monetization and its implications, perhaps, less so.[24]

The findings of the foregoing chapters suggest that the history of market economics runs deeper than was previously thought and that the Roman economy had many 'modern' traits. At the same time, market imperfections in the Roman empire, conversely, call into question the strictly economic views of price theory and reinforce the sociological and neo-institutional approaches to the historical economy. In the case of urban labour in early imperial Italy, therefore, a focus on social structures of the family and non-familial labour collectives has proven to be particularly helpful.

Classification of occupations

With an extensive catalogue of job titles like mine, it would be tempting to start historical comparison from occupational classification: the grouping of job titles of individuals under economically significant headings. The tool to do so is available in HISCO.[25] HISCO is the historical counterpart of ISCO (the International Standard Classification of Occupation), a system developed by the International Labour Office in the mid-twentieth century to classify and codify occupations. HISCO, adding an H for 'historical', has been adapted to bridge time and language boundaries in comparisons

[21] De Vito (2013) has recently made a strong case for the inclusion of pre-industrial societies in global labour history. De Vito and Lichtenstein eds (2015) on global convict labour include a chapter on ancient Rome: Groen-Vallinga and Tacoma (2015); so does a special issue of ***Workers of the World*** on global labour history edited by De Vito: Zuiderhoek (2013). Earlier, tentative attemps to include pre-industrial societies in what is largely a history of ideas on work and labour may be found in Ehmer and Lis eds (2009); Lis and Soly (2012).

[22] J. Lucassen (2013) 22; Lucassen (2007).

[23] J. Lucassen (2013) 22: "deeply monetized societies must have had market economies". See also Temin (2013a); Kessler and Temin (2008); Temin (2001).

[24] Cf. De Ligt (2003); De Ligt (1990); Hopkins (1980).

[25] Van Leeuwen et al. (2002).

of occupational title. It was initially created for the nineteenth and early twentieth centuries. Cross-referencing from HISCO allows us to connect these data with social classification systems for work, such as HISCLASS and HISMA (social mobility analysis).[26]

Analysing the occupational inscriptions from the Latin provinces, Rada Varga has taken on the encoding of job titles into HISCO, only to find that there was a lack of overlap, which necessitated assigning double codes, unspecific codes, and other ancient occupations that were simply absent from the system;[27] in part this is due to the obscure meaning of occupational titles for Roman society, as discussed in the introductory chapter: quite apart from the difficulties of distinguishing producers and traders, for example, it remains an open question what exactly an *aquarius* might have done with water. The resulting makeshift encoding into HISCO feeds directly into the social classification systems of HISCLASS and others, so it is no wonder that Varga has had to conclude that these social classification systems are "completely inappropriate for the Roman era".[28] Roman job titles cannot, in my view, be usefully encoded for comparison using HISCO, as Varga's brave attempt may underline. There are, however, other lines of comparison through historical taxonomies that prove to be especially fruitful in view of the present book.

Roman labour relations

Urban work and labour in Roman Italy gave rise to a wide spectrum of labour relations, including, but not restricted to, self-subsistence, wage labour, and small independent producers for the market. The existence of slavery in Rome is, of course, particularly distinctive.

In 2007, a vast project was initiated under the guidance of Karin Hofmeester, entitled the Global Collaboratory on the History of Labour Relations 1500–2000.[29] The associated labour historians have developed a universal classification system for labour relations, "intended to cover the whole world, from 1500 and in principle also for earlier periods".[30] In what follows, therefore, I will attempt to fit Roman labour relations into this taxonomy.[31] The purpose of this exercise is twofold: first, it provides

[26] For references and current status of the projects: historyofwork.iisg.nl.

[27] Varga (2020) Chapter 3.

[28] Varga (2020) Chapter 3 for HISCLASS, HISCAM, and SOCPO, with references, there 14.

[29] See https://collab.iisg.nl/web/labourrelations.

[30] Hofmeester (2018) 318.

[31] Stapel (2016), "Taxonomy of Labour Relations", https://hdl.handle.net/10622/OJYQOR, IISH Data Collection, V2. For ease of reference the taxonomy is included as Appendix 3. Definitions of the various categories in Hofmeester (2018) 323–27.

a schematic overview of the Roman labour market through its labour relations, and second, it is a first attempt to apply the taxonomy to the Roman situation, testing its applicability in an ancient economy. Table 6.1 presents a schematic overview of Roman labour relations, divided by household type. I have included the rural household, and I have distinguished between two categories of non-elite household on the basis of their main income: self-employed or waged.

Table 6.1. Schematic view of Roman labour relations from the perspective of the family by means of the classification system of the Global Collaboratory on the History of Labour Relations (Appendix 3).

	Taxonomy category	
Agricultural family		
Housework	5	Kin non-producers
Slave labour	17.1	Working for proprietor
	17.2	For hire
Hiring additional seasonal labour	13.1	Employer of free wage earners
	14.2	Piece-rate wage labourers
	14.3	Time-rate wage labourers
	17.2	Slaves for hire
Seasonal rural–urban migration	14.2	Piece-rate wage labourers
	14.3	Time-rate wage labourers
Non-elite family (a) entrepreneur		
The entrepreneur (m/f)	12a	Self-employed leading producers
	13.1	Employer of free wage earners
	13.2	Employer of indentured labourers (freedmen *operae*)
	13.4	Employer of slaves
Kin	12b	Self-employed kin producers
Housework	5	Kin non-producers
Slaves	17.1	Working for proprietor
	17.2	For hire
Freedmen	12b	Self-employed kin producers (freedmen viewed as extended family)
	15	Indentured labourers (*operae*)
Wage-earning family members	14.2	Piece rate
(including those apprenticed out)	14.3	Time rate
Extra hired hands, freeborn/	14.2	Piece rate
freedmen/slaves/apprentices	14.3	Time rate
	17.2	Slaves for hire

		Taxonomy category
Non-elite family (b) wage-earning family		
Housework	5	Kin non-producers
Wage-earning family members	14.2	Piece rate
	14.3	Time rate
	14.4	Cooperative subcontracting
Elite *domus*		
Ruling family	13.1	Employer of free wage earners
	13.2	Employer of indentured labourers (freedmen *operae*)
Slaves' housework	6	Household servants
Free hired labour	14.2	Piece-rate wage labourers
	14.3	Time-rate wage labourers
Freedmen	12b	Self-employed kin producers (viewed as extended family)
	15	Indentured labour (freedmen *operae*)
Slaves	17.1	Working for proprietor
	17.2	For hire

Most rural families are likely to have been largely self-sufficient, allowing for small-scale market transactions (4a and 4b).[32] I have included their contribution to urban labour as employers and employees in the seasonal labour cycle in Table 6.1.

The full range of labour relations brings out the importance of labour for the market, categorized as the third goal of production, in an urban context (= all classifications within the range 12–17). Its frequent recurrence shows that the category of wage labourers (14) is likely to have been substantial, and the flexibility necessary to deal with market insecurity predicts that many Romans will have turned to one form of wage labour or another at some point in their life. This is how the individual life cycles of workers should be understood, something that was shown to be especially obvious in the case of women.

Indeed, one of the most noteworthy findings from the Global Collobo-ratory on the History of Labour Relations, to my mind, is that combinations of different labour relations for both individuals and households are the rule rather than an exception.[33] What is more, the exercise brings out the vagueness of the distinctions between various groups of Roman labourers: slavery recurs in all households, and in various forms (6, 17.1–2), reflecting

[32] Hofmeester (2018) 321 n. 10; cf. De Ligt (2003).

[33] Hofmeester (2018) 321–22.

interconnecting slaving strategies.[34] In Rome, seasonality and the labour cycle predict that many free labourers will also have conformed to a similar pattern of multiple labour relations or occupational pluralism. Conversely, the overview indicates that the same assignment in a non-elite household might be executed by any one of no less than twelve types of labourer.

An attempt to place servile labourers within the taxonomy immediately reveals that labour relations are not determined by legal status or economic position per se. Slave, freed, and free can all be understood as part of one integrated labour market, even though they functioned as imperfect substitutes. It is significant that parallel developments of 'reconceptualizing the working class' can be found in global labour history, identifying a similar heterogeneous nature within the category of slave labour as well as a feeble dividing line from free wage labour in other historical societies.[35] Instead of slavery, the dichotomy between free and unfree labour and the spectrum of dependency that lies in between takes precedence in the new labour history.[36] In Roman society, moreover, the boundaries between legal categories were not fixed: freeborn people could become slaves, slaves became freedmen, freedmen's children were freeborn. The life and labour cycles of an individual are therefore likely to have seen someone progress through various labour relations. Slaves could go from dependent slave labour (6, 17.1 and/or 17.2) to a shop of their own with a family or *colliberti* (12a and 12b) and with their own employees (13).

Table 6.1 visualizes a remarkable variety of possible labour relations within the non-elite family, particularly the entrepreneurial non-elite family. A small slave workforce, the option of manumission, and the continued economic bonds between patrons and freedmen ensured that non-elite households in the city had a variety of economic strategies available to them. This flexibility is probably one of the reasons why slavery remained so popular for so long.

The taxonomy includes a category of tributary labour (8–11) that does not recur in my Table 6.1. The category concerns various types of labour largely left out of the present book, such as convict labour and conscripts (both category 8), though soldiers from Roman Italy in the early empire were mainly a very particular group of wage earners (14.3); tributary labour

[34] Chapters 3 and 4 above; Vlassopoulos (2021) 58–74.

[35] Van der Linden (2012) 63–66, 67–68 ('reconceptualizing the working class').

[36] The research of the Bonn Center for Dependency and Slavery Studies works with the concept of 'asymmetrical dependencies', https://www.dependency.uni-bonn.de/en; Brown and Van der Linden (2010); Engerman (1999); Palmer (1998); Brass and Van der Linden eds (1997).

could also include debt bondage, or the *servus quasi colonus*.[37] The collective slaves and freedmen of associations are a very particular group of labourers that strain the limits of the taxonomy. Similarly, public slaves are difficult to classify. Their position on the margins of the city and of society more generally has largely excluded them from the current investigation.[38] They might be incorporated into the taxonomy with minor adaptations.

The taxonomy of labour relations should be commended for its explicit attempt to cover the entire population. Indeed, the unremunerated work of household members is explicitly included, and could be subsumed under categories 5 or 12b. On the whole, the taxonomy proves to be a useful tool for mapping Roman work and labour relations, at least as far as vertical labour relations are concerned; that is, relationships of dependence. Horizontal labour relations (outside the household) are notably lacking. Horizontal labour relations in Roman Italy would include an apprenticeship, a *societas* between *colliberti*, for example, or a business partnership on equal terms between *collegiati*. Associations and other informal, non-familial labour collectives clearly played an important part in labour relations of early imperial Italy, but they cannot be accommodated in this scheme.

Concluding remarks

Much is to be gained from the cooperation between ancient historians and global historians. Initiatives like the taxonomy for labour relations indicate to the ancient historian where to look for the unseen Romans, and for useful comparisons. Conversely, it is hoped that labour historians of other periods will take note of the fact that Roman work, labour, and labour relations were just as complex as in any other historical society, which may provide provocative hypotheses for researching later periods. This monograph, for example, has argued that work and labour in the cities of Roman Italy under the early empire was shaped and structured by the social relations of the family as well as by means of other intersecting and overlapping non-familial associations. It was demonstrated that market forces applied to labour supply and demand, but that markets were fragmented geographically, and were segmented along lines of gender, legal status, and skill. Such segmentation was determined and maintained through social institutions. The importance of family, horizontal labour relations, and trust networks for work and labour throughout history should not be underestimated.

[37] Groen-Vallinga and Tacoma (2015).

[38] They are another category that challenges the suggested slaving contexts of Vlassopoulos (2021) 74–83.

Appendices

Appendix 1

Catalogue of Job Titles

This list started from the combined catalogues of Joshel, Treggiari, and Von Petrikovits.[1] The resulting list was then expanded with many job titles from epigraphy, literature, and legal sources that were not previously included. The translations provided are a combination of those by the three authors mentioned, the Lewis and Short Latin dictionary, Hemelrijk (2020), and my own interpretations.

a manu, amanuensis	secretary
abietarius, abetarius	timber merchant
accomodator	unknown
acroamatica Graeca	Greek actress/singer
actarius	scribe, record keeper
actor	agent, administrator
acuarius, acuclarius	maker of needles (*acuarius* may also be a variant of *aquarius*?)
acutarius	maker of sharp objects
admissione, ab	usher
adplumbator, applumbator	solderer
advocatus	lawyer
aedifex, aedificator	builder
aedificia, ad/supra	superintendent of urban property
aedituus	keeper of a temple
aequator monetae	coinage tester(?)
aerarius statuarius	maker of copper statues
aerarius vascularius	maker of copper vessels
aerarius	coppersmith
agrimensor	land surveyor
albarius	worker in stucco
alicarius	maker/dealer of things in halica (spelt)
alipilus	plucker of armpit hair
aluminarius	dealer in alum
ampullarius	maker of miniature amphorae (*ampullae*)
anaglyptarius	maker of reliefs

[1] Joshel (1992) 176–82; Von Petrikovits (1981) 83–119; Treggiari (1980) 61–64.

anagnostes, anagnostria	reader
anatiarius	dealer in ducks
antiquaries	teacher of palaeography
anularius, anellarius	ring-maker
aquarius	workman for a household's water supply?
aquilegus	water diviner
arbitrix emboliarium	arbiter of actresses
arcarius, arcuarius	treasurer, cashier
archimagirus	chef
archimimus, -a	first leading mime player
architectus, arcitectus	architect
arcularius	chest or cupboard maker
argentarius artifex	silversmith
argentarius vascularius	maker of silver vessels
argentarius	banker, money changer
argento, ab	person in charge of silver, or the treasury?
armamentarius, armamintarius	one engaged with *armamenta*, weaponry
armariarius	cabinetmaker, carpenter
armiger	armor bearer
armillarius	bracelet maker
aromatarius	spice dealer
artifex	artisan
asinarius	ass driver
asturconarius	breeder and/or driver of *asturcones* (horses from Asturia in Spain)
atellana	actress in Atellan farce
atriensis	majordomo and servants who cleaned and maintained the house
aurarius	goldsmith
aurator, ad statuas aurandas	gilder (of statues)
auri acceptor	goldsmith/dealer in gold?/pawnbroker?
auri netrix	gold spinner
auri vestrix	gold embroiderer
auricaesor	gold cutter
auricoctor	gold smelter?
auriductor in lamina	gold embosser in sheets of gold
aurifex brattiarius	gold-leaf beater
aurifex, aurufex	goldsmith
aviarius altiliarius	dealer in fattened birds (bird fattener?)
aviarius	dealer in birds
axearius	axle maker, wheelwright
ballistarius, ballistrarius	maker of *ballistae* (catapults)
balneator, balneator privatarius	bath attendant

baltearius	belt maker (?)
barbaricarius, barbaricas	brocade maker, embroiderer
baxiarius, baxearius	sandal maker
blattiarius	purple worker
botularius	sausage maker
bracarius	tailor
brattiarius inaurator	goldbeater, gilder
brattiarius, -a	goldbeater, maker of gold leaf
bucaeda, bucida	butcher
buccularius	maker of cheek flaps for helms
burdonarius	hinny driver
bybliopola	bookseller
cabator (cavator)	engraver, gem cutter, excavator
caelator, gelator	engraver
caementarius, cementarius	bricklayer, mason
calcariensis	lime burner
calcarius, -ia	chalk burner
calceolarius	shoemaker
calciator, calceator	shoemaker
calcis coctor	lime burner
calculator	mathematician?
caligarius	bootmaker
cameliarius	camel driver
candelabrarius	maker of candelabrae, lampstands
candidarius	white-bread baker
cantor, -trix	singer
capistrarius	holster maker
capsarius	servant who carried a child's bookcase, scroll-holder carrier
capulator, caplator	one who carries oil from the presses
carbonarius	coal dealer
carinarius	dyer in a modish tint
carpentarius	wagonwright
cassidarius	helmet maker
castellarius	superintendent of reservoirs
caudicarius	lighterman, bargee
caupo, copo, caupona	innkeeper
cellarius, cellariarius	provisioner, storeskeeper
centonarius	patchwork maker, ragman
cerarius	wax-figure maker
cerdo	handworker
ceriolarius	wax-candle maker
ceromatita	gymnastics instructor
cervesarius	beer brewer

chartarius	dealer in paper, paper-maker
choraula	flute player (m)
chorographiarius, chorographus(?)	geographer, map designer
ciliciarius	wig maker
circi nuntius	announcer of the circus
circitor, circu(m)itor	overseer of waterway management (repair man?)
cisiarius, gisiarius, cisianus(?)	cab driver/owner
cistarius	guardian of a chest or wardrobe
citharoedus, -a	lyre player and singer
citrarius	workers in citrus wood
clavarius, -a	nailsmith
clavicularius, clavicarius	keymaker, locksmith
cloacarius	sewer cleaner
clostrarius, claustrarius, clastrarius	locksmith
coactor	collector
cocio	dealer
cocus, coquus, coctor; supra cocos	cook; supervisor of cooks
colorator	painter of houses?
columnarius	pillar maker
comoedus	comic actor
conditarius, -a	chef de cuisine?
conditor	seasoner
coriarius subactarius	preparer of hides for tanning
coriarius, corarianus	tanner
corinthiarius	worker in Corinthian bronze
corinthis, a	caretaker of Corinthian ware
cornicularius	assistant, aid, secretary (in civil offices)
coronarius	garland maker
crepidarius	maker of sandals, slippers
crustarius	one who makes embossed figures
crustularius	confectioner
cubicularius	bedchamber servant
cubiculo, a	servant in charge of bedroom
culinari	kitchen servant
cullearius	maker of *cullei* (leather bags?)
cultrarius	knife maker, cutler
cunaria	infant attendant
cuparius	cellar master
curator aedificiorum	superintendent of urban property
custodiarius	jailer
custos	guard, keeper

dealbator	plasterer
deaurator	gilder
decempedator	land surveyor
diabathrarius	shoemaker for light shoes (*diabathra*)
diatretarius	cage cup maker
diffusor olearius, diffusitrix	one who taps oil from a larger amphora to a smaller one
dispensator	steward
dissignator	usher/undertaker
dolearius	vessel maker
dulciarius	confectioner
eborarius, eburarius	worker in ivory
educator, -trix	tutor, nanny
embaenitarius	unknown, but regularly attested
emboliaria	actress of interludes
ep(h)ippiarius	maker of horsecloths, saddler?
equiso	groom, stableman
essedarius	maker of *esseda* (war chariots)?
exactor	collector or overseer
exemptor	quarryman
exonerator calcariarius	lime unloader
exstructor	builder
fabarius	bean seller
faber argentarius	silversmith
faber automatarius	maker of *automata* (machines)
faber balneator	provider of services in the baths?
faber dolabrarius	cooper
faber eborarius	worker in ivory
faber ferrarius	ironsmith
faber ferrius	ironworker
faber intestinarius	joiner, inlayer (carved fine interior woodwork)
faber intestinus	woodworker
faber lecticarius, lectarius	maker of beds
faber oculariarius, ocularius	maker of eyes for statues
faber soliarius baxiarius	maker of woven footwear
faber subaedianus	builder working on interiors
faber tignuarius	carpenter
faber	worker; esp. builder or carpenter
fabricator	craftsman
factor	oilpresser
faenarius	hay salesman
faenerator, -trix	moneylender

falcarius	sickle smith
ferramentarius	worker with iron equipment
ferrariarius	someone in iron mining
ferrarius, -a	ironsmith
fictiliarius	potter
fictor, finctor	sculptor?
figlinator	brickmaker
figularius, figulator, figulus, figelus	potter
flammarius, flammearius	dyer in very red colour
flator argentarius aerarius	moulder, esp. in minting
flaturarius	caster
florentinarius	damast weaver?
focarius	kitchen servant
fontanus	someone who has to do with a water source (*fons*)
fossor, fosor	grave digger?
frumentarius	grain dealer
frumento, a	custodian of household grain
fullo	fuller
funerarius, funerator	undertaker
furnarius, -a	baker?
fusor (olearius)	moulder, in metal or oil
gallicarius	maker of Gallic shoes
gallinarius, -a	poulterer
gaunacarius	furrier
gemmarius sculptor	gem engraver, gem sculptor
gemmarius, -a	jeweller
geometres	geometrician
gerdius, -a	weaver
germanus	bodyguard
gerulus	bearer, porter
gladiarius, gladiator	swordmaker
glutinarius	maker of glue or paste
glutinator	papyrus gluer
grammaticus	grammar teacher, teacher of language
gregarius	shepherd
gypsarius, gupsarius	maker of plaster casts
hariolus, -a	prophet, prophetess
harundinarius	seller of reeds (for hunting or fishing, or roofs) or writing pens?
haruspex, haruspica	soothsayer

hereditates, ad	financial administrator or account keeper of inheritances
holitor, hilitores	greengrocer
hordearius	barley seller
horologiarius	watchmaker
horrearius	storehouse man
hospitiis (et paedagogus puerorum), ab	host (and attendant/teacher of slave children)
hymnologus	singer of hymns
iatralipte, iatraliptes	doctor who cures by ointments and massage, masseuse
iatromea	midwife
imagines, ad	in charge of paintings/statues
inaurator	gilder
indusiarius	maker/dealer of over-tunics
infector	dyer
inpaestator	metal embosser
inpedimenta, ad	caretaker of baggage
inpiliarius	maker of felt footwear
insignarius, insignitor	gem cutter
institor unguentarius	perfume seller
insularius	rent collector or supervisor of an *insula*
inundator	flooders?
iumenta, supra	person in charge of pack and draft animals
iumentarius	driver or supplier of coacher and carts, dealer in baggage animals
lactarius, lactearius	dealer in milk/milk cakes?
lagonarius, -a; lagunarius, -a	bottle seller, potter
lanarius carminator	wool carder
lanarius coactilarius, –coactiliarius	maker of felt, felter
lanarius	maker of woollen cloth
lanifica circulatrix	street vendor of woollen cloth
lanifricarius	cloth cleaner
lanipendus, -a	wool weigher, spinning supervisor
lanista	trainer/owner of gladiators
lanius, lanio, laniarius	butcher
lanternarius	lighterman
lapicida, lapicidinarius	stonecutter
lapidaries, lapidaries structor	stoneworker
laquearius	maker of panelled ceilings
lavator, lotor	washer

lectarius, lectuarius	bedmaker
lecticarius	litter bearer
lector, -trix	reader
lena	madam
lenuncularius	barge skipper
libarius	cake baker
libitinarius	undertaker
librarius a manu	scribe, secretary
librarius, -a	scribe, copyist, secretary
librator	land measurer, equalizer
libripens	weigher?
lignarius	dealer in wood
limarius, faber limarius	file hewer
limbularius	maker of girdles, ribbons, and so on
linarius, -ia	linen weaver/dealer
lintearius, linteo, -earia	linen weaver
linyfarius, linyfio	linen weaver/dealer
loc(u)larius	maker of *loculi* (niches)?, box maker
locationes, ad	administrator or account keeper of contracts or leases?
lorarius	harness maker
lyntrarius	boatman
macellarius	provisions dealer
macellensis	market man
machinarius	engineer
machinator	engineer
magister	teacher
magister chori	choir director
magister magnus ovium	chief overseer of sheep flocks
malleator, malliator	beater (minting)
manceps	dealer, usually in slaves
manicarius	worker with *manicae* (bandages for the sword arm of a gladiator)
manticularius	maker of handbags and so on
manulearius	maker of clothing with long sleeves
manupretiarius burrarius	one who creates *burrae* for an hourly wage
margarita, ad	caretaker of pearls
margaritarius, -a	pearl setter
marmorarius, marmarius	marble mason, marble cutter
materiarius	timber merchant
mediastinus	servant, medical assistant
medicamentarius	apothecary
medicus chirurgus	surgeon

medicus equarius et venator	horse doctor and huntsman
medicus iumentarius	doctor of draft animals
medicus ocularius	eye doctor
medicus, -a	doctor
mellarius, -ia	dealer in honey
membranarius	parchment maker
memoria, a	in charge of written accounts
mensor aedificiorum	surveyor/measurer of buildings
mensor machinarius	grain measurer
mensor (metator)	surveyor
mercator bovarius	dealer in cattle
mercator olei hispani ex provincia Baetica	dealer in Spanish oil from the province of Baetica
mercator sagarius	dealer in cloaks
mercator venalicius	slave dealer
mercator	dealer, trader, merchant
metallarius, metallicus	mine worker
mimus, -a	mime
miniarius, minaria	one who makes paint from tin
minister, -tra	servant
ministrator	waiter
molendinarius	mill worker
molinarius, molitor	miller
molochinarius, molocinarius	maker of clothes from tree mallow
monetarius	minter
monodiaria	solo singer
mulio	mule driver
mulomedicus	veterinarian
multicarius	maker of *multicia* (thin cloth)
murilegulus	one who fishes for purple-fish
museiarius, musaearius, musarius, musivarius	mosaicist
musicarius	person in charge of music?
musicus	musician
myrrepsius	maker of salves and oils
naupegus aupiciarius	maker of auspicious signs on ships?
naupegus, naupegiarius	shipbuilder
navicularius	shipowner
negotia(n)s coriariorum	dealer in tanned hides
negotians lagonaris	dealer in wine bottles
negotians perticaruis	dealer in poles or rods
negotians pigmentarius	dealer in paints and cosmetics

negotians salsamentarius et vinariarius maurarius	dealer in salted fish and Moroccan wine
negotians salsarius et malacitanus	dealer in salted fish and fish sauce from Malaga
negotians siricarius	dealer in silk
negotians vinarius, navicularius	dealer in wines, shipper
negotians, negotiator	tradesman, dealer
negotiator aerarius et ferrarius	dealer in copper and iron
negotiator fabarius	dealer in beans
negotiator frumentarius	dealer in grain
negotiator lanarius	dealer in woollens
negotiator lintiarius	dealer in linens
negotiator marmorarius	dealer in marble
negotiator olearius ex Baetica	dealer in oil from Baetica
negotiator penoris et vinorum	dealer in food and wine
negotiator sagarius	dealer in cloaks
negotiator suariae et pecuariae	dealer in pigs and cattle
negotiator vestiarius	dealer in clothing
negotiator	slave manager of master's business
negotiator, negotians ferrarius	dealer in iron
negotiator, negotians vinarius	dealer in wines
negotiatrix frumentaria et legumenaria	dealer in grain and pulse
nomenclator	name teller
notarius, -a	shorthand writer, stenographer
numida	messenger or outrider
nummularius	money changer
nutritor, -trix	child nurse
obstetrix, opstetrix	midwife
offector	dyer
officinator, -trix	manager/owner of a workshop
olearius, oleareus, olarius	oil dealer
operarius	workmen
opifex	worker, artist
orator	rhetor
ornatrix, ornator	hairdresser
ostiarius, -a	porter, doorkeeper
paedagogus, -a	child attendant
paenularius	cloak seller
panarius	baker
panchrestarius	confectioner
pantomimus	mime

parmularius	shield maker
pastillarius, pastilarius	pill maker (or bread maker)
pastor	shepherd
patagiarius	lace maker
pavimentarius	paviour
pectinarius, pectenarius, pectinator	wool comber or comb maker
pedisequus, -a	attendant, footservant
pellio, pellionarius	furrier
pernarus, pernarius	seller of ham
philosophus Epicureus	Epicurean philosopher
philosophus Stoicus	Stoic philosopher
philosophus, -pha	philosopher
phrygio, frygio	gold embroiderer
picarius (coll)	tar burner
pictor imaginarius	figure painter
pictor parietarius	wall painter?
pictor	painter
pigmentarius	dealer in paints and cosmetics
pilicrepus	ballplayer
pincerna	mixer (of drinks)
piscator, -trix	fisherman (-woman)
pistor	baker
pistricarius	baker
pistrinarius	baker
placentarius	baker
plastis, plastes, plasta	pottery, statuary, model sculptor
plicatrix	clothes folder (f)
plostrarius (plaustrarius)	foreman, cart maker
plumarius	embroiderer, brocader with feathers
plumbarius, plombarius	maker of (lead) pipes, plumber
plutiarius	maker of balustrades
poeta	poet
politor eborarius	ivory polisher
politor	polisher
pollinctor	washer and anointer of corpses
pollio	polisher
pomarius, -a	fruit seller
popa, popinaria, popinarius, popinator	keeper of a cookshop
praebitor vinarius	supplier of wine
praeceptor	teacher, instructor
praeco vinorum	crier of wines
praeco	crier, herald

praegustator	taster
procurator	manager
promus	distributor of provisions
psecas	girl servant who oils hair
pugillariarius	maker of writing tablets
pullarius	poulterer, chicken keeper
purpurarius, -a	dyers and seller of purple cloth
putearius	fountain builder
quadratarius, quadratatorius	stonemason
quasillaria	spinning woman
raedarius, rhedarius	coachman, coach builder
redemptor	contractor
refector pectinarius	comb repairman?
resinaria	dealer in resin
restio, restiarius	rope maker
retiarius	net knitter (gladiatorial?)
retifex	net knitter
rhyparographus	painter of offensive material
rogator	questioner
rosarius	garland maker with roses, cf. *violarii* and *coronarii*
saccarius, sacarius	porter of sacks
sacomarius	weighter/weight dealer
sagarius	maker of cloaks
sagittarius	arrow maker
salarius (salinator?)	dealer in salted fish
salgamarius	dealer/maker of salted produce
salinator	dealer in cooking salt
salsamentarius	dealer in salted fish
salsarius	salter
samiarius, samiator	polisher
sandalarius	shoemaker
sandapilarius	corpse bearer
saponarius	soap maker
sarcinatrix, -tor, sarcitor, -trix, sartor, -trix	mender, seamstress
scabillarius	ritual musicians?
scalarius	stair maker
scalptor	stone carver
scandularius	clapboard maker
scapiaria	maker of seller or vessels called *scaphia*

scaurarius	slag worker
scissor	pruner
scordiscarius	saddler
scriblitarius	pie baker
scriniarius	maker of *scrinia* (cases)
scriptor titulorum	signwriter
sculptor, scultor	sculptor
scutarius	shield maker
sector, – serrarius, – zonarius, – materiarum roborearum	sawyer
securicularius	axle maker
segmentarius	maker of *segmenta* (decorative strips for clothes)
sellularius, artifex -	maker of litters, chairs
seminaria	seller of seeds
seplasiarius	salve maker
sericarius, -a; siricarius	silkworker, seller of silk
sigillarius, sigillariarius	maker of *sigilla* (statuettes)
signarius, artifex -	skilled sculpture worker
silentiarius	silence maintainer
silicarius	street plasterer
siliginarius, pistor	white-bread baker
silvicaedus	lumberjack
similaginarius, pistor	white-bread baker
sindoniacus, sintoniacus	weaver of sindon
sofista	teacher of public speaking
solatarius, solatarus	maker of women's shoes
solearius, soliarius	shoemaker
spadicarius	brown-dyer
spatharius	someone to do with longswords
spec(u)larius, spec(u)lariarius, ars ispeclararia	worker in mica or isinglass, mirror maker?, glazier
speculum, a	caretaker of mirrors
staminaria	weaver
statuarius	maker of statues
strator	groom
strophiarius	brassiere maker
structor lapidarius	stone worker
structor parietarius (varietarius)	builder of walls
structor	carver, builder
stuppator	worker with flax?
subaedianus, subidianus, subedianus	worker on interiors
subornatris	beautician servant?
subrutor	demolition man

suffossor	digger
sumptuarius	agent in charge of household expenditures, cashier
supellectilarius, ad supellectilem	caretaker of furniture
sutor cerdo	shoemaker
sutor institor caligarius	shoemaker
sutor veteramentarius	shoemaker
sutor, -trix	shoemaker, cobbler
symphoniacus	musician
tabellarius	courier
tabellio	notary
tabernacularius	tent maker
tabernarius, -a	shopkeeper, tavern keeper
tabularius	accountant, bookkeeper
tector lignarius	carpenter
tector	plasterer, stucco worker, carpenter
tector, albarius -	plasterer
tegularius	brick worker
tesselarius, tessalarius, tessellator	maker of *tesselae* or dice
tesserarius lignarius	maker of wooden(?) dice
testarius	ore smelter
textor, -trix	weaver
thurarius, -a	incense dealer
tibiarius	maker of reed pipes, flute maker
tibicina	flute player (f)
tignarius, ticnarius, tignuarius	carpenter
tignor	carpenter
tignoserrarius	timber worker
tinctor	dyer
tonsor peccorum	sheep shearer
tonsor, -trix; tosor, tostrix, tussor, tosillaria	barber, shearer of nap on woollen cloth
topiarius	ornamental gardener
torcularius	winepress maker
toreutes	metal engraver
toreuticensis	embosser
tractator, -trix	masseur, masseuse
tricliniarcha	caterer?
tritor argentarius	chaser of silver
tubarius	dealer in tubes
tubularius	= tubarius?
tudiator = χαλκοτόπος	bronze beater

unctor, -trix	masseur, masseuse
unguentarius, -a	perfumer
urinator	diver
ustor	corpse-burner
valetudinarium, ad/supra	infirmary staff/supervisor
valvarius	maker of double doors?
vascularius, vasarius	maker of metal vessels
velarius	curtain closer, curtain or awning maintenance man
venalicius	slave dealer
vespillo, vispillo	corpse bearer
veste, a/ ad vestem	caretaker of clothing
vestiarius tenuarius	tailor of fine clothing
vestiarius, -a	tailor
vestifex	tailor
vestificus, -a	tailor
vestiplex	clothes folder
vestiplicus, -a	clothes folder, presser
vestispica	caretaker of clothing
vestitor	tailor
veterinarius	veterinarian
vexillarius	maker of *vexilla*
victimarius	assistants at sacrifice
vietor, vitor	basket maker
vilicus	overseer, manager
viminarius	tracer
vinarius	wine dealer
violarius	violet-dyer; garland maker with violets
viridarius	gardener
vitriarius, vitrearius	glazier
vitricus	glazier
zonarius, sonarius	girdle maker

Appendix 2

Apprenticeship Contracts

This collection includes all documents securely attesting to an apprenticeship, including contracts, apprenticeship registrations, and one letter.

	Reference	Date	Origin	Profession	Free/ slave	M/F
1	P. Heid. 226	215/213 BC	Unknown	Medicine	Free	M
2	BGU 4.1124	18 BC	Alexandria	?	Free	M
3	BGU 4.1125 = SB 22.15538	13 BC	Alexandria	Flute player	Slave	M
4	SB 6.9445	AD 5/6	Oxyrhynchus	Stonemason	Free?	M
5	P Tebt 2.384	AD 10	Tebtunis	Weaver	Free	M
6	P. Mich. 5.346a	AD 13	Tebtynis	Weaver	Slave	F
7	P. Mich. 5.346b	AD 16	Tebtynis	Builder	Free	M
8	P. Oxy. 2.322 = SB 10.10236	AD 36	Oxyrhynchus	Weaver	Free	M
9	P. Mich. 2.121, recto II, 8	AD 42	Tebtynis	Weaver	Free	M
10	P. Fouad. 1.37	AD 48	Oxyrhynchus	Linen weaver?	Free	M
11	P. Mich. 3.170	AD 49	Oxyrhynchus	Weaver	Free	M
12	P. Osl. 3.141	AD 50	Karanis	Weaver	Free	M
13	P. Wisc. 1.4 = Papyrologica Lugduno Batava XVI	AD 53	Oxyrhynchus	Weaver	Free	M
14	P. Oxy. Hels. 29	AD 54	Oxyrhynchus	Weaver	Free	M
15	P. Mich. 3.171	AD 58	Oxyrhynchus	Weaver	Free	M
16	PSI 10.1132	AD 61	Talei	?	Free	M
17	P. Mich. 3.172	AD 62	Oxyrhynchus	Weaver	Free	M
18	PSI 8.871	AD 66	Oxyrhynchus	?	Free	M
19	P. Oxy. 2.275	AD 66	Oxyrhynchus	Weaver	Free	M
20	P. Oxy. 41.2971	AD 66	Oxyrhynchus	Weaver	Free	M

	Reference	Date	Origin	Profession	Free/ slave	M/F
21	P. Osl. Inv. 1470 = SB 24.16186	AD 70	Oxyrhynchus	Weaver	Free	M
22	P. Heid. 4.326	AD 98	Ankyron	?	Free	F
23	P. Heid. 4.327	AD 99	Ankyron	Dancer?	Free	M
24	SB 24.16253 = SB 12.10946	AD 98–117	Oxyrhynchus	?	Free	M
25	P. Tebt. 2.442 = SB 12.10984	AD 113	Tebtynis	Weaver	Free	M
26	P. Tebt. 2.385	AD 117	Tebtynis	Weaver	Free	M
27	P. Col. Inv 164	AD 118–138	Oxyrhynchus e.o.		Free	M
28	P. Mich. Inv. 4238	AD 128	Theadelpheia	Carpentry	Free	M
29	P. Ross. Georg. 2.18.450	AD 140	Arsinoite		Free	F
30	St. Pal. 22.40	AD 150	Soknopaiou Nesos	Weaver	Slave	M
31	P. Oxy. 4.724	AD 155	Oxyrhynchus	Shorthand writer	Slave	M
32	P. Vars. S.n. 7 = SB 6.9374	AD 170 (169?)	Ptolemais Drymou	Weaver	Free	M
33	P.Oxy. 4.725	AD 183	Oxyrhynchus	Weaver	Free	M
34	P. Grenf. 2.59	AD 189	Soknopaiou Nesos	Weaver	Slave	M
35	P. Oxy. 41.2988	AD 100–200	Oxyrhynchus	Shorthand writer	Slave? (*Pais*)	M
36	PSI 10.1110, verso I	AD 150–200	Theogonis	?	Free	M
37	P. Oxy. 14.1647	AD 150–200	Oxyrhynchus	Weaver	Slave	F
38	BGU 11.2041	AD 201	Arsinoite	Weaver	Free	M
39	P. Oxy. 38.2875	AD 200–250	Oxyrhynchus	Builder?	Free	M
40	P. Oxy. 41.2977	AD 239	Oxyrhynchus	Wool carder/ hairdresser?	Slave *verna*	M
41	P. Oxy. 31.2586	AD 264	Oxyrhynchus	Linen weaver?	Free	M
42	P. Oxy. 67.4596	AD 264	Oxyrhynchus	Weaver	Free	F
43	P. Mich. Inv. 5191a = SB 8.13305 was P. Mich. Inv. 5191b	AD 271	Karanis	Weaver	Slave?	F
44	P. Kell. G. 19a appendix = SB 24.16320	AD 293–304	Kellis	Weaver	Slave	F

	Reference	Date	Origin	Profession	Free/ slave	M/F
45	BGU 4.1021	AD 200–300	Oxyrhynchus	Wool carder/ hairdresser?	Slave	M
46	PSI 3.241	AD 200–300	Antinoopolis	Weaving?	Slave	F
47	P. Mich. Inv. 337 = SB 14.11588	late 4th c.?	Unknown	Linen weaver?	Free	M
48	P. Aberd. 59	AD 300–500	Panopolis (?)	?	Free	F
49	PSI inv. 195 = SB 14.11982	AD 554	Oxyrhynchus	?	Free	M
50	P. Lond. 5.1706	AD 500–600	Aphrodites Kome	?	Free	M

Appendix 3

Taxonomy of Labour Relations

Stapel, R. 2016. "Taxonomy of Labour Relations", https://hdl.handle.net/10622/OJYQOR, IISH Data Collection, V2. Reproduced under a CC-BY licence: https://creativecommons.org/licenses/by/4.0/.

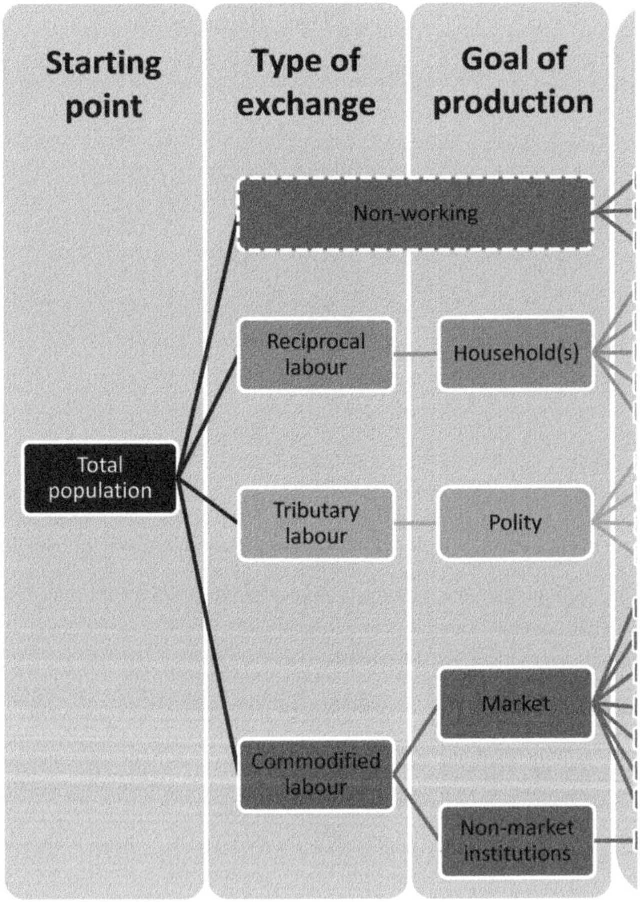

© 2015–18 Global Collaboratory on the History of Labour Relations, 1500-2000
http://www.historyoflabourrelations.org

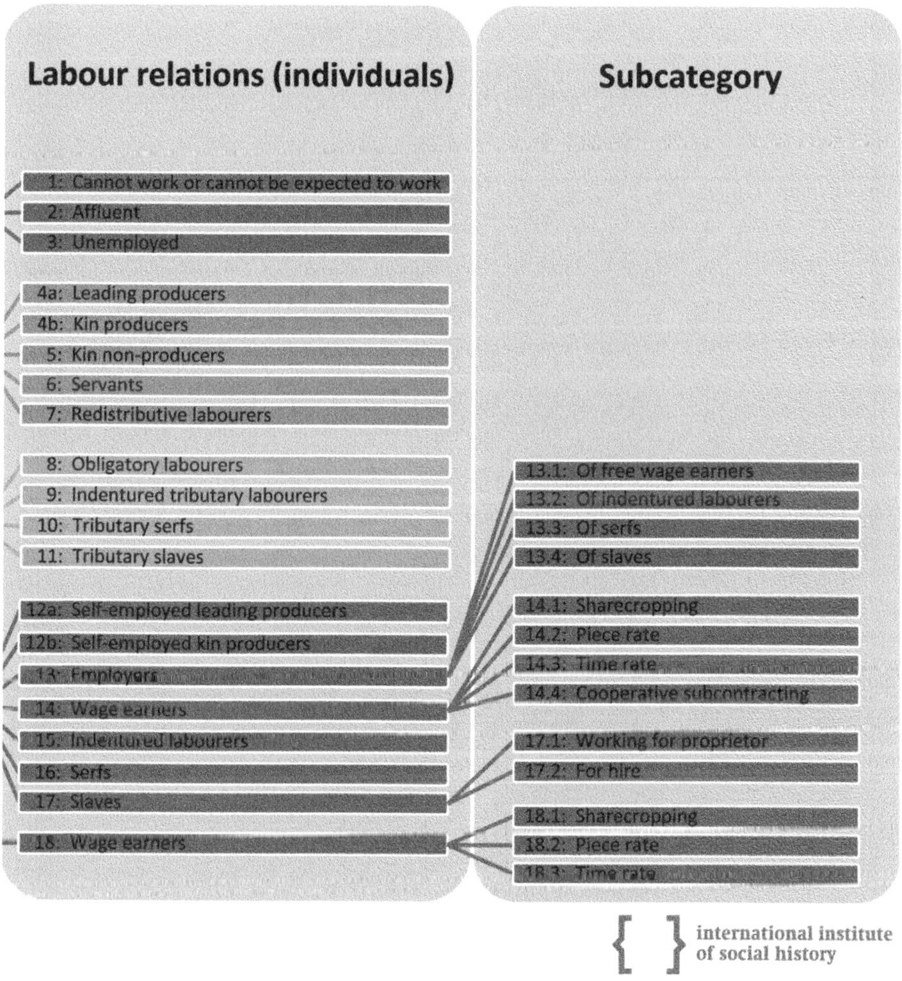
Labour relations (individuals)
Subcategory
1: Cannot work or cannot be expected to work
2: Affluent
3: Unemployed
4a: Leading producers
4b: Kin producers
5: Kin non-producers
6: Servants
7: Redistributive labourers
8: Obligatory labourers
9: Indentured tributary labourers
10: Tributary serfs
11: Tributary slaves
12a: Self-employed leading producers
12b: Self-employed kin producers
13: Employers
14: Wage earners
15: Indentured labourers
16: Serfs
17: Slaves
18: Wage earners
13.1: Of free wage earners
13.2: Of indentured labourers
13.3: Of serfs
13.4: Of slaves
14.1: Sharecropping
14.2: Piece rate
14.3: Time rate
14.4: Cooperative subcontracting
17.1: Working for proprietor
17.2: For hire
18.1: Sharecropping
18.2: Piece rate
18.3: Time rate
international institute of social history

Bibliography

Adams, B. 1964. *Paramone und verwandte Texte.* Berlin.

Aldrete, G.S., and D.J. Mattingly. 1999. "Feeding the City: The Organization, Operation and Scale of the Supply System for Rome". In *Life, Death and Entertainment in the Roman Empire,* edited by D.S. Potter and D.J. Mattingly, 171–204. Ann Arbor.

Alföldy, G. 1986. "Die Freilassung von Sklaven und die Struktur der Sklaverei in der römischen Kaiserzeit". In *Die römische Gesellschaft: Ausgewählte Beiträge,* 286–331. Stuttgart. First published in *Rivista Storica dell'Antichità* 2 (1972) 97–129.

Allen, R.C. 2009. "How Prosperous Were the Romans? Evidence from Diocletian's Price Edict (AD 301)". In *Quantifying the Roman Economy: Methods and Problems,* edited by A.K. Bowman, 327–45. Oxford.

Allison, P.M. 2001. "Placing Individuals: Pompeian Epigraphy in Context". *Journal of Mediterranean Archaeology* 14: 53–74.

Allison, P.M. 2004. *Pompeian Households: An Analysis of the Material Culture.* Los Angeles.

Andreau, J. 1999. *Banking and Business in the Roman World.* Cambridge.

Andreau, J. 2002. "Twenty Years after Moses I. Finley's *The Ancient Economy*". In *The Ancient Economy,* edited by W. Scheidel and S. von Reden, 33–49. New York.

Aparaschivei, D. 2019. "Physicians and Medicine in the Roman Army of Moesia Inferior", *Dacia N.S.* 56: 99–118.

Applebaum, H. 1992. *The Concept of Work: Ancient, Medieval, and Modern.* Albany, NY.

Aubert, J.-J. 1994. *Business Managers in Ancient Rome: A Social and Economic Study of Institores, 200 BC–AD 250.* Leiden and New York.

Ausbüttel, F.M. 1982. *Untersuchungen zu den Vereinen im Westen des Römischen Reiches.* Kalmünz.

Baba, M. 1990. "Slave-Owning Slaves and the Structure of Slavery in the Early Roman Empire". *Kodai* 1: 24–35.

Bagnall, R.S. 1996. *Egypt in Late Antiquity.* 4th ed. Princeton.

Bagnall, R.S. 2002. "The Effects of Plague: Model and Evidence". *Journal of Roman Archaeology* 15: 114–20.

Bagnall, R.S., and B.W. Frier. 2006. *The Demography of Roman Egypt.* Cambridge. 1st ed. 199e4.

Baldwin, B. 1978. "Trimalchio's Domestic Staff". *Acta Classica* 21: 87–97.

Bang, P.F. 2008. *The Roman Bazaar: A Comparative Study of Trade and Markets in a Tributary Empire*. Cambridge etc.

Bang, P.F. 2009. "The Ancient Economy and New Institutional Economics". *Journal of Roman Studies* 99: 194–206.

Barber, E.J.W. 1994. *Women's Work: The First 20,000 Years. Women, Cloth, and Society in Early Times*. New York etc.

Béal, J.-C. 2000. "La dignité des artisans: Les images d'artisans sur les monuments funéraires de Gaule romaine". *Dialogues d'histoire ancienne* 26: 149–82.

Becker, G.S. 1964. *Human Capital: A Theoretical and Empirical Analysis, with Special Reference to Education*. New York.

Becker, G.S. 1985. "Human Capital, Effort, and the Sexual Division of Labor". *Journal of Labor Economics* 3 (1): S33–S58.

Bellemore, J., and B. Rawson. 1990. "Alumni: The Italian Evidence". *Zeitschrift für Papyrologie und Epigrafik* 83: 1–19.

Beltrán Lloris, F. 2015. "The 'Epigraphic Habit' in the Roman World". In *The Oxford Handbook of Roman Epigraphy*, edited by C. Bruun and J. Edmondson, 131–48, Oxford.

Bendlin, A. 2011. "Associations, Funerals, Sociality, and Roman Law: The Collegium of Diana and Antinous in Lanuvium (*CIL* 14.2112) Reconsidered". In *Aposteldekret und antikes Vereinswesen: Gemeinschaft und ihre Ordnung*. Wissenschaftliche Untersuchungen zum Neuen Testament 1, edited by M. Öhler, 207–96. Tübingen.

Beresford, J. 2012. *The Ancient Sailing Season*. Mnemosyne Supplements, History and Archaeology of Classical Antiquity. Leiden.

Berg, C. 2014. "Capitalism in Ancient Rome". *IPA Reviews* 65 (4): 34–37.

Berg, R. 2016. "Dominae Apothecarum: Gendering Storage Patterns in Roman Houses". In *The Material Sides of Marriage: Women and Domestic Economies in Antiquity*, edited by R. Berg, 175–89. Acta Instituti Romani Finlandiae 43. Rome.

Bergamasco, M. 1995. "Le Didaskalikai Nella Ricerca Attuale". *Aegyptus* 75: 95–167.

Bergamasco, M. 1997. "Una Petizione per Violazione di un Contratto di Tirocinio: P.Kell.G 19a". *Aegyptus* 77: 7–26.

Bergamasco, M. 2004. "Tre Note a Tre Didaskalikai". *Studi di Egittologia e di Papirologia* 1: 31–41.

Bergamasco, M. 2006a. "La Didaskalika di P. Col. Inv. 164". *Zeitschrift für Papyrologie und Epigrafik* 158: 207–12.

Bergamasco, M. 2006b. "Orfani e Didaskalikai: Il Caso di SB XIV 11588". *Studi di Egittologia e di Papirologia* 3: 55–59.

Berger, A. 1911. *Die Strafklauseln in den Papyrusurkunden: Ein Beitrag zum Gräko-ägyptischen Obligationenrecht*. Leipzig etc.

Bernard, S.G. 2017. "Workers in the Roman Imperial Building Industry". In *Work, Labour and Professions in the Roman World*, edited by K. Verboven and C. Laes, 62–86. Leiden.

Biscottini, M.V. 1966. "l'Archivio di Tryphon, Tessitore di Oxyrynchos". *Aegyptus* 46: 186–292.

Bisel, S.C., and J.F. Bisel. 2002. "Health and Nutrition at Herculaneum: An Examination of Human Skeletal Remains". In *The Natural History of Pompeii*, edited by W.F. Jashemski and F.G. Meyer, 451–75. Cambridge.

Bodel, J. 2000. "Dealing with the Dead: Untertakers, Executioners and Potter's Fields in Ancient Rome". In *Death and Disease in the Ancient City*, edited by V.M. Hope and E. Marshall, 128–51. London and New York.

Bodel, J. 2005. "Caveat Emptor: Towards a Study of Roman Slave-Traders". *Journal of Roman Archaeology* 18: 181–95.

Bodel, J. 2008. "From Columbaria to Catacombs: Collective Burial in Pagan and Christian Rome". In *Commemorating the Dead: Texts and Artifacts in Context. Studies of Roman, Jewish and Christian Burials*, edited by L. Brink and D. Green, 177–242. Berlin etc.

Bodel, J. 2011. "Slave Labour and Roman Society". In *The Cambridge World History of Slavery, Volume I*, edited by K.R. Bradley and P. Cartledge, 311–36. Cambridge.

Bodel, J., and W. Scheidel, eds. 2017. *On Human Bondage: After Slavery and Social Death*. Chichester.

Bollmann, B. 1998. *Römische Vereinshäuser: Untersuchungen zu den Scholae der römischen Berufs-, Kult- und Augustalen-Kollegien in Italien*. Mainz.

Bond, S. 2016. *Trade and Taboo: Disreputable Professions in the Roman Mediterranean*. Ann Arbor: University of Michigan Press.

Bond, S. 2017. "Currency and Control: Mint Workers in the Later Roman Empire". In *Work, Labour and Professions in the Roman World*, edited by K. Verboven and C. Laes, 227–45. Leiden.

Bonsangue, M.L. 2002. "Aspects économiques et sociaux du monde du travail À Narbonne, d'après la documentation épigraphique (1er siècle av. J.-C.–1er siécle ap. J.-C.)". *Cahiers du Centre G. Glotz* 13: 201–32.

Booth, A.D. 1979. "The Schooling of Slaves in First-Century Rome". *Transactions and Proceedings of the American Philological Association* 109: 11–19.

Borbonus, D. 2008. "Review of the Familia Urbana during the Early Empire: A Study of Columbaria Inscriptions by K. Hasegawa". *Klio* 90 (2): 505–6.

Borbonus, D. 2014. *Columbarium Tombs and Collective Identity in Augustan Rome*. Cambridge.

Bosworth, D., P. Dawkins, and T. Stromback. 1996. *The Economics of the Labour Market*. Harlow.

Boulvert, G. 1974. *Domestique et fonctionnaire sous le haut-empire romain: La condition de l'affranchi et de l'esclave du prince*. Paris.

Bowman, A.K., ed. 2009. *Quantifying the Roman Economy: Methods and Problems*. Oxford.

Bracher, M. 1992. "Breastfeeding, Lactational Infecundity, Contraception and the Spacing of Birth: Implications of the Bellagio Consensus Statement". *Health Transition Review* 2: 19–47.

Bradley, J.W. 2018. *The Hypogeum of the Aurelii: A New Interpretation as the Collegiate Tomb of Professional Scribae*. Oxford.

Bradley, K.R. 1987a. "On the Roman Slave Supply and Slavebreeding". *Slavery and Abolition* 8: 42–64.

Bradley, K.R. 1987b. *Slaves and Masters in the Roman Empire: A Study in Social Control.* New York and Oxford.

Bradley, K.R. 1991. *Discovering the Roman Family: Studies in Roman Social History.* New York and London.

Bradley, K.R. 1994. *Slavery and Society at Rome.* Key Themes in Ancient History. Cambridge.

Bradley, K.R. 2012. *Apuleius and Antonine Rome: Historical Essays.* Phoenix Supplementary Volume 50. Toronto.

Bradley, K.R., and P. Cartledge, eds. 2011. *The Cambridge World History of Slavery, Volume I.* Cambridge.

Bransbourg, G. 2012. "Rome and the Economic Integration of Empire". *Instute for the Study of the Ancient World Papers* 3. http://dlib.nyu.edu/awdl/isaw/isaw-papers/3/#endnote-asterix.

Brass, T., and M. van der Linden, eds. 1997. *Free and Unfree Labour: The Debate Continues.* Bern.

Braudel, F. 1981. *Civilization and Capitalism, 15th–18th Century. I. The Structures of Everyday Life: The Limits of the Possible.* 2nd ed. New York.

Brewster, E.H. 1927. "A Weaver of Oxyrhynchus: Sketch of a Humble Life in Roman Egypt". *Transactions and Proceedings of the American Philological Association* 58: 132–54.

Brodsky, V. 1986. "Widows in Late Elizabethan London: Remarriage, Economic Opportunity and Family Orientations". In *The World We Have Gained: Histories of Population and Social Structures*, edited by R. Smith and K. Wrightson, 122–54. Oxford.

Broekaert, W. 2011. "Partners in Business: Roman Merchants and the Potential Advantages of Being a Collegiatus". *Ancient Society* 41: 221–56.

Broekaert, W. 2012. "Welcome to the Family! Marriage as Business Strategy in the Roman Economy". *Marburger Beiträge zur Antiken Handels-, Wirtschafts- und Sozialgeschichte* 30: 41–65.

Broekaert, W. 2017. "Conflicts, Contract Enforcement, and Business Communities in the Archive of the Sulpicii". In *The Economy of Pompeii*, edited by M. Flohr and A.I. Wilson, 387–414. Oxford.

Broekaert, W. 2019. "Between Coercion and Compulsion? The Impact of Occupations and Economic Interests on the Relational Status of Slaves and Freedmen". In *The Single Life in the Roman and Later Roman World*, edited by C. Laes and S.R. Hübner, 85–102. Cambridge.

Brown, C., and M. van der Linden. 2010. "Shifting Boundaries between Free and Unfree Labor: Introduction". *International Labor and Working-Class History* 78 (1): 4–11.

Brown, P. 1967. *Augustine of Hippo: A Biography.* London and Boston.

Brown, P. 2012. *Through the Eye of a Needle: Wealth, the Fall of Rome, and the Making of Christianity in the West, 350–550 AD.* Princeton and Oxford.

Brunt, P.A. 1974. "The Roman Mob". In *Studies in Ancient Society*, edited by M.I. Finley, 74–102. London and Boston.

Brunt, P.A. 1980. "Free Labor and Public Works at Rome". *Journal of Roman Studies* 70: 81–100.

Bruun, C. 2011. "Water, Oxygen Isotopes, and Immigration to Ostia-Portus". *Journal of Roman Archaeology*, 109–32.

Bruun, C. 2013. "Greek or Latin? The Owner's Choice of Names for Vernae in Rome". In *Roman Slavery and Roman Material Culture*, edited by M. George, 19–42. Toronto.

Bruun, C. 2015. "Slaves and Freed Slaves". In *The Oxford Handbook of Roman Epigraphy*, edited by C. Bruun and J. Edmondson, 605–26. Oxford.

Buckler, W.H. 1923. "Labour Disputes in the Province of Asia". In *Anatolian Studies Presented to Sir William Mitchell Ramsay*, edited by W.H. Buckler and W.M. Calder, 27–50. Manchester.

Buonocore, M. 1984. *Schiavi e Liberti dei Volusii Saturnini: Le Iscrizioni del Colombario sulla via Appia Antica*. Rome.

Burford, A. 1972. *Craftsmen in Greek and Roman Society*. London.

Bürge, A. 1990. "Der Mercennarius und die Lohnarbeit". *Zeitschrift für Rechtsgeschichte* 107: 80 135.

Burton-Jones, A., and J.C. Spender, eds. 2011. *The Oxford Handbook of Human Capital*. Oxford.

Calabi Limentani, I. 1958. *Studi sulla Società Romana: Il Lavoro Artistico*. Milano.

Caldelli, M.L., and C. Ricci. 1999. *Monumentum Familiae Statiliorum: Un Riesame*. Rome.

Camodeca, G. 2016. "Unguentarii e turarii in Campania: Nuovi dati da Puteoli e Cumae". In *Puteoli: Studi di storia ed archeologia dei Campi Flegrei*, edited by G. Camodeca and M. Giglio, 23–39. Naples.

Camodeca, G., and M. Giglio, eds. 2016. *Puteoli: Studi di storia ed archeologia dei Campi Flegrei*, Naples, 2016.

Cantarella, E. 2005. "Roman Marriage: Social, Economic and Legal Aspects". In *Hoping for Continuity: Childhood, Education and Death in Antiquity and the Middle Ages*, edited by K. Mustakallio, J. Hanska, H.-L. Sainio, and V. Vuolanto, 25–32. Rome.

Casson, L. 1978. "Unemployment, the Building Trade and Suet. Vesp. 18". *Bulletin of the American Society of Papyrologists* 15: 43–51.

Champlin, E. 1991. *Final Judgments: Duty and Emotion in Roman Wills, 200 B.C.–A.D. 250*. Berkeley.

Chantraine, H. 1967. *Freigelassene und Sklaven im Dienst der romischen Kaiser: Studien zu ihrer Nomenklatur*. Wiesbaden.

Checchi, D. 2006. *The Economics of Education: Human Capital, Family Background and Inequality*. Cambridge etc.

Cherry, D. 1995. "Re-figuring the Roman Epigraphic Habit". *Ancient History Bulletin* 9: 143–56.

Chevallier, R. 1997. "Perspectives de recherche sur le scènes de métiers (Gaule cisalpine et transalpine)". *Archeologia Classica* 49: 47–63.

Cigno, A. 1991. *Economics of the Family*. Oxford.

Clauss, M. 1994. Review of F.P. Rizzo, *La Menzione del Lavoro nelle Epigrafi della Sicilia Antica (Per Una Storia della Mentalità)*, *Klio* 76: 525.

Cohn-Haft, P. 1957. "A Note on the 'didaskalikai' [GR] and a Correction in the Reading of P. Vars. Ser Nov 7". *Aegyptus* 37 (2): 266–70.

Corbier, M. 1980. "Salaires et salariat sous le haut-empire". In *Les dévaluations à Rome, époque républicaine et impériale*, 2: 61–101. Paris and Rome.

Corbier, M. 1991. "Divorce and Adoption as Roman Familial Strategies". In *Marriage, Divorce, and Children in Ancient Rome*, edited by B. Rawson, 47–78. Oxford.

Corbier, M. 1999. *Adoption et fosterage*. Paris.

Corbier, M. 2001. "Child Exposure and Abandonment". In *Childhood, Class and Kin in the Roman World*, edited by S. Dixon, 64–98. London.

Cotter, W. 1996. "The Collegia and Roman Law: State Restrictions on Voluntary Associations, 64 BCE–200 CE". In *Voluntary Associations in the Graeco-Roman World*, edited by J.S. Kloppenborg and S.G. Wilson, 74–89. London.

Cristofori, A. 2004. *Non Arma Virumque: Le Occupazioni nell'epigrafia del Piceno*. 2a ed. riv. et ampliata. Bologna.

Cristofori, A. 2006. "Medici 'stranieri' e medici 'integrati' nella documentazione epigrafica del mondo romano". In *Medicina e società nel mondo antico: Atti del convegno di Udine (4–5 ottobre 2005)*, edited by A. Marcone, 111–41. Florence.

Cristofori, A. 2011. "Le occupazioni nell'epigrafia dell'Epiro e dell'Illiria meridionale di età romana". In *Sulla rotta per la Sicilia: l'Epiro, Corcira et l'Occidente*, edited by G. De Sensi Sestito and M. Intrieri, 133–72. Pisa.

Cristofori, A. 2016. "Lavoro e identità sociale", in *Storia del Lavoro in Italia. L'Età Romana: Liberi, Semiliberi e Schiavi in una Società Premoderna*, edited by A. Marcone, 149–74. Rome.

Crook, J.A. *Law and Life of Rome*. London, 1967.

Cuvigny, H. 1996. "The Amount of Wages paid to the Quarry-Workers at Mons Claudianus". *Journal of Roman Studies* 86: 139–45.

D'Ambra, E. 1988. "A Myth for a Smith: A Meleager Sarcophagus from a Tomb in Ostia". *American Journal of Archaeology* 92 (1): 85–100.

D'Arms, J.H. 1981. *Commerce and Social Standing in Ancient Rome*. Cambridge, MA etc.

De Callataÿ, F., ed. 2014. *Quantifying the Greco-Roman Economy and Beyond*. Bari.

DeLaine, J. 1997. *The Baths of Caracalla: A Study in the Design, Construction, and Economics of Large-Scale Building Projects in Imperial Rome*. Portsmouth, RI.

DeLaine, J. 2005. "The Commercial Landscape of Ostia". In *Roman Working Lives and Urban Living*, edited by A. Mac Mahon and J. Price, 29–47. Oxford.

De Ligt, L. 1990. "Demand, Supply, Distribution: The Roman Peasantry between Town and Countryside. Rural Monetization and Peasant Demand". *Münstersche Beiträge zur antiken Handels-, Wirtschafts- und Sozialgeschichte* 9 (2): 24–56.

De Ligt, L. 1991. "The Roman Peasantry: Demand, Supply, Distribution between Town and Countryside, 2. Supply, Distribution and a Comparative Perspective". *Münstersche Beiträge zur antiken Handels-, Wirtschafts- und Sozialgeschichte* 10 (1): 33–77.

De Ligt, L. 1993. *Fairs and Markets in the Roman Empire.* Amsterdam.

De Ligt, L. 1999. "Legal History and Economic History: The Case of the Actiones Adiecticiae Qualitatis". *Tijdschrift voor Rechtsgeschiedenis/Revue d'histoire du droit/Legal History Review* 67 (3): 205–26.

De Ligt, L. 2000. "Governmental Attitudes towards Markets and Collegia". In *Mercati Permanenti e Mercati Periodici nel Mondo Romano: Atti degli Incontri Capresi di Storia dell'Economia Antica, Capri 13–15 Ottobre 1997*, edited by E. Lo Cascio, 237–52. Bari.

De Ligt, L. 2001. "D. 47.22.1 Pr-1 and the Formation of Semi-public Collegia". *Latomus* 60: 345–58.

De Ligt, L. 2003. "Taxes, Trade and the Circulation of Coin: The Roman Empire, Mughal India and T'ang China Compared". *Medieval History Journal* 6: 231–48.

De Ligt, L. 2004. "Poverty and Demography: The Case of the Gracchan Land Reforms". *Mnemosyne*, Series 4 57 (6): 725–57.

De Ligt, L. 2005. "Review of Lelis, Percy and Verstraete 2003". *Tijdschrift voor Geschiedenis* 118 (1): 75–77.

De Ligt, L. 2012. *Peasants, Citizens and Soldiers: Studies in the Demographic History of Roman Italy, 225 BC–AD 100.* Cambridge etc.

De Ligt, L. 2013. "Population and Migration". In *The Oxford Handbook of Cities in World History*, edited by P. Clark, 147–63. Oxford.

De Ligt, L. 2016. "Urban Systems and the Political and Economic Structures of Early-imperial". *Rivista di Storia Economica* 32 (1): 17–75.

De Ligt, L., and J. Bintliff, eds. 2019. *Regional Urban Systems in the Roman World 150 BCE–250 CE*, Leiden.

De Ligt, L., P. Garnsey. 2012. "The Album of Herculaneum and a Model of the Town's Demography". *Journal of Roman Studies* 25: 69–94

De Ligt, L., and P. Garnsey, 2019. "The Album of Herculaneum Revisited". In *Popolazione, Risorse e Urbanizzazione nella Campania Antica*, edited by M. Maiuro and M. Balbo, 197–209. Bari.

De Ligt, L., and L.E. Tacoma, eds. 2016. *Migration and Mobility in the Early Roman Empire.* Leiden.

DeMause, L. (1974). "The Evolution of Childhood". In *The History of Childhood*, edited by L. deMause, 1–73. New York.

De Robertis, F.M. 1946. *I Rapporti di Lavoro nel Diritto Romano.* Milan.

De Robertis, F.M. 1963. *Lavoro e Lavoratori nel Mondo Romano.* Bari.

De Robertis, F.M. 1971. *Storia delle Corporazioni e del Regime Associativo nel Mondo Romano*. Bari.

Dessau, H. 1892–1916. *Inscriptiones Latinae Selectae*. Berlin.

De Vito, C. 2013. "New Perspectives on Global Labour History: Introduction". *Workers of the World: International Journal on Strikes and Social Conflicts* 1 (3): 7–31.

De Vito, C., and A. Lichtenstein, eds. 2015. *Global Convict Labour*. Leiden.

De Vries, J. 1984. *European Urbanization, 1500–1800*. London.

De Vries, J. 2008. *The Industrious Revolution: Consumer Behaviour and the Household Economy, 1650 to the Present*. New York.

Dey, H.W. 2011. *The Aurelian Wall and the Refashioning of Imperial Rome, AD 271–855*. Cambridge.

Di Giacomo, G. 2010. "Les aurifices de Rome: Relectures et nouvelles interprétations". *Epigraphica* 72: 395–405.

Dillon, M., and L. Garland. 2015. *Ancient Rome: Social and Historical Documents from the Early Republic to the Death of Augustus*. 2nd ed. London.

Di Porto, A. 1984. *Impresa Collettiva e Schiavo "manager" in Roma Antica (II Sec. a.C.–II Sec. d.C)*. Istituto di Diritto Romano e dei Diritti dell'Oriente Mediterraneo 64. Milan.

Dixon, S. 1984. "Infirmitas Sexus: Womanly Weakness in Roman Law". *Legal History Review* 52 (4): 343–71.

Dixon, S. 1988. *The Roman Mother*. London etc.

Dixon, S. 1991. "The Sentimental Ideal of the Roman Family". In *Marriage, Divorce, and Children in Ancient Rome*, edited by B. Rawson, 99–113. Oxford.

Dixon, S. 1992. *The Roman Family*. London.

Dixon, S. 2001a. "Familia Veturia: Towards a Lower-Class Economic Prosopography". In *Childhood, Class and Kin in the Roman World*, edited by S. Dixon, 115–27. London and New York.

Dixon, S. 2001b. "How Do You Count Them if They're Not There? New Perspectives on Roman Cloth Production". *Opuscula Romana* 25–26: 7–17.

Dixon, S. 2001c. *Reading Roman Women*. London: Duckworth.

Drexhage, H.-J. 1991. *Preise, Mieten/Pachten, Kosten und Löhne im römischen Ägypten, bis zum Regierungsantritt Diokletians*. Skt. Katharinen.

Drexhage, H.-J. 2004. "Vorläufige Liste der bislang ausschliesslich literarisch belegten Berufs- bzw. Tätigkeitsbezeichnungen". *Münstersche Beiträge zur antiken Handelsgeschichte* 23 (1): 41–65.

Duncan-Jones, R.P. 1978. "Two Possible Indices of the Purchasing Power of Money in Greek and Roman Antiquity". *Publications de l'École française de Rome* 37 (1): 159–68.

Duncan-Jones, R.P. 1996. "The Impact of the Antonine Plague". *Journal of Roman Archaeology* 9: 108–36.

Dyson, S. 2011. "The Family and the Roman Countryside". In *A Companion to Families in the Greek and Roman Worlds*, edited by B. Rawson, 431–44. Malden, MA etc.

Eck, W. 1998. "Grabmonumente und sozialer Status in Rom und Umgebung". In *Bestattungssitte und kulturelle Identität: Grabanlagen und Grabbeigaben der frühen römischen Kaiserzeit in Italien und den Nordwest-Provinzen*. Xanthener Berichte 7, edited by P. Fasold, T. Fischer, H. von Hesberg, and M. Witteyer, 29–40. Cologne.

Eck, W. 2017. "Ordo Senatorius und Mobilität: Auswirkungen und Konsequenzen im Imperium Romanum". In *The Impact of Mobility and Migration in the Roman Empire: Proceedings of the Twelfth Workshop of the International Network Impact of Empire (Rome, June 17–19, 2015)*, edited by E. Lo Cascio and L.E. Tacoma, with the assistance of M.J. Groen-Vallinga, 100–15. Leiden.

Eckerman, C. 2011. "P. Mich. inv. 4238". *Bulletin of the American Society of Papyrologists* 48: 47–49.

Edmondson, J. 2011. "Slavery and the Roman Family". In *The Cambridge World History of Slavery, Volume I*, edited by K.R. Bradley and P. Cartledge, 337–61. Cambridge.

Edmondson, J. 2015. "Roman Family History". In *The Oxford Handbook of Roman Epigraphy*, edited by C. Bruun and J. Edmondson, 559–81. Oxford.

Edwards, C. 1997. "Unspeakable Professions: Public Performance and Prostitution in Ancient Rome". In *Roman Sexualities*, edited by J.P. Hallett and M.B. Skinner, 66–95. Princeton.

Ehmer, J. 2014. "Attitudes to Work, Class Structures, and Social Change: A Review of Recent Historical Studies". *International Review of Social History* 59 (1): 99–117.

Ehmer, J., and C. Lis, eds. 2009. *The Idea of Work in Europe from Antiquity to Early Modern Times*. Farnham.

Eichenauer, M. 1988. *Untersuchungen zur Arbeitswelt der Frau in der römischen Antike*. Frankfurt am Main etc.

Eide, E.R., and M.H. Showalter. 2010. "Human Capital". In *International Encyclopedia of Education*, 3rd ed., edited by P. Peterson, E. Baker, and B. McGaw, 282–87. Oxford. http://www.sciencedirect.com/science/article/pii/B9780080448947012136.

Elliott, T. 2015. "Epigraphy and Digital Resources". In *The Oxford Handbook of Roman Epigraphy*, edited by C. Bruun and J. Edmondson, 78–86. Oxford.

Ellis, S.J.R. 2018. *The Roman Retail Revolution: The Socio-economic World of the Taberna*. Oxford.

Engelen, Th. 2002. "Labour Strategies of Families: A Critical Assessment of an Appealing Concept". *International Review of Social History* 47 (3): 453–64.

Engelen, Th., A. Knotter, J. Kok, and R. Paping. 2004. "Labor Strategies of Families: An Introduction". *History of the Family* 9 (2): 123–35.

Engelen, Th., J. Kok, and R. Paping. 2004. "The Family Strategies Concept: An Evaluation of Four Empirical Case Studies". *History of the Family* 9 (2): 239–51.

Engerman, S.L. 1999. "Introduction". In *Terms of Labor: Slavery, Serfdom, and Free Labor*, edited by S.L. Engerman, 1–23. Stanford CA.

Erdkamp, P.M. 1999. "Agriculture, Underemployment, and the Cost of Rural Labour in the Roman World". *Classical Quarterly* 49 (2): 556–72.

Erdkamp, P.M. 2005. *The Grain Market in the Roman Empire: A Social, Political and Economic Study*. Cambridge and New York.

Erdkamp, P.M. 2008. "Mobility and Migration in Italy in the Second Century B.C". In *People, Land, and Politics: Demographic Developments and the Transformation of Roman Italy 300 BC–AD14*, edited by L. de Ligt and S. Northwood, 417–49. Leiden.

Erdkamp, P.M. 2012. "Urbanism". In *The Cambridge Companion to the Roman Economy*, edited by W. Scheidel, 241–65. Cambridge.

Erdkamp, P.M. 2014. "How Modern was the Market Economy of the Roman World?" *Oeconomia: History, Methodology, Philosophy* 4 (2): 225–35.

Erdkamp, P.M. 2016. "Seasonal Labour and Rural–Urban Migration in Roman Italy". In *Migration and Mobility in the Early Roman Empire*, edited by L. de Ligt and L.E. Tacoma, 33–49. Leiden.

Erdkamp, P.M. 2018. "Famine and Hunger in the Roman World". In *The Routledge Handbook of Diet and Nutrition in the Roman World*, edited by P.M. Erdkamp and C. Holleran, 296–307. London and New York.

Erdkamp, P.M., and C. Holleran, eds. 2018. *The Routledge Handbook of Diet and Nutrition in the Roman World*. London and New York.

Erickson, A.L. 2008. "Married Women's Occupations in Eighteenth-Century London". *Continuity and Change* 23 (2): 267–307.

Esposito, D. 2017. "The Economics of Pompeian Painting". In *The Economy of Pompeii*, edited by M. Flohr and A.I. Wilson, 261–88. Oxford.

Evans Grubbs, J. 2002. *Women and the Law in the Roman Empire: A Sourcebook on Marriage, Divorce and Widowhood*. London etc.

Evans Grubbs, J. 2013. "Infant Exposure and Infanticide". In *Oxford Handbook of Childhood and Education in the Roman World*, edited by J. Evans Grubbs, T.G. Parkin, and R. Bell, 83–107. Oxford.

Evans Grubbs, J. and T.G. Parkin. 2013. "Introduction". In *The Oxford Handbook of Childhood and Education in the Roman World*, edited by J. Evans Grubbs, T.G. Parkin, and R. Bell, 1–13. Oxford.

Fantham, E. 1995. "Aemilia Pudentilla: Or the Wealthy Widow's Choice". In *Women in Antiquity*, edited by R. Hawley and B.M. Levick, 221–32. London.

Fenoaltea, S. 1984. "Slavery and Supervision in Comparative Perspective: A Model". *Journal of Economic History* 44: 635–68.

Finley, M.I. 1973. *The Ancient Economy*. 2nd ed. Berkeley etc.

Finley, M.I. 1980. *Ancient Slavery and Modern Ideology*. Cambridge.

Finley, M.I. 1983. "The Slave Trade in Antiquity: the Black Sea and Danubian Regions". In *Economy and Society in Ancient Greece*, edited by B.D. Shaw and R.P. Saller, 3rd ed., 167–75. Virginia.

Finley, M.I. 1985. *Ancient History: Evidence and Models*. London.

Finley, M.I. 1998. *Ancient Slavery and Modern Ideology*. Edited by B.D. Shaw. 2nd ed. Princeton.

Finley, M.I. 1999. *The Ancient Economy*. 3rd ed. with a foreword by I. Morris. Berkeley etc.

Flemming, R. 2000. *Medicine and the Making of Roman Women: Gender, Nature, and Authority from Celsus to Galen*. Oxford.

Flohr, M. 2007. "Nec Quicquam Ingenuum Habere Potest Officina? Spatial Contexts of Urban Production at Pompeii, AD 79". *Bulletin Antieke Beschaving = Annual Papers on Classical Archaeology* 82 (1): 129–48.

Flohr, M. 2012. "Working and Living under One Roof: Workshops in Pompeian Atrium Houses". In *Privata Luxuria: Towards an Archaeology of Intimacy*, edited by A. Anguissola, 51–72. Munich.

Flohr, M. 2013. *The World of the Fullo: Work, Economy, and Society in Roman Italy*. Oxford.

Flohr, M. 2017. "Constructing Occupational Identities in the Roman World". In *Work, Labour and Professions in the Roman World*, edited by K. Verboven and C. Laes, 147–72. Leiden.

Flohr, M. 2019. "Artisans and Markets: The Economics of Roman Domestic Decoration". *American Journal of Archaeology* 123 (1): 101–25.

Flohr, M., and A.I. Wilson, eds. 2017. *The Economy of Pompeii*. Oxford.

Flory, M.B. 1978. "Family in Familia: Kinship and Community in Slavery". *American Journal of Ancient History* 3: 78–95.

Forbes, C.A. 1955. "The Education and Training of Slaves in Antiquity". *Transactions and Proceedings of the American Philological Association* 86: 321–60.

Foubert, L. 2013. "Female Travellers in Roman Britain: Vibia Pacata and Julia Lucilla". In *Women and the Roman City in the Latin West*, edited by E.A. Hemelrijk and G. Woolf, 391–403. Leiden.

Freu, C. 2011. "Apprendre et exercer un métier dans l'Égypte romaine (Ier–VIe siècles ap. J.-C". In *Les savoirs professionels des gens de métier: Études sur le monde du travail dans les sociétés urbaines de l'empire romain*, edited by N. Tran and H. Dessales, 27–40. Collection du Centre Jean Bernard 37. Naples.

Freu, C. 2016. "Disciplina, Patrocinium, Nomen: The Benefits of Apprenticeship in the Roman World". In *Urban Craftsmen and Traders in the Roman World*, edited by A. Wilson and M. Flohr. Oxford.

Frézouls, E. 1991. "Les noms de métier dans l'épigraphie de la Gaule et de la Germanie romaines". *Ktema* 16: 33–72.

Frier, B.W. 1994. "Natural Fertility and Family Limitation in Roman Marriage". *Classical Philology* 89 (4): 318–33.

Gagos, T., L. Koenen, and B.E. McNellen. 1992. "A First Century Archive from Oxyrynchos or Oxyrynchite Loan Contracts and Egyptian Marriage". In *Life in a Multi-cultural Society: Egypt from Cambyses to Constantine and Beyond*, edited by J.H. Johnson, 181–205. Chicago.

Gallivan, P., and P. Wilkins. 1997. "Familial Structures in Roman Italy: A Regional Approach". In *The Roman Family in Italy: Status, Sentiment, Space*, edited by B. Rawson and P.R.C. Weaver, 239–79. Oxford.

Gambash, G. 2017. "Between Mobility and Connectivity in the Ancient Mediterranean: Coast-Skirting Travellers in the Southern Levant". In *The Impact of Mobility and Migration in the Roman Empire: Proceedings of the Twelfth Workshop of the International Network Impact of Empire (Rome, June 17–19, 2015)*, edited by E. Lo Cascio and L.E. Tacoma, with the assistance of M.J. Groen-Vallinga, 155–72. Leiden.

Gardner, J.F. 1995. "Gender-Role Assumptions in Roman Law". *Echos du monde classique/Classical Views* 39 (3): 377–400.

Garnauf, R. 2009. "Slaves Doing Business: The Role of Roman Law in the Economy of a Roman Household". *European Review of History/Revue europeenne d'histoire* 16 (3): 331–46.

Garnsey, P. 1979. "Where Did Italian Peasants Live?", *Proceedings of the Cambridge Philological Society* 25: 1–25.

Garnsey, P., ed. 1980. *Non-slave Labour in the Greco-Roman World.* Proceedings of the Cambridge Philological Society, supplementary volume 6. Cambridge.

Garnsey, P. 1981. "Independent Freedmen and the Economy of Roman Italy under the Principate'. *Klio* 63 (2): 359–71.

Garnsey, P. 1988. *Famine and Food Supply in the Graeco-Roman World: Responses to Risk and Crisis.* Cambridge etc.

Garnsey, P. 1991. "Child-Rearing in Ancient Italy". In *The Family in Italy from Antiquity to the Present*, edited by D.I. Kertzer and R.P. Saller, 48–65. New Haven.

Garnsey, P. 1998. *Cities, Peasants, and Food in Classical Antiquity: Essays in Social and Economic History*, edited by W. Scheidel. Cambridge.

Garnsey, P., and L. de Ligt. 2016. "Migration in Early-Imperial Italy: Herculaneum and Rome Compared". In *Migration and Mobility in the Early Roman Empire*, edited by L. de Ligt and L.E. Tacoma, 72–94. Leiden.

Garnsey, P., and R.P. Saller. 1987. *The Roman Empire: Economy, Society and Culture.* London.

George, A. 2011. "Within Salvation: Girl Hawkers and the Colonial State in Development Era Lagos". *Journal of Social History* 44 (3): 837–59.

George, M. 2006. "Social Identity and the Dignity of Work in Freedmen's Reliefs". In *The Art of Citizens, Soldiers and Freedmen in the Roman World*, edited by E. d'Ambra and G.P.R. Métraux, 19–29. Oxford.

Gibbs, M. 2011. "Trade Associations in Roman Egypt: Their Raison D'être". *Ancient Society* 41: 291–315.

Gibbs, M. 2012. "Manufacture, Trade and the Economy". In *The Oxford Handbook of Roman Egypt*, edited by C. Riggs, 38–56. Oxford etc.

Gibbs, M. 2013. "Artisans, Trades, and Guilds, Late Antiquity". In *The Encyclopedia of Ancient History Online*, edited by R.S. Bagnall, K. Brodersen, C.B. Champion, A. Erskine, and S. Hübner. https://doi.org/10.1002/9781444338386.wbeah12020.pub2.

Gilbert, A. 2013. "Poverty, Inequality, and Social Segregation". In *The Oxford Handbook of Cities in World History*, edited by P. Clark, 683–99. Oxford etc.

Golden, M. 1988. "Did the Ancients Care When Their Children Died?" *Greece & Rome* 35 (2): 152–63.

Goldsmith, R.W. 1984. "An Estimate of the Size and Structure of the National Product of the Roman Empire". *Review of Income and Wealth* 30: 263–88.

Goodman, P. 2016. "Working Together: Clusters of Artisans in the Roman City'. In *Urban Craftsmen and Traders in the Roman World*, edited by M. Flohr and A.I. Wilson, 301–33. Oxford.

Goody, J. 1990. *The Oriental, the Ancient and the Primitive: Systems of Marriage and the Family in the Pre-industrial Societies of Eurasia*. Cambridge.

Gorz, A. 1989. *Critique of Economic Reason*, translated by G. Handyside and C. Turner. New York.

Gowland, R.L., and P. Garnsey. 2010. "Skeletal Evidence for Health, Nutritional Status and Malaria in Rome and the Empire". In *Roman Diasporas: Archaeological Approaches to Mobility and Diversity in the Roman Empire*, edited by H. Eckardt, 131–56. Journal of Roman Archaeology, Supplement 78. Portsmouth.

Groen-Vallinga, M.J. 2013. "Desperate Housewives? The Adaptive Family Economy and Female Participation in the Roman Urban Labour Market". In *Women and the Roman City in the Latin West*, edited by E.A. Hemelrijk and G. Woolf, 295–312. Leiden.

Groen-Vallinga, M.J., and L.E. Tacoma. 2015. "Contextualising Condemnation to Hard Labour in the Roman Empire". In *Global Convict Labour*, edited by C. De Vito and A. Lichtenstein, 49–78. Leiden.

Groen-Vallinga, M.J., and L.E. Tacoma. 2017. "The Value of Labour: Diocletian's Prices Edict". In *Work, Labour and Professions in the Roman World*, edited by K. Verboven and C. Laes, 104–32. Leiden.

Gummerus, H. 1913. "Darstellungen aus dem Handwerk auf römischen Grab- und Votivsteinen in Italien". *Jahrbuch des Deutschen Archäologischen Institut* 28: 63–123.

Gummerus, H. 1915. "Die Römische Industrie: Wirtschaftsgeschichtliche Untersuchungen I, II". *Klio* 14: 129–89.

Gummerus, H. 1918. "Die Römische Industrie: Wirtschaftsgeschichtliche Untersuchungen III". *Klio* 15: 256–302.

Gummerus, H. 1926. "Cognomen als Beruf". In *Commentationes Philologicae in Honorem Professoris Emeriti Heikel I.A.*, edited by his disciples (n.n.), 48–74. Helsinki.

Gummerus, H. 1932. *Die Ärztestand im römischen Reiche nach den Inschriften*. Helsinki.

Günther, R. 1987. *Frauenarbeit – Frauenbindung: Untersuchungen zu Unfreien und freigelassenen Frauen in den Stadtrömischen Inschriften*. Munich.

Hallett, J.P. 1984. *Fathers and Daughters in Roman Society: Women and the Elite Family*. Princeton.

Händel, A. 1983. "Zu Produktion und Distribution in der Stadt Rom während des Prinzipats in Auswertung der Inschriften". In *Studien zur römischen Stadtentwicklung in Italien und Thrakien: Sonderband des Jahrbuchs für Wirtschaftsgeschichte*, 87–149. Berlin.

Händel, A. 1985. "Zur Interpretation von Inschriften mit Berufsbezeichnungen von Handwerkern und Händlern im Rom der Prinzipatszeit". *Klio* 67: 498–501.

Hänninen, M.-L. 2005. "From Womb to Family: Rituals and Social Conventions Connected to Roman Birth". In *Hoping for Continuity: Childhood, Education and Death in Antiquity and the Middle Ages*, edited by K. Mustakallio, J. Hanska, H.-L. Sainio, and V. Vuolanto, 49–59. Rome.

Hanson, J.W., and S.G. Ortman. 2017. 'A Systematic Method for Estimating the Populations of Greek and Roman Settlements'. *Journal of Roman Archaeology* 30: 301–24.

Hanson, J.W., S.G. Ortman, and J. Lobo. 2017. 'Urbanism and the Division of Labour in the Roman Empire'. *Journal of the Royal Society Interface* 14: 20170367. http://dx.doi.org/10.1098/rsif.2017.0367.

Hareven, T.K. 1987. "Family History at the Crossroads". *Journal of Family History* 12: ix–xxiii.

Harkness, A.G. 1896. 'Age at Marriage and at Death in the Roman Empire'. *American Philological Association* 27: 35–72.

Harland, P.A. 2005. "Familial Dimensions of Group Identity (I): 'Brothers' (ΑΔΕΛΦΟΙ) in Associations of the Greek East". *Journal of Biblical Literature* 124 (3): 491–513.

Harland, P.A. 2007. "Familial Dimensions of Group Identity (II): 'Mothers' and 'Fathers' in Associations and Synagogues of the Greek World". *Journal for the Study of Judaism* 38: 57–79.

Harlow, M., and L. Larsson Lovén, eds. 2012. *Families in the Imperial and Late Antique World*. London and New York.

Harlow, M., and R. Laurence, eds. 2002. *Growing Up and Growing Old in Ancient Rome: A Life Course Approach*. London.

Harper, J. 1972. "Slaves and Freedmen in Imperial Rome". *American Journal of Philology* 93 (2): 341–42.

Harper, K. 2010. "Slave Prices in Late Antiquity". *Historia: Zeitschrift für alte Geschichte* 59 (2): 206–38.

Harper, K. 2011. *Slavery in the Late Roman World, AD 275–425*. Cambridge etc.

Harper, K. and W. Scheidel. 2018. "Roman Slavery and the Idea of 'Slave Society'". In *What Is a Slave Society? The Practice of Slavery in Global Perspective*, edited by N. Lenski and C.M. Cameron, 86–105. Cambridge.

Harris, E. 2002. "Workshop, Marketplace and Household. The Nature of Technical Specialization in Classical Athens and Its Influence on Economy and Society". In *Money, Labour and Land: Approaches to the Economies of Ancient Greece*, edited by P. Cartledge, E.E. Cohen, and L. Foxhall, 67–99. London.

Harris, W.V. 1980. "Towards a Study of the Roman Slave Trade". In *The Seaborne Commerce of Ancient Rome*, edited by J.H. d'Arms and E.C. Kopff, 117–40. Rome.

Harris, W.V. 1989. *Ancient Literacy*. Cambridge, MA etc.

Harris, W.V., ed. 1993. *The Inscribed Economy: Production and Distribution in the Roman Empire in the Light of Instrumentum Domesticum. The Proceedings of a Conference Held at the American Academy in Rome on 10–11 January, 1992.* Journal of Roman Archaeology, Supplementary Series 6. Ann Arbor.

Harris, W.V. 1994. "Child Exposure in the Roman Empire". *Journal of Roman Studies* 84: 1–22.

Harris, W.V. 1999. "Demography, Geography and the Sources of Roman Slaves". *Journal of Roman Studies* 89: 62–75.

Harris, W.V. 2006. "A Revisionist View of Roman Money". *Journal of Roman Studies* 96 (January): 1–24.

Harris, W.V. 2011. *Rome's Imperial Economy: Twelve Essays.* Oxford etc.

Hasegawa, K. 2005. *The Familia Urbana during the Early Empire: A Study of Columbaria Inscriptions.* Oxford.

Hawkins, C. 2013. "Labour and Employment". In *The Cambridge Companion to Ancient Rome*, edited by P.M. Erdkamp, 336–51. Cambridge.

Hawkins, C. 2017. "Contracts, Coercion, and the Boundaries of Roman Manufacturing Firms". In *Work, Labour and Professions in the Roman World*, edited by K. Verboven and C. Laes, 36–61. Leiden.

Hawkins, C. 2021. *Roman Artisans and the Urban Economy.* Cambridge. First published 2016.

Hawkins, C. forthcoming. "Manumission and the Organization of Labour". In *The Oxford Handbook of Economies in the Classical World*, edited by A. Bresson, E. Lo Cascio, and F. Velde. Oxford.

Helttula, A, T. Gestrin, M. Kahlos, R. Pentti-Tuomisto, P. Tuomisto, R. Vainio, and R. Valjus. 2007. *Le Iscrizioni Sepolcrali Latine nell'Isola Sacra.* Acta Instituti Romani Finlandiae 30. Rome.

Hemelrijk, E.A. 2001a. "De Laudatio Turiae: Grafschrift voor een Uitzonderlijke Vrouw?" *Lampas* 34 (1): 62–80.

Hemelrijk, E.A. 2001b. "Inleiding: De Laudatio Turiae". *Lampas* 34 (1): 5–17.

Hemelrijk, E.A. 2004. "Masculinity and Femininity in the Laudatio Turiae". *Classical Quarterly*, new series 54 (1): 185–97.

Hemelrijk, E.A. 2008. "Patronesses and 'Mothers' of Roman Collegia". *Classical Antiquity* 27 (1): 115–62.

Hemelrijk, E.A. 2010. "Women's Participation in Civic Life: Patronage and 'Motherhood' of Roman Associations". In *De Amicitia: Friendship and Social Networks in Antiquity and the Middle Ages*, edited by K. Mustakallio and C. Krötzl, 49–62. Acta Instituti Romani Finlandiae 36. Rome.

Hemelrijk, E.A. 2012. "Fictive Motherhood and Female Authority in Roman Cities". *Journal of Gender Studies in Antiquity* 2: 201–20.

Hemelrijk, E.A. 2015. *Hidden Lives, Public Personae: Women and Civic Life in the Roman West.* Oxford.

Hemelrijk, E.A. 2020. *Women and Society in the Roman World: A Sourcebook of Inscriptions from the Roman West.* Cambridge.

Hengstl, J. 1972. *Private Arbeitsverhältnisse freier Personen in den hellenistischen Papyri bis Diokletian.* Bonn.

Herfst, P. 1922. *La travail de la femme dans la Grèce ancienne*. Utrecht.
Herrmann-Otto, E. 1994. *Ex ancilla natus: Untersuchungen zu den "hausgeborenen" Sklaven und Sklavinnen im Westen des römischen Kaiserreiches*. Stuttgart.
Herz, P. 2017. "Die Mobilität römischer Soldaten in Friedenszeiten". In *The Impact of Mobility and Migration in the Roman Empire: Proceedings of the Twelfth Workshop of the International Network Impact of Empire (Rome, June 17–19, 2015)*, edited by E. Lo Cascio and L.E. Tacoma, with the assistance of M.J. Groen-Vallinga, 80–99. Leiden.
Hin, S. 2011. "Family Matters: Fertility and Its Constraints in Roman Italy". In *Demography and the Graeco-Roman World: New Insights and Approaches*, edited by C. Holleran and A. Pudsey, 99–116. Cambridge.
Hin, S. 2013. *The Demography of Roman Italy: Population Dynamics in an Ancient Conquest Society 201 BCE–14 CE*. Cambridge.
Hin, S. 2016. "Revisiting Urban Graveyard Theory: Migrant Flows in Hellenistic and Roman Athens". In *Migration and Mobility in the Early Roman Empire*, edited by L. de Ligt and L.E. Tacoma, 234–63. Leiden.
Hirschmann, V.E. 2004. "Methodische Überlegungen zu Frauen in antiken Vereinen". In *Roman Rule and Civic Life: Local and Regional Perspectives. Proceedings of the Fourth Workshop of the International Network Impact of Empire (Roman Empire, c.200 B.C.–A.D. 476) Leiden, June 25–28. 2003*, edited by E.A. Hemelrijk and L. de Ligt, 401–14. Amsterdam.
Hofmeester, K. 2018. "Labour Relations: Introductory Remarks". In *Handbook Global History of Work*, edited by K. Hofmeester and M. van der Linden, 317–27. Berlin.
Hofmeester, K., and C. Moll-Murata. 2011. "The Joy and Pain of Work: Global Attitudes and Valuations, 1500–1650. Introduction". *International Review of Social History* 56 (Supplement S19): 1–23.
Hofmeester, K., and M. van der Linden. 2018. *Handbook Global History of Work*. Berlin.
Holderness, B.A. 1984. "Widows in Pre-industrial Society: An Essay upon Their Economic Functions". In *Land, Kinship, and Life-Cycle*, edited by R.M. Smith, 423–42. Cambridge.
Holleran, C. 2011. "Migration and the Urban Economy of Rome". In *Demography and the Graeco-Roman World: New Insights and Approaches*, edited by C. Holleran and A. Pudsey, 155–80. Cambridge.
Holleran, C. 2012. *Shopping in Ancient Rome: The Retail Trade in the Late Republic and the Principate*. Oxford.
Holleran, C. 2013. "Women and Retail in Roman Italy". In *Women and the Roman City in the Latin West*, edited by E.A. Hemelrijk and G. Woolf, 313–30. Leiden.
Holleran, C. 2016. "Labour Mobility in the Roman World: A Case Study of Mines in Iberia". In *Migration and Mobility in the Early Roman Empire*, edited by L. de Ligt and L.E. Tacoma, 95–137. Leiden.
Holleran, C. 2017. "Getting a Job: Finding Work in the City of Rome". In *Work, Labour and Professions in the Roman World*, edited by K. Verboven and C. Laes, 87–103. Leiden.

Holleran, C. 2018. "Market Regulation and Intervention in the Urban Food Supply". In *The Routledge Handbook of Diet and Nutrition in the Roman World*, edited by P.M. Erdkamp and C. Holleran, 283–95. London and New York.

Holleran, C., and A. Pudsey, eds. 2011a. *Demography and the Graeco-Roman World.* Cambridge.

Holleran, C., and A. Pudsey. 2011b. "Introduction". In *Demography and the Graeco-Roman World: New Insights and Approaches*, edited by C. Holleran and A. Pudsey, 1–13. Cambridge.

Honeyman, K., and J. Goodman. 1991. "Women's Work, Gender Conflict and Labour Markets in Europe, 1500–1900". *Economic History Review* 44: 608–28.

Hope, V.M. 2009. *Roman Death: The Dying and the Dead in Ancient Rome.* London and New York.

Hopkins, K. 1965. "The Age of Roman Girls at Marriage". *Population Studies* 18: 309–27.

Hopkins, K. 1966. "On the Probable Age Structure of the Roman Population". *Population Studies* 20: 245–64.

Hopkins, K. 1978. *Conquerors and Slaves.* Sociological Studies in Roman History 1. Cambridge, London, New York etc.

Hopkins, K. 1980. "Taxes and Trade in the Roman Empire (200 B.C.–A.D. 400)". *Journal of Roman Studies* 70: 101–25.

Hopkins, K. 1983. *Death and Renewal.* Sociological Studies in Roman History 2. Cambridge.

Hopkins, K. 1987. "Graveyards for Historians". In *La mort, les morts, et l'au-dèla dans le monde romain: Actes du colloque de Caen*, edited by F. Hinard, 113–26. Caen.

Howgego, C. 1992. "The Supply and Use of Money in the Roman World 200 BC–AD 300". *Journal of Roman Studies* 82: 1–31.

Hübner, S.R. 2007. "'Brother–Sister' Marriage in Roman Egypt: A Curiosity of Humankind or a Widespread Family Strategy?" *Journal of Roman Studies* 97: 21–49.

Hübner, S.R. 2011. "Household Composition in the Ancient Mediterranean: What Do We Really Know?" In *A Companion to Families in the Greek and Roman Worlds*, edited by B. Rawson, 73–91. Malden, MA etc.

Hübner, S.R. 2013. *The Family in Roman Egypt: A Comparative Approach to Intergenerational Solidarity and Conflict.* Cambridge etc.

Hübner, S.R. 2019. "Single Men and Women in Pagan Society: The Case of Roman Egypt". In *The Single Life in the Roman and Later Roman World*, edited by C. Laes and S.R. Hübner, 37–56. Cambridge.

Hübner, S.R., and D.M. Ratzan, eds. 2021. *Missing Mothers: Maternal Absence in Antiquity.* Leuven.

Huttunen, P. 1974. *The Social Strata in the Imperial City of Rome: A Quantitative Study of the Social Representation in the Epitaphs Published in the Corpus Inscriptionum Latinarum Volumen VI.* Acta Universitatis Ouluensis, Series B, Humaniora 3. Oulu.

Ivanov, P. 2013. "Book Review: The Roman Market Economy". *London School of Economics Blog*, May 17. http://blogs.lse.ac.uk/lsereviewofbooks/2013/05/17/book-review-the-roman-market-economy/.

Jackson, R. 2005. "The Role of Doctors in the City". In *Roman Working Lives and Urban Living*, edited by A. MacMahon and J. Price, 202–20. Oxford.

Jaschke, K. 2010. *Die Wirtschafts- und Sozialgeschichte des antiken Puteoli.* Rahden.

Johnson, A.C. 1936. *Roman Egypt: To the Reign of Diocletian.* Baltimore.

Jones, A.H.M. 1956. "The Economics of Slavery in the Ancient World". *Economic History Review* 9: 185–204.

Jongman, W. 1988. *The Economy and Society of Pompeii.* Amsterdam.

Jongman, W. 1990. "Het Romeins Imperialisme en de Verstedelijking van Italië". *Leidschrift* 7: 43–58.

Jongman, W. 2003. "Slavery and the Growth of Rome". In *Rome the Cosmopolis*, edited by G. Woolf and C. Edwards, 100–22. Cambridge.

Jongman, W. 2007. "Consumption". In *The Cambridge Economic History of the Greco-Roman World*, edited by W. Scheidel, I. Morris, and R.P. Saller, 592–618.

Jongman, W. 2014. "Why Modern Economic Theory Applies, Even to the Distant Roman Past'. In *TRAC 2013: Proceedings of the Twenty-Third Theoretical Roman Archaeology Conference. King's College, London 2013*, 27–36. Oxford and Havertown, PA.

Jonkers, E.J. 1933. *Economische en Sociale Toestanden in het Romeinsche Rijk blijkende uit het Corpus Juris.* Wageningen.

Joshel, S.R. 1986. "Nurturing the Master's Child: Slavery and Roman Child Nursing". *Signs* 12: 5–22.

Joshel, S.R. 1992. *Work, Identity and Legal Status at Rome: A Study of the Occupational Inscriptions.* Norman etc.

Judd, E.R. 2010. "Family Strategies: Fluidities of Gender, Community and Mobility in Rural West China". *China Quarterly* 204: 921–38.

Kampen, N. 1981. *Image and Status: Roman Working Women in Ostia.* Berlin.

Keegan, P. 2013. "Reading the 'Pages' of the Domus Caesaris: Pueri Delicati, Slave Education, and the Graffiti of the Palatine Paedagogium". In *Roman Slavery and Roman Material Culture*, edited by M. George, 69–98. Toronto.

Kelly, J.M. 1966. *Roman Litigation.* Oxford.

Kessler, D., and P. Temin. 2008. "Money and Prices in the Early Roman Empire". In *The Monetary System of the Greeks and Romans*, edited by W.V. Harris, 137–59. Oxford.

King, H., ed. 2005. *Health in Antiquity.* London etc.

Kirschenbaum, A. 1987. *Sons, Slaves and Freedmen in Roman Commerce.* Washington DC and Jerusalem.

Kleijwegt, M. 1991. *Ancient Youth: The Ambiguity of Youth and the Absence of Adolescence in Greco-Roman Society.* Amsterdam.

Kleijwegt, M. 2006. "Freedpeople: A Brief Cross-cultural History". In *The Faces of Freedom: The Manumission and Emancipation of Slaves in Old World and New World Slavery*, edited by M. Kleijwegt, 3–68. Leiden and Boston.

Kloppenborg, J.S. 1996. "Collegia and Thiasoi: Issues in Function, Taxonomy and Membership". In *Voluntary Associations in the Graeco-Roman World*, edited by J.S. Kloppenborg and S.G. Wilson, 16–30. London and New York.

Kloppenborg, J.S., and S.G. Wilson, eds. 1996. *Voluntary Associations in the Graeco-Roman World*, London and New York.

Kneissl, P. 1994. "Die Fabri, Fabri Tignuarii, Fabri Subaediani, Centonarii und Dolabrarii als Feuerwehern in den Städten Italiens und der westenlichen Provinzen". In *E Fontibus Haurire: Beitrage zur römischen Geschichte und zu ihren Hilfswissenschaften*, edited by R. Günther and S. Rebbenich, 133–46. Paderborn.

Knotter, A. 1994. "Problemen van de Family Economy: Gezinsarbeid en Arbeidsmarkt in Pre-Industrieel Europa". In *Samen Wonen, Samen Werken? Vijf Essays over de Geschiedenis van Arbeid en Gezin*, edited by M. Baud and Th. Engelen, 35–71. Hilversum.

Knotter, A. 2004. "Poverty and the Family-Income Cycle: Casual Laborers in Amsterdam in the First Half of the 20th Century". *History of the Family* 9: 221–37.

Koestner, E. 2017. "The Linouphoi of P. Giss. 40 II Revisited: Applying the Sociological Concept of Ethnic Colonies to Alexandria's Linen-Weavers". In *The Impact of Mobility and Migration in the Roman Empire: Proceedings of the Twelfth Workshop of the International Network Impact of Empire (Rome, June 17–19, 2015)*, edited by E. Lo Cascio and L.E. Tacoma, with the assistance of M.J. Groen-Vallinga, 191–204. Leiden.

Kok, J. 2002. *Rebellious Families: Household Strategies and Collective Action in the Nineteenth and Twentieth Centuries*. New York etc.

Köves-Zulauf, T. 1990. *Römische Geburtsriten*. Munich.

Koyama, M. 2013. "Preindustrial Cliometrics". *Economic Affairs* 33 (2): 268–78.

Kroon, C. 2002. "How to Write a Ghost Story? A Linguistic View on Narrative Modes in Pliny Ep. 7.27". In *Donum Grammaticum: Studies in Latin and Celtic Philology and Linguistics in Honour of Hannah Rosén*, edited by D. Shalev and L. Szawicky, 189–200. Louvain-la Neuve.

Laes, C. 2010. "The Educated Midwife in the Roman Empire: An Example of 'Differential Equations'". In *Hippocrates and Medical Education: Selected Papers Read at the XIIth International Hippocrates Colloquium, Universiteit Leiden, 24–26 August 2005*, edited by H.F.J. Horstmanshoff and C. van Tilburg, 261–86. Leiden.

Laes, C. 2011a. *Children in the Roman Empire: Outsiders Within*. Cambridge etc.

Laes, C. 2011b. "Midwives in Greek Inscriptions in Hellenistic and Roman Antiquity". *Zeitschrift für Papyrologie und Epigrafik* 176: 154–62.

Laes, C. 2013. "Raising a Disabled Child". In *Oxford Handbook of Childhood and Education in the Roman World*, edited by J. Evans Grubbs, T.G. Parkin, and R. Bell, 125–46. Oxford.

Laes, C. 2015a. "Children and Their Occupations in the City of Rome (300–700 CE)". In *Children and Family in Late Antiquity: Life, Death and Interaction*, edited by C. Laes, K. Mustakallio, and V. Vuolanto, 79–109. Leuven.

Laes, C. 2015b. "Masters and Apprentices". In *A Companion to Ancient Education*, edited by M. Bloomer, 474–82. Oxford.

Laes, C. 2016. "Educators in the Late Ancient City of Rome". *Revue belge de philologie et d'histoire/Belgisch Tijdschrift voor Filologie en Geschiedenis* 94: 183–207.

Laes, C. 2018. "Women, Children and Food". In *The Routledge Handbook of Diet and Nutrition in the Roman World*, edited by P. Erdkamp and C. Holleran, 177–88. London and New York.

Laes, C., and S.R. Hübner, eds. 2019. *The Single Life in the Roman and Later Roman World.* Cambridge.

Laes, C., and J. Strubbe. 2008. *Jeugd in het Romeinse Rijk: Jonge Jaren, Wilde Haren?* Leuven.

Langner, M. 2001. "Szenen aus Handwerk und Handel auf gallo-römischen Grabmälern". *Jahrbuch des Deutschen Archäologischen Institut* 116: 299–356.

Larsson Lovén, L. 1998. "'Lanam fecit'. Woolworking and female virtue". In *Aspects of Women in Antiquity: Proceedings of the First Nordic Symposium on Women's Lives in Antiquity, Göteborg, 12–15 June 1997*, edited by L. Larsson Lovén and A. Strömberg, 85–95. Studies in Mediterranean archaeology and literature 153. Jonsered.

Larsson Lovén, L. 2003. "Funerary Art, Gender and Social Status: Some Aspects from Roman Gaul". In *Gender, Cult and Culture in the Ancient World from Mycenae to Byzantium: Proceedings of the Second Nordic Symposium on Gender and Women's History in Antiquity, Helsinki 20–22 October 2000*, edited by A. Strömberg and L. Larsson Lovén, 54–70. Partille.

Larsson Lovén, L. 2007. "Male and Female Work in Roman and Gallo-Roman Funerary Iconography". In *Geschlechterdefinitionen und Geschlechtergrenzen in der Antike*, edited by E. Hartmann, U. Hartmann, and K. Pietzner, 169–86. Stuttgart.

Larsson Lovén, L. 2016. "Women, Trade, and Production in Urban Centres of Roman Italy". In *Urban Craftsmen and Traders in the Roman World*, edited by M. Flohr and A. Wilson, 200–21. Oxford.

Laslett, P. 1972. "Introduction: The History of the Family". In *Household and Family in Past Time*, edited by P. Laslett and R. Wall, 1–89. Cambridge.

Laslett, P., and R. Wall, eds. 1972. *Household and Family in Past Time.* Cambridge.

Laurence, R. 1999. *The Roads of Roman Italy: Mobility and Cultural Change.* London etc.

Laurence, R. 2005. "Health and the Life Course at Herculaneum and Pompeii". In *Health in Antiquity*, edited by H. King, 83–96. London and New York.

Laurence, R. 2012. "Introduction: From *Oikos* to *Familia*: Looking Forward?" In *Families in the Greco-Roman World*, edited by R. Laurence and A. Strömberg, 1–9. London and New York.

Laurence, R., and F. Trifilò. 2012. "Vixit plus Minus. Commemorating the Age of the Dead: Towards a Familial Roman Life Course?" In *Families in the Imperial and Late Antique World*, edited by M. Harlow and L. Larsson Lovén, 23–40. London and New York.

Laurence, R., and A. Wallace-Hadrill, eds. 1997. *Domestic Space in the Roman World: Pompeii and Beyond.* Journal of Roman Archaeology. Supplementary series 22. Portsmouth, RI.

Lazer, E. 2017. "Skeletal Remains and the Health of the Population at Pompeii". In *The Economy of Pompeii*, edited by M. Flohr and A.I. Wilson, 135–59. Oxford.

Le Gall, J. 1970. "Les métiers des femmes au Corpus Inscriptionum Latinarum". *Revue des études latines* 47 (2): 123–30.

Le Gall, J. 1971. "Rome, ville de fainéants?" *Revue des études latines* 49: 266–77.

Lelis, A.A., W.A. Percy, and B.C. Verstraete. 2003. *The Age of Marriage in Ancient Rome.* Lewiston, NY.

Lemercier, C. 2012. 'Apprenticeship, Wages and Contracts during the Industrial Revolution: Lessons from the Parisian Case'. Paper presented at the ESSHC, Glasgow, April 14.

León, V. 2007. *Working IX to V: Orgy Planners, Funeral Clowns, and Other Prized Professions of the Ancient World.* New York: Walker Books.

Le Play, F. 1871. *L'organisation de la famille selon le vrai modèle signalé par l'histoire de toutes les races et de tous les temps.* Paris.

Lewis, Ch.T., and C. Short, eds. 1958. *A Latin Dictionary.* Oxford. First edition 1879.

Lightman, M., and W. Zeisel. 1977. "Univira: An Example of Continuity and Change in Roman Society". *Church History* 46: 19–32.

Lindsay, H. 2001. "Adoption and Its Function in Cross-cultural Contexts". In *Childhood, Class and Kin in the Roman World*, edited by S. Dixon, 190–204. London and New York.

Lindsay, H. 2009. *Adoption in the Roman World.* Cambridge etc.

Lis, C., and H. Soly. 2012. *Worthy Efforts: Attitudes to Work and Workers in Pre-industrial Europe.* Leiden.

Liu, J. 2008a. "The Economy of Endowments: The Case of the Roman Collegia". In *Pistoi dia tèn Technèn': Bankers, Loans and Archives in the Ancient World. Studies in Honour of Raymond Bogaert*, edited by K. Verboven, K. Vandorpe, and V. Chanowski-Sable, 231–56. Studia Hellenistica 44. Leuven.

Liu, J. 2008b. "Pompeii and Collegia: A New Appraisal of the Evidence". *Ancient History Bulletin* 22 (1): 53–69.

Liu, J. 2009. *Collegia Centonariorum: The Guilds of Textile Dealers in the Roman West*. Leiden.

Liu, J. 2013. "Professional Associations". In *The Cambridge Companion to Ancient Rome*, edited by P.M. Erdkamp, 352–68. Cambridge.

Liu, J. 2017. "Group Membership, Trust Networks, and Social Capital: A Critical Analysis". In *Work, Labour and Professions in the Roman World*, edited by K. Verboven and C. Laes, 203–26. Leiden.

Loane, H.J. 1938. *Industry and Commerce of the City of Rome*. The John Hopkins University Studies in Historical and Political Science 56. Baltimore.

Lo Cascio, E. 2009. "Urbanization as a Proxy of Demographic and Economic Growth". In *Quantifying the Roman Economy: Methods and Problems*, edited by A.K. Bowman, 87–106. Oxford.

Lo Cascio, E., and P. Malanima. 2009. "GDP in Pre-modern Economics (1–1820 AD)". *Rivista di Storia Economica* 25 (3): 391–419.

Lo Cascio, E., and L.E. Tacoma, eds, with the assistance of M.J. Groen-Vallinga. 2017. *The Impact of Mobility and Migration in the Roman Empire: Proceedings of the Twelfth Workshop of the International Network Impact of Empire (Rome, June 17–19, 2015)*. Leiden.

Lopez Barja de Quiroga, P. 1998. "Junian Latins: Status and Number". *Athenaeum* 86: 133–63.

Louis, P. 1965. *Ancient Rome at Work: An Economic History of Rome from the Origins to the Empire*. 2nd ed. London.

Lucassen, J. 2006. *Global Labour History: A State of the Art*. Bern etc.

Lucassen, J. 2007. *Wages and Currency: Global Comparisons from Antiquity to the Twentieth Century*. Bern etc.

Lucassen, J. 2013. *Outlines of a History of Labour* (IISH research paper). Amsterdam. https://hdl.handle.net/10622/AE6A0AA2-0A58-4CB2-9D77-9A10CA4CE3EA.

Lucassen, J.M.W.G., T. De Moor, and J. Luiten van Zanden. 2008. "The Return of the Guilds: Towards a Global History of the Guilds in Pre-industrial Times". *International Review of Social History* 53 (Supplement S16): 5–18.

Lucassen, L. 2013. "Population and Migration". In *The Oxford Handbook of Cities in World History*, edited by P. Clark, 664–82. Oxford etc.

Maat, G. 2005. "Two Millennia of Male Stature Development". *Journal of Osteoarchaeology* 58: 803–21.

McCann, L. 1999. "Seasons of Labor: Family, Work, and Land in a Nineteenth-Century Novia Scotia Shipbuilding Community". *History of the Family* 4 (4): 485–527.

McDermott, W.C. 1972. "M. Cicero and M. Tiro". *Historia* 21: 259–86.

McGuire, R.H., J. Smith, and W.H. Martin. 1986. "Patterns of Household Structures and the World-Economy". *Review* 10 (1): 75–97.

MacMahon, A., and J. Price, eds. 2005. *Roman Working Lives and Urban Living*. Oxford.

MacMullen, R. 1966. *Enemies of the Roman Order: Treason, Unrest and Alienation in the Empire*. Cambridge, MA etc.

MacMullen, R. 1974. *Roman Social Relations, 50 B.C. to A.D. 284.* New Haven etc.

MacMullen, R. 1982. "The Epigraphic Habit in the Roman Empire". *American Journal of Philology* 103: 233–46.

Maddison, A. 2007. *Contours of the World Economy, 1–2030 AD.* Oxford.

Maiuro, M., and M. Balbo, eds. 2019. *Popolazione, Risorse e Urbanizzazione nella Campania Antica: Dall'età preromana alla tarda antichità.* Bari.

Malaspina, E. 2003. "La Terminologia Latina delle Professioni Femminili nel Mondo Antico". *Mediterraneo Antico* 6 (1): 347–91.

Manacorda, D. 2005. "Appunti sull'Industria Edilizia a Roma". In *Interpretare i Bolli Laterizi di Roma e della Valle del Tevere: Produzione, Storia Economica e Topografia. Atti del Convegno all'École française de Rome e all'Institutum Romanum Finlandiae, 31 Marzo e 1 Aprile 2000, Organizzato da Christer Bruun e François Chausson*, edited by C. Bruun, 25–52. Acta Instituti Romani Finlandiae 32. Rome.

Martin, D.B. 1996. "The Construction of the Ancient Family: Methodical Considerations". *Journal of Roman Studies* 86: 39–60.

Martin, S.D. 2001. "The Responsibility of Skilled Workers in Classical Roman Law". *American Journal of Philology* 122 (1): 107–29.

Maxey, M. 1938. *Occupations of the Lower Classes in Roman Society.* Chicago.

Mayer, E. 2012. *The Ancient Middle Classes: Urban Life and Aesthetics in the Roman Empire.* Cambridge MA and London.

Meiggs, R. 1960. *Roman Ostia.* Oxford.

Mennella, G. and G. Apicella. 2000. *Le Corporazioni Professionali nell'Italia Romana: Un Aggiornamento al Waltzing.* Napoli.

Meyer, E. 1990. "Explaining the Epigraphic Habit in the Roman Empire: The Evidence of Epitaphs". *Journal of Roman Studies* 80: 74–96.

Migliardi Zingale, L. 2007. "Riflessioni in Tema di Apprendistato Femminile e Arte della Tessitura: In Margine a P. Oxy. LXVII 4596". *Aegyptus* 87: 199–208.

Millar, F. 1984. "Condemnation to hard labour in the Roman empire, from the Julio-Claudians to Constantine". *Proceedings of the British School at Rome* 52: 124–47.

Mincer, J., and S. Polachek. 1974. "Family Investments in Human Capital: Earnings of Women". In *Economics of the Family: Marriage, Children and Human Capital*, edited by T.W. Schultz, 397–429. Chicago and London.

Moatti, C. 2017. "Migration et droit dans l'empire romain: Catégories, contrôles et intégration". In *The Impact of Mobility and Migration in the Roman Empire: Proceedings of the Twelfth Workshop of the International Network Impact of Empire (Rome, June 17–19, 2015)*, edited by E. Lo Cascio and L.E. Tacoma, with the assistance of M.J. Groen-Vallinga, 222–45. Leiden.

Moen, P. and E. Wethington. 1992. "The Concept of Family Adaptive Strategies". *Annual Review of Sociology* 18 (1): 233–51.

Mohler, S.L. 1940. "Slave Education in the Roman Empire". *Transactions and Proceedings of the American Philological Association* 17: 262–80.

Möller, C. 1993. "Die Mercennarii in der Römischen Arbeitswelt". *Zeitschrift für Rechtsgeschichte* 110: 296–330.

Mommsen, Th. 1843. *De Collegiis et Sodaliciis Romanorum*. Kiel.

Morel, J.-P. 1992. "l'Artigiano". In *De Wereld van de Romeinen*, translated by F. de Haan, edited by A. Giardina, 229–60. Amsterdam.

Morley, N. 1996. *Metropolis and Hinterland: The City of Rome and the Italian Economy 200 BC–AD 200*. Cambridge.

Morley, N. 2008. "Urbanisation and Development in Italy in the Late Republic". In *People, Land and Politics: Demographic Developments and the Transformation of Roman Italy*, edited by L. de Ligt and S. Northwood, 121–37. Leiden.

Morley, N. 2011. "Slavery under the Principate". In *The Cambridge World History of Slavery, Volume I*, edited by K.R. Bradley and P. Cartledge, 265–86. Cambridge.

Morley, N. 2013. "Review of Temin". *Sehepunkte* 13 (7–8). http://www.sehepunkte.de/2013/07/23247.html.

Mossé, C. 1969. *The Ancient World at Work*, translated by J. Lloyd. London.

Mouritsen, H. 2011a. "The Families of Roman Slaves and Freedmen". In *A Companion to Families in the Greek and Roman Worlds*, edited by B. Rawson, 129–44. Malden, MA etc.

Mouritsen, H. 2011b. *The Freedman in the Roman World*. Cambridge.

Mouritsen, H. 2013. "Slavery and Manumission in the Roman Elite: A Study of the Columbaria of the Volusii and the Statilii". In *Roman Slavery and Roman Material Culture*, edited by M. George, 43–68. Toronto.

Mouritsen, H. 2019. "Slavery and Manumission in Imperial Italy: The Album from Herculaneum Revisited". In *Popolazione, Risorse e Urbanizzazzione nella Campania Antica*, edited by M. Maiuro and M. Balbo, 211–31. Bari.

Mrozek, S. 1975. *Prix et rémunération dans l'occident romain (31 av.n.è.–250 de n.è.)*. Gdańsk.

Mrozek, S. 1986. "Zur Verbreitung der freien Lohnarbeit in der römischen Kaiserzeit". In *Studien zur alten Geschichte: Siegfried Lauffer zum 70. Geburtstag am 4. August 1981 dargebracht von Freunden, Kollegen und Schülern*, edited by H. Kalcyk, B. Gullath, and A. Graeber, Volume II: 705–16. Rome.

Müller, I. 2010. "Single Women in the Roman Funerary Inscriptions". *Zeitschrift für Papyrologie und Epigrafik* 175: 295–303.

Munck, B.D., S.L. Kaplan, and H. Soly. 2007. *Learning on the Shop Floor: Historical Perspectives on Apprenticeship*. New York.

Murphy, E.A. 2017. "Roman Workers and Their Workplaces: Some Archaeological Thoughts on the Organization of Workshop Labour in Ceramic Production". In *Work, Labour and Professions in the Roman World*, edited by K. Verboven and C. Laes, 133–46. Leiden.

Netting, R. McC., E.J. Arnould, and R.R. Wilk. 1984. "Introduction". In *Households: Comparative and Historical Studies of the Domestic Group*, xiii–xxxviii. Berkeley, Los Angeles, and London.

Neumann, G. 1981. “Zur Bildung der lateinischen Handwerkerbezeichnungen”. In *Das Handwerk in Vor- und Frühgeschichtlicher Zeit*, edited by H. Jankuhn, W. Janssen, R. Schmidt-Wiegand, and H. Tiefenbach, 133–40. Göttingen.

Nicolet, C., and S. Panciera, eds. 1994. *Epigrafia della produzione e della distribuzione*. CEFR 193. Rome.

Nörr, D. 1965. “Zur sozialen und rechtlichen Bewertung der freien Arbeit in Rom”. *Zeitschrift für Rechtsgeschichte* 82: 67–105.

North, D.C. 1990. *Institutions, Institutional Change and Economic Performance*. Cambridge.

North, D.C. 2005. *Understanding the Process of Economic Change*. Princeton.

North, J. 2013. “Gender and Cult in the Roman West: Mithras, Attis”. In *Women and the Roman City in the Latin West*, edited by E. A. Hemelrijk and Greg Woolf, 109–27. Leiden.

Noy, D. 2000. *Foreigners at Rome: Citizens and Strangers*. London.

Oerlemans, A.P.A, and L.E. Tacoma. 2014. “Three Great Killers: Infectious Diseases and Patterns of Mortality in Imperial Rome”. *Ancient Society* 44: 213–41.

Ogilvie, S.C. 2007. “Whatever Is, Is Right? Economic Institutions in Pre-industrial Europe”. *Economic History Review* 60: 649–84.

Ogilvie, S.C. 2011. *Institutions and European Trade: Merchant Guilds, 1000–1800*. Cambridge Studies in Economic History. Second series. Cambridge etc.

O’Hara, S.F. 1998. “Patria Potestas”. In *Ancient History in a Modern University*, Volume I: 210–16. Grand Rapids and Cambridge.

Ojo, M.O.D. 2013. “A Sociological Investigation of the Determinant Factors and the Effects of Child Street Hawking in Nigeria: Ageg E, Lagos State, under Survey”. *International Journal of Asian Social Science* 3 (1): 114–37.

Oleson, J., ed. 2009, *The Oxford Handbook of Engineering and Technology*, Oxford.

Oppenheimer, V.K. 1974. “The Life-Cycle Squeeze: The Interaction of Men’s Occupational and Family Life Cycles”. *Demography* 11: 227–245.

Oppenheimer, V.K. 1982. *Work and the Family: A Study in Social Demography*. New York.

Ornstein, M., and G.J. Stalker. 2013. “Canadian Families’ Strategies for Employment and Care for Preschool Children”. *Journal of Family Issues* 34 (1): 53–84.

Oyefara, J.L. 2005. “Family Background, Sexual Behaviour, and HIV/AIDS Vulnerability of Female Street Hawkers in Lagos Metropolis, Nigeria”. *International Social Science Journal* 57 (186): 687–98.

Palmer, P.A. 1998. *The Worlds of Unfree Labour: From Indentured Servitude to Slavery*

Paping, R. 2004. “Family Strategies Concerning Migration and Occupations of Children in a Market-Oriented Agricultural Economy”. *History of the Family* 9 (2): 159–91.

Park, M.E. 1918. *The Plebs in Cicero's Day: A Study of Their Provenance and of Their Employment.* Cambridge, MA.

Parker, H. 1997. "Women Physicians in Greece, Rome, and the Byzantine Empire". In *Women Physicians and Healers: Climbing a Long Hill,* edited by L.R. Furst, 131–50. Lexington.

Parkin, T.G. 1992. *Demography and Roman Society.* Baltimore etc.

Parkin, T.G. 2003. *Old Age in the Roman World : A Cultural and Social History.* Baltimore.

Parkin, T.G. 2011. "The Roman Life-Course and the Family". In *A Companion to Families in the Greek and Roman Worlds,* edited by B. Rawson, 276–90. Malden MA etc.

Parkin, T.G. 2013. "The Demography of Infancy and Early Childhood in the Ancient World". In *Oxford Handbook of Childhood and Education in the Roman World,* edited by J. Evans Grubbs, T.G. Parkin, and R. Bell, 40–61. Oxford.

Parkin, T.G., and J. Evans Grubbs. 2013. "Introduction". In *The Oxford Handbook of Childhood and Education in the Roman World,* edited by J. Evans Grubbs, T.G. Parkin, and R. Bell, 1–13. Oxford.

Patterson, J. 1998. "Trade and Traders in the Roman World: Scale, Structure, and Organisation". In *Trade and Traders in the Ancient City,* edited by H. Parkins and C. Smith, 149–67. London.

Patterson, J.R. 1992. "Patronage, Collegia and Burial in Imperial Rome". In *Death in Towns: Urban Responses to the Dying and the Dead, 100–1600,* edited by S.R. Bassett, 15–27. Leicester.

Patterson, J.R. 1994. "The Collegia and the Transformation of the Towns of Italy in the Second Century AD". In *L'Italie d'Auguste à Dioclétien: Actes du colloque international organisé par l'École française de Rome,* 227–38. Rome.

Patterson, J.R. 2006. *Landscapes and Cities: Rural Settlement and Civic Transformation in Early Imperial Italy.* Oxford etc.

Patterson, O. 1982. *Slavery and Social Death: A Comparative Study.* Cambridge, MA and London.

Pearl, O. 1985. "Apprentice Contract". *Bulletin of the American Society of Papyrologists* 22 (1–4): 255–59.

Pearse, J.L.D. 1976. "Three Alba of the Collegium Fabrum Tignariorum at Rome". *Bullettino della Commissione Archeologica Comunale di Roma* 85: 163–76.

Penner, L. 2012. "Gender, Household Structure and Slavery: Re-interpreting the Aristocratic Columbaria of Early Imperial Rome". In *Families in the Greco-Roman World,* edited by R. Laurence and A. Strömberg, 143–58.

Penner, L. 2013. "The Epigraphic Habits of the Slaves and Freed Slaves of the Julio-Claudian Households". Diss. University of Calgary.

Perry, J.S. 2006. *The Roman Collegia: The Modern Evolution of an Ancient Concept.* Leiden.

Perry, M.J. 2021. "Control of Roman Slave Sexuality: Authority, Profit, and Resistance". In *Slavery and Sexuality in Classical Antiquity,* edited by D. Kamen and C.W. Marshall, 254–70. Madison, WI.

Pestman, P.W., and W. Clarysse. 1989. *Familiearchieven uit het Land van Pharao: Een Bundel Artikelen samengesteld naar Aanleiding van een Serie Lezingen van het Papyrologisch Instituut van de Rijksuniversiteit van Leiden in het Voorjaar van 1986*. Zutphen.

Petermandl, W. 1997. "Kinderarbeit im Italien der Prinzipatszeit: Ein Beitrag zur Sozialgeschichte des Kindes". *Laverna* 8: 113–36.

Petersen, L.H. 2003. "The Baker, His Tomb, His Wife, and Her Breadbasket: The Monument of Eurysaces in Rome". *Art Bulletin* 85 (2): 230–57.

Petersen, L.H. 2006. *The Freedman in Roman Art and Art History*. Cambridge.

Petersen, L.H., and P. Salzman, eds. 2012. *Mothering and Motherhood in the Ancient World*, Austin.

Petrikovits, H. von. 1981. "Die Spezialisierung des römischen Handwerks". In *Das Handwerk in Vor- und Frühgeschichtlicher Zeit*, edited by H. Jankuhn, W. Janssen, R. Schmidt-Wiegand, and H. Tiefenbach, 63–132. Göttingen.

Piccolo, M. 2003. "Osservazioni ad alcuni Papiri dell'Archivio di Tryphon". *Aegyptus* 83: 197–213.

Pleket, H.W. 1988. "Labor and Unemployment in the Roman Empire: Some Preliminary Remarks". In *Soziale Randgruppen und Aussenseiter im Altertum: Referate vom Symposium "Soziale Randgruppen und Antike Sozialpolitik", in Graz (21. bis 23. September)*, edited by I. Weiler, 267–76. Graz.

Porena, P. 2016. "Il Lavoro Infantile'. In *l'Età Romana: Liberi, Semilibere e Schiavi in una Societa Premoderna*, edited by A. Marcone, 663–85. Rome.

Potter, D.S. 2009. *Ancient Rome: A New History*. New York.

Prior, M. 1985. "Women and the Urban Economy: Oxford 1500–1800". In *Women in English Society 1500–1800*, edited by M. Prior, 93–117. London.

Prowse, T.L. 2016 "Isotopes and Mobility in the Ancient Roman World". In *Migration and Mobility in the Early Roman Empire*, edited by L. de Ligt and L.E. Tacoma, 205–33. Leiden.

Pudsey, A. 2011. "Nuptiality and the Demographic Life Cycle of the Family in Roman Egypt". In *Demography and the Graeco-Roman World: New Insights and Approaches*, edited by C. Holleran and A. Pudsey, 60–98. Cambridge.

Pudsey, A. 2012. "Death and the Family: Widows and Divorcées in Roman Egypt". In *Families in the Imperial and Late Antique World*, edited by M. Harlow and L. Larsson Lovén, 157–80. London and New York.

Pudsey, A. 2013. "Children in Roman Egypt". In *Oxford Handbook of Childhood and Education in the Roman World*, edited by J. Evans Grubbs, T.G. Parkin, and R. Bell, 484–508. Oxford.

Purcell, N. 1987. "Tomb and Suburb". In *Römische Gräberstrassen: Selbstdarstellung, Status, Standard. Kolloquium in München vom 28.–30. Oktober 1985*, edited by H. von Hesberg and P. Zanker, 25–41. Munich.

Ramin, J., and P. Veyne. 1981. "Droit romain et société: Les hommes libres qui passent pour esclaves et l'esclavage volontaire". *Historia: Zeitschrift für alte Geschichte* 30 (4): 472–97.

Rathbone, D. 2006. "Poverty and Population in Roman Egypt". In *Poverty in the Roman World*, edited by M. Atkins and R. Osborne, 100–14. New York.

Rathbone, D. 2009. "Earnings and Costs: Living Standards and the Roman Economy (First to Third Centuries A.D.)". In *Quantifying the Roman Economy: Methods and Problems*, edited by A.K. Bowman, 299–326. Oxford.

Rawson, B. 1966. "Family Life among the Lower Classes at Rome in the First Two Centuries of the Empire". *Classical Philology* 61 (2): 71–83.

Rawson, B. 1986a. "Children in the Roman Familia". In *The Family in Ancient Rome*, edited by B. Rawson, 170–200. London.

Rawson, B. 1986b. *The Family in Ancient Rome: New Perspectives.* London etc.

Rawson, B., ed. 1991. *Marriage, Divorce, and Children in Ancient Rome.* Canberra.

Rawson, B. 2003. *Children and Childhood in Roman Italy.* Oxford etc.

Rawson, B. 2005. "Circulation of Staff between Roman Households". *Zeitschrift für Papyrologie und Epigraphik* 151: 223–24.

Rawson, B., ed. 2011. *A Companion to Families in the Greek and Roman Worlds.* Malden, MA etc.

Rawson, B. 2013. "Vernae". In *The Encyclopedia of Ancient History Online*, edited by R.S. Bagnall, K. Brodersen, C.B. Champion, A. Erskine and S. Hübner. https://onlinelibrary.wiley.com/doi/10.1002/9781444338386.wbeah22271.

Ray, N.M. 2017. "Consumer Behaviour in Pompeii". In *The Economy of Pompeii*, edited by M. Flohr and A.I. Wilson, 87–109. Oxford.

Reden, S. von. "Arbeitsmarkt", in: *Der Neue Pauly*, Antiquity volumes edited by H. Cancik and H. Schneider. http://dx.doi.org.ezproxy.leidenuniv.nl:2048/10.1163/1574-9347_dnp_e131620 (accessed 26 October 2016). First published online 2006.

Reden, S. von. "Unemployment", in *Der Neue Pauly*, Antiquity volumes edited by H. Cancik and H. Schneider. http://dx.doi.org.ezproxy.leidenuniv.nl:2048/10.1163/1574-9347_dnp_e131620 (accessed 31 August 2022). First published online 2006.

Reden, S. von. 2014. "The Roman Market Economy by Peter Temin (Review)". *Journal of Interdisciplinary History* 44 (4): 535–36.

Remijsen, S., and W. Clarysse. 2008. "Incest or Adoption? Brother–Sister Marriage in Roman Egypt Revisited". *Journal of Roman Studies* 98: 53–61.

Remus, H.E. 1996. "Voluntary Association and Networks: Aelius Aristides at the Asclepieion in Pergamum". In *Voluntary Associations in the Graeco-Roman World*, edited by J.S. Kloppenborg and S.G. Wilson, 146–75. London and New York.

Richardson, L. 1992. *A New Topographical Dictionary of Ancient Rome.* Baltimore etc.

Riddle, J.M. 1992. *Contraception and Abortion from the Ancient World to the Renaissance.* Cambridge and London.

Ridgeway, C.L. 2011. *Framed by Gender.* Oxford.

Rink, B. 1983. "Zur Bedeutung des Handwerks im italienischen Raum zur Zeit der späten römischen Republik". In *Studien zur römischen Stadtentwicklung in Italien und Thrakien: Sonderband des Jahrbuchs für Wirtschaftsgeschichte*, 55–86. Berlin.

Rives, J.B. 1999. *P. Cornelius Tacitus – Germania*. Clarendon Ancient History Series. Oxford.

Rizzo, F.P. 1993. *La Menzione del Lavoro nelle Epigrafi della Sicilia Antica (per una Storia della Mentalità)*. Palermo.

Robinson, D. 2017. "Wealthy Entrepreneurs and the Urban Economy". In *The Economy of Pompeii*, edited by M. Flohr and A.I. Wilson, 243–62. Oxford.

Rosafio, P. 2016. "Lavoro e Status Giuridico: Lavoro Libero e Lavoro Servile nelle Campagne dell'Italia Romana in Età Repubblicana". In *l'Eta Romana: Liberi, Semiliberi e Schiavi in una Società Premoderna*, edited by A. Marcone, 91–112. Rome.

Rose, H. 2007. "Vom Ruhm des Berufs: Darstellungen von Händlern und Handwerkern auf römischen Grabreliefs in Metz". In *Römische Bilderwelten: Von der Wirklichkeit zum Bild und Zurück. Kolloquium der Gerda Henkel Stiftung am Deutschen Archäologischen Institut Rom 15.–17. März 2004*, edited by F. Hölscher and T. Hölscher, 145–80. Archäologie und Geschichte 12. Heidelberg.

Rowan, E. 2017. "Sewers, Archaeobotany, and Diet at Pompeii and Herculaneum". In *The Economy of Pompeii*, edited by M. Flohr and A.I. Wilson, 111–33. Oxford.

Rowland, R.J. 1977. "Some New Medici in the Roman Empire". *Epigraphica* 39: 174–79.

Rowlandson, J. 1998. *Women and Society in Greek and Roman Egypt: A Sourcebook*. Cambridge.

Rowlandson, J., and R. Takahashi. 2009. "Brother–Sister Marriage and Inheritance Strategies in Greco-Roman Egypt". *Journal of Roman Studies* 99: 104–39.

Royden, H. 1988. *The Magistrates of the Roman Professional Collegia in Italy from the First to the Third Century AD*. Pisa.

Ruffing, K. 2008. *Die berufliche Spezialisierung in Handel und Handwerk*. 2 vols. Rahden.

Ruffing, K. 2016. "Driving Forces for Specialization: Market, Location Factors, Productivity Improvements". In *Urban Craftsmen and Traders in the Roman World*, edited by M. Flohr and A. Wilson, 115–31. Oxford.

Ruffing, K., and H.-J. Drexhage. 2008. "Antike Sklavenpreise". In *Antike Lebenswelten: Konstanz, Wandel, Wirkungsmacht. Festschrift für Ingomar Weiler zum 70. Geburtstag*, edited by P. Mauritsch, 321–51. Wiesbaden.

Sallares, R. 2002. *Malaria and Rome: A History of Malaria in Ancient Italy*. Oxford.

Sallares, R. 2007. "Ecology". In *The Cambridge Economic History of the Greco-Roman World*, edited by W. Scheidel, I. Morris, and R.P. Saller, 27–34. Cambridge.

Saller, R.P. 1984. "Familia, Domus and the Roman Conception of the Family". *Phoenix* 38: 336–55.

Saller, R.P. 1986. "Patria Potestas and the Stereotype of the Roman Family". *Continuity and Change* 1 (1): 7–22.

Saller, R.P. 1987. "Men's Age at Marriage and Its Consequences in the Roman Family". *Classical Philology* 82: 21–34.

Saller, R.P. 1994. *Patriarchy, Property and Death in the Roman Family.* Cambridge.

Saller, R.P. 1997. "Roman Kinship: Structure and Sentiment". In *The Roman Family in Italy: Status, Sentiment, Space*, edited by B. Rawson and P.R.C. Weaver, 7–34. Oxford.

Saller, R.P. 2002. "Framing the Debate over Growth in the Ancient Economy". In *The Ancient Economy*, edited by W. Scheidel and S. von Reden, 251–69, Edinburgh; reprinted in 2005 in *The Ancient Economy: Evidence and Models,* edited by J. Manning and I. Morris, 223–38. Stanford.

Saller, R.P. 2003. "Women, Slaves, and the Economy of the Roman Household". In *Early Christian Families in Context*, edited by D. Balch and C. Osiek, 185–204. Grand Rapids.

Saller, R.P. 2007. "Household and Gender". In *The Cambridge Economic History of the Greco-Roman World*, edited by W. Scheidel, I. Morris, and R.P. Saller, 84–112. Cambridge.

Saller, R.P. 2011. "The Roman Family as Productive Unit". In *A Companion to Families in the Greek and Roman Worlds*, edited by B. Rawson, 116–28. Oxford.

Saller, R.P. 2013. "Human Capital and Economic Growth". In *The Cambridge Companion to the Roman Economy*, edited by W. Scheidel, 71–86. Cambridge.

Saller, R.P., and B.D. Shaw. 1984. "Tombstones and Roman Family Relations in the Principate: Civilians, Soldiers and Slaves". *Journal of Roman Studies* 74: 124–56.

Salvaterra, C. and A. Cristofori, 2016. "Twentieth-Century Italian Scholarship on Roman Craftsmen, Traders, and Their Professional Organizations", In *Urban Craftsmen and Traders in the Roman World,* edited by A.I. Wilson and M. Flohr, 55–76. Oxford.

Salway, B. 2010. "Mancipium Rusticum Sive Urbanum: The Slave Chapter of Diocletian's Edict on Maximum Prices". In *By the Sweat of Your Brow: Roman Slavery in Its Socio-economic Setting*, 1–20. Bulletin of the Institute of Classical Studies Supplements. London.

Scheidel, W. 1994. *Grundpacht und Lohnarbeit in der Landwirtschaft des römischen Italien.* Frankfurt.

Scheidel, W. 1995. "The Most Silent Women of Greece and Rome: Rural Labour and Women's Life in the Ancient World (I)". *Greece & Rome* 42 (2): 202–17.

Scheidel, W. 1996. "Reflections on the Differential Valuation of Slaves in Diocletian's Price Edict and in the United States". *Münstersche Beiträge zur antiken Handelsgeschichte* 15 (1): 67–79.

Scheidel, W. 1997. "Quantifying the Sources of Slaves in the Early Roman Empire". *Journal of Roman Studies* 87: 160–63.

Scheidel, W., ed. 2001a. *Debating Roman Demography.* Leiden etc.

Scheidel, W. 2001b. "Progress and Problems in Roman Demography". In *Debating Roman Demography*, edited by W. Scheidel, 1–81. Leiden.

Scheidel, W. 2002. "A Model of Demographic and Economic Change in Roman Egypt after the Antonine Plague". *Journal of Roman Archaeology* 15: 97–114.

Scheidel, W. 2003. "Germs for Rome". In *Rome the Cosmopolis*, edited by C. Edwards and G. Woolf, 158–76. Cambridge etc.

Scheidel, W. 2004. "Human Mobility in Roman Italy, I: The Free Population". *Journal of Roman Studies* 94: 1–26.

Scheidel, W. 2005a. "Human Mobility in Roman Italy, II: The Slave Population". *Journal of Roman Studies* 95: 64–79.

Scheidel, W. 2005b. "Real Slave Prices and the Relative Cost of Slave Labor in the Greco-Roman World". *Ancient Society* 35: 1–17.

Scheidel, W. 2006. "Stratification, Deprivation and Quality of Life". In *Poverty in the Roman World*, edited by M. Atkins and R. Osborne, 40–59. Cambridge.

Scheidel, W. 2007a. "Demography". In *The Cambridge Economic History of the Greco-Roman World*, edited by W. Scheidel, I. Morris, and R.P. Saller, 38–86. Cambridge.

Scheidel, W. 2007b. "Roman Funerary Commemoration and the Age at First Marriage". *Classical Philology* 102 (4): 389–402.

Scheidel, W. 2008. "The Comparative Economics of Slavery in the Greco-Roman World". In *Slave Systems, Ancient and Modern*, 105–26. Cambridge.

Scheidel, W. 2009. "Sex and Empire: A Darwinian Perspective". In *The Dynamics of Ancient Empires: State Power from Assyria to Byzantium*, edited by I. Morris and W. Scheidel, 255–324. Oxford.

Scheidel, W. 2010a. "Economy and Quality of Life". In *The Oxford Handbook of Roman Studies*, edited by A. Barchiesi and W. Scheidel, 593–608. Oxford.

Scheidel, W. 2010b. "Real Wages in Early Economies: Evidence for Living Standards from 1800 BCE to 1300 CE". *Journal of the Economic and Social History of the Orient* 53 (3): 425–62.

Scheidel, W. 2011a. "Monogamy and Polygyny". In *A Companion to Families in the Greek and Roman Worlds*, edited by B. Rawson, 108–15. Oxford.

Scheidel, W. 2011b. "The Roman Slave Supply". In *The Cambridge World History of Slavery, Volume I*, edited by K.R. Bradley and P. Cartledge, 287–310. Cambridge.

Scheidel, W., ed. 2012a. *The Cambridge Companion to the Roman Economy.* New York etc.

Scheidel, W. 2012b. "Epigraphy and Demography: Birth, Marriage, Family, and Death". In *Epigraphy and the Historical Sciences.* Proceedings of the British Academy 177, edited by J. Davies and J. Wilkes, 101–29. Oxford.

Scheidel, W. 2012c. "Physical Well-Being". In *The Cambridge Companion to the Roman Economy*, edited by W. Scheidel, 321–33.

Scheidel, W. 2012d. "Roman Wellbeing and the Economic Consequences of the Antonine Plague". In *l'Impatto della Peste Antonina*, edited by E. Lo Cascio, 265–95. Bari.

Scheidel, W. 2014. "Roman Real Wages in Context". In *Quantifying the Greco-Roman Economy and Beyond*, edited by F. de Callataÿ, 209–18. Bari.

Scheidel, W. and S.J. Friesen. 2009. "The Size of the Economy and the Distribution of Income in the Roman Empire". *Journal of Roman Studies* 99: 61–91.

Scheidel, W., I. Morris, and R.P. Saller, eds. 2007. *The Cambridge Economic History of the Greco-Roman World*. Cambridge.

Scheidel, W., and S. von Reden, eds. 2002. *The Ancient Economy*. Edinburgh.

Schmidt, A. 2001. *Overleven na de Dood: Weduwen in Leiden in de Gouden Eeuw*. Amsterdam.

Schmidt, A. 2007. "Survival Strategies of Widows and Their Families in Early Modern Holland, C. 1580–1750". *History of the Family* 12: 268–81.

Schoevaert, J. 2018. *Les boutiques d'Ostie: L'économie urbaine au quotidien. Ier s. av. J.-C.–Ve s. ap. J.-C.* Rome: École française de Rome.

Schultz, T.P. 1990. "Women's Changing Participation in the Labor Force: A World Perspective". *Economic Development and Cultural Change* 38 (3): 457–88.

Schultz, T.P., ed. 1995. *Investment in Women's Human Capital*. Chicago and London.

Schultz, T.W. 1961. "Investment in Human Capital". *American Economic Review* 51 (1): 1–17.

Schultz, T.W. 1980. *Investing in People: The Economics of Population Quality*. Berkeley etc.

Schulze, H. 1998. *Ammen und Pädagogen: Sklavinnen und Sklaven als Erzieher in der antiken Kunst und Gesellschaft*. Mainz am Rhein.

Schulz-Falkenthal, H. 1972. "Zur Lehrlingsausbildung in der Römischen Antike: *Discipuli* und *Discentes*". *Klio* 54: 193–212.

Schumacher, L. 2001. "Hausgesinde – Hofgesinde: Terminologische Überlegungen zur Funktion der '*familia Caesaris*' im 1. Jh. n. Chr". In *Fünfzig Jahre Forschungen zur antiken Sklaverei an der Mainzer Akademie 1950–2000: Miscellanea zum Jubiläum*, edited by H. Heinen and H. Bellen, 331–52. Stuttgart.

Scott, J., and G. Marshall. 2009. *A Dictionary of Sociology*. Oxford reference online 2009, version 1994 (3rd edition).

Scott, J.C. 1976. *The Moral Economy of the Peasant: Rebellion and Subsistence in Southeast Asia*. Princeton.

Shaw, B.D. 1987a. "The Age of Roman Girls at Marriage: Some Reconsiderations". *Journal of Roman Studies* 77: 30–46.

Shaw, B.D. 1987b. "The Family in Late Antiquity: The Experience of Augustine". *Past & Present* 115 (1): 3–51.

Shaw, B.D. 2001. "Raising and Killing Children: Two Roman Myths". *Mnemosyne* 54 (1): 31–77.

Sigismund-Nielsen, H. 1987. "Alumnus, a Term of Relation That Denotes Quasi-adoption". *Classica et Mediaevalia* 38: 142–88.

Sigismund-Nielsen, H. 1991. "Ditis Examen Domus? On the Use of the Term Verna in Roman Epigraphic and Literary Sources". *Classica et Mediaevalia* 42: 221–39.

Sigismund-Nielsen, H. 2006. "Collegia: A New Way for Understanding the Roman Family". *Hephaistos* 24: 201–14.

Sigismund-Nielsen, H. 2013. "Slave and Lower-Class Roman Children". In *Oxford Handbook of Childhood and Education in the Roman World*, edited by J. Evans Grubbs, T.G. Parkin, and R. Bell, 286–301. Oxford.

Sijpesteijn, P.J. 1967. *The Wisconsin Papyri I.* Leiden.

Silver, M. 2011. "Contractual Slavery in the Roman Economy". *Ancient History Bulletin* 25: 73–132.

Silver, M. 2016. "The Role of Slave Markets in Migration from the Near East to Rome". *Klio* 97 (2): 184–202.

Sirks, A.J.B. 1991. *Food for Rome: The Legal Structure of the Transportation and Processing of Supplies for the Imperial Distributions in Rome and Constantinople.* Studia Amstelodamensia ad Epigraphicam, Ius Antiquum et Papyrologicam Pertinentia. Amsterdam.

Smith, A. 1776. *An Inquiry into the Nature and Causes of the Wealth of Nations.*

Solin, H. 1971. *Beiträge zur Kenntnis der griechischen Personennamen in Rom.* Commentationes humanarum litterarum 48. Helsinki etc.

Solin, H. 2000. "Nouvelle interprétation, nouvelle lecture et identité d'inscriptions". *Arctos* 34: 156–92.

Spicksley, J. 2012. *The Business and Household Accounts of Joyce Jeffreys, Spinster of Hereford, 1638–1648.* Oxford.

Stapel, R. 2016. "Taxonomy of Labour Relations", https://hdl.handle.net/10622/OJYQOR, IISH Data Collection, V2.

Stewart, E., E. Harris, and D. Lewis, eds. 2020. *Skilled Labour and Professionalism in Ancient Greece and Rome.* Cambridge.

Strauss, J. 2017. "Les contrats d'apprentissage et d'enseignement relatifs a des esclaves dans la documentation papyrologique d'Égypte". In *En marge du serment hippocratique: Contrats et serments dans le monde gréco-romain*, edited by M.-H. Marganne and A. Ricciardetto, 119–34. Leuven.

Strobel, K. 1991. "Handwerk im Heer – Handwerk im zivilen Sektor: Neue Zeugnisse zu Berufsbezeichnungen und zur Verknüpfung zweier sozialer und wirtschaftlicher Sektoren mit einem Anhang zum neuen Pridianum aus Vindolanda". *Ktema* 16: 19–32.

Strong, A.K. 2012. "Working Girls: Mother–Daughter Bonds among Prostitutes'. In *Mothering and Motherhood in the Ancient World*, edited by L.H. Petersen and P. Salzman, 121–39. Austin.

Strong, D., and D. Brown. 1976. *Roman Crafts.* London.

Syme, R. 1987. "Marriage Ages for Roman Senators". *Historia* 36: 318–32.

Syme, R. 1989. *The Augustan Aristocracy.* 2nd ed. Oxford.

Szaivert, W., and R. Wolters. 2005. *Löhne, Preise, Werte: Quellen zur römischen Geldwirtschaft.* Darmstadt.

Szilágyi, J. 1963. "Prices and Wages in the Western Provinces of the Roman Empire". *Acta Antique Academiae Hungaricae* 11: 325–89.

Tacoma, L.E. 2006. *Fragile Hierarchies: The Urban Elites of Third-Century Roman Egypt*. Leiden.

Tacoma, L.E. 2013. "Migrant quarters at Rome?" In *Integration in the Roman World: Impact of Empire 10*, edited by S. Benoist and G. de Kleijn, 127–46. Leiden.

Tacoma, L.E. 2016. *Moving Romans: Migration to Rome in the Principate*. Leiden.

Tacoma, L.E. 2017. "Bones, Stones, and Monica: Isola Sacra Revisited". In *The Impact of Mobility and Migration in the Roman Empire: Proceedings of the Twelfth Workshop of the International Network Impact of Empire (Rome, June 17–19, 2015)*, edited by E. Lo Cascio, L.E. Tacoma, and M.J. Groen-Vallinga, 132–54. Leiden.

Tacoma, L.E. 2018. "The Labor Market", In *A Companion to the City of Rome*, edited by C. Holleran and A. Pudsey, 425–42. Chicester.

Tacoma, L.E., and R. Tybout. 2016. "Moving Epigrams: Migration and Mobility in the Greek East". In *Migration and Mobility in the Early Roman Empire*, edited by L. de Ligt and L.E. Tacoma, 345–89. Leiden.

Tate, G. 1991. "Les métiers dans les villages de la Syrie du nord". *Ktema* 16: 73–78.

Taylor, D. 1979. *Work in Ancient Greece and Rome*. London. First edition 1975.

Temin, P. 1980. "Modes of Behavior". *Journal of Economic Behavior and Organization* 1 (2): 175–95.

Temin, P. 2001. "A Market Economy in the Early Roman Empire". *Journal of Roman Studies* 91: 169–81.

Temin, P. 2004. "The Labor Market of the Early Roman Empire". *Journal of Interdisciplinary History* 34 (4): 513–38.

Temin, P. 2006. "Estimating the GDP of the Early Roman Empire". In *Innovazione Tecnica e Progresso Economico nel Mondo Romano*, edited by E. LoCascio, 31–54. Rome.

Temin, P. 2013a. *The Roman Market Economy*. Princeton.

Temin, P. 2013b. "Statistics in Ancient History", working paper, Department of Economics, Massachusetts Institute of Technology. http://dspace.mit.edu/handle/1721.1/77609.

Terpstra, T. 2008. "Roman Law, Transaction Costs and the Roman Economy: Evidence from the Sulpicii Archive". In *Pistoia dia tèn Tèchnen: Bankers, Loans and Archives in the Ancient World*, edited by K. Verboven, K. Vandorpe, and V. Chankowski, 345–69. Leuven.

Terpstra, T. 2013. *Trading Communities in the Roman World: A Micro-economic and Institutional Perspective*. Leiden.

Thoma, M. 2016. "Women's Role in Domestic Economy of Roman Egypt: The Contribution of the Gnomon Idios Logos (BGU V 1210)". In *The Material Sides of Marriage: Women and Domestic Economies in Antiquity*, edited by R. Berg, 145–51. Acta Instituti Romani Finlandiae 43. Rome.

Thonemann, P. 2013. "Who Made the Amphora Mountain?" *Times Literary Supplement*, 9 August 2013, 10–11.

Tilly, C. 2005. *Trust and Rule*. Cambridge.

Tilly, C., and C. Tilly. 1998. *Work under Capitalism*. Boulder, CO etc.

Tilly, L.A., and Scott, J.W. 1978. *Women, Work and the Family*. New York, London, etc.

Todd, B. 1985. "The Remarrying Widow: A Stereotype Reconsidered". In *Women in English Society 1500–1800*, edited by M. Prior, 54–91. London.

Tol, G., and T. de Haas, eds. 2017. *The Economic Integration of Roman Italy: Rural Communities in a Globalising World*. Leiden.

Tran, N. 2006. *Les membres des associations romaines: Le rang social des collegiati en Italie et en Gaules, sous le haut-empire*. Rome.

Tran, N. 2007a. "La mention épigraphique des métiers artisanaux et commerciaux en Italie centro-méridionale". In *Vocabulaire et expression de l'économie dans le monde antique*, edited by J. Andreau and V. Chankowski, 119–41. Bordeaux.

Tran, N. 2007b. "Les procédures d'exclusion des collèges professionels et funéraires sous le haut-empire: Pratiques épigraphiques, norme collective et non-dits". In *Les exclus dans l'antiquité. Actes du colloque organisé par l'Université Lyon III les 23 et 24 Septembre 2004*, edited by C. Wolff, 119–38. Paris.

Tran, N. 2011. "Les collèges professionnels romains: 'Clubs' ou 'corporations'? L'exemple de la Vallée du Rhône et de *CIL* XII 1797 (Tournon-sur-Rhône, Ardèche)". *Ancient Society* 41: 197–219.

Treggiari, S. 1969a. "The Freedmen of Cicero". *Greece & Rome* 16 (2): 195–204.

Treggiari, S. 1969b. *Roman Freedmen during the Late Republic*. Oxford.

Treggiari, S. 1973. "Domestic Staff at Rome during the Julio-Claudian Period". *Histoire sociale/Social History* 6: 241–55.

Treggiari, S. 1975a. "Family Life among the Staff of the Volusii". *Transactions of the American Philological Association (1974–)* 105: 393–401.

Treggiari, S. 1975b. "Jobs in the Household of Livia". *Papers of the British School at Rome* 43: 48–77.

Treggiari, S. 1976. "Jobs for Women". *American Journal of Ancient History* 1: 76–104.

Treggiari, S. 1979a. "Lower Class Women in the Roman Economy". *Florilegium* 1: 65–86.

Treggiari, S. 1979b. "Questions on Women Domestics in the Roman West". In *Schiavitù, Manumissione e Classi Dipendenti nel Mondo Antico*, edited by Maria Capozza, 185–201. Rome.

Treggiari, S. 1980. "Urban Labour in Rome: Mercenarii and Tabernarii". In *Non-slave Labour in the Greco Roman World*. Proceedings of the Cambridge Philological Society 6, edited by P. Garnsey, 48–65. Cambridge.

Treggiari, S. 1991. *Roman Marriage: Iusti Coniuges from the Time of Cicero to the Time of Ulpian*. Oxford.

Ulrich, R.B. 2008. *Roman Woodworking.* New Haven.

Umar, F.M. 2009. "Street Hawking: Oppressing the Girl Child or Family Economic Supplement?" *Journal of Instructional Psychology* 36 (2): 169–74.

Van Bavel, B.J.P. 2008. "Markt, mensen, groei en duurzaam welzijn? Economie en samenleving van de Middeleeuwen als laboratorium", inaugural lecture, Utrecht University.

Van den Heuvel, D. 2008. "Partners in Marriage and Business? Guilds and the Family Economy in Urban Food Markets in the Dutch Republic". *Continuity and Change* 23 (2): 217–36.

Van den Hoven, B. 1996. *Work in Ancient and Medieval Thought: Ancient Philosophers, Medieval Monks and Theologians and Their Concept of Work, Occupations and Technology.* Amsterdam.

Van der Linden, M., ed. 1993. *The End of Labour History?* International Review of Social History Supplement 1. Cambridge.

Van der Linden, M. 2002. "Introduction". In *Rebellious Families: Household Strategies and Collective Action in the Nineteenth and Twentieth Centuries*, edited by J. Kok, 1–23. New York, etc.

Van der Linden, M. 2006. "The 'Globalization' of Labour and Working-Class History and Its Consequences". In *Global Labour History: A State of the Art*, edited by J. Lucassen, 13–36. Bern etc.

Van der Linden, M. 2008. *Workers of the World: Essays toward a Global Labor History.* Leiden etc.

Van der Linden, M. 2011. "Studying Attitudes to Work Worldwide, 1500–1650: Concepts, Sources, and Problems of Interpretation". *International Review of Social History* 56 (Supplement S19): 25–43.

Van der Linden, M. 2012. "The Promise and Challenges of Global Labor History". *International Labor and Working-Class History* 83: 57–76.

Van der Linden, M. 2013. "Global Labor History: Promising Challenges". *International Labor and Working-Class History* 84: 218–25.

Van der Linden, M., and J. Lucassen. 1999. *Prolegomena for a Global Labour History.* Amsterdam.

Van der Linden, M., and L. Lucassen. 2012. *Working on Labor: Essays in Honor of Jan Lucassen.* Leiden etc.

Vandoni, M. 1974. *Testi per il Corso di Papirologia: I Documenti di Trifone (dai Papiri di Ossirinco).* Milan.

Van Leeuwen, M.H.D., I. Maas, and A. Miles. 2002. *HISCO: Historical International Standard Classification of Occupations.* Leuven.

Van Minnen, P. 1987. "Urban Craftsmen in Roman Egypt". *Münstersche Beiträge zur antiken Handelsgeschichte* 6 (1): 31–88.

Van Minnen, P. 1998. "Did Ancient Women Learn a Trade Outside the Home? A Note on SB XVIII 13305". *Zeitschrift für Papyrologie und Epigrafik* 123: 201–3.

Van Nijf, O. 1997. *The Civic World of Professional Organisations in the Roman East.* Amsterdam.

Van Nijf, O. 2002. "Collegia and Civic Guards: Two Chapters in the History of Sociability". In *After the Past: Essays in Ancient History in Honour of H.W. Pleket*, edited by W. Jongman and M. Kleijwegt, 305–39. Mnemosyne Supplementum 233. Leiden.

Varga, R. 2020. *Carving a Professional Identity: The Occupational Epigraphy of the Roman Latin West.* Oxford.

Venticinque, P.F. 2010. "Family Affairs: Guild Regulations and Family Relationships in Roman Egypt". *Greek and Roman Byzantine Studies* 50 (2): 273–94.

Venticinque, P.F. 2016. *Honor among Thieves: Craftsmen, Merchants, and Associations in Roman and Late Roman Egypt.* Ann Arbor.

Verboven, K. 2002. *The Economy of Friends: Economic Aspects of Amicitia and Patronage in the Late Republic.* Brussel.

Verboven, K. 2007. "The Associative Order: Status and Ethos among Roman Businessmen in Late Republic and Early Empire". *Athenaeum* 95: 861–93.

Verboven, K. 2011a. "Professional Collegia: Guilds or Social Clubs?" *Ancient Society* 41: 187–95.

Verboven, K. 2011b. "Resident Aliens and Translocal Merchant Collegia in the Roman Empire". In *Frontiers in the Roman World: Proceedings of the Ninth Workshop of the International Network Impact of Empire* (Durham, 16–19 April 2009), edited by O. Hekster and T. Kaizer, 335–48. Leiden.

Verboven, K. 2012a. "City and Reciprocity: The Role of Cultural Beliefs in the Roman Economy". *Annales: Histoire, sciences sociales:* 67 (4): 597–627.

Verboven, K. 2012b. "The Freedman Economy of the Roman Empire". In *Free at Last! The Impact of Freed Slaves on the Roman Empire*, edited by S. and T.R. Ramsby, 88–109. London.

Verboven, K. 2015. "The Knights who say NIE. Can Neo-Institutional Economics Live Up to Its Expectation in Ancient History Research?" In *Structure and Performance in the Roman Economy: Models, Methods and Case Studies*, edited by P.M. Erdkamp and K. Verboven, 33–58. Leuven.

Verboven, K. 2017a. "Currency and Credit in the Bay of Naples in the First Century AD", in *The Economy of Pompeii*, edited by M. Flohr and A. Wilson, 363–86. Oxford.

Verboven, K. 2017b. "Guilds and the Organisation of Urban Populations during the Principate". In *Work, Labour and Professions in the Roman World*, edited by K. Verboven and C. Laes, 173–202. Leiden.

Verboven, K. 2017c. "Work, Labour, Profession: What's in a Name?" In *Work, Labour and Professions in the Roman World*, edited by K. Verboven and C. Laes, 1–19. Leiden.

Verboven, K., and C. Laes, eds. 2017. *Work, Labour and Professions in the Roman World.* Impact of Empire 23. Leiden: Brill.

Vlassopoulos, K. 2021. *Historicising Ancient Slavery.* Edinburgh.

Walker-Ramisch, S. 1996. "Voluntary Associations and the Damascus Document: A Sociological Analysis". In *Voluntary Associations in the Graeco-Roman World*, edited by J.S. Kloppenborg and S.G. Wilson, 128–45. London.

Wall, R. 1986. "Work, Welfare and the Family: An Illustration of the Adaptive Family Economy". In *The World We Have Gained: Histories of Population and Social Structure. Essays Presented to Peter Laslett on His Seventieth Birthday*, edited by L. Bonfield, R.M. Smith, and K. Wrightson, 261–94. Oxford.

Wall, R. 2007. "Widows and Unmarried Women as Taxpayers in England before 1800". *History of the Family* 12 (4): 250–67.

Waltzing, J-P. 1895–1900. *Étude historique sur les corporations professionnelles chez les romains depuis les origines jusqu'à la chute de l'empire d'occident.* Brussels.

Watson, J.L. 1980. "Slavery as an Institution: Open and Closed Systems". In *Asian and African Systems of Slavery*, 1–16. Berkeley and Los Angeles.

Weaver, P.R.C. 1972. *Familia Caesaris: A Social Study of the Emperor's Freedmen and Slaves.* Cambridge.

Weaver, P.R.C., *Repertorium Familiae Caesarum.* http://www.uni-koeln.de/phil-fak/ifa/altg/eck/weaver.htm.

Welwei, K.-W. 2000. *Sub Corona Vendere: Quellenkritische Studien zu Kriegsgefangenschaft und Sklaverei in Rom bis zum Ende des Hannibalkrieges.* Stuttgart.

Wen, S. 2018. "Communal Dining in the Roman West: Private Munificence towards Cities and Associations in the First Three Centuries AD". Diss. Leiden University. https://hdl.handle.net/1887/64935.

White, L.H. 2008. "Can Economics Rank Slavery against Free Labor in Terms of Efficiency?" *Politics Philosophy Economics* 7: 327–40.

Wilensky, H. 1963. "The Moonlighter: A Product of Relative Deprivation". *Industrial Relations* 3: 105–24.

Williams, C.A. 2004. *Martial's Epigrams Book Two.* Oxford.

Wilson, A., and K. Schörle. 2009. "A Baker's Funerary Relief from Rome". *Proceedings of the British School at Rome* 77: 101–24.

Wilson, A., and M. Flohr, eds. 2016. *Urban Craftsmen and Traders in the Roman World.* Oxford.

Wilson, S.G. 1996. "Voluntary Associations: An Overview". In *Voluntary Associations in the Graeco-Roman World,* edited by J.S. Kloppenborg and S.G. Wilson, 1–15. London and New York.

Winn, P. 2012. "Global Labor History: The Future of the Field?" *International Labor and Working-Class History* 82: 85–91.

Woolf, G. 1992. "Imperialism, Empire and the Integration of the Roman Economy". *World Archaeology* 23 (3): 283–93.

Woolf, G. 2000. "Literacy". In *The Cambridge Ancient History, Volume XI: The High Empire, AD 70–192*, 857–97. Cambridge.

Woolf, G. 2006. "Writing Poverty in Rome". In *Poverty in the Roman World,* edited by M. Atkins and R. Osborne, 83–99. Cambridge.

Woolf, G. 2013. "Female Mobility in the Roman West". In *Women and the Roman City in the Latin West*, edited by E.A. Hemelrijk and G. Woolf, 351–68. Leiden.

Woolf, G. 2017. "Moving Peoples in the Early Roman Empire". In *The Impact of Mobility and Migration in the Roman Empire: Proceedings of the Twelfth Workshop of the International Network Impact of Empire (Rome, June 17–19, 2015)*, edited by E. Lo Cascio and L.E. Tacoma, with the assistance of M.J. Groen-Vallinga, 25–41. Leiden.

Zambon, A. 1935. "Didaskalikai [Greek]". *Aegyptus* 35: 3–66.

Zimmer, G. 1982. *Römische Berufsdarstellungen*. Berlin.

Zuiderhoek, A. 2013. "Workers of the Ancient World: Analyzing Labour in Classical Antiquity". *Workers of the World: International Journal on Strikes and Social Conflicts* 1 (3): 32–48.

Index

Printed and bound by CPI Group (UK) Ltd, Croydon, CR0 4YY

13/09/2026

14961102-0006